Revolutionary Nonviolence

REVOLUTIONARY NONVIOLENCE
Essays by Dave Dellinger

The Bobbs-Merrill Company, Inc.
Indianapolis • New York

The editor is grateful to the following for permission to reprint the essays cited: *Retort* for "Statement on Entering Prison"; *Direct Action* for "Declaration of War"; *Individual Action* for "Why Were the Rosenbergs Killed?"; *Studies on the Left* for "The Future of Non-violence"; Dell Publishing Co. for "Where Things Stand Now." The remaining essays first appeared in *Liberation*.

The Bobbs-Merrill Company, Inc.
A Subsidiary of Howard W. Sams & Co., Inc., Publishers
Indianapolis • Kansas City • New York

Designed by Martin Stephen Moskof & Associates Inc.
Printed in the United States of America

To my mother and father
   Lib, Nancy and Fiske
   Betty
   Patch and Lissa
   Ray and Mary Gray
   Tasha, Val and Michele Lissa
   Danny
   Michele
   Howie and Fiske
the beloved inner family through whom I have been enabled to
keep believing in the reality of the family of all human beings

Acknowledgments

Since I believe in a dialectical relationship between the individual and the collective, and between thought and action, the ideas and formulations in this book reflect the influence and insights of a wide range of people with whom I have collaborated in a common, existential search for truth—both in the Movement and in various collective enterprises—but in the end the responsibility is mine alone.

Particularly helpful were Willa and Meredith Dallas, Janice Mitchell Forman, Frances Lee (now deceased), Don Benedict, Bill Sutherland, Al Harris, Ralph DiGia, Charlotte and Bill Kuenning, Bill Lovett, Al Uhrie (also deceased), Rita and Marty Corbin, all of whom I knew at one time or another during the twenty-five years I spent living and working communally in New Jersey, first in Newark and then in Glen Gardner. With all the men, except Marty Corbin, I shared a prison experience as well, as also with Paton Price, whose caustic criticisms I have found particularly helpful from that day to this.

Most of the articles that appeared originally in *Liberation* were influenced by discussions I had or movement enterprises I shared with successive managing editors Dick Gilpin, Lamar Hoover, and Dave Gelber and with fellow editors A. J. Muste, Staughton Lynd, Paul Goodman, Barbara Deming, and Sid Lens. I was also aided, beginning long before *Liberation,* by exchanges with former editors Roy Finch and Bayard Rustin, though we later came to a sharp parting of the ways politically. A number of the articles reflect the suggestions and criticisms of Steve Halliwell, John Wilson, and Dan Dewees.

The greatest influence and assistance have come from my wife, Betty, as we have tried to live out the underlying attitudes and beliefs of these essays during the last twenty-eight years, and from my children, Patch, Ray, Tasha, Danny and Michele. Contrary to the prejudice of our culture that children are not capable of genuine insight and at least equal collaboration with adults, the children exerted a profound influence from an early age. In the Glen Gardner commune where *Liberation* was published for ten years, Patch, Ray, and I used to set the articles in type and run them on the press, discussing and revising all the while.

I want to express special appreciation for the assistance of Barbara Webster, my partner in practically all the enterprises of the last few years on which the articles are based, and of Bob Ockene, my editor at Bobbs-Merrill and intimate friend. Bob never lost patience or faith in the worthwhileness of the projected book, even though I kept delaying the work as I became overextended in each new phase of the movement to end United States aggression in Vietnam. After he became ill with leukemia, he redoubled his efforts, forcing through the final selections and editing at a time when he knew he would not live to see the published book.

Finally, I hope that the concluding chapters begin to reflect the stimulus and inspiration I have received since April 1969 from working intimately with my fellow conspirators, Bobby Seale, Rennie Davis, Tom Hayden, Lee Weiner, John Froines, Jerry Rubin, and Abbie Hoffman. Our life-styles, thought processes and tactical judgments vary widely—in the end none of them believes that the society of our common dreams can be won through nonviolence alone—but I have a profound respect for all of them. My collaboration with Rennie, Tom, and Jerry predated by several years the government's prescient selection of the eight of us to form a working coalition against militarism, capitalism, imperialism, and racism. And let us not forget our conspiracy against an obsolete and authoritarian judicial system that faithfully represents the values of capitalism, and a joyless culture that moralistically interferes with the freedom of every individual to select his own pleasures and sources of enlightenment. I consider such freedom inalienable as long as it does not abridge the similar rights of anyone else. Fred Hampton (Chairman Fred of the Illinois Black Panther Party) was not one of those so honored by the government, but from the time of our indictment in April 1969 to the time, on December 4, when Illinois State's Attorney Edward Hanrahan rectified the oversight by having him murdered in his bed, he was an invaluable member of our conspiracy.

Contents

Introduction

Sometimes when I am speaking against the war in Vietnam, a heckler will try to undermine my credibility by asking about my opposition to World War II. Usually, I welcome the challenge because it enables me to raise more fundamental criticisms of American society and its wars than might otherwise seem relevant at an anti-Vietnam-war meeting. Or, if I have already argued that the war against Vietnam is a logical expression of America's profit-oriented economy and self-righteous foreign policy, both of which have been with us from the beginning, my refusal to support one of America's "good wars," World War II, emphasizes the point existentially in a way that opposition to its "bad war" in Vietnam does not. It is for that reason, rather than because of chronology, that I begin this book with an article written in the middle of World War II.

This is, after all, a country characterized by humanitarian rhetoric and, at the same time, actual disregard for the dignity of millions of persons who fall into negative categories—blacks, criminals, Communists, welfare recipients, young people, etc. In such a context there is a danger that social protest may function not as a revolutionizing force but as a soporific. Mass marches and reform candidacies become opiates of people whose consciences have been disturbed by intrusions of reality. The existence of moderate (ineffective) dissent encourages the illusion that the country's goals are proper and its "shortcomings" are being taken care of within a context of political freedom. What other country in the world would allow a half million people to register their dissent in the nation's capital in the midst of an enervating war? But then, what kind of country is it in which the government can cushion and absorb widespread public protest without altering its policies of death and domination? At some point—some fifty to a hundred thousand senseless casualties later—the government will do a little fancy footwork and withdraw all or most of its overt combat troops from Vietnam while continuing its imperialist policies throughout the world. Similarly, in the normal course of events, the country will elect more and more black mayors and fund more and more black capitalists while continuing to deny the masses of people, black and white, the joys and dignity of political and economic equality.

For Americans of goodwill who are not themselves prime victims of the current society, the temptation is to think in terms of restoring or bringing up to date the "normal" functionings of a basically humane and democratic system; they rarely trace the connections between the immediate abuse under attack and the fundamental assumptions and institutions of the society. Some abuses are thought to be carry-overs from the past, such as poverty and the oppression of black people—which is characteristically called the black problem, though it is clearly a problem created by white people and perpetuated by institutions that white people have established. Other problems, like the war in Vietnam, are thought to result from the mistakes or bad politics of individual office-holders, who can be persuaded to respond to reason or, if they do not, can be defeated in the next election. In the days since the United States dropped its atom bombs on Hiroshima and Nagasaki and launched the Cold War, we have exchanged Truman and Acheson for Eisenhower and Dulles; Eisenhower and Dulles for Kennedy, Johnson, Rostow, and Rusk; Johnson, Rostow, McNamara, and Rusk for Nixon, Agnew, Laird, and Mitchell. Just a rundown of the names is a reminder that changes in management have produced no fundamental changes in policy.

The truth is, as Randolph Bourne wrote early in World War I, that "war is the health of the state." And three quarters of a century earlier, Pierre Joseph Proudhon enunciated the maxim that "property is theft." The failure of most Americans to believe and connect these two truths and to become revolutionaries rather than reformers, helps explain not only America's repeated participation in imperialist wars, but also the continued existence of poverty and injustice in the richest, most technologically advanced country in the world.

The health of the state conflicts with the health of the citizenry, and the prerogatives of property prevent the fulfillment of the people. In the sixties, more than any other time in this country's history, pressures from the outside combined with pressures from the inside to make the country explode in chaos and conflict. The present disorders are not apt to be terminated short of a repression so severe that it resembles fascism, or institutional changes so far reaching that they will constitute a second American Revolution. In either case the name assigned will probably be neither fascism nor communism, but the reality will be an up-to-date, peculiarly American version of one or the other.

"America was promises," says an early poem by Archibald MacLeish. And large numbers of Americans have believed the promises, a fact which has encouraged domestic liberalism and stalled completion of the unfinished American Revolution. We have a genuine history of liberal reforms and elementary civil liberties. But neither the liberalism nor the civil liberties have extended far beyond the educated, white middle and upper classes. In a moment of tense drama in the courtroom of the Chicago Conspiracy trial, Bobby Seale, who had momentarily removed the gag imposed by Judge Julius Hoffman, told an astonished court that George Washington and Benjamin Franklin, whose pictures were displayed behind the judge's bench, were slave owners and that the court in which he was being tried was a racist and fascist institution. To the judge, this was criminal "contempt of court." With touching irrelevance—or actually with a relevance that he did not comprehend—he reminded Bobby that George Washington was "the father of our country."

The Declaration of Independence, the first of the great promises, proclaimed that all men are created equal, but it was an in-group document which was aimed at the overseas rivals and exploiters of the early colonists. It did not apply to the people whom the colonists themselves wanted to exploit and control—the lower-class whites, the blacks, and the "underdeveloped" Indians, whose country our forefathers seized for the pursuit of their own happiness.

This early dualism provided a model for what followed in the schizophrenic history of the country. The Monroe Doctrine warned of foreign exploiters and Old World tyrannies in idealistic language reminiscent of the Declaration, but failed to protect the people of Latin America from U.S. Marines, the United Fruit Company, or the Chase Manhattan Bank. Both Puerto Rico and Cuba had more freedom under the Spanish monarchy than under the protection of their "democratic liberators." Today Puerto Rico has approximately the same status that India had under the British when Gandhi began his nonviolent campaigns for independence. Its youths are drafted to fight in America's imperialist wars, but Puerto Rico has no voice in U.S. foreign policy. After "freeing" the Philippines from Spain, the United States used the techniques it had perfected against the Indians (and some of the identical military personnel) to massacre and suppress the Filipinos. No, the American aggression against Vietnam was not a "mistake." It flowed inexorably from America's earliest drive southward and westward to "open up" new territories to the benefit of the American way of life.

If the tyranny of the opposing side and the loftiness of one's own announced goals were sufficient to justify a war, World War I would indeed be one of America's "good" wars. But shortly after the successful prosecution of the holy war to end all war and to make the world safe for democracy, Woodrow Wilson, who had articulated much of the idealism, cried out in disillusionment: "Is there any man, woman, or child in this country who does not know—let me repeat, is there any child who does not know that this was an industrial and commercial war?"

Having beaten back the challenge of their industrial and commercial rivals, the Allies showed little interest in freedom or justice or democracy for the German people, who were, after all, the first victims of the Kaiser and of the German landowners and industrialists. When I was in Germany in 1936 and 1937, I had contact with members of the anti-Nazi underground and was made aware of the intimate ties between German fascism and American finance and industry. I also knew other decent Germans who reluctantly supported Hitler. Their rationalization was: "We don't like some of his methods, but there is no one else strong enough to break the Anglo-American stranglehold." Earlier, near the end of World War I, when the Russians had thrown off the tyranny of the Czars and were trying to rid themselves of the tyranny of property as well, the U.S. blockaded and invaded that country, thereby bringing upon itself at least a share of the responsibility for the tyrannical forms that disgraced communism there.

These constant contradictions between the highly publicized idealism of America's war aims and the sordid self-serving actions that followed hard on its military victories had their roots in a similar contradiction in the domestic economy. Perhaps the early Americans believed that "all men (except blacks and Indians) are *created* equal," but if so they were determined that they should not remain equal. The same year that the colonists produced the Declaration of Independence, the mother country produced Adam Smith's *The Wealth of Nations,* the theoretical and moral justification for capitalism. Smith, a conventionally religious man, argued that if every man pursued his own selfish economic interest, the invisible hand of God would see to it that the result would be a prosperous and just society. Although the colonists rejected the British monarchy and British rule, they embraced the mother country's emergent capitalism. Capitalism exalts not equality, liberty, and fraternal solidarity, but private ownership of the natural resources and accumulated productive capital, usury (all interest and other payments on capital are usury, as the Jewish prophets and early Christians well knew), and private profit from the labor of others. This was the Achilles' heel of the great American experiment. It sanctioned selfishness, excused vast inequalities in wealth and power, and denied the legitimacy of economic equality even as a goal.

Without economic democracy, political democracy didn't amount to much. In the first place, capitalism removes one of the most important areas of a person's life from even the pretense of democratic decision-making: the factory or other enterprise where he works. The sacrifices of thousands of heroes and martyrs finally established the legitimacy of labor unions, thus giving some workers some bargaining power over their wages and conditions of work, but to this day the unions do not claim the necessary right of the workers to own and manage the enterprises democratically.

Secondly, in a money economy, inequalities in wealth automatically create an unequal political competition between rich and poor, much as an inequality in weapons would rule out the possibility of a fair duel. In theory, a poor man has an equal chance in political decision-making in this country. In fact, the poor man's legal right to finance an effective campaign, address the public on television, or organize a lobby is of the same general utility as his legal right to buy a yacht, gain control of General Motors, or own a newspaper. When effectively disfranchised people try to redress the balance by taking to the streets or progressing from electoral politics to active resistance, the government has property laws, trespass laws, permit regulations, antiriot laws, police and national guard procedures to curb them.

All of America's foreign wars were fought in the name of political democracy but increased the wealth and power of those whose businesses were exempt from democracy and subject only to the most minor and indirect controls. Thus, in World War II, the country's youth were conscripted on the theory that the preservation of civilization was at stake. Those who refused to offer up their lives to the military were put in jail. Private Edward Slovik, who deserted, was shot as an example to others. But it was taken for granted that industry would not offer its cooperation unless guaranteed substantial profits. So industry was not conscripted. War contracts were issued on a guaranteed cost-plus-profits basis. Occasionally, a manufacturer who was caught supplying shoddy material or unduly padding expenses was slapped on the wrist with a small fine. Even if the costs had not been inflated; even if the government had not in many cases supplied the capital for plant expansion and then turned the new plant over to private ownership; even if the profits had not been astronomical, the appalling principle should have been clear. In time of war, as in time of peace, this is a society in which profits and property are more sacred than human life itself.

In a naïve and inexperienced way I had been anti-Nazi and antifascist before World War II, during the period when America's power elite was supporting Hitler, Mussolini, Franco, and Tojo. This was the period when the United States, under Franklin Roosevelt, imposed an arms embargo on democratic Spain but did not interfere with the highly profitable business of American corporations which were shipping oil, scrap iron, and munitions all over the world, including to fascist Japan. The U.S.-Nazi alliance of the thirties was just as real as the Nazi-Soviet pact of 1940, but less formal. In part its informality was because Big Business carries out its international maneuvers in relative secrecy. In part it was to preserve the democratic façade, with its usefulness in providing tyranny by consent. But the United States was attracted by Hitler's no-nonsense anti-communism much as the Soviet Union was attracted by his blistering condemnations of British and American imperialism. Both the United States and the Soviet Union collaborated shamelessly with Hitler, each attempting to turn his destructive force against the other. Ironically, Hitler became overconfident after his easy conquest of France and the Low Countries and attacked the Soviet Union. Russia and the United States became emergency allies.

However, the basis of the Cold War rivalry, in which each attempted to dominate the post-war world for its own selfish purposes, had already been established. It was never far from the surface, during the war itself, as each of the giants tried not only to defeat the common enemy of the moment but to strengthen its own position relative to the other. After the defeat of Germany and the increasingly hopeless situation in which Japan found itself, both the Soviet Union and the United States ignored Japanese peace feelers—Russia because it was anxious to get its troops into the Orient, and the United States because it did not want the war to end before it could use the newly developed A-bomb, thus establishing itself, it thought, as the dominant power in the post-war world.

Long before this, in 1940 and 1941, the United States had finally turned against Hitler and imposed an oil embargo on Japan in a calculated attempt to provoke reprisals, thereby overcoming the widespread popular opposition to American participation in the war. The attack on Pearl Harbor was Franklin Roosevelt's greatest political triumph. Until then he had not succeeded in reducing unemployment below the danger point or in uniting the country behind capitalist democracy, conscription, and an expansionist foreign policy.

Despite the stampede to the war, my experience as a "premature antifascist" and as a community organizer in the slums of Harlem and Newark, New Jersey, had taught me that the United States was an unreliable ally whose goals were not my goals and whose methods were not my methods. I knew from bitter personal experience that the United States was not interested in the dignity or economic well-being of black people or of any of the residents of America's slums. Given the conflict of interest between the requirements of corporate capitalism and human need, it was interested only in pushing through enough reform to pacify the poor and to turn them into profit-yielding consumers, producers, and tenants for the power elite. Until the outbreak of World War II, it had only partially succeeded in attaining even that limited objective. In the neighborhood of Newark where I lived and worked, most of the young men got the first paycheck of their lives, their first regular meals and adequate clothing when they were drafted (or yielded to economic and political pressure by volunteering). I knew from personal experience that the government wasn't interested in aiding the Jewish victims of Nazism. I had been involved for years in an unsuccessful campaign to get the United States to lower its immigration barriers to provide asylum for Jews and antifascists. Similarly, I was certain that the military-industrial complex (in those days we spoke of the War Department and Big Business) was not interested in freedom for the peasants of Indochina or the other countries overrun by Japan.

In World War II, Ho Chi Minh and the Indochinese nationalists cooperated with the United States against the occupying Japanese. But when Japan was defeated and when, on September 2, 1945, Vietnam declared its independence, the Allies used Japanese fascist troops to suppress the Vietnamese independence forces. Forty thousand Japanese troops, who had been disarmed and were awaiting repatriation, were given back their arms and turned loose on the Vietnamese. Technically the British Labour government was in charge of Saigon at the time and did the dirty deed, but by that time the United States was clearly the dominant power. It didn't even bother to make a protest for the public record. In October 1966, when I first visited Hanoi, a Vietnamese member of parliament asked me rather naïvely why the United States had reversed its long history of anticolonialism in 1945 and betrayed its war-time goals by opposing self-determination in Vietnam. I explained to him that the United States had always had two sides to its foreign policy: the promises and the reality. The fact that many Americans believed in the promises and laid down their lives or otherwise labored heroically to make them come true did not mean that they were ever the dominant reality.

On my departure from Hanoi, I traveled homeward by way of China. In Peking I spent my first evening at the North Vietnamese embassy, dining with the ambassador. Hardly had we settled in our chairs in the anteroom and had the first round of toasts, when he turned to me and said: "We know of your struggle against the American aggressions in Vietnam and Korea, and we are curious what role you played in the fight against fascism in World War II." I groaned inwardly and thought that, whereas I was prepared to discuss pacifism with the Vietnamese in Peking, as I had done in North Vietnam itself, it was hardly the most appropriate subject with which to begin our acquaintance. But I took a deep breath and began by analyzing America's role in World War II and the years immediately leading up to and following it, somewhat as I have done in the last few pages. Not surprisingly, he quickly indicated his sympathy with the political reservations I had had about relying on American imperialism to act as a genuine opponent of fascism and colonialism. Then I discussed the second factor in my refusal to support World War II: my distrust of violence as a method for building a new society and my belief that nonviolence can and must be developed as a viable method of all-out resistance to tyranny and aggression. To my amazement he again expressed agreement and reminded me that during World War II Gandhi had developed a plan for nonviolent resistance to the Japanese if they had invaded India, as had seemed likely at the height of the Japanese military and naval successes in the Pacific. Clearly the Vietnamese ambassador was not an advocate of nonviolence in his country's current plight, but far more than many of America's current "revolutionists," he realized that nonviolence did not need to be synonymous with either moderation or appeasement, and was motivated by the sufferings of his countrymen to feel the urgency of experimentation with alternative methods of resistance and liberation. For my part, I had just come from Vietnam where I had been inspired by the heroic struggle of the Vietnamese. I had seen at first hand that a people engaged in violent resistance to tyranny and aggression are not automatically corrupted, hardened, and desensitized by the struggle, in the manner outlined in classical pacifist theory (and reflected in the opening sentences of my 1943 Statement on Entering Prison).

We need not only a moral equivalent to war, as William James called for, but also a politically effective substitute. It will not come either by an aloofness from the struggle or from a purist condemnation of those who, seeing no alternative, pick up the rifle or man the antiaircraft gun when their country is attacked. Nor will it come by acquiescence in the institutionalized violence of the current American status quo, as if the violence of slum and property and money were any less destructive than the violence of an armed liberation struggle. I am convinced that an armed revolt in this country against capitalism would be a disaster for everyone. But I am equally convinced that capitalism is already a disaster—not only for the blacks, the poor, the disadvantaged, and the foreign victims, but for the so-called privileged classes as well. Those who supposedly benefit from capitalism sell their birthright of love, self-respect, and human solidarity for a mess of plastic pottage. Law and order under the present distribution of wealth and power and privilege is not an answer to the current trend to violence in the movement. Those of us who oppose the violence of the status quo and reject the violence of armed revolt and class hatred bear a heavy responsibility to struggle existentially to provide nonviolent alternatives.

I wish I could say that the following pages provide convincing answers to this dilemma. They don't. But I hope they will help some people to focus on the right questions. And I hope they provide some preliminary analysis and raw materials that, combined with other sources, will contribute to the eventual discovery of viable alternatives to the violence of the status quo and the violence of would-be liberation. In any case, I do not believe that the answers will be discovered by reading or writing books, except insofar as those who read or write them engage in the concrete struggle. Histories are *written* by intellectuals, who generally give undue credit to other intellectuals for making history. But history is *made* by people who commit themselves, their lives, and their energies to the struggle. The best history is made by people who struggle against war, oppression, and hypocrisy and who also struggle to incorporate into their own lives and organizations the values that led them to oppose these evils in the first place.

Revolutionary Nonviolence

Part One

World War II

Introduction to Part I

The opening statement in this section was written in 1943, just before I went to Lewisberg Penitentiary to serve a two-year sentence for refusing to accept assignment, under the draft, to a Civilian Public Service Camp for conscientious objectors. Previously I had served a sentence of a year and a day for publicly refusing to register under America's first peacetime conscription law. I was a student at Union Theological Seminary at the time, and assistant minister of a church, so registration would have exempted me from all further military obligation, under the automatic exemption granted the clergy.

On the first occasion, in 1940, I co-authored an explanatory statement, which was signed by twenty Union Seminary students. In the end only eight of us refused to register and went to prison—the first antidraft prisoners of World War II. Naturally, the statement was intended to convey our position to the wider world, and hopefully to win recruits. After a few months in prison I began to feel that it was so burdened with the specialized language and modes of thought of the theological world that it was of little general value. For that reason I have not included it here. (For the curious, the more intelligible sections of it are printed in Staughton Lynd's anthology, *Nonviolence in America* [Bobbs-Merrill, 1965]).

The Statement that is printed here still includes some of the formal religious language that I seldom use these days. I stopped using it not because I do not still believe in the attitudes and experiences that lie behind the once noble words, but because, given the sectarianism of the church and its lack of moral leadership, such words no longer communicate their original energizing content, except to a very few.

There follows a "Declaration of War," written shortly after my release from Lewisberg and occasioned by the atom bombing of Hiroshima and Nagasaki. As I reread it today, it seems to me one of the clearest and most concise expressions in the book of the convictions that caused me to be indicted, twenty-four years later, under the infamous antiriot act.

One interesting change between the Declaration and the earlier Statement is that, whereas in 1943 I had condemned sabotage as an essentially violent act, after two years in a maximum security prison I drew a distinction between violence against people (which I continue to oppose to this day) and violence against property. In a society which exalts property rights above human rights, it is sometimes necessary to damage or destroy property, both because property has no intrinsic value except insofar as it contributes to human welfare, and also in order to challenge people to discover a new sense of priorities. As Fathers Philip and Daniel Berrigan said when they destroyed the draft files of a Baltimore draft board, there is some property, including concentration camps and draft files, that has no right to exist. On the other hand, the use of violence against property presents many problems, not the least of them the pressures toward promiscuity, attended by a hardening of attitude toward the persons who protect property and toward passersby. Already the anti-imperialist movement tends to attract some who are driven by despair, impatience, or boredom to focus on destruction and to neglect the building of enduring human relationships and institutions. Physical assaults on the primacy of property are more apt to accomplish the legitimate purpose of exalting the rights of people if they are an adjunct of revolutionary nonviolence than if they are accompanied by contempt for those persons who, as brainwashed tools of the dominant society, happen to be one's "enemies" of the moment. The current trend in some circles toward "pig-baiting," Movement factionalism, and self-coronation of one's little group as the revolutionary vanguard do not furnish a good context in which to experiment with blowing up, burning down, or trashing property. The combined excitement and drama of such actions can foster an illusion of revolutionary serious-ness and effectiveness while actually discouraging hard organizing, critical analysis, and tactical imagination.

In other sections of the book, I touch from time to time both on the radicalizing effect of my three years in prison and on the im-portance, for a true understanding of American history, of getting be-yond the conventional myths about World War II. On the first point, I disagree with those who think that "doing time" is necessarily wast-ing time. Naturally we should try to stay out of prison as long as we can do so without compromising our basic beliefs or so restricting our activities that we have, in effect, imprisoned ourselves outside prison. But prison is a teeming ghetto where the realities of society are writ large and harshly for all to perceive. Ironically, some of the very sections of the anti-imperialist movement that eulogize the work-ing class often go to absurd lengths to stay out of prison. But prison is one of the native habitats of some of the most courageous and per-ceptive members of the working class. Any movement which dis-misses convicts as politically useless "lumpen proletariat" betrays its own elitist hang-ups and cuts itself off from an important part of reality. Leadbelly, Caryl Chessman, Malcolm X, and Eldridge Cleaver are four of many who were "organized"—or organized themselves—in prison.

Concerning World War II, there can be no doubt that inter-national fascism was a catastrophic evil that had to be resisted. But it is my contention now, as it was in 1940, that for those who under-stand that social evils are created less by bad men than by bad systems, of which capitalism is surely one of the worst, it was also catastrophic for people who believed in human dignity to think that they could resist fascism under the leadership and by the methods of big busi-ness, big government, and the military. I believe that history bears this out, whether one reads such historical studies as David Horowitz's *Free World Colossus* and Gabriel Kolko's *Politics of War; the World and U.S. Foreign Policy, 1943-1945,* or whether one examines such contemporary phenomena as the United States aggression in Vietnam and the worldwide encroachments of the American military-industrial complex, which was the real winner of World War II.

Statement on
Entering Prison

1943 I. I believe that all war is evil and useless. Even a so-called war of defense is evil in that it consists of lies, hatred, self-righteousness, and the most destructive methods of violence that man can invent. These things corrupt even the most idealistic supporters of the war. They harm even the most innocent children of "enemy" countries.

Even a war fought with the highest idealism is useless in that it can produce no good result that could not be secured better in other ways. Just as it would be stupid to plant weeds and to try to harvest vegetables, so it would be stupid to encourage the lies, conscription and murder of war, and to hope to produce democracy, freedom, and brotherhood. War is a Trojan horse from which emerge at home the enemies that destroy us.

The fact that some people sincerely believe that war will help us cannot persuade me to cooperate in their mistake. Instead it makes it all the more important to do everything possible to help free them from their error and to show them a substitute for war.

II. I believe that when anyone supports war he violates the life and teachings of Jesus.

III. I believe that the so-called United Nations and each individual resident of them bear a tremendous responsibility for this present war.

A. The rest of the world has been driven to desperation by the economic cruelty of the United States, with its Big Business Empire, and of England with her Colonial Empire. We produced the economic, social, and psychological conditions that made war inevitable. Russia, for all her social reforms, is a bloody dictatorship that has followed a policy of selfish nationalism for years. As part of this policy she has subsidized political parties, all over the world, that have poisoned the left wing movement with dishonesty, opportunism, and violence.

B. So far as Germany and Italy are concerned, British and American politicians and industrialists supported the rise of Hitler and Mussolini. One reason they did this was to make private profits out of various business deals. A second reason was that Hitler and Mussolini were destroying the labor and socialist movements of Europe, which had the power to introduce economic and social democracy to oppressed peoples everywhere. If you find this hard to believe, let me remind you that the United States government is following a similar policy today. Of course they cannot support the two individuals, Hitler and Mussolini, but they are supporting totalitarian forces in every country—Giraud, Peyroutan, Franco, Prince Otto Hapsburg, the Junkers of Germany, the land owners and business interests of Italy, the dictators of Latin America, etc. At the same time they are opposing the democratic forces of Europe—and their representatives in this country.

Even after the early honeymoon with Hitler and Mussolini, when these men began to emerge as dangerous Frankensteins, the United States and England were still ready to sell the democratic freedoms of Spain, Austria, Czechoslovakia, etc., down the river. They resisted every suggestion that we offer the hungry people of Europe the economic and social equality that would have uprooted both fascism and war.

C. So far as Asia is concerned, we introduced modern violence and robbery to the Japanese, by our rape of the orient.

Later we were partners of Japan in her invasion of China. American oil, steel, and munitions were sold at huge profits for that purpose. President Roosevelt, the State Department, and politicians all conspired in this. *Every one of them is as guilty of murder as are the Japanese whom they accuse.*

We began to boycott Japan only when it began to threaten our damnable mastery of the orient, and when we needed an incident to strengthen the propaganda by which we were trying to sell the war to our own peace-loving people.

Churchill himself has admitted in Parliament that President Roosevelt committed us to war against Japan in August 1941, four months before Pearl Harbor. Shortly afterward we started issuing ultimatums and threats for *the sole purpose* of carrying out this promise—that we would wage war against Japan before the year was out.

We also began a policy of limited naval warfare. Naval officers have admitted that *before Pearl Harbor,* they were sent on secret expeditions with orders to shoot Japanese ships and aircraft—on sight and without warning. See Jeannette Rankin's speech in the House of Representatives on December 8, 1942. The same policy was pursued in the Atlantic. Rather brazen proof of this terrible policy of our government has just been given by the Navy Department in General Order No. 190, whereby the Navy, Marine Corps, and Coast Guard personnel have been ordered to wear a bronze letter A on their American defense medal service ribbon "to commemorate service on ships operating in actual or potential belligerent contact with Axis forces in the Atlantic Ocean prior to December 7, 1941."

How many Japanese ships were sunk in this way, we do not know. Nor do we know how many peace-loving Japanese reluctantly accepted the war because of our treachery. But the governments of the United States and Japan each exploited the treachery of the other, forcing war upon its own people.

D. We also went to war to avoid facing up to the failures

of our selfishly organized private-ownership, private-profit system.

At home we have a system whereby the mines, factories, and other means of production are owned and operated —not for the good of all but for the private profit of a few. *Such organized selfishness will not work.* It produced years of mass unemployment, depression and unrest. But even the misery of millions did not persuade the privileged classes to give up their stranglehold on God's material gifts and to embrace the total democracy and brotherhood that alone will work. Instead, after seven desperate years of bread lines and boondoggling, they turned to the manufacture of armaments. Roosevelt himself, in an interview recorded in the *New York Times,* pointed to Nazi Germany and said that she had lots of armaments plants and no unemployment.

At the same time they played up war scares and international hatreds as an excuse for making bombs instead of bread, and as a scapegoat on which to blame the sufferings of the people.

After a time "national defense" was an insufficient excuse for slavery and injustice. The people were restless. Our privileged classes had to choose: brotherhood or war. The Axis threatened the financial and business empire of certain private interests. War offered an excellent smoke-screen for profiteering, for feeling important, and for suppressing American freedom, with all its dangers to economic selfishness. Finally, the brutality of the Axis presented the idealistic mask without which neither the people nor most of their masters would have been able to face the terrible choice they made.

Very few people actually chose war. They chose selfishness and the result was war. Each of us, individually and nationally, must choose: total love or total war.

Most people are afraid to choose total love and brotherhood. It is too new, too daring. It seems to require too many sacrifices. For the privileged classes who control the normal instruments for manufacturing public opinion and making public decisions, it means abandoning certain traditional privileges which bring no real happiness—so long as they are private privileges—but which possess a superficial glitter and attractiveness. For all of us it means abandoning our pride, our self-centeredness, and whatever special privileges we have or hope to have some day.

The selfishness of all of us underlies the dishonesty of our Roosevelts and Tojos, the brutality of our Hitlers and Churchills.

IV. I believe that there is a practical alternative to war and that the world is capable of accepting it in the near future.

A. The basic alernative to war is brotherhood. Even today the United States and England could end the war within a month. Suppose we said *to the peoples of the world:*

1. We will lift the blockade immediately and ship food and supplies to the peoples of Europe.

2. We will free all of our far-flung colonies and economic subjects at once. We will not seek any special privileges in India, Africa, Malay, Latin America, etc. We will not exploit any native populations or natural resources for our own private profit against the interest of the rest of the world.

3. We will share our raw materials, natural resources and manufactured goods with other people, in the spirit of equal brotherhood.

4. Our factories, natural resources and large farms will be democratically owned and operated, not for the private profit of a few, but for the good of the whole world.

5. We will forget all past wrongs, confess our great share in the guilt, and renounce all claim to special privileges.

6. We will demobilize our army, navy and marines and destroy all munitions that cannot be converted to useful ends.

7. We will no longer persecute our Negroes, our Jews and our foreigners. We will accept within our shores any people who care to come here. Under our policy of social equality, economic brotherhood and production for use, there will be room for all.

If instead of invasion and threats we offered an announcement of this kind, do you think Hitler and Mussolini could force their people to fight? What could any dictator anywhere offer to his people to persuade them to destroy us?

Even the so-called material costs (of sharing our wealth with other nations who, remember, would soon share their wealth with us) could not be one-tenth the cost of war. Actually, the world's productive power would be used productively for the first time. And spiritually, for the first time we would be free. We would discover the infinite happiness that is possible for all men.

Such practical brotherhood would put an end to international war and an end to the cruel class war that exists in every country today. It would benefit everyone: the misled workers who sacrifice their freedom today—and their jobs and self-respect tomorrow; the draftees who are bathing the world in blood—and losing their own bodies and souls in the process; the self-deceiving politicians and businessmen who are selling the anguish of their fellowmen for "profits" that wither their souls.

B. But the weapons of the spirit are not limited to the methods of fraternity. There are weapons of resistance as well. True pacifists are uncompromising fighters against fascism, totalitarianism, and every form of injustice and oppression. But we believe in fighting with methods that are successful.

Remember, the "democracies" fought and won a violent war from 1914 to 1918. But it achieved nothing—at tremendous cost. It increased all the evils we hoped it would overcome. So it is time to discard this unsuccessful method of fighting and to embrace a new method, one that will work. That method is the method of nonviolent opposition to all evil.

Already the occupied countries show that there are ways of resisting an aggressor without huge armies and fleets. The noncooperation, the sabotage, the slowdown, and the secret press of countries like Norway, Holland, and Belgium have done more to insure the real defeat of Hitlerism than all the military might of the United States.

We need to go but one step further. We need a resistance that will renounce sabotage, sniping, deception, terrorism and all other essentially violent acts. We need to embrace a type of resistance that is equally unyielding to tyranny, but at the same time is humble, straightforward and loving.

The strike can be such a method. Although violence and threats have often been associated with the strike, they can be renounced. And the strongest government in the world is powerless against coal miners who persist in their refusal to operate the mines. If American coal miners will go as far as they have against their own government, and if their sons will die on foreign battlefields for lies—then coal miners and their sons can learn to strike unyieldingly, at home, against foreign invaders, for truth.

Besides the strike, there are many other methods of nonviolent resistance to evil. Thus if Hitler could keep Europe under control and persuade his armies to invade the United States, Americans need not waste time starving, bombing and invading the common people of Europe. We could stay at home. We could treat every individual German soldier as our brother, giving him every good thing of hospitality, food and shelter that would help him. But we could conscientiously refuse to cooperate in any of his orders to teach falsehood in the schools, to persecute Jews or Negroes, to operate factories or railroads for the conscription of goods. We could constantly circulate papers and pamphlets against fascism. Our courageous, kindly, nonviolent resistance would undermine the morale of the German invaders. It would stimulate sympathetic strikes and action all over Europe.

If all our workers treated individual Germans as brothers but refused to operate a single factory until certain national evils were eliminated; if we combined this with sincere announcements of international economic brotherhood, no dictator could force German conscripts to kill or imprison the population. He would be faced with rebellion. The dictators would be forced to give up their ideas of conquest—and to relinquish their authority. The soldiers would become our friends.

This is but a bare outline—the product of one mind. But I hope it shows the spirit and some of the typical steps by which the genius of a nation can renounce war and win a real victory for all mankind.

Believing these things, I must be true to them. This means that I try, as sincerely as I can, to live in love and brotherhood with my fellowmen. Therefore I have renounced all claim to the illusory privileges of the upper classes. I live as a working man in a working-class district. I live with a group of people who try to share with our fellowmen our time, our energy, and whatever of God's love or goods we have.

For instance, we have accepted gifts to buy a farm. This farm we try to make available for the physical and spiritual creativity of the people from the underprivileged neighborhood where we live. In addition, we share our ideas with our neighbors, learning from them and imparting to them. We participate in a "People's Peace Now Committee" which is trying to arouse people to a nonviolent struggle against both war and fascism.

By these and other methods, we try to live in such a way that some of our neighbors and ourselves will gradually lose our pride, selfishness, violence, and fear and absorb the love and beauty that is the heritage of all men.

It would be dishonest for me to abandon this life that I believe in to patch up a truce with the war system that I oppose.

For me, there is no choice between going to a camp for conscientious objectors and going to jail. I have only one choice—my ministry in response to God. If the government puts me in jail for following that ministry, that is its choice, not mine. Then my ministry will be in jail. But civilian public service would be a confusing, semi-voluntary withdrawal from my lifework in order to avoid certain penalties of the war-making government.

To me the C.P.S. system is a method of draft evasion—not of draft opposition. It is a device whereby persons who know the wrongness of war and conscription tone down their opposition in return for the theoretical advantage of avoiding open prosecution and jail. For most pacifists it is a faithless sellout whereby we accept relative isolation and silence at a time when we should be among people, actively expressing the total brotherhood and love of God in which we believe. At a certain stage in a person's development, going to C.P.S. camp can be a significant step forward representing the first major break with a world of nationalism and war. But it should be a stage, not a resting place, and thousands of us have passed beyond that stage. Further, C.P.S. is a method by which the government maintains an illusion of democracy and freedom and is thus able to keep people relatively happy and docile while it destroys them with totalitarianism and war.

It is my observation that large numbers of those pacifists who accept the C.P.S. system do so because they are afraid of jail or because they think they can be more effective outside jail, as semifree, semiresponsible, law-abiding citizens.

But: If we compromise with war and conscription in order to carry on activities outside jail, the test is our activities. How many of us pass such a test? No series of acts is so worthless as those based on compromise. When the law directs the conscription of American boys and men, the growing destruction of American freedom, the scandalous profiteering of war contracts, the deliberate starvation and nightly bombing of Europe, the ruthless murder of "our enemies"—then neither I nor any honest man is bound by it.

Of course we have built up defenses against this. We do not want to think we are partners in murder, oppression, dishonesty. We never tell ourselves openly that it is so.

In that lies the horror of it. You and I are murderers against our wills. Our businessmen and politicians profiteer from the blood of their sons and brothers with clear consciences. Most judges and FBI men suppress and silence those who champion honesty and brotherhood and Christ—without knowing what they are doing. Finally, those of us who see these things cannot express them adequately. Both our lives and our statements get poisoned with that very spirit of pride and antagonism to which we are opposed. But underneath it all lies the truth. Somehow more and more people must face up to the murder and universal suicide in which we needlessly participate. Somehow we must all become more and more conscious of the love of God which is the only practical thing in man's life, and the only solution to all our striving.

Each in his own way, let us search our hearts and purify our *lives*.

Declaration of War

1945   The atom bombing of Hiroshima and Nagasaki destroyed whatever claims the United States may have had to being either a "democratic" or a "peace-loving" nation. Without any semblance of a democratic decision—without even advance notice of what was taking place—the American people waked up one morning to discover that the United States government had committed one of the worst atrocities in history.

Hiroshima and Nagasaki were atomized at a time when the Japanese were suing desperately for peace. The American leaders were acting with almost inconceivable treachery by denying that they had received the requests for peace, rumors of which had been trickling through censorship for several months.

The atom bombs were exploded on congested cities filled with civilians. There was not even the slightest *military* justification, because the military outcome of the war had been decided months earlier. The only reason that the fighting was still going on was the refusal of American authorities to discontinue a war which postponed the inevitable economic collapse at home, and was profitable to their pocketbooks, their military and political prestige, their race hatred, and their desires for imperialist expansion.

The "way of life" that destroyed Hiroshima and Nagasaki (and is reported to have roasted alive up to a million people in Tokyo in a single night) is international, and dominates every nation of the world. But we live in the United States, so our struggle is here. With this "way of life" ("death" would be more appropriate) there can be no truce nor quarter. The prejudices of patriotism, the pressures of our friends, and the fear of unpopularity, imprisonment, or death should not hold us back any longer. It must be *total war* against the infamous economic, political, and social system which is dominant in this country. The American system has been destroying human life in peace and in war, at home and abroad, for decades. Now it has produced the crowning infamy of atom bombing. Beside these brutal facts the tidbits of token democracy mean nothing. *Henceforth no decent citizen owes one scrap of allegiance (if he ever did) to American law, American custom, or American institutions.*

There is a tendency to think that the bombing of Hiroshima and Nagasaki was an excess that can be attributed to a few militarists and politicians at the top. That is the easy way out. It enables us to express our horror at the more obvious atrocities of our civilization while remaining "respectable" supporters of the institutions which make them inevitable. But obliteration bombing by blockbusters, incendiaries, and atom bombs was a logical part of the brutal warfare that had been carried on for nearly four years with the patriotic support of American political, religious, scientific, business, and labor institutions. The sudden murder of 300,000 Japanese is consistent with the ethics of a society which is bringing up millions of its own children in city slums. The lives of 300,000 "enemies" are distant and theoretical to business and labor leaders who find excuses for enjoying $15,000 incomes (and $150,000 incomes) while hiring workers for less than $1,500. Workers who passively accept starvation wages, periodic unemployment, and relief checks, at the order of private owners and civic authorities, will also accept orders to put on a uniform and mutilate their fellow men.

No, the evil of our civilization cannot be combated by campaigns which oppose militarism and conscription but leave the American economic and social system intact. The fight against military conscription cannot be separated from the fight against the economic conscription involved in private ownership of the country's factories, railroads, and natural resources. The fight against the swift destruction of human life which takes place in modern warfare cannot be separated from the fight against the slow debilitation of the human personality which takes place in the families of the rich, the unemployed, and the poor. *The enemy is every institution which denies full social and economic equality to anyone. The enemy is personal indifference to the consequences of acts performed by the institutions of which we are a part.*

There is no solution short of all-out war. But there must be one major difference between our war and the war that has just ended. The war against the Axis was fought as a military campaign against people, with all the destructive fury, violent hatred, regimentation, and dishonesty of military warfare. The combatants were conscripts rather than free men. Every day that the war went on they were compelled to act in contradiction to the ideals which motivated many of them. Therefore "victory" was predestined to be a hollow farce, putting a partial end to killing that never should have begun, but entrenching white imperialism as the tyrant of the Pacific, and contributing unemployment, slums, and class hatred to the United States. The American people won half the world and lost their souls.

The war for total brotherhood must be a nonviolent war carried on by methods worthy of the ideals we seek to serve. The acts we perform must be the responsible acts of free men, not the irresponsible acts of conscripts under orders. We must fight against institutions but not against people.

There must be strikes, sabotage, and seizure of public property now being held by private owners. There must be civil disobedience of laws which are contrary to human welfare. But there must be also an uncompromising practice of treating everyone, including the worst of our opponents, with all the respect and decency that he merits as a fellow human being. We can expect to face tear gas, clubs, and bullets. But we must refuse to hate, punish, or kill in return. We must respect the owners, policemen, conservatives, and strike-breakers for what they are—potentially decent people who have been conditioned by a sick society into playing anti-social roles, the basic inhumanity of which they do not understand.

This is a diseased world in which it is impossible for anyone to be fully human. One way or another, everyone who lives in the modern world is sick or maladjusted. Slick businessmen and bosses, parasitical coupon clippers, socially blind lawyers, scientists, and clergymen are as much victims of "a world they never made" as are the rough and irresponsible elements of America's great slums. The only way we can begin to break the vicious circle of blindness, hatred, and inequality is to combine an uncompromising war upon evil institutions with an unending kindness and love of every individual—including the individuals who defend existing institutions.

This is total war. But it is a war in which our allegiance transcends nationalities and classes. Every act we perform today must reflect the kind of human relationships we are fighting to establish tomorrow.

Adolf Eichmann and
Claude Eatherly

1962 Adolf Eichmann and Claude Eatherly suffer from opposing types of insanity. If we can overlook for the moment the fact that Eichmann was on the "wrong" side and killed the "wrong" people, we can see that he was a "normal maniac"; that is, his actions were motivated by the need for respectability, security, and personal advancement within the dominant society rather than by concern for the effect of his actions on other people. How is one to distinguish morally (or clinically) between Eichmann and, for example, the men in the Strategic Air Command, on Polaris submarines, or at missile bases throughout the world, who are ready at a signal from Washington to press the buttons that will turn vast cities into crematoria— and perhaps the earth into a cinder? All lack the imagination—the saving contact with reality—to visualize what they are really doing. All lack the habit of conscientious examination of the routine acts of society and their frequently bloody consequences. If they have momentary hesitations or doubts, they set them aside, shrinking from the lonely, arduous, seemingly arrogant, and ultimately dangerous path of developing their individual consciences.

Normal insanity extends far beyond acquiescence in war and preparation for war and is particularly virulent in the economic life of society, where, for example, few Americans establish a realistic connection between North American prosperity and Latin American (or African or Asian) hunger, disease, and squalor. Like Eichmann we keep our eyes on getting ahead—or at least surviving—within the system rather than on the dolorous consequences of the system on the lives of its victims. As a matter of fact, what helps keep us both "normal" and "insane" is the fact that its victims don't really appear in our consciousness as human beings—just as the bulk of the Jews weren't quite people to Eichmann (or to the British who refused to let them into Palestine and the Americans who wouldn't let them into the United States). Instead they are such things as immigrants-to-be-absorbed and threats-to-our-standard-of-living, or, in other cases, criminals, subversives, bums, enemies, employees (units of labor-cost), tenants, consumers, customers, etc. And we particularly fail to face them as human beings if they wear the scars of privation and exploitation—if they are not our social and economic equals or if they revolt illegally or irrationally (not necessarily synonymous). In this way the system carries its own built-in justifications and tends to be psychologically self-perpetuating.

The reduction of people to objects (Marx spoke of the reduction of working persons to commodities—"hands," "labor power") is the mark of society's insanity and makes it possible for otherwise honest and decent people to acquiesce in routine inhuman practices. Some day, let us hope, our children will look back with amazement on many of our institutions and customs (absentee ownership, with the right to receive rent, profits, and dividends and to control the labor and the product of other persons; the crowding of Negroes, Puerto Ricans and others into rat-infested tenements, often at higher rents per square foot than their employers are charged for luxury apartments; financial and political control by American companies of whole countries in Africa and Latin America; the American court and prison system) just as we are appalled by the witch-burning and chattel slavery of our ancestors. Unfortunately, the failure of the left, as exemplified by the Communists, has been its similar failure to see *all* people as fellow human beings (its reduction of persons to class enemies, fascists, deviationists) and its resultant failure to introduce a new sanity, a new awareness, into human relationships.

Milton Mayer has shown some of the ramifications of society's involvement in the murder of the Jews in the following excerpt from an imaginary dialogue between Eichmann and an Israeli:

> EICHMANN: Why not hang the man who sold us the Cyclon-B for the gas chambers, or the man who had the contracts for the crematories, or the man who used the Jews for slave labor in his munitions plants? *He* is the greatest industrialist in Germany now, and on his last birthday Adenauer sent him a telegram of congratulations. Why not hang Adenauer?
>
> ISRAELI: We'll start with you.
>
> EICH. Why me? Why not the local policemen, thousands of them? They would have been shot if they had refused to round up the Jews for the death camps. Why not hang *them* for not wanting to be shot? Why me? *Everybody killed the Jews.*
>
> ISR. We can't put everybody on trial.
>
> EICH. You must, you must. *Everybody killed the Jews.*
>
> (The *Progressive,* April 1961)

Claude Eatherly was a "normal maniac" at one time, too. He was carried along the assembly line of society, without significant protest, and one day he found himself piloting the plane which led the atomic bombing of Hiroshima. A few days later he participated in the bombing of Nagasaki. Perhaps he might have remained a normal member of society all his life (there is no way of knowing) but the American Military Command took the men who had atomized Hiroshima and Nagasaki to see the results of their work. From that day to this Claude Eatherly has been haunted by the cries of those whom he, like Eichmann, helped incinerate. But there is a difference. Eatherly was on "our side" and Eichmann was not (even though his side has become our side now and the men who hired Hitler and Eichmann are now not only our valued allies but at times even seem to be our masters, forcing us closer to the brink than we might otherwise go). If we are to continue preparing for more and greater crematoria, and at the same time preserve the illusions of sanity and morality, Eichmann must be condemned and Eatherly must be a "hero." Perhaps it is especially important that Eichmann be condemned at this late date (once the Israelis have raised the embarrassing question) because

Krupp and Globke and Wernher von Braun and hundreds of others have risen so high. And certainly Eatherly, since he refuses to be a hero, must be got out of the way as quietly as possible because the automation of genocide has raised new questions for Americans about the morality of war, has given them intimations, as it were, of sanity. But the terrible logic of history appears to be that we shall not be permitted to have the protective curtain of social insanity lifted from one area (to be able, for instance, to visualize the victims of war as fellow human beings and so to renounce the military madness) without the inconvenience of having it at least partially lifted in some other areas as well. If the military domination of the great powers is diminished, how shall we keep the Africans, the Latin Americans, and the Asians from forcing themselves on us as human beings instead of expendable suppliers of labor and raw materials and profits? In many ways the Kennedys, the Schlesingers, etc., are more realistic, as they claim, than most pacifists in that they realize that to abandon our military protection would be to abandon our way of life. The unjustifiable special privileges that have been won and defended by violence *cannot* be defended by nonviolence. (But how are we going to build a peace movement if we admit that? Isn't it unconventional enough to be against military protection without being against the things that need protection? In other words we want to be against war without having to be against the things that cause war.)

Like all empires of the past, the United States is doomed to lose its preeminence anyway (and the pace of history is greatly speeded up these days). But few Americans are prepared to face up to the dissolution of an empire whose existence they don't even like to recognize. The problem has to be rephrased something like this: Would you want *your* daughter to marry an African tribesman? Would you be willing for your son to share a standard of living somewhere between the one he is "entitled" to and that of an impoverished Guatemalan peasant (who presently works for a few cents a day for the United Fruit Company)?

The American press has been revealingly silent about Eatherly. We hear more about the triumphs of Wernher von Braun, who is now doing for the Pentagon, on a more devastating scale, what he formerly did for Hitler, than of the tortured apostasy of Eatherly. The same week that Eichmann was condemned to die James Wechsler, of the *New York Post,* picked up a story from a Canadian magazine that told of Eatherly's escape some months earlier from the Waco insane asylum. His whereabouts are unknown and Wechsler speculates that somewhere in some obscure bar Eatherly may be trying to tell his story to some skeptical drunken companion. My acquaintance with two other victims of war led me to speculate along different lines. I refer to two war heroes who served in World War II under the Office of Strategic Services, parachuting behind enemy lines and carrying out strategic murders and acts of demolition and sabotage. After the war they were psychologically unable to abandon the life of adventure, danger, and high pay to which they had become accustomed. For sixteen years they have been employed by various branches of the government, and occasionally by American corporations with foreign holdings, to continue their work of strategic murder and sabotage. One of them told me that he kills with everything from piano wire and his bare hands to conventional weapons. They are part of the "paramilitary" operations which President Kennedy said must play an increasingly important role in the New Frontier, since, as he put it, "It is the soft societies that perish." Both men have been used in the campaign to overthrow the Cuban revolution.

Perhaps it was because of my contact with these men that I began to wonder about Eatherly. Are his whereabouts really unknown? Has he, perhaps, been quietly captured and salted away, more securely this time? Oh has he, perhaps, been done away with, by those who cannot afford to have him around to raise embarrassing questions? Since the American conscience is shielded as much as possible from knowledge of these "paramilitary" realities, we may never know.

In any event we owe Eatherly a debt of gratitude. He was willing not only to refuse riches and the mantle of a hero but to sacrifice something which most men value more highly than their consciences and cling to more desperately than their lives—his respectability— in order to help us prevent the reappearance, on an even larger scale, of the death camps and death cities of World War II.

The dramas of these two men, Eatherly and Eichmann, revolve around their responses to the social ethics of their day when each was asked to participate in the incineration of millions of his fellows. (The toll in Nagasaki and Hiroshima was but a fraction of the total burned alive by American and British saturation bombing of the cities of Europe and Japan.) The challenge to each of us today is that *our* "leaders" are asking *us* to participate, actively or by discreet silence, in preparations to incinerate far greater numbers of our fellows. Eichmann stands condemned for being anti-Semitic. Will we who condemn him accept the role prepared for us of being anti-human? Or will we, while there is perhaps still time, understand what Eatherly understood too late—that no "patriotic duty," timidity, or opportunism can justify us in cooperating, either actively or by the moderation of our opposition, in this madness?

Part Two

The War Against Vietnam

Political Realism and Moral Disaster

It is easy to learn whether there is much iron in the sun, and what metals there are in the sun and the stars; but it is hard, yes frightfully hard, to discover that which convicts us of immorality.

— Leo Tolstoi, *The Kreutzer Sonata.*

1966 I can imagine no more distressing reading matter than Eric Norden's survey of American atrocities in Vietnam.* It is a compilation and concentration of events that originally came to us in driblets, like small doses of poison whose lethal properties we did not recognize because they were mixed with our regular diet. Americans have been genuinely troubled by reports and pictures of brutality in Vietnam. We have not seen that they reflect a persistent pattern of infamy that is inseparable from continuation of the war and yet is so intolerable that it cannot be justified by the pressures of a losing military campaign.

* *First published in the same issue of* Liberation *as this article (February 1966). Reprinted as a pamphlet "American Atrocities in Vietnam."* Liberation.

The immediate political implications of this dilemma are difficult enough for most Americans: that we must accept the "loss of face" involved in military withdrawal from Vietnam and victory for the National Liberation Front. Even more intolerable are the long-run cultural and political implications, in terms of our knowledge of ourselves and our society. The very mention of German atrocities in the same breath as America's "indiscretions" and circumstantial "excesses" in Vietnam is offensive to us. Far from serving as a warning of the evils that lie in wait for any self-righteous and powerful nation which considers itself above the law (whether as a result of racial superiority or the peculiar virtue of its form of government), the German atrocities have been interpreted from the beginning as lying outside the context of our own political dynamics. They have been portrayed as the willful perversities of insane or evil men, men who gloried in brutal and uncivilized values that are the exact opposite of those treasured (though not always lived up to) by our own culture.

No doubt there were such men, as there are in every culture, though their links to the rest of us are closer than we like to imagine or trace. But the real lesson of Nazi Germany we have hidden from ourselves—with obviously unfortunate results today and even greater danger for the future, as the United States finds its hegemony challenged all over the world. The lesson we should have taken to heart was the number of ordinary, "decent," humane and enlightened men and women, persons very much like ourselves, who collectively formed the cast of the German tragedy. Hannah Arendt has pointed out that even Adolf Eichmann fits for the main into this category:

> Half a dozen psychiatrists had certified him as "normal"—"More normal, at any rate, than I am after having examined him," one of them was said to have exclaimed, while another had found that his whole psychological outlook, his attitude toward his wife and children, mother and father, brother, sisters, and friends, was "not only normal but most desirable"—and finally the minister who had paid regular visits to him in prison . . . reassured everybody by declaring Eichmann to be "a man with very positive ideas."
> . . . The judges . . . were too good, and perhaps also too conscious of the very foundations of their profession, to admit that an average, "normal" person, neither feeble-

minded nor indoctrinated nor cynical, could be perfectly incapable of telling right from wrong.

Paradoxically, along with our isolation of the Nazis and their accomplices as being basically different from ourselves or anything that we might easily become—under the pressure of a deteriorating political situation, as in Vietnam—we have found it hard to believe that the average German was not "aware" of what was going on under the Nazis. We conveniently overlook the personal defense mechanisms which protected the Germans (as they protect us today) from emotional and spiritual awareness, even when the facts were available. We know that the average German did not consciously will evil, as we do not today, but fail to recognize what Hannah Arendt has called "the banality of evil," in certain periods of historical stress, when our merited prerogatives are being denied (Germany) or threatened (the United States). At such times, evil insinuates itself into our daily lives and makes us its accomplices, without any major effort or decision on our parts. In fact all that it requires of most of us, at least for a very long time, is that we do nothing. More convenient still, we can work constructively, for civil rights, in anti-poverty programs, in medicine, education, civil liberties, or what-have-you; and just not weaken our influence or endanger our financing (as S.N.C.C. has recently done) by speaking out too insistently on behalf of those who are being murdered.

In our own case, the damning facts are presented to us almost daily in the mass media. With a sophistication possible only in a corrupt and calloused society which has lost its capacity for human relatedness, we interpret this as evidence that we live in a free society and that therefore America's role in Vietnam cannot be quite as indefensible as is sometimes charged. We turn our knowledge into anti-knowledge. Our possession of institutional "freedom" robs us of the capacity to act as free persons—much as our self-image of being the Free World becomes our justification for suppressing the freedom of others.

In the main, though, we find it possible to digest our atrocities without gagging only because they form such a small part of our diet. They come to us diluted by:

The normality of our daily lives, which by and large have survived unchanged (so far), with their customary allotments of freedom, decency, material prosperity, minor tribulations, and satisfactions.

Homey little comments and descriptions from the front, which convey (quite accurately, I might add) the essential humanness of American soldiers, the majority of whom are as likably American as Willie Mays, Bob Hope, and the kid next door. They have an unpleasant duty to perform on behalf of freedom, we are told, and are performing it with true American greatness.

Depersonalization of the victims, not only as Reds, Vietcong, aggressors, and, terrorists, but as bodies to be counted, like tallies in a ball game or some other computation of gain. Here is a typical report from today's paper:

> A massive U.S.-Australian drive began *paying dividends* yesterday. New fighting brought guerrilla dead to 207. . . . U.S. officers' disappointment over the results of Operation Crimp [which had not brought many "dividends," in the form of bodies, or human beings killed] was replaced with a feeling of *satisfaction* . . . . "When you're on to a *good thing* you stay with it," an Army spokesman said. (A.P. dispatch from Saigon, January 13, 1966. Emphasis added.)

Unless one has previously rejected the assumed framework of values within which the war is reported and analyzed (even by most of the critics), it is hard to be moved by such accounts to awareness and compassion, let alone indignation and revolt. The "innocent" victims of torture and napalm tend to excite greater concern, but for the most part we relate to them much as we do to victims of auto accidents or innocent bystanders who are caught in a dragnet or killed in a battle between cops and bank robbers. We ask for cautions and safeguards, in order to minimize accidents and "excesses" in the future; assurances that the hearts (aims) of our war lords are pure and democratic—or at least as pure and democratic as it is "politically realistic" to expect, hemmed in as they are by Communists on the left and impetuous "extremists" on the right. Finally, some of us even ask for negotiations—to achieve America's basic war aims without further, unnecessary slaughter.

The shallow optimism and basic pro-Americanism of the critics. If we do reject the fundamental myths of American foreign policy for the past twenty years (American virtue, despite occasional lapses, and the democratic burden of protecting the weak and hungry peoples of the world from aggressive, totalitarian communism), if we begin to apply the normal laws of cause and effect to American actions and draw logical conclusions from the regularity of the pattern (instead of seeing each new aggression as a mistake, each new atrocity as an "excess," each new lie as an overzealousness in public relations), then the good shepherds of the peace flock warn us against the neurotic errors of "alienation" and "anti-Americanism." To protect us from these heresies, they remind us of the evils of communism (both real and imagined), thereby distracting us from our primary responsibility of being true to ourselves and the society of which we are a part. It becomes a matter of "maturity," "goodwill," and "constructive" faith in mankind to view the American state as basically healthy, democratic, and free. We are encouraged to believe that the addition or repeal of a few laws, the replacing of a few misguided leaders, the dissemination of a few "facts," or the coming together of a new liberal coalition (the more enlightened leaders of organized labor, organized religion and the responsible civil rights movement, who secured the 1964 civil rights law, the anti-poverty legislation, and the election of Johnson over Goldwater) will get it back on the right track. We are told that we must move "from protest to politics," where the governing principles are realistic compromise and the art of the possible, within the existing framework and assumptions, rather than indulge ourselves in a no-win policy of calling for a revolutionary reorientation, with new values, the development of new (parallel) institutions, and the emergence of new, egalitarian revolutionists, of whom we have seen forerunners in S.N.C.C. and here and there in S.D.S. and other sectors of the New Left.

Since American democracy, with its admitted defects, is nonetheless assumed to be the best system known to man—and certainly a lesser evil than the totalitarianism to which all un-American and anti-American experiments in economic egalitarianism and organic democracy are bound to lead—even peace lovers tend to be reassured by reports of American military success and impending military victory.

Promises that "The corner has been definitely turned toward victory" (Secretary of Defense Robert NcNamara, May 1962); that "The major part of the U.S. military task can be completed by the end of 1965" (McNamara, October 1963); that "We have stopped losing the war" (McNamara, October 1965).

As James Reston has pointed out,

> The day-to-day communiqués give the impression that
> we win almost every encounter, but we somehow merely ad-
> vance deeper into the bog. . . . Officials go on talking as if
> one more summer or one more winter of American action
> will bring the desired result, but in private they concede that
> this kind of war could easily go on for years. (The *New
> York Times,* November 14, 1965).

These promises, however disingenuous, give us the feeling that
soon the atrocities will be ended (so why get ourselves in trouble, or
endanger our usefulness?), pursuit of the Great Society will become
our rallying point, and American liberalism will be triumphant. We
forget that it is the liberals and moderates who have been in control
for thirty-three years and have guided us every step of the way into
moral disaster. We forget that the only real victory in Vietnam for
the American ideals of the Declaration of Independence and the Revolutionary War would be defeat for the Pentagon and complete military withdrawal, in the manner of George III and the British Red-
coats.

When we toy with subversive formulations of this kind and
are tempted to apply the Golden Rule to foreign relations (seeing the
Vietnamese war, for example, through the eyes of the Vietnamese),
we are brought back into the fold by the pious public-relations copy
of the White House, which reads like a wise and loving father's combination of the realism of Machiavelli and the good intentions of the
Sermon on the Mount. Since it is a cardinal tenet of Niebuhrian Prot-
estantism, political liberalism, social-democratic socialism, and even
the American Communist Party, that political realism requires a combination of moral aims and immoral means, our defenses against this
kind of appeal are minimal. The resoluteness of our opposition is un-
dermined by:

Pious assurances, which reaffirm our self-image as an idealistic
and humanitarian nation, a myth which conflicts with the known
facts but is important to our self-respect. We are reminded that the
United States is providing generous economic, educational, and medical aid, even in the midst of war, and has offered billions for development, once the war is over. Our main targets are said to be bridges,
munitions depots, power plants, and supply routes. (The people just

get in the way.) The administration is eager to enter into "unconditional discussions" as soon as the stubborn and aggressive Communists give a signal of a genuine desire for peace (such as abandoning their "condition" of American military withdrawal). President Johnson weeps over the deaths of American soldiers and Vietnamese civilians (as some of the Roman Emperors wept over the deaths of the Christians in the Coliseum).

These and a host of other professed pieties may be largely sincere, but even so are hardly relevant. Neither the juxtaposition of ruthless murder and flamboyant financial compensation, nor the preference, when convenient, for peaceful methods of maintaining domination and control, nor the spiritual torments of sado-masochism are acceptable substitutes for egalitarianism and respect for the dignity and freedom of those who, under even the most generous interpretation, are now our vassals.

In these and other ways, we are restrained from facing up to the full implications of the rumors, disclosures, and charges that have left us worried and uneasy. It really is hard to recognize "that which convicts us [us!] of immorality." But what happens when we spend a concentrated hour or so reading the Norden article, exposing ourselves to events so gruesome and beyond justification on any terms (comprehension even), that knowledge of them drove intelligent and conscientious persons like Alice Herz, Norman Morrison, and Roger LaPorte to immolate themselves? No doubt these three acted in part out of a sense of helplessness, aware as they were that nothing else any of us had devised or done had been even remotely adequate to the need. But they also acted with faith, faith that human beings can be touched and, in the end, will respond.

Perhaps it is harder for most Americans to discard their illusions about their country and its underlying decency in world affairs than it was for these three to burn themselves to death. Perhaps it is harder for any of us to live adequately day after day, handicapped by our limitations of intellect and will and our proneness to distraction and tactical error, than it is to die in one supreme sacrifice. In any event, there comes a time when we cannot wait to straighten out our ideology or be certain that we have hit upon the most effective tactics; a time when we must respond as human beings—as a number of anti-Semites did in Germany, when they helped Jews to escape the wrath of the S.S.; in the manner of those courageous white Southern-

ers who have spoken out against lynching and terror, even while
clinging to the myths of white paternalism and black inferiority.

Naturally, the nature of our opposition will vary according to
our differing temperaments and circumstances, but we must ask ourselves whether the time has not come when to refrain from acting to
our personal utmost is to commit spiritual suicide. Indeed, if we lack
the compassion and selfhood to cry out now, with the insistency of
panic, we must ask ourselves if we are not already dead.

Of course life does not work quite that way. We grow and develop erratically, not only in response to the events that beset us but
also in accord with our own internal times and seasons. But if we are
aware, we cannot evade our responsibility for long without perishing
along with those whose murder we will have sanctioned by our
silence.

There is another problem of a different sort presented by accounts of American atrocities in Vietnam. Why just American?
What of terror by the National Liberation Front? One cannot dismiss it all on the basis of Senator Young's disclosure that the C.I.A.
hires Vietnamese to pose as members of the Vietcong and to commit
both murder and rape. (The *New York Times,* October 21, 1965.)
One may wonder why the C.I.A. conceives it to be politically advantageous to commit this ultimate depravity. Is it for propaganda reasons, because the Vietcong does not commit enough atrocities of its
own? Or is it a customary, double-barreled routine in which the C.I.A.
gets rid of its political enemies and blames the Communists? With
murder, perhaps; but rape?

It is instructive for Americans who still pride themselves on the
basic morality of American society and its democratic government to
reflect on this practice. What does it say about the state of the Republic that such a disclosure caused no significant public outcry, no crisis
in government, no perceptible disillusionment among the masses of
loyal Americans? What will serve to unmask our government and
shatter our self-image as defenders of human dignity in world affairs?

Be that as it may, we know better than to think that the United
States commits *all* the atrocities on both sides. Neither the N.L.F. nor
Hanoi claim to be pacifists or act as such. Relatively innocent Vietnamese suffer almost every time an attempt is made to blow up facilities used by Americans in Saigon. This is perhaps "normal" in war
(though no less deplorable, and certainly an argument in favor of

equally resolute all-out nonviolent resistance, as a substitute for violent wars of liberation.) But there is revolting evidence, as well, of the disembowelling of native quislings and Benedict Arnolds, and according to some reports, sometimes of their children as well.

Who can gainsay the political and psychological pressures to commit such acts—as warnings to collaborators and as the traditional response of most humanitarians and patriots to the ravages of a foreign invader? Who but the most protected or self-righteous among us can dismiss these pressures or predict how he would act under similar provocations; that is, if he had grown up as a native of Vietnam, which has suffered active invasion and foreign treachery for nearly thirty years? Apparently the N.L.F. has succeeded till now in keeping acts of revenge (as distinct from the selective political murder of key traitors) at a minimum. As near as we can tell, this is in part an expression of its humanistic values, in part a result of its reliance on overwhelming popular support (a partially humanizing characteristic of guerrilla warfare that is not always noted by pacifist critics). But now that the United States has refused to accept the verdict rendered by native guerrilla warfare and is increasingly turning the struggle into a large-scale war between regular armies of the United States and North Vietnam, this moderating pressure may well be minimized.

In any case, acts of terror or reprisal, whatever their "justification," tend to corrupt rather than preserve or enhance the humanism of those who perform them. Life becomes cheap after a while, and human beings tend to become objects, obstacles, abstractions, in the eyes of conscientious revolutionaries as well as of the naïvely idealistic anti-Communists who fly bombing missions or man machine guns in behalf of the white man's democratic burden.

In revolutionary movements of the past, there has been a tendency for violence to feed on itself and cumulatively corrupt the movement. History is replete with examples, ranging from several branches of nineteenth century anarchism through twentieth century Stalinists to contemporary anarchists and social democrats among Cuban and middle-European exiles. Wars of liberation that have not dragged on too long or provoked large-scale foreign intervention (bringing full-scale war, as distinct from guerrilla conflict) have suffered less from this internal corruption. Such was the case in Cuba, where the United States supplied military materiel and advisers to Batista, as in Vietnam, but did not impose full-scale war when he was defeated, "realistically" expecting, on the basis of past experiences, to be able to buy off Castro on his accession to power. The Revolution was able to take power on January 1, 1959, at a stage roughly comparable to that attained by the Vietnamese liberation front in 1964.

In the bitter and exhausting Spanish Civil War, which involved significant intervention by Germany, Italy and the Soviet Union, the initial enthusiasm and solidarity of the people, in 1936, was comparable to that in Cuba in late 1958 and in Vietnam in 1964. The imposition of "revolutionary justice," which began as a form of political reprisal against fascists and their collaborators, was gradually extended to include anarchists, social democrats, and Trotskyists. Political "deviationists" in the International Brigade, men who gave up the comfort and security of their homeland to risk their lives fighting fascism, ended up, in countless cases, being shot in the back by men on their own side. Franco triumphed as much from the resulting collapse of revolutionary morale as he did from superiority in arms. Revolutionary abuses of this kind helped disillusion and distract a whole generation of Americans, who grew up in the revolutionary school of the depression. Many of them were turned from potential revolutionists to paranoiac anti-Communists. It would be false to attribute their tragic loss of way entirely to the seductions of American affluence or the persecutions of Red-baiting. Certainly it was harder for many of them to stand up to these pressures because of their internal anguish and disillusionment.

I mention these sad historical facts, not to take the curse of American atrocities and aggression, which are the primary and immediate evils with which the world is presently confronted, and not as evidence of the malevolence of the Stalinists. Rather they are warning of the traps and pitfalls that lie in wait for good men who regretfully conclude that their methods cannot be as revolutionary as their goals. This is a problem that must be faced up to, honestly and sensitively, by today's aspiring revolutionists. For us to fall into the same trap that history sprang on the Stalinists would be less excusable for us than it was for them. It would compound the present disaster:

North Vietnam: Eyewitness Report

1966 *Moscow, October 14, 1966 .*　　　　Enroute to Hanoi.

Tomorrow I leave for Peking and Hanoi. Before I go I want to record some of what I have seen and learned during the past two months in the course of a trip that has already taken me to Saigon, Phnom Penh (Cambodia) and Bangkok, to Tokyo, Hong Kong, Delhi, Cairo and Moscow.

In Phnom Penh and Moscow, I had a series of conferences with spokesmen of the National Liberation Front and with representatives of the Democratic Republic of Vietnam. In Saigon I met with leaders of the opposition to the U.S.-Ky government. These opponents included not only Buddhist monks, students and intellectuals, but also early members of the Diem government who resigned when they became convinced that the United States insists on a policy which is the exact opposite of its public rhetoric of peace, political freedom and social justice.

Let me start in Saigon. At midnight I saw a mother gather four little children around her, one at the breast, to catch what troubled sleep they could on a rain-drenched sidewalk. Nearby a group of eight- to twelve-year-olds, without either homes or parents, tugged at my sleeves for a *piastre*. Some whimpered plaintively while others smiled eagerly and looked up with the irresistible faces of innocence. Most heartrending of all was the fact that the whole performance was obviously rehearsed for maximum impact. Victims of war that do not appear in the statistics or the military reports: children not only orphaned and desolate but progressively hardened and corrupted in order to survive.

A TV man who has been in Saigon for eighteen months told me that these particular children will not be on the streets for long. There is a constant influx and a high turnover. He said that juvenile delinquency work (and a lot of the other nonmilitary operations in Saigon) is being taken over by West Germany. The Germans are more efficient than the Vietnamese, and besides there is a shortage of reliable Vietnamese collaborators. Periodically the authorities "clean" the streets by having the homeless waifs arrested. Kids as young as ten are given sentences of ten to fifteen years on trumped-up charges, and then trained as suicide squads. They can gain their "freedom" by risking death or mutilation while betraying their countrymen to the hated foreign invader. (Given the depth of that hatred, I wonder how many of them actually carry out their missions. But where do they go, what do they do, if they don't?)

At the entrance to my hotel, a little girl, perhaps eight years old, asks for money. After she gets a little, she runs back a few steps and cries out defiantly: "*Ka Ka Do* Americans; *Ka Ka Do* Americans." ("Cut the Americans' throats.") Just then two American M.P.'s ride slowly by in a jeep, chins and guns protruding menacingly. The little girl turns from me and screams at the soldiers: "*Ka Ka Do* M.P.'s; *Ka Ka Do* M.P.'s." In the background the voice of someone who is obviously half drunk can be heard complaining, "Nobody likes the Americans and I look like an American, but I'm not. I'm Canadian."

Early in the morning, in the men's room of my Saigon hotel, a boy about ten years old, with a drawn and pinched face, smiles wanly, makes obscene gestures with his hands, and invites me to follow him. It is not clear whether it is he or his mother I am supposed to "enjoy," but that is all that is left obscure as he pushes a finger of one hand back and forth through a hole formed by the thumb and fingers of the other.

I follow the hotel doorman instead. He has offered to "change money." I shall not do it, but I want to find out a little about the black market. He starts by offering me one and a half times the official rate and gradually climbs to more than double, taking my continued refusals and disclaimers as sharp bargaining.

I apologize for having wasted his time and wander into the street. Packages of American cigarettes catch my eye. There are strange white labels under the cellophane wrapping. Looking more closely, I read on a pack of Pall Malls:

FOR USE OUTSIDE U.S.
DONATED BY M & O CHEVROLET CO.
427 FRANKLIN ST.
FAYETTEVILLE, N. C.

I decide to buy a pack as a "souvenir" and select a package of Lucky Strike Filters. The label says:

FOR USE OUTSIDE U.S.
DONATED BY
COLONIA MEMORIAL POST 6061 V.F.W.
606 INMAN AVE.
COLONIA, N. J. 07067

On the top is printed

TAX EXEMPT
NOT TO BE SOLD

This routine and perhaps minor perversion of the generosity and idealism of the donors back home strikes me as symbolic of the perversion and corruption of all the varied idealism and self-sacrifice which innumerable Americans have poured and are pouring into Vietnam. Most heartbreaking of all, of course, are the sacrifices of those who fight and die there, believing, for a time at least, what the government has told them.

If they arrive in Saigon thinking that they have come to help the Vietnamese, they soon find that the Vietnamese have a different view. Saigon is the heartland of the "pro-American" sector. Besides the hit-and-run attacks of the N.L.F. guerrillas, there is the sullen aloofness and hostility of the general population, which is not above making a fast dollar off the Americans but never really fraternizes with them—and always protects and shelters its own. A bomb explodes, a symbolic assault is made at the very center of Saigon in full view of hundreds of people, and the perpetrators are almost never caught. The population opens up and swallows its own.

The Venerable Thich Thien Hoa, President of the United Buddhist Church, explained the universal hostility toward Americans in the following manner:

> We realize that many Americans want to help us. We thank them for this. But the policy of the United States government is not to help the Vietnamese people but to help a small group which oppresses the people. The American government has been here more than ten years and it has always supported dictator governments, so the Vietnamese people are against the American government.

Similarly, members of an underground student group told me

> All the present collaborators were collaborators and hirelings (*serviteurs*) of France. During the Japanese occupation they collaborated with the Japanese. This tiny oppressing minority collaborates with whatever foreign power is seeking to rule over us. They profit from colonialism so they don't want independence. They profit from the war, so they don't want peace. But the people are against the Americans. That is for sure. One hundred percent of the people are against the United States.

Like others I talked with, these students made it clear that it was not Ky but the United States which was responsible for the brutal suppression of last spring's Buddhist demonstrations. They spoke with anguish of the number of people who had been killed or put in jail. They said that the suppressions were so extensive that they were unable to plan and launch an offensive just now. But they emphasized that new uprisings were inevitable.

Despite the persuasiveness of American money and power, the ranks of the collaborators are thinning out. In Phnom Penh I spoke with wealthy and conservative refugees who talked with tears in their eyes of their disillusionment with the United States. One of them had served in the governments of both Bao Dai and Ngo Dinh Diem. In 1951 he was declared by the Viet Minh to be under sentence of death as a notorious collaborator with the French. In 1955, the Americans sought him out in Paris and made him a member of the Diem government. Still looking and talking like an aristocrat, but obviously a man of both courage and integrity, he said to me:

No one can accuse me of being anti-American. On the contrary, I collaborated with the Americans under Diem. But I resigned when it became clear that the United States did not want peace. I wanted to collaborate with the Americans, but I wanted to collaborate for peace, not for war. I wanted to work with them for the good of my country, not for its destruction. . . . After the assassination of Diem, your government contacted me again and asked me to serve in the new government. I refused, making clear that I still wanted to follow a policy of peace and would not serve in a government that was set up by the Americans in order to wage war.

A second man had studied at M.I.T. in the early sixties and looked me up at my hotel in Phnom Penh. He explained that he thought he had heard me speak on the radio in the United States, but as he talked I realized that his real reason was that he needed to work out his ambivalence by discussing it with an American. This man also appeared quite aristocratic in his manner and in general was both so mild and nonpolitical that he took me completely by surprise when he said:

I hesitate to take up a gun and fight because I know so many Americans. They are my friends. But I am very much opposed to what the Americans are now doing and before long I may decide that I have to join the war against them.

As he spoke I had the feeling that he had just about made up his mind but had needed to "explain" his action to an American first.

In Saigon itself, I spoke at length, behind locked doors and drawn blinds, with an important public official *of the present government*. He also was an aristocrat, one of the "tiny minority" who until recently had had no difficulty getting along with the various foreign rulers that have occupied his country. But as he put it to me:

We have had war since 1939. My hair has become gray. War, always war, and everyone suffers. And since the United States is insistent on continuing the war, I have come to feel that it would be better for us to form a new government, one that will deal with the National Liberation Front. One that would initiate a cease-fire, bring peace, and try to absorb the N.L.F. It would have to be a new nationalist government for peace. Ky is where he is today only because of the Americans. In the end whichever group wins out in the peaceful competition between ourselves and the N.L.F., it will be better than what we have now.

At Tansonnhut Airport in Saigon, youthful Vietnamese are leaving the country to study in France, Canada, and the United States. At the same time youthful Americans are arriving, many of them to die in the paddies and jungles of Vietnam. I had the opportunity to interview a number of the departing students. None of them seemed too troubled over who wins the war. When I asked one of them, as gently as I could, if he felt any hesitation about leaving his country to study in the United States while Americans were coming there to risk mutilation and death, he replied:

> As a human being, yes. But you must remember that it is the United States which insists on continuing the war.

REPORT FROM NORTH VIETNAM

I hope that I may be forgiven for beginning this report by saying that I recoil from the prospect of writing it, because of the difficulties of communication involved. The problem is partly the superficiality of our most cherished words and concepts before the abrupt finality of premature, man-made death and the lingering horror of dismembered or faceless survivors. But there is a cultural and political problem as well, involving the gap between American experience and Vietnamese experience, American political assumptions and Vietnamese assumptions.

What words are there with which to talk to any young mother who tearfully hands one a snapshot of her three dead children? But what does an American say to a young Vietnamese mother who hands him such a snapshot and says: "We Vietnamese do not go to the United States to fight your people. Why have they come over here to kill my children?"

What can one say to a twenty-year-old girl, swathed in bandages and still in a state of shock because her mother, father, three brothers and sisters were all killed at their noonday meal when American bombers attacked the primitive agricultural village in which they lived? She herself was pulled unconscious and severely burned from the straw hut in which the rest of the family perished.

"Ask your President Johnson," she said to me, "if our straw huts were made of steel and concrete" (a reference to the President's claim that our targets in North Vietnam are military structures of steel and concrete). "Ask him if our Catholic church that they destroyed was a military target, with its 36 pictures of the Virgin, whom we revere. Tell him that we will continue our life and struggle no matter what future bombings there will be, because we know that without independence and freedom nothing is worthwhile."

I went with her to a nearby "Hate Memorial." It was not dedicated to hatred of those whom the United States labels as aggressors and villains. Instead, on one side of the monument, the inscription said:

> In Hatred against the U.S. Pirates
> Who Killed our Countrymen
> of Phuxa Village
> Nhât Tân Commune
> On August 13, 1966

The other side read:

> Firmly Hold the Plow
> Firmly hold the Rifle
> Be Determined to Fight and Win
> Over the American Aggressors
> In order to Avenge our Fellow Countrymen
> of Phuxa, Nhât Tân

Of the 237 houses in Phuxa, 40 were destroyed on August 13. Thirty-two persons were killed.

Meanwhile an American mother mourns the death of her son, drafted into the armed forces and shot down on a bombing raid over Vietnam. In the United States we are told that he was defending the Vietnamese people against Chinese aggression, but there are no Chinese soldiers in Vietnam. In fact, the Vietnamese will tell you that the last Chinese soldiers to invade Vietnam were 180,000 U.S.-supported Chiang Kai-shek troops, in the winter of 1945-46. They helped the Allies suppress the Vietnamese independence which the United States had promised Vietnam when we needed her help during World War II. Earlier, when the Vietnamese first declared their independence, on September 2, 1945, the Allies hastily rearmed 90,000 Japanese soldiers who had been waiting shipment back to Japan. During the next nine years, the United States supplied eighty percent of the cost of the unsuccessful "French" war to preserve Western colonialism in Indochina. President Eisenhower's refusal, in 1956, to allow democratic elections and reunification of Vietnam, as promised in the Geneva Accords, was not our first flagrant betrayal of Vietnamese independence. Most Americans are ignorant of these facts, or dimly aware of them as unfortunate mistakes committed in a confused and distant past, but there is hardly a Vietnamese family that does not measure America's broken promises in terms of the death of one or more loved ones.

How does one greet a seventeen-year-old boy who limps painfully across the room, looking as if he were fifty (though he will never reach that age) because his face and neck, legs and arms are covered with welts and abscesses from napalm burns? I don't know, but I remember protest meetings in the United States at which Christian clergymen have said: "It may be true that our tax money buys napalm but you can't expect Americans to refuse to pay their income taxes in protest. After all, whatever mistakes the United States may make, this is a democratic country and we must obey its laws."

We weep for your wounds, Thai Binh Dan, and those of your countrymen. But we hope that you don't expect us to be so rash as to revolt against the society that inflicted them. Don't be discouraged. There is a solution and we will tell it to you. You can revolt against your government. Tell your brothers and sisters who are not yet wounded that if they are anxious to avoid your fate, that is what they must do.

We admit that the United States had no business getting involved in Vietnam in the first place, but you must remember that we are a big and powerful country. Now that we are there we can't just withdraw; that is, we can't just stop the murder, stop trying to dictate to your people what kind of economic and political system they can have, stop pretending that our massive terrorization of your people is somehow a way of protecting them against intimidation and terror.

So it's up to you, Thai Binh Dan. You must get your people to come over to our side. You must get them to turn against your government so that it will be forced to surrender. ("Come to the conference table" is the way we put it in the United States; surely you can see how reasonable that sounds.) Meanwhile we shall continue the napalm and the other bombing, which, if you stop to think of it, will help you in your struggle against your government.

Be of good cheer, Dan. After the peace that we all desire so earnestly, if your country lines up satisfactorily on our side of the Cold War, our government will probably permit us, after a few years, to bring dozens, possibly even hundreds of your people to the United States. Here in our warm-hearted, rich, and democratic country, they will be given every consolation. Our women will weep over them, our skilled plastic surgeons will remove the worst of the scars, and the most enlightened of our businessmen will write tax-deductible checks to cover their expenses.

What does one say to a seven-year-old lad who (if he manages to survive future attacks) will have to go through life with only one arm, because his right arm was severed near the shoulder in a bombing raid? When I talked with him and a twelve-year-old friend, who had lost a leg in a different attack, I tried to get away from the horrors of war. I asked them about their school and told them about the daily life of my ten- and fourteen-year-olds in the United States.

We had a good conversation. There were the beginnings, at least, of trust and affection. But there was no way we could get away from the war, as one can do in the United States by turning off the news or changing the topic.

School? Seven-year-old Dai had lost his arm when his kindergarten was bombed. Ten of his classmates and the teacher were killed; nine were wounded. Twelve-year-old Chinh had been on his way to his school one morning with a friend when:

> There was the explosion of bombs and I didn't know that my leg was cut but only that I couldn't stand up and that I couldn't walk any longer. . . . My friend Ve put me on his back and got me near the trenches. Then another explosion knocked us into the trenches where there was water and we got all wet. Ve kept pulling me through the water to get away from the bombs. He put me in a dry place and saw that there was lots of blood and was afraid and went to the village to get my father. . . . When my father was carrying me to the first aid station I still could see everything all around and I saw a number of my friends and some of the

villagers lying dead on the ground. Then I lost my consciousness and couldn't see anything.

My notes say: "It is amazing how simply and naturally he speaks, without a trace of self-consciousness or self-pity. I wonder if he will be able to preserve such a healthy attitude as he goes through life without a leg."

While we were talking, American planes came suddenly upon us (as they do, day and night, all over Vietnam), roaring over the little complex of primitive shelters and the communal well at which women were washing their supper dishes and the three of us were talking. We took to shelter and continued the conversation. They told me that some of their friends had been killed while herding water buffalo: "The planes swoop down on the fields and machine gun the beasts and the people."

Earlier that day Miss Tuyen, a twenty-year-old peasant girl in the village of Nam Ngan, told me that two of her brothers, one eight and one three, had been killed less than a month earlier in the field where they had been taking care of buffalo. Miss Tuyen had been introduced to me as a "village hero" who had carried twice her weight in ammunition on her shoulders during an attack, transporting crates of shells through the narrow trenches to the anti-aircraft stations. It was only when I tried to turn the conversation to personal subjects, asking about her family, that I learned about the strafing of her brothers. An older brother had been killed at the age of eighteen, at the battle of Dien Bien Phu, the last major battle of the French Resistance War, which led to the Geneva Agreements and (supposedly) recognition of the independence and sovereignty of the unified country of Vietnam.

Perhaps it is worth quoting part of what Miss Tuyen said to me:

> When the planes come bombing and strafing our native land we feel a great indignation. We are making every effort to shoot them down, in order to avenge our young people who have been cut down by the American aggressors. . . . What would young Americans think if they were living peacefully and suddenly another country came and started killing them? For this reason, in spite of the planes all over the skies, we do not fear them. . . . When I was carrying ammunition a bomb exploded near me and covered me

with dirt but I struggled free in order to continue fighting. We only have rifles in the ground forces but we are making every effort to bring down the planes. Since August 5, 1964, we have participated in more than a hundred battles (I can't remember the exact number), but we are still firm in the battle.

At night when the planes come, I volunteer to cook rice. I reach every difficult place to serve the soldiers. During the day I go to the fields and gather vegetables for the army. They come, we open fire; they go, we continue picking vegetables. . . . Bombing is continuous but we never feel tired. . . . It is very clear that the young people in my village are ready to sacrifice their lives if necessary to defend our independence. The struggle may last for years, but we realize that we will win.

During the resistance against the French colonialists, when we won our independence, one of my brothers lost his life. He was eighteen at the time. Now the Americans have come, massacring the people in our village. That has fanned our hatred. We know that the American aggressors may commit more crimes against our village, but we have no alternative but to stand firm.

Recently, as I told you, my aunt and my two younger brothers were killed and I can't help feeling a great hatred. I am determined to avenge this blood debt. . . . We know that our battle is very difficult but we can see our victory ahead.

It's hard to find the words to tell you all our experiences but I realize that you can see much for yourself. On your return I hope that you can help the American people to understand the truth and, if you don't mind, I send my regards both to the peace movement in your country and also to your wife and to my brothers and sisters in your family. As for me I have no alternative but to go on fighting. When one day our country is reunited in freedom, I hope to greet you in our village on your way to Saigon.

The village in which this interview took place was another of those unbelievably primitive agricultural villages, similar to Phuxa, which cover the countryside. There was no way in which it could be considered a military target, except perhaps that its people fire back at attacking American planes. Yet because of the frequency with which bombs are dropped in the vicinity, every primitive straw hut had an individual underground concrete shelter that the family could slip into during night attacks. In addition there was a network of trenches, some of them concrete and some brick-lined. These trenches led away from the houses to larger shelters and to anti-aircraft stations. Before such villages have electricity, plumbing or paved roads, they have concrete trenches and bomb shelters to protect them from the advocates of the Great Society. While I was at Nam Ngan, I watched the peasants thresh rice by hand. Although they have no threshing machines, or for that matter sewing machines, washing machines, refrigerators—any of the things most Americans take for granted—they have to have machine guns and rifles to fight off the American attackers.

Now, a few hours after my conversation with Miss Tuyen, I was in another little hamlet, a few miles away, talking with Dai and Chinh and listening to the bombs explode. We estimated by the blast and illumination that they were falling in an area between a mile and perhaps five miles away. I tried to calculate whether some of them might be falling on Nam Ngan village, and wondered whether Miss Tuyen was cooking rice or carrying ammunition. I knew that I would probably never find out, because in a few minutes I would be on the road. It was dark already and nighttime is the only time it is "safe" to travel in North Vietnam. Now the planes were dropping flares, bathing everything in an eerie light, and despite myself I found myself wondering whether this was to make it easier to strafe "anything that moved," as the Vietnamese charge is the common practice.

In the minds of the American gunners, anything that moved would almost certainly be a Red totalitarian or terrorist, or, at the very least, an ignorant and inferior "Gook." I looked at seven-year-old Dai, with his missing arm, and twelve-year-old Chinh, with his missing leg, and thought of Miss Tuyen's three- and eight-year-old brothers who had been shot down a few weeks earlier while tending buffalo. I didn't want to think about what might be happening to any children who had been caught cowering in a field when the flares were dropped. So I turned to Dai and Chinh and tried to explain to them that many American airmen think that they are helping the

Vietnamese people when they bomb and strafe Vietnamese villages. It wasn't easy.

As long as I was in Hanoi, I was able to keep a relatively open mind and raise questions when I was told about the "deliberate bombing" of residential areas, schools and hospitals. Something, perhaps my own type of Americanism, rose up inside me and I tried to deny that Americans would knowingly bomb and strafe civilians, at least as part of deliberate governmental policy.

At dusk I sometimes sat on a bench by the lake and enjoyed the beauty of the thunder and lightning in the background—until I became adjusted to the fact that it was not really thunder and lightning but the explosion and illumination of bombs in the outskirts. Occasionally in Hanoi in November, one's eardrums would be threatened by particularly loud explosions, which generally turned out to be Vietnamese anti-aircraft fire from the roofs of nearby buildings. Twice while I was there, after shelter alarms and deafening blasts on all sides, the Vietnamese told me that they had shot down pilotless reconnaissance planes over the inner city. I saw the wreckage of one such plane. I could lie on my bed in the Thong Nhat hotel and watch the flames at the mouths of the guns on the roof of an adjacent building as they fought off occasional intruders. I talked with several people who had had fuel tanks or an isolated bomb crash on their houses as an American pilot tried to lighten his load in order to facilitate his getaway. A Polish diplomat told me that from inside the Polish embassy he had caught on tape the explosion of American bombs which fell in the embassy district in June. He said that it caused a sensation in Warsaw when he played the tape on his leave. But the inner city of Hanoi had not suffered any major attack, and, during the time I was in North Vietnam, it was indeed a small island of relative safety.

The Vietnamese, who have suffered from ceaseless escalation, even as President Johnson assured the world that "We seek no wider war," considered the partial sparing of inner Hanoi as a temporary public relations gimmick that would not last much longer. In North Vietnam they say that there are two events which are invariably followed by particularly brutal bombing raids. One is a severe military set-back in the South. ("After they have lost a battle on the ground they seem to need to reassure themselves by dropping tons and tons of bombs on our towns and cities.") The other is a speech by Presi-

dent Johnson assuring the world of his love for little children and his
devotion to world peace. (A Vietnamese writer said to me: "We are
as offended by Johnson's hypocrisy as by his cruelty." A doctor said:
"You have no idea how angry Johnson makes us with his 'carrot' of
a million dollars for economic aid. He is as cynical as he is barbarous.
Why, do you realize that some days the planes come dropping bombs
and killing our children, and then the next day they may drop toys
and candy, and leaflets urging us to surrender?")

For my part I shared the Vietnamese expectations of the worst
for Hanoi (though I remembered hopefully that even the Nazis did
not bomb Paris during World War II, apparently for fear of pro-
voking world-wide indignation). At the same time I could not help
being grateful for the delay in bombing the inner city. In a strange
way, perhaps the American peace movement, which tends to be rather
too quickly discouraged by its inability to reverse twenty years of
American foreign policy with a few demonstrations, might take some
credit (along with world public opinion) for having saved many
Vietnamese lives by forcing the military-industrial complex to accelerate its aggression at a slower rate than it might otherwise have done,
thus giving the Vietnamese the opportunity to disperse and decentralize. They had evacuated half or more of the population (including most of the children and older people) and had scattered most of
Hanoi's factories and schools throughout rural and jungle areas.

My first trip outside Hanoi was a brief one, to the village of
Phuxa, which did not provide conclusive evidence of civilian bombing as governmental policy. Phuxa was clearly not a military target
itself and was not near anything that appeared a likely military target.
In fact it was surrounded by fields and dikes. Thirty-two civilians had
been killed but the damage had been done by three airplanes which
dropped a total of five bombs and fourteen rockets. In August, in the
United States, I had talked with an ex-Marine, returned from service
in Vietnam, who had hold me that out of a combination of irritation
and boredom he and his buddies had opened fire on civilians in a
South Vietnamese village that lay beneath the spot on a hillside where
they had been standing guard all day. It is not hard to imagine that
from time to time enraged or frightened airmen might drop bombs
on "Communist villages" without great qualms of conscience. Clearly
such incidents need not reflect governmental policy. While I was in
Phuxa, an alarm was sounded by the ringing of the village bell and

all lights were extinguished but the planes passed noisily overhead to drop their bombs on other targets. I was prepared to believe—and still am—that the three offending planes, on August 13, might have been over-anxious to get rid of their load and return to safety, rather than to carry out their original assignment.

Later, however, when I made two extensive trips outside Hanoi, I reluctantly agreed with the Vietnamese that the United States has consciously and deliberately attacked the civilian population in a brutal attempt to destroy civilian morale. The best defense my American pride could muster was to say that the American people would not knowingly tolerate such practices. I urged Vietnamese officials to invite other non-Communist observers, including perhaps a few American newsmen or even someone like Senator Fulbright, to see the damage and report the facts to the American people. I argued that when the American people found out the nature and effects of the bombings, they would put an end to them.

Even apart from the widespread destruction of villages, cities and towns, I see no way to explain away the universal use of fragmentation bombs. Fragmentation bombs are useless against bridges and buildings of any kind but are deadly against people. In fact another name of them is anti-personnel bombs. I saw these bombs everywhere I went in North Vietnam.

There are different types of fragmentation bombs, but they all start with a "mother" bomb. (The term itself tells us something about our culture. Do we know nothing more about motherhood than this? Or is it that we have accepted the fact that mothers produce offspring who are destined to become killers?) The mother bomb explodes in the air over the target area, releasing 300 smaller bombs, typically the size of either a grapefruit or a pineapple. Each of the smaller bombs then ejects a spray of 150 tiny pellets of steel, which are so small that they bounce uselessly off concrete or steel, though they are very effective when they hit a human eye or heart. Vietnamese doctors told me that they have difficulty operating on patients wounded by these bombs, because the steel is so small that it is hard to locate, except through X rays. (There are more target areas in Vietnam than there are X-ray machines.) According to the Vietnamese, the general pattern of most attacks is to drop heavy explosive bombs and then to follow a few minutes later with fragmentation bombs and strafing, so as to interfere with relief operations and to kill those who are trying to flee the bombed-out area. From personal observation, I learned that the fragmentation bombs are equipped with timing devices so that they do not all eject their murderous barrage right away. When relief workers are trying to rescue the wounded, or later when the planes have departed and the all-clear has been sounded, hundreds of fragmentation bombs may explode, wounding or killing the innocent.

On my return to the United States, I discussed the uses of fragmentation bombs with a representative of the State Deparment. The only justification that he could offer was that they cut down the activities of guerrillas. But of course there are no guerrillas in North Vietnam and will be none unless the United States extends its land invasion to the North. And I talked with a mother in Than Hoa province who complained that it is difficult for children and parents to find one another after a raid because of the delayed-action fragmentation bombs.

In practice I know of only two possible explanations for the use of fragmentation bombs: 1) as part of a deliberate attempt to terrorize the civilian population. This explanation is held by everyone I talked with in Vietnam; and 2) as a way of trying to kill any soldiers who might be on their way south. (Perhaps the State Department representative meant "soldiers" when he said "guerrillas.") Technically this would fit in with the American claim that the bombing is aimed at military targets, but it would rob such a claim of any moral attractiveness or humanitarian meaning, since fragmentation bombs obviously cannot distinguish between soldiers in transit and children in search of their mothers, or any other category of human beings.

Even if one gives the United States the benefit of the doubt as to intent, the results can only be classified as criminal. Widespread use of fragmentation bombs in the North becomes the equivalent, on a large scale, of the practice in the South of shelling, napalming or setting fire to a village which is suspected of harboring a few guerrillas. There have been some practical restraints on this practice in the South, because of occasional publicity and attendant public reaction, but until now Americans have not been made aware of the nature and implications of their bombing of the North. They have preferred to believe, for the sake of their own illusory peace of mind, that it is possible to send an average of nearly a thousand bombers a day to attack the small country of Vietnam in an essentially sanitary and surgical operation that impedes "aggression" and spares civilians.

The figure of a thousand planes a day is the Vietnamese estimate of the daily average during the period I was in Vietnam (from October 28 through November 15, 1966). The American estimate is somewhat lower but, with typical deception, does not include attacks originating in Thailand, where the United States has built seven large bases, with as little publicity as it could get away with. According to Arthur Cook, Bangkok correspondent of the *London Daily Mail, more than half of all the air attacks on North Vietnam now originate in Thailand (Viet Report,* October 1966). Even the American figures would imply that Vietnam has a virtually limitless supply of "military targets."

About thirty-five miles south of Hanoi I visited the ruins of what once had been Phu Ly, a city with a population of over ten thousand. It was a gruesome Vietnamese Guernica. Not a building was still standing. Despite the fact that I think that the Air Force and the White House have grossly exaggerated American ability to carry out "pin-point," "precision" bombing, I do not see how the total destruction of a city of this size can be passed off as an accident—as if a city of more than ten thousand people could be reduced to rubble and ashes by a few bombs that were aimed at a bridge or railroad terminal but missed their mark.

Phu Ly was attacked on six different occasions, five of them between July 14 and November 5, 1966 (when I happened to be in the outskirts). The heaviest attacks were on the mornings of October 1 and 2, when an estimated 250 heavy bombs were dropped on the city. Survivors told me that after the heaviest bombings planes returned at intervals of twenty to thirty minutes to strafe anything that moved.

Before I went to Nam Dinh, North Vietnam's third largest city, I met the mayor, Mrs. Tran Thi Doan, in a rural hideaway some five or six miles outside the city, where it was considered safer to talk. Nam Dinh is a textile city of about 93,000 population, about sixty miles southwest of Hanoi and eighteen miles from the seacoast. It is about twenty-five miles from Phu Ly.

In view of the American suspicion that the Vietnamese exaggerate the extent of bombing damage, it is interesting to note that Mayor Doan supplied me with statistics that appear to have underestimated the damage to Nam Dinh. For example, she told me that 881 houses had been destroyed in thirty-three attacks, rendering 12,000 people homeless. She said that thirteen percent of the city had been destroyed. When one walks through block after block that has been completely flattened and in addition surveys dozens and dozens of other buildings that turn out, on examination, to be empty shells, with a section of the roof caved in or a wall shattered, it is hard to estimate percentages. This was particularly true in my case because planes had been in the province off and on all day and my Vietnamese guides, including Mayor Doan, rushed me from location to location in a speeding jeep and kept urging me to hurry when I wandered through the debris. Even so, I had the definite impression that something more than the announced thirteen percent of the city had been destroyed. Later, when we were back in the rural hideaway and bombs could be heard exploding in the background, thereby reminding me of the frequency of attacks, I told my impression that more than thirteen percent had been destroyed and asked if the statistics included damage from raids that had taken place last week. It turned out that the statistics were only up-to-date as of September 20, two weeks earlier, and that since that time there had been seven additional attacks whose grim results had not yet been itemized and added to the totals.

(Since writing the above, I have learned of Harrison Salisbury's visit to Nam Dinh. Interestingly enough, reporting on his visit, which took place on December 25, during the Christmas truce, he repeats the figure of thirteen percent destruction. On the other hand, he speaks of fifty-one attacks, which is an increase of eleven since my visit on November 4 and 5 and eighteen since September 20. He still gives the figure of eighty-nine killed and 405 wounded, which I had been told was the total up to September 20. Salisbury has been criticized for passing Vietnamese statistics as if they were credible, but in the case of Nam Dinh the real statistics are undoubtedly more damaging to American claims than those he used. Certainly he would have been better advised to say in his first dispatch, that the statistics came from the Vietnamese and the visual observations were his own. But what did his critics imagine—that he counted the 881 houses that had been destroyed, most of which had been so totally demolished that no one could possibly have counted them anyway? Obviously an intelligent and honest reporter can only be asked to indicate whether his own observation of the damage makes the official statistics appear credible. The only incredible aspect of these statistics is that with such pulverization of the area, only eighty-nine persons would have been killed. It is a tribute both to Vietnamese honesty and to the success of their evacuation procedures and other safety measures that they announce such a low death rate.)

When I visited Nam Dinh, areas almost totally destroyed included the working class residential areas of Hang Thao Street, where according to official statistics 17,680 persons had lived, and Hoang Van Thu Street, which had housed nearly 8,000. Because of the precautionary policy of evacuating the large cities and other areas of concentrated population, less than 2,600 persons still lived on these two streets when they were subjected to repeated attacks. In passing, let me point out that Mayor Doan's estimate of 12,000 rendered homeless for the entire city apparently could not have been based on the population before evacuation, since more than 25,000 persons lived on Hang Thao and Hoang Van Thu streets in normal times. On the other hand, I cannot state definitely that her figures included only those who remained after evacuation—in this case the 2,600 thought to have lived on these two streets at the time of the attacks—since unfortunately I did not notice the discrepancy until too late to inquire. In any event, the damage was massive—far out of line with any comforting thoughts Americans may have about precision bombing of purely military targets—and the human effects incalculable.

Judging from the neighborhood and from an occasional shell of a building that was not completely demolished, I would call Hang Thao Street a "slum" area. On the other hand, Hoang Van Thu Street appeared to be more "middle class," or at least the buildings adjacent to the gutted area gave this impression. On Hoang Van Thu Street a Catholic church, a Buddhist temple, and the headquarters of the Overseas Chinese Businessmen's Association had all been rendered unusable, but not flattened. At least half a mile from either of these streets, I walked in the ruins of the new "social welfare" section, where a hospital, two schools, a kindergarten and some model "workers apartments" had been destroyed.

On the outskirts of the city, I saw three different places where bombs had fallen on dikes and on the brick retaining wall that kept the Black River from flooding the city. I did not see enough or know enough to be able to judge whether or not these attacks on the dikes were deliberate, as charged by the Vietnamese. In any event, here and in many other places the damage to the dikes was indisputable and the Vietnamese have very wisely taken precautions by building auxiliary dikes, through a tremendous expenditure of labor power, and by piling huge mounds of materials ready to plug any gaps. A huge auxiliary dike runs right through the city of Nam Dinh, cutting it in half.

The real impact of the bombing—both human and political—cannot be estimated by a catalogue of the physical damage. To understand this, one must talk as much as possible with the "ordinary people," whom the United States claims to be rescuing from communism. Let me quote excerpts from just two of my conversations with residents of Nam Dinh. The details differ but the response to the bombings is typical of the response of everyone with whom I talked.

Vu Thi Minh spoke to me about the death of her brother, a young poet by the name of Vu Dinh Tanh:

> My brother was a young talented man who was working night and day to sharpen his poems. When the American Norman Morrison burned himself in front of the Pentagon, my brother was inspired by the sacrifice and made a poem which he dedicated to Mrs. Morrison and the children. Tanh was killed at a time when his talents were being developed. The cowardly Americans misused the cloudy skies to intrude in our city and bomb and strafe our people. My brother died on the way to the first aid station. [At this point she handed me a photo of her brother, who was twenty-one when killed. He had an open, sensitive appearing face and wore glasses.]
>
> Since Tanh's death all of his sixteen brothers and sisters are working harder in their posts in order to avenge him. My father is sixty-four and had retired, but he has come back to the city to carry on. My younger brother Kim, seventeen, volunteered to join the army to avenge his brother. Sister Ngoc has graduated from the Polytechnic college but her dream is to serve in the people's army to avenge her brother. For myself and the other teachers, after his death we asked to share his teaching work. In addition we are ready to take arms against the American planes. . . . We are determined to fight until final victory. Only when the U.S

aggressors go home can we have peace and independence
and be finished with all the hardships you have seen in
our city.

Mrs. Trung Thi Mai appeared to be in her late twenties or early
thirties. She told me that her children had been evacuated to the countryside, because of the expectation of attacks. They lived with their
grandmother, while Mrs. Mai and her husband stayed in the city to
continue their work at the textile factory. After the children had been
gone about a year, the Mais had another child and the other children
came to the city to see their new brother.

In view of the American attacks, we prepared for them
to be evacuated again. Binh, my oldest son [aged thirteen],
brought water to the house from the well and bathed his
brother and sister before they were to go to the evacuation
place the next morning. As we were going to be separated,
we sat up late talking and visiting, till 1 A.M.

When we were sleeping I heard a bomb explode and
the house fell down on me and the three children. We didn't
know what time it was. I had only enough time to call my
husband: "Darling, save us," and Binh only enough time to
cry out, "Father, save us." My husband heard our voices but
it was impossible to dig us out of the debris. I felt my
youngest dying by my side and the others too, but it was
impossible to do anything. I fainted and then people dug
us out and took me and my children to the hospital. I recovered consciousness at the first aid station and saw my
father. I asked him where my husband and children were
and he said: The children are all dead and your husband is
out in the street helping other people. I lost consciousness
again. Then I woke up and saw my three children lying dead
by me and I couldn't do anything but cry the whole day.

I didn't expect that the U.S. aggressor was so barbarous. We Vietnamese people do not go to the United States
to fight their people, why have they come here to kill my
three children? At present when I see other children of the
same age as my children I can't help crying. My second son,
whose name is Long, when he sees that I am ill, he comes to
my bed and consoles me. He says, "Mother you must keep

up your health so that you can bring me up. When I am grown up I will avenge the family." The more we grieve at the death of our children, the more we swear not to live under the same skies as the U.S. aggressors.

On another trip through the provinces, I visited the city of Than Hoa, which is about 110 miles south of Hanoi. Here the Vietnamese estimated that by early November about 200 houses, or one dwelling in ten, had been destroyed. The entire city of Than Hoa was wiped out in the French Resistance War of 1945 to 1954 and painfully rebuilt after the Geneva accords, only to suffer this new destruction.

One must remember, in evaluating the areas of damage, whether in Phu Ly, Nam Dinh or Than Hoa (the three cities that I visited) that the tallest buildings are three stories, and most buildings don't even have a second story. In Than Hoa, block after block of rubble included the ruins of a Franciscan seminary, a Buddhist pagoda and the general hospital. Here again I saw damage to the dikes that protected the city. Outside the city limits, I saw the ruins of the 600-bed Than Hoa tuberculosis sanitorium, which had been attacked on five different occasions. It had the usual identifying huge red crosses and was sitting by itself in an area of rice paddies and irrigation dikes. There was no conceivable military target for miles around. Let me quote from the testimony, undoubtedly biased, of Mrs. Nguyen Thi Tien, a seventy-one-year-old peasant lady from the village of Kieu Dai:

> Last year on the seventh day of the seventh month of the lunar calendar (you'll have to forgive me, I never did learn the new way of figuring the months), when I was doing some housework the American planes came, dropping bombs and cutting off my arm. . . . When my wound was cured and I returned to my village, the villagers helped me in every way. I am very moved by their help. At the same time I feel a great indignation at those who have come and attacked us. The pain in my heart is as big as the pain in my body. More than thirty persons were killed during that attack. Twenty-four were wounded. Probably more than twenty roofs [meaning houses] were knocked down. Before that, in the sixth month of the lunar new year, during the

bombing of Than Hoa tuberculosis hospital, two old people were killed and another young person was killed that day. I don't remember the day but I remember it was the sixth month and some other people on the dikes near the hospital were also killed. The crater of the bomb looked like a river. There were a lot of people, about twenty-seven I think, who entered the cave under the dam and they were killed. If we speak of indignation and hatred, we have no words to describe them. The people now working in the fields do not do anything to the Americans, why do they come here to kill us? . . . The more we hate the Americans the more we unite with each other. We must have unity in order to produce our food and serve our sons in the army. We will keep up this hatred forever. We can never live under the same sky as the American aggressors. I am very old, but I am thinking very much about the children.

Americans often argue that the destruction of villages and the killing of civilians in North Vietnam is an unpleasant but largely unavoidable byproduct of the bombing of tactical military targets, such as bridges and railroad depots. Mrs. Tien describes circumstances under which two old people, a young person and about twenty-seven others "who entered the cave under the dam" were killed. It is my belief, based on the testimony of Mrs. Tien and other eyewitnesses and based on my own personal visit to the scene, that these thirty peasants died as a result of a deliberate attack on a tactical *political* target, the Than Hoa tuberculosis sanitorium.

Actually Vietnam has very few cities, and is mostly rural. As I traveled through the countryside I saw many villages that had been attacked, as well as an occasional one that seemed to have been spared completely. At first I thought that I might be getting an exaggerated sense of the rural destruction because of the fact that I was traveling on main highways, which probably could be thought by the American Air Command to be the main routes for military infiltration from the North to the South. But the frequency of the attacks soon forced us off the main routes, which are only two-lane highways at best. Each time I traveled we detoured through narrow dirt roads and traveled on dikes that might not have been intended as roads at all, except for carts pulled by oxen and on occasion by Vietnamese peasants.

After a while I learned that no matter how many miles we left the highway we were never very far from bomb craters and bombed-out villages.

Traveling always by night (and making only occasional brief sorties by daytime) I was unable to get a clear picture of the statistics of the damage, but there was no doubt that it was extensive and ghastly. In Y Ngo, a village of 300 primitive houses, none of which would normally be considered suitable habitation for an American, 100 houses had been destroyed. In Yen Vuc, out of 262 houses, only nine still remained.

When we came to a section that looked like a layman's visualization of the surface of the moon—barren and pockmarked with craters—I could imagine that we were approaching a bridge, but this did not always turn out to be the case. Sometimes it was clear that a whole hamlet had been wiped out in a determined effort to destroy a bridge that was at most twenty to thirty feet long. The stream had been quickly spanned again. More than once we crossed a river an hour or two after its bridge had been knocked out. When a sizable bridge was destroyed, apparently it took a little longer—perhaps half a day—to throw up a crude floating bridge (which would be torn down by day and reassembled at night) or create a ferry (actually a hastily constructed barge powered by a small motor boat). Unfortunately, though the bridges could be quickly restored, at least to a rough but serviceable state, the houses and the people could not.

Vietnam and the International Liberation Front

1965 Arnold Toynbee, the British historian, recently wrote a remarkable article which has been virtually ignored in this country. Yet the views expressed by Toynbee not only reflect the attitude of a growing number of non-Communist Europeans toward the United States and its holy wars, but have significant implications for the American antiwar movement, engaged as it is in an examination of questions of principle and strategy. Toynbee writes:

> For the past twenty years the government and people of the United States have been acting on the belief that communism is on the march for the conquest of the world and that it is the manifest destiny of the United States to save the world from suffering this fate. . . . Americans have believed that America has practically the whole human race on her side in her anti-Communist stand. . . . This picture is not founded on facts.
>
> . . . The revolt of the "native" majority of mankind against the domination of the Western minority—this, and not the defense of freedom against communism by the leading Western country, the United States, is the real major

issue in the world today. . . . Is the United States St. George fighting against the dragon? Or is she Goliath fighting David? The question is important, because St. George is a winner but Goliath is not. . . . The President manifestly believes that he is speaking with Churchill's voice—the Churchill of 1940—but to the ears of people who have suffered Western domination in the past, his voice sounds like the Kaiser's and like Hitler's.

. . . The spectacle of overwhelming American military power will not impress an Englishman who has lived through two world wars. . . . If I were a South Vietnamese guerrilla fighter today, I should remember 1940 and should continue audaciously to resist the mighty United States. The American picture of aggressive ecumenical communism is a mirage, but the reality which America is up against today is something much more formidable. She is up against the determination of the non-Western majority of mankind to complete its self-liberation from Western domination. (*Vancouver Times,* May 11; reprinted from the *London Observer.*)

If Toynbee's interpretation is substantially correct, as I believe it is, it undercuts the argument that the United States must protect its prestige by winning military victories in Vietnam (killing more "natives") or at least gaining a stalemate. The claim is that this is necessary to provide a basis for sound negotiations in Vietnam and for influencing other Southeast Asians to choose allies and forms of government acceptable to the United States. But in the pattern of Western-Asian relations, every show of military strength merely reinforces the Asian conviction that the United States is a ruthless invader who is determined to perpetuate its domination as long as possible, no matter how many Asian lives it may cost. Military victories may produce Asian quislings and appeasers or evoke huzzas in suburbia. They cannot coerce popular support in Asia. It is significant that even the pro-American Japanese government recently compared the Vietcong to the anti-Nazi resistance forces during the German occupation of Europe.

What is more, from the point of view of Asian self-liberation from Western domination, it makes little difference whether the criteria for American approval of Asian governments are those presently held by the Johnson administration (under which a democratically elected centrist like Juan Bosch was unacceptable in the Dominican Republic) or new liberal standards currently being advanced by sections of the peace movement. SANE and Democratic Party coalitionists Michael Harrington, Norman Thomas, and Bayard Rustin are so offended by the slaughter that they are campaigning for a cease-fire—and this is certainly a crucial lowest common denominator for the antiwar movement—but they cling to the notion that the United States has the right to negotiate the terms and extent of its military withdrawal. In other words, they argue that American troops should not be withdrawn until the government has secured satisfactory assurances from the National Liberation Front, Hanoi and Peking as to what the domestic arrangements shall be. They advance the slogan, "One man, one vote—in Selma and Saigon, Hanoi and Peking." Such a demand may sound noble to some Americans, but it is hard to imagine that self-respecting Vietnamese can look upon it as other than a product of American self-righteousness, an attempt to transplant in Asia the American system of parliamentary democracy and Presidential elections under which the United States has launched a pitiless economic and military aggression against Asians. It should hardly be surprising if they are a little skeptical about the demand and prefer to experiment with other forms of political organization. It may be that their experiments will turn out badly, particularly in view of the heritage of bitterness which we have helped impose on them. Or it may be that they will work their way through to attainments of freedom, dignity, and forms of "participatory democracy" as yet unknown to us. In any case, it is not our right to demand that they follow our system. Nor to make withdrawal of American troops contingent on their doing so.

To call for the immediate unconditional withdrawal of American military power is not isolationist. Nor does it imply that the situation will become idyllic once the American military threat is removed. It does emphasize that whatever economic aid or constructive influence Americans may provide will have to be dissociated from American military pressures. For the United States to stop bombing and attacking would be an important human gain. It would hardly give the United States the right to negotiate about the internal affairs of Vietnam or to continue its military occupation during such negotiations.

Material aid and political advice must be freely offered and freely accepted. Cambodia has refused American economic aid for several years and Norodhom Sihanouk, head of the Cambodian government, argues convincingly that his country is better off because of the refusal. At this point, the only legitimate course for the United States is to offer economic aid to Vietnam as an indemnity rather than as either charity or a bribe.

Ultimately we will have to accept on a world-wide basis the proposition of the Triple Revolution that every human being has an inalienable right to a guaranteed annual income. (I prefer Robert Theobald's term Basic Economic Security, because it minimizes the cash nexus.) The early Christians had the belief that if we have luxuries while others lack necessities, we are stealing their goods and are responsible for their death or degradation. If Jesus was hundreds of years ahead of his time, as the "realists" have been claiming for the last two thousand years, the galloping revolutions in productive techniques, weaponry, and assertion of human rights by the left-outs have brought us to the point where we must follow this primitive Christian insight soon or probably perish. But for the moment, to recognize the principle that we owe an indemnity to the Vietnamese would be a considerable step forward. Of course no one should think that paying such an indemnity would make up for the death and suffering we have inflicted, but it could signify repentance and the beginnings of treating the Vietnamese with respect and as equals.

We should never forget that offers of negotiations are received with bitterness by those who feel themselves the victims of aggression. Toynbee makes clear in *The Observer* article that even if the President's offers can be taken at face value, they strike Asians differently than Americans:

> Today, President Johnson is willing to negotiate without making it a condition that America's opponents in Vietnam shall first stop fighting. He has, however, made it a condition that South Vietnam shall remain separate from North Vietnam, whatever the wishes of the Vietnamese people may be. The United States also insists that South Korea

shall remain separate from North Korea, and Taiwan from continental China, and in all these three cases the United States is enforcing her fiat by military action. Now the imposition of the fiats of Western governments by force is the humiliation that has been inflicted on the non-Western peoples during the last 200 years. When they got rid of the European and Japanese imperialists . . . the Americans . . . jumped in and are dictating, in their turn, to the Asians what the Asians may or may not do. In other words, the Americans, in their turn, are treating the Asians as "natives," and this is infuriating them.

Even without the help of Toynbee's analysis, Americans should realize that for Johnson to offer negotiations now (as he may be smart enough to do shortly, as a gimmick) is apt to be at least as offensive to the Vietnamese as a Japanese offer to negotiate would have been to most Americans shortly after the attack on Pearl Harbor.

I have quoted Toynbee at length because Americans tend to be ignorant of the underlying political dynamics of the Vietnamese conflict—and of the United States role in Africa and Latin America as well. Most of the conventional American argumentation *on both sides* of such questions as whether (or how) to end the war is based on false assumptions derived from American ethnocentrism. Even when we think we are aware of the historical realities, our knowledge is mostly intellectual and we are not apt to feel what almost any Asian, African or Latin American does. White Americans should be able to get some sense of the gap if they consider how offensive Malcolm X was to white liberals and what a hero he was in the black ghettoes. Even those who disagreed with his program used to say: "Malcolm is the only one who tells it like it is."

Failure to understand the deep-seated Asian revulsion against everything white, Western, and pseudo-democratic is compounded by the conditioning most of us have had to feel that our culture is superior. Murray Kempton recently told a *Liberator** conference in Harlem that he was forty-five years old before he realized that as a white man he had a "built-in superiority complex." He said: "If I can't face up to this truth about myself, I will go on lying to others."

* Liberator *is a black nationalist magazine, edited by Daniel Watts.*

Unfortunately, when it comes to world politics, most of us find it such a wrench to break with the lies of the government, crude and flagrant though they are, that we stop short of facing up to the more subtle lies that we have absorbed from birth. American ethnocentricity is as much a part of our political ambiance as polluted air is part of the atmosphere of our large cities.

To make matters worse, there is a great deal of talk about taking the peace message to the "mainstream" of American society and insufficient recognition that the American mainstream is isolated from and running counter to the mainstream of world politics. Sections of the peace movement come up with proposals that seem eminently fair and even a little daring, if our focus is upper-middle-class America. They call for negotiations (backed of course by American military might) or for United States efforts to put together a democratic regime in Saigon as a constructive alternative to *both* Nguyen Cao Ky (or whoever is in at the moment) and the National Liberation Front. Inevitably such proposals are rejected in Asia as hypocritical or touching on matters that are none of our business. We build a peace movement that is easily maneuvered by the government into thinking that the United States has been reasonable and the National Liberation Front (or Hanoi, Peking, Havana) "intransigent" and "reckless." Most Americans expect our victims to be grateful—and to offer a few concessions on their part—if we offer to stop killing them.*

All of the foregoing can be said regardless of one's convictions about violence and nonviolence, as ways of life or as alternative methods of self-liberation. It is an indication of the unconscious pro-Americanism and historical disorientation of a number of peace leaders that they look upon the expression of such views about America's role not as "speaking truth to power" but as unhealthy anti-Americanism and an implied abandonment of pacifism. Perfectly willing themselves to campaign for Johnson in the last election or to call for Federal troops to protect the Selma march, they nonetheless view any expressions of sympathy for the Vietcong as betrayals of nonviolence. As an advocate of nonviolence, I do not wish to seize upon their inconsistency to

---

* *Since I wrote this, a news story has appeared in the* New York Times, *which begins as follows: "Washington, July 4—Secretary of State Dean Rusk disclosed today that the United States had made several fruitless efforts to learn what North Vietnam would offer in exchange for a halt in air attacks on North Vietnamese targets."*

obscure the difficulties involved in being pro-liberation and anti-violence at a time when most of the active liberation movements of the world rely on guerrilla warfare. One thing we can do is to step up the tempo of our nonviolent action here in the United States, to try to stop American aggression at its source rather than leave the whole burden on those who suffer its impact. This can be a way of expressing solidarity with the liberation movement and at the same time working for the development of nonviolence as a more effective method. If we feel that nonviolent resistance is potentially superior to guerrilla warfare, we had better set about freeing American nonviolence from its unfortunate pro-American bias. We had better learn to commit ourselves actively to the historic struggles for liberation rather than taking an isolationist stance of "a plague on both sides, since both use violence."

There is a tendency on the part of some pacifists to treat questions of violence and nonviolence as if they were absolute (and therefore abstract) moral questions existing in a historical vacuum. It is as if all movements using violence were absolutely (and therefore equally) evil and all nonviolence absolutely and equally good. We need to get back to Gandhi's insight that the best way to resist injustice is nonviolently but that it is nonetheless better to resist oppression violently than not to resist it at all. To the extent that we agree with Gandhi in this, we will remain nonviolent ourselves and will attempt to persuade others that this is the better way. It seems to me that we will also offer nonviolent assistance to those who are struggling in their own way for freedom and justice, dignity and self-liberation from Western domination. This involves a major shift in emphasis for the American peace movement. Specifically, I am calling for the opening of an active nonviolent corps for the liberation of Vietnam, Korea, Taiwan, the Dominican Republic and other subjects of American suzerainty.

I do not wish to minimize the problems. Let me give an example, which is partially academic for most of us at the present time but underlines the dilemma. Recently, in a review of *The New Face of War,* by Malcolm W. Browne, I came across the following passage:

> (Browne) says that of thousands of officials he has known in the government sponsored by the United States, he can think of none who does not more or less hold the

Vietnamese people in contempt. The feeling is reciprocated. As a result, he says, ". . . When Vietcong terrorists publicly behead some hamlet or province official and then disembowel the wife and children as well, Americans tend to assume that this will result in a powerful reaction by the people against the Vietcong. Nothing could be farther from the truth in most cases. The Vietcong often liquidates a government official precisely because it knows such an act will please the local people." (*The Nation,* June 12.)

No matter how convinced we may be that the ruthlessness of American bombings and torture contribute to the ruthlessness of the reprisal, we must never justify or overlook such regressions. I would consider it the duty of a nonviolent supporter of Vietnamese liberation to offer refuge to the potential victims, if it were at all within his power. Without accepting exaggerated American contentions of the extent of Vietcong terrorism, we should call such practices to the attention of those who speak as if all terror were on one side and every action of the Vietcong justified. But is it beyond possibility to look approvingly on the *struggle* of the National Liberation Front without endorsing or applauding its violence? Particularly in the absence of a nonviolent force for liberation? Particularly in view of our own failure to risk as much in our dedication to the overthrow of American aggression nonviolently as the Vietnamese are risking in guerrilla warfare? We may try to excuse ourselves by saying that, after all, *they* are the victims, and are bound to feel the hurt and risk their lives in a way that Americans are not apt to do. But then whose victims are they? What kind of nonviolence is it that allows those who savor the fruits of American military power (as all of us do, willy-nilly) to dissociate ourselves self-righteously from the struggles of our victims because they are unwilling to adopt a method whose validity we are unwilling or unable to establish ourselves?

Report from the International War Crimes Tribunal*

I

1967-1968 *As an American I was naturally uneasy at the prospect of sitting on an International War Crimes Tribunal to investigate and sift evidence of alleged American war crimes. One has only to know neighbors and friends who are serving in the U.S. armed forces—and other friends and neighbors who are convinced that the American aim in Vietnam is to defend the freedom of the Vietnamese people against "Vietcong" terror and Communist aggression—to realize that there is no conscious criminality of intent in most of the ordinary Americans who support the war. But then, "to understand all is to forgive all," and meanwhile one whole people is being destroyed physically and another one morally. Ways have to be found, even harsh ways, to let people know that their society has embarked on a course of disaster.*

There is considerable evidence that there was signally little criminality of intent among ordinary Germans either, at a time when the Jews were being systematically isolated, robbed of their rights and, in the end, cremated. Random conversations in the United States today often remind me of conversations I had in Germany in 1936 and 1937. At the time there was little of the bloodthirsty spirit and

* Condensed

*wild contempt for human life that Americans identify as the hall-
mark of a country capable of committing atrocities and war crimes.
Liberal and humane Germans complained of Hitler's extremism (his
"methods," they used to say). They laughed, loved, and traded; skirted
the ghetto; deplored "extremists" of both the right and the left; and
mainly left foreign policy and other complicated questions to the
government. Most political questions are complicated—unless of
course you are one of the victims. Whatever uneasiness most Germans
felt, they refused to question the fundamental assumptions of German politics: underlying German righteousness, anti-Communism
and a conception of patriotism that was willing to sacrifice the rights
of human beings, especially foreigners, to the requirements of national prestige and "honor." Step by step decent Germans were carried along to disgrace and disaster.*

*Ironically, Americans today find it difficult to conceive of them-
selves and their government as capable of playing an evil role in history, in part because we are still misled by the crude anti-Nazi propaganda of World War II, which ignored mixed motivations, human
inertia, man's capacity for patriotic self-deception and the complicated historical interactions that took many years to produce world
war and death camps. The oversimplified good-guys, bad-guys psychology reinforced our self-image of Americans as the good guys of
history, whose foreign interventions are always in defense of freedom.
(It was quickly forgotten that Communists were "good guys" too, during World War II.) At the same time, our shallow approach to Nazism set up a caricature of the "bad guys" with which it is impossible
for most Americans to identify even a crude charlatan like Johnson,
let alone themselves and their neighbors.*

*Too many Americans assume that if the tone of the public ut-
terances is calm and measured, the announced aims are lofty and the
rights of dissent are preserved at home, then it is ludicrous to speak
of deliberate aggression and "war crimes." It matters not that no one
believes Johnson any more. Or that the dissenters are rendered impotent by the complicated controls and indirections of American democracy—even though they may well represent a majority of those
who concern themselves with public affairs. So long as the soft sell is
maintained and there is not too much talk of bombing Vietnam back
into the Stone Age (General Curtis Le May) or of bleeding them until
it will be felt for generations to come (General William C. West-*

moreland), then most Americans may criticize and dissent, but they will resist facing up to the full truth of what the United States is doing in Vietnam—and what this portends for the future.

Against this background of public incredulity, the U.S. press has had a relatively easy time libeling the motives and procedures of the War Crimes Tribunal and overlooking the mass of truly overwhelming evidence that was produced in Stockholm. For eight days the incontrovertible evidence piled up that the United States is committing acts in Vietnam that are both so contemptuous of human life and so deliberate and systematic that they make one ashamed not just to be an American but to be a human being at all.

The truth, once revealed so clearly, is bound to become known —even in the United States. The question is whether, given the resistance of the American people and the distortions of the liberal press, it will be known soon enough to avert even greater catastrophe. Greater, that is, not in qualitative terms but in numbers and extent, until most of the human race ends up bought, bullied, or killed.

Whatever the Tribunal's shortcomings, real and imagined, it sent more than thirty experts to Vietnam in the months immediately preceding the first hearings. Investigators included scientists, doctors, hydraulic engineers, agronomists, political scientists, lawyers, historians, journalists, still- and motion-picture photographers. They traveled thousands of miles and were often under direct attack in air raids or by shelling from the Seventh Fleet. For example, one team of Japanese investigators traveled more than 2,600 miles through seven hard-hit provinces of North Vietnam. Some of the experts left Vietnam barely in time to reach Stockholm for the sessions.

The Tribunal's investigators examined or interviewed patients and other survivors, observed the patterns of attack at firsthand and photographed corpses, the evacuation of the wounded, collapsing buildings, villages in flames and cities in ruins. They brought back everything from fragments of bombs, missiles and rockets, and cinders of napalm, to counterfeit money, dolls and surrender leaflets that had been dropped on the smoldering ruins of destroyed villages. They salvaged unexploded bombs that were subsequently tested and analyzed in laboratories and weapons-testing centers in Tokyo and Paris. The accumulation of reports from these and other witnesses who traveled to Stockholm (including Vietnamese victims of napalm, phosphorus and pellet bombs) laid bare for the first time the nature

of the U.S. war in the North. The truth was far more ugly than anyone had imagined. A tremendous amount of new material was reported by the various witnesses and the juxtaposition of reports and
evidence revealed unexpected new patterns of warfare that none of
the witnesses or members of the Tribunal (and quite possibly not
even the Vietnamese) had been aware of.

Dr. Jean-Pierre Vigier, a weapons expert and retired French
colonel, was the most authoritative witness on C.B.U.'s (cluster bomb
units) and the deadly "pellet bombs" that are released from them. A
Resistance leader during World War II and former member of the
French General Staff, he traveled extensively in Vietnam with one of
the Tribunal's investigating teams.

In a dry, matter-of-fact way, Vigier described the cluster bombs
as a military improvement on the atomic bomb. Atomic bombs not
only kill the population, but destroy military and economic installations as well. Hence their use is "uneconomic." The advantage of the
pellet bombs is that they kill people without damaging property.

Vigier did not point out that certain psychological and political
restraints interfere with the use of atomic bombs, because of the widespread knowledge of their nature, the campaigns that have been
waged against them and the almost universal horror with which they
are viewed. By contrast, the United States has been using pellet bombs
since February 1966 with a minimum of public reaction. Few Americans realize that their very use gives the lie to U.S. claims that it is
not deliberately attacking the civilian population of North Vietnam.

Buttressing his presentation with references to the U.S. Army's
Military Review, Vigier stated that pellet bombs are "a new event
in the annals of war. Like combat gas they are a weapon designed to
harm noncombatants and civilian populations. Their development
makes it possible to carry out massive destructions of civilian populations." All this, Vigier pointed out, involves a minimum of danger to
the attacker and no damage to property—except for straw houses,
which are not damaged by the tiny pellets but can be set afire if the
bomblet containing the pellets makes a direct hit and explodes on the
roof.

Under questioning, mainly by Courtland Cox of the Student
Nonviolent Coordinating Committee (who was sitting at this session
as a deputy for Stokely Carmichael), Vigier expressed his opinion
that "the cluster bombs have been developed for use in underdevel-

oped countries," where there is a minimum of protective steel and concrete and the main target is the people.

According to *Fundamentals of Aerospace Weapons Systems,* a manual of the U.S. Air Force issued on May 20, 1966 and in use at the Air University (mimeographed copies of which were made available to the Tribunal), a target is defined as follows:

> A military target is any person, thing, idea, entity, or location selected for destruction, inactivation or rendering nonusable with weapons which will reduce or destroy the will or ability of the enemy to resist. (Chapter Eight)

A few pages later, the manual states:

> Targets within a nation fall into four categories: military, economic, political, and psychosocial. . . . As targets such components must be analyzed to determine which should be destroyed in order to cause the entire instrument or organization they make up to malfunction or break down completely.

Drawing on his experience as a military strategist and his study of the targets hit and weapons used in Vietnam, Vigier offered the following analysis:*

> Field commanders can no longer be left free to choose their own targets. Selection can only be made by computers. The specific weight of the targets (military, economic, political, and psychosocial) varies according to the culture, economy, etc. In Vietnam the political targets are movable. The guerrilla leaders move from place to place, whereas in a country like France, Paris would be the nerve center, and vulnerable to a different type of attack. In Vietnam the villages are largely self-reliant cells and each is a center of opposition. The same type of consideration applies to military installations in underdeveloped countries. They are small, decentralized, and highly mobile. The psychosocial targets become the primary targets.

* *I have strung together from my notes a series of statements made by Vigier, mostly in response to questioning by members of the Tribunal. I refer the reader to the complete proceedings of the Stockholm hearings,* Against the Crimes of Silence, *edited by John Duffet (O'Hara Books, 1968).*

It is logical that the computers would choose the very targets that in fact have been bombed. The bombing has been concentrated on schools, hospitals, churches, dams, dikes, and the civilian population.

In the end, the main military objectives in underdeveloped countries turn out to be the people. There are no tactical objectives of a military nature other than the people. In developed countries you can destroy morale by destroying the industrial centers, the military installations and the communications networks, but not in a peasant country like Vietnam. That is why the United States is using such a high proportion of C.B.U.'s, which are strictly antipersonnel weapons. They are useless against military targets, because with their methods of launching and their scatter effect they cannot be aimed on the battlefields or against specific military objectives. If they occasionally strike military objects they are useless because they cannot penetrate wood, metal, sandbags, etc.

In case Vigier's conclusions seem extreme, it might be wise to quote once more from Chapter Eight of *Fundamentals of Aerospace Weapons Systems*. It will be seen that Vigier's analysis is in line with the Air Force philosophy (though it should be pointed out that the Air Force manual is a general one and is not referring specifically to Vietnam) :

Some of the conventional targets for morale attacks have been water supplies, food supplies, housing areas, transportation centers, and industrial sites. The objectives of these attacks in the past have been to dispel the people's belief in the invincibility of their forces, to create unrest, to reduce the output of the labor force, to cause strikes, sabotage, riots, fear, panic, hunger, and passive resistance to the government, and to create a general feeling that the war should be terminated. . . . In any prolonged war, whether fought with non-nuclear weapons or with low yield nuclear weapons, the concepts for attacking a nation's psychosocial structure—concepts which were developed in recent wars— would generally be applicable.

The evidence presented at Stockholm indicated overwhelmingly that the targets that have actually been hit most extensively in North Vietnam have been the "psychosocial" structure and the civilian population.

II

There is no possibility of summing up the evidence presented at the second session of the International War Crimes Tribunal, held at Roskilde, Denmark, from November 20 to December 1, 1967. For much of the time I sat numbed by the accumulation of horrors, convinced intellectually of the reality of the events being described but too limited emotionally to be able to grasp them.

I doubt if Americans will ever be able to comprehend the depravity represented by United States actions in Vietnam or the nightmare of Vietnamese suffering, as both were revealed at the Tribunal. Most Germans have never come to grips with Dachau and Buchenwald and most Communists, in and out of the Soviet Union, are as yet unable to grasp the reality of Stalin's purges and death camps. Still, neither German nor Stalinist atrocities were adequately documented while they were taking place, though of course there were rumors and some evidence. The Tribunal performed a historic task by gathering and sifting volumes of evidence while the crimes are still being enacted and in the very midst of the denials and justifications of their perpetrators. We owe a debt of gratitude to Bertrand Russell for launching the Tribunal and to the investigators who risked their lives and their Western "careers" by gathering the information.

No matter that the U.S. press chose to ignore most of the evidence. (The *New York Times* correspondent did not attend on the days that ex-G.I.'s Peter Martinsen and David Tuck gave their testimony of G.I. tortures of prisoners, though he was in town and forewarned.) Anyone who reads the documents will realize that this dereliction condemns the mass media and seriously handicaps the developing American conscience but does not nullify the work of the Tribunal, which will out in the end.

Hardly a word of the statements by Martinsen, Tuck and former Green Beret Sergeant Donald Duncan (who placed the events described by the other two in the context of the world-wide counter-insurgency apparatus and policy of the United States) reached the

American public. Yet every pious assertion of U.S. idealism by President Johnson, Secretary Rusk and General Westmoreland is trumpeted to our attention, overshadowed only by the commercials and the trivia. We are misled by the fact that opposition is reported and a certain amount of muckraking takes place. We congratulate ourselves on the contrast with the one-party press of most Communist countries and forget that looking better than the Communist press is not much of a test since this is one of the worst aspects of those regimes. Erroneously we conclude that the Free World's press is significantly free and the truth available to those who have the wit to discern it. So the slaughter continues and we are not really aware of its extent or of what it portends for our society and for the human race.

At the opening sessions of the Tribunal, we learned that the pattern of psychosocial targeting that had been exposed at Stockholm has been extended and intensified during the last few months.

In April, at Stockholm, we learned that eighty Catholic churches had been destroyed from the air in North Vietnam during the twenty-three months of 1965 and 1966 in which bombing took place, as against thirty Buddhist pagodas. At Roskilde we learned that during the first ten months of 1967, an additional 227 Catholic churches were destroyed and 86 Buddhist pagodas. Thus there was a major increase in the number of attacks on religious institutions and the concentration continued to be on the Catholic institutions. In primitive Vietnam, the Catholic churches are big and easily identifiable, usually sitting in somewhat isolated splendor in the midst of extensive church properties.

In addition to churches, key psychosocial targets in Vietnam are schools and hospitals, livestock and agriculture, civilian housing and the people. Frank Harvey, who is not a Tribunal witness but a military specialist chosen by the Air Force to write an authoritative report on the air war, gives the feeling, from within the master race, of the bombing of houses and people. Harvey writes:

> A pilot going into combat for the first time is a bit like a swimmer about to dive into an icy lake. He likes to get his big toes wet and then wade around a little before leaping off the high board into the numbing depths. So it was fortunate that young pilots could get their first taste of combat under

the direction of a forward air controller over a flat country in bright sunshine where nobody was shooting back with high-powered ack-ack. *He learns how it feels to drop bombs on human beings and watch huts go up in a boil of orange flame when his aluminum napalm tanks tumble into them. He gets hardened to pressing the fire button and cutting people down like little cloth dummies, as they sprint frantically under him.* He gets his sword bloodied [in the South] for the rougher things to come [in the North, where there are antiaircraft defenses]. (*Air War—Vietnam,* Bantam Books; emphasis added)

The Tribunal was impatient with reports of devastation in the North, since the pattern of the bombing had already been established at Stockholm. It cut short all such reports and moved on to new matters, most notably the types of weapons and patterns of attack in the South, the destruction of villages and herding of the surviving population into concentration camps, the treatment of prisoners and the drastic escalation of attacks on Laos. First though, it took note of recent "improvements" in the dreaded C.B.U.'s, the antipersonnel bombs which scatter a deadly broadside of tiny steel pellets. In one raid, it was estimated that over three million of these pellets saturated an area of approximately one and a half square kilometers. (A kilometer is .62 miles.)

In recent months, many of the baseball-sized secondary bombs (guavas), each of which holds approximately three hundred pellets, have been equipped with timing devices and other mechanisms for delaying firing of the lethal pellets until hours or days after the attack or until they are set off by activity in the area. In this way, vast areas are turned into death traps for rescue workers, people emerging from their shelters, peasants returning to the fields, children going to school. A second recent "improvement" is the development of a model in which "flechettes" or barbed steel splinters the thickness of a needle are substituted for the rounded, pea-sized pellets. Currently this type is being manufactured near San Jose, California. (One ironic result of the Tribunal's earlier work is that the Pentagon has declassified the original pellet bombs, whose use it denied from their first employment on February 8, 1965 until after they had been exhibited and analyzed by weapons experts at the Tribunal's first session in April of 1967. Now it has released the design for competitive bidding and has openly contracted for their delivery.)

As the Tribunal moved its searchlight from North to South Vietnam and on to Laos, Thailand, and Cambodia, there emerged a pattern of gradually escalating contempt for Asian life and dignity and a resulting scale of death and destruction that stuns the imagination and legitimizes—nay requires—use of the term genocide. Significantly, former G.I.'s Martinsen and Tuck indicated that they were content to kill "Communists" in Vietnam but that their disillusionment began when they discovered that the *entire* Vietnamese population was subject to attack unless they left their native homesteads and moved into the U.S.-occupied areas.

A team of three French investigators traveled for three weeks through an N.L.F. zone. They reported:

> During those three weeks we have not seen a single hamlet, a single house which was spared by bombings or strafing. . . .
>
> For two months, the whole Tay Ninh province was particularly well combed by "search and destroy" teams. All the hamlets were razed, all the rice plantations poisoned by chemical products, samples of which we have brought back. The grain reserves were annihilated and the civilians discovered were deported to concentration camp zones. . . .
>
> Many peasants we talked with had escaped from concentration camps, many others had fled from the advancing U.S. troops or simply hid in the forests and escaped the tank columns.
>
> Civilians are now forced to lie in hiding in the forests. They build miserable huts. . . . Each family has dug an underground shelter, they live like primitive men to avoid being located.
>
> This so-called "white" or "free-fire" zone is now declared by the Americans as totally "Vietcong," where all signs of life must be systematically extinguished. From the military bases . . . the American artillery shoots at random to maintain a constant state of anxiety and insecurity. [The U.S. military admits to this practice and calls it "H & I," or harassment and interdiction.]

The reconnaissance planes fly methodically over the whole zone in large concentric circles. As soon as some movement appears as a sign of human presence, as soon as a field appears to be cultivated, orders are given for a concentrated artillery attack. The least sign of life located by reconnaissance planes is immediately followed by an attack of fighter-bombers which fire rockets, drop fragmentation bombs, napalm and phosphorus bombs. . . .

If we believe the reports of the . . . officials, since the beginning of . . . the policy of attack on "everything that moves" [February 1967], the average expended ordnance is two tons of projectiles per inhabitant and one killed or wounded in every eight persons. . . . Peasants are obliged to cultivate by night tiny kitchen gardens and the rice paddies on the fringe of the forests. Otherwise any rice patch slightly showing cultivation would be automatically destroyed by defoliants dropped from planes or helicopters. We saw a number of metallic drums dropped on rice paddies and then shot full of holes by the same planes in order to permit the chemical products to dissolve into the water or the rice field and to pollute and contaminate the produce.

Particularly shocking to me were reports from Laos of a parallel policy of total destruction of all life in the Pathet Lao districts. One of the Tribunal investigators reported that he walked more than 300 kilometers zigzig through that part of Laos and did not see a single village that has not been destroyed. Here too the entire surviving population is forced to live in caves or underground shelters, or as nomads in the forests. The only agriculture that is possible is the cultivation of tiny patches deep in the forest at night. According to Tribunal witnesses, an estimated one thousand Laotian villages had been destroyed by November 1, 1967. When I was in Vientiane, Laos, in May 1967, numerous clean-cut, well-dressed, pleasant Americans dominated the airport. Some of them joked about the daily bombing run which was launched at 5 P.M. Sure enough, at 5 P.M. I watched twenty-four small planes take off, each with two bombs on the wings. A few minutes later, Nick Egleson and I finished our beer and boarded the International Control Commission plane for Hanoi and took off on the same runway previously used by the bombers. As happens to American TV

viewers who sit in security and see war scenes on their screens, sand-
wiched in between the luxuriant commercials, it was hard for me to
realize the significance of what I was seeing. The Tribunal was told
that bombers also take off daily for Laos from Thailand.

Facts such as these render obsolete the present level of debate
and opposition in the Western world. Given the systematic destruction of people, habitations and countryside about which there can be
no question for those interested enough to find out, Johnson's talk
about North Vietnamese aggression becomes both as fanciful and irrelevant as Hitler's catalog of Jewish crimes against Germany. One
would have to think less of the North Vietnamese if they failed to
help their South Vietnamese brothers—not just because Vietnam is
one country, as guaranteed by the Geneva accords and violated by the
United States under Eisenhower, Kennedy and Johnson, but because
elementary human solidarity requires standing together. And the frequent claim that the war should be ended by mutual concessions and
compromise rather than by U.S. withdrawal becomes like arguing, as
many Germans did in the thirties, that you were against Hitler's excesses but would not dream of calling for an end to his political program. What reciprocal acts should the Jews have offered in return for
a suspension of cremations?

Our capacity to comprehend evils as great as those taking place
in Southeast Asia may be limited, but within the normal limits of
human understanding one can react by refusal and resistance. The
Vietnamese have made this clear. In fact, the ability of resisters like
Mrs. Pham Thi Yen and Mrs. Nguyen Thi Tho to undergo the tortures described in their testimony before the Tribunal without yielding is almost as incomprehensible to most of us as the ability of their
torturers to inflict such barbarities. Apparently each course of action
has its own internal momentum which carries its practitioners far beyond the realms of ordinary human behavior—though in opposite di-
rections. Thus ex-G.I. Peter Martinsen, whose job was to interrogate
prisoners of war, testifies:

> None of us ever thought we would actually torture or
> even beat a prisoner . . . until after members of the detach-
> ment were killed. . . . Then you realize that everyone par-
> ticipates in the torture, unless we have a special group of
> sadists working as interrogators, which I don't believe. I be-
> lieve that they are just normal people. . . .

> It's so horrifying to recall an interrogation where you beat the fellow to get an effect [i.e., information] and then you beat him out of anger and then you beat him out of pleasure.

On the other hand, it is doubtful if anyone, including Mrs. Yen and Mrs. Tho themselves, would have been able to predict in advance of their ordeal that these women could stand up to the treatment they received. Perhaps the first lesson in all this is that we must do everything in our power to stop society from putting ourselves or others in Peter Martinsen's predicament—and that we should not be deterred in our resistance by fear of ending up in Mrs. Yen's or Mrs. Tho's situation. That sounds far braver than I feel or than I imagine most people will feel after reading the documents, but can we do less without suffering moral deterioration?

In any event, no one listening to Mrs. Yen or Mrs. Tho could believe that they were "ordinary persons" any longer, after their ordeal and triumphs. On the other hand the preponderance of evidence from Vietnam, not just at the Tribunal but from a variety of sources, including statements by American fighting men, indicates that otherwise "ordinary" Vietnamese take on extraordinary powers of resistance to hardship and suffering in the ranks of the Vietcong. By contrast, of course, the complaint about the Vietnamese who side with the United States is just the opposite—that they won't fight, that they lack motivation, etc. Notice the testimony of former G.I. David Tuck:

> Our officers told us . . . that the only good Vietnamese was a dead Vietnamese, that they were no good, that they would not fight.

But describing acts of torture against a captured V.C., he says:

> They had the man tied on the ground, he was spread-eagled. They were using a knife to sort of pry under his toenails and the soles of his feet. When this got no results they went on to other more sensitive parts of the body. Well this still got no results, because evidently this man was, as we say in America, a tough nut to crack. So then . . . they put the knife under his eyeball . . . and he still would not talk.

The behavior of both torturers and the tortured goes so far beyond our normal experience that any isolated account automatically arouses our suspicions, or alternatively makes us think in terms of an occasional sadist or hero. But Martinsen makes it clear that he participated in "several hundred formal interrogations" and that:

> I cannot think of an interrogation that I saw in Vietnam during which a war crime, as defined by the Geneva Convention, was not committed. I cannot think of one without harassment or coercion.

Reading testimonies like that of Mrs. Yen and Mrs. Tho in N.L.F. literature in the past, I have found myself automatically discounting them, wondering if they were not exaggerated in places to make propaganda. But it is the war itself which offends credibility and I don't believe that anyone who listened to Mrs. Yen and Mrs. Tho in person doubted a syllable that they uttered.

After the Tribunal's first session in Stockholm, in April 1966, a TV and radio tycoon from Texas who had attended some of the sessions (Gordon McLendon) held a press conference in New York at which he attacked the Tribunal by repeating some of the evidence it had listened to—evidence that the United States had deliberately attacked a Vietnamese leprosarium on thirty-nine separate occasions. Undoubtedly Mr. McLendon had a sound sense of public credibility and succeeded in discrediting the Tribunal. The sad reality is that the leprosarium had indeed been attacked in the manner described.

Thus an honest investigatory body like the Tribunal—or the aggrieved victims of genocide, the Vietnamese, who have no need to exaggerate—are confronted with a credibility problem far more serious than that faced by President Johnson. Almost everyone knows that the government lies regularly about what it is doing in Vietnam. Its lies have been exposed time after time. But even knowing this, the nature of our daily lives and the handling of the war by the mass media makes it easier for us to believe the government's version of what is happening in Vietnam, give or take a few details, than to accept that of the Tribunal or of the Vietnamese. The reality is too far-fetched—but we ignore it at our peril.

At Roskilde I was convinced of the authenticity and pervasiveness of the atrocities because the same incredible pattern was described to us by the victims and the practitioners, by independent nonpolitical observers and by committed partisans on both sides, by journalists who lived and traveled with the Americans and journalists who lived and traveled with the Vietnamese. We heard descriptions of what goes on in Vietnam and we saw it in photographs and films and in the seared flesh and mutilated bodies of the Vietnamese witnesses. We saw it in sample weapons brought from the battlefields and it was confirmed in the testimony of doctors, chemists, weapons analysts, historians, lawyers and social scientists.

On the last day of testimony, Erich Wulff, a West German doctor who had served on the Faculty of Medicine and in the hospitals of Hué for six years (from September 1961 to November 1967), flew into Copenhagen to report on what he had seen in this American-occupied Vietnamese city. Without much idea of what the American G.I.'s, the Vietnamese victims or the other witnesses had said, he supported their evidence by delineating the same realities. Six years ago he was an anti-Communist humanitarian who went to Vietnam to supplement U.S. efforts to aid the Vietnamese. He said that step by step the war in Vietnam has become a war against the whole population. A profoundly fair man, he argued that the average American official in Vietnam successfully shielded himself from perceiving this reality, but that the primitive understanding of the less sophisticated Marine—that he must kill every "gook"—comes closer to the actuality of the present U.S. policy than the rationalizations of the officials.

Let me conclude by summarizing one example of the concatenation of evidence from diverse sources—the use and effects of poison gas. All quotations, including statements by U.S. officials, which appeared first in American periodicals, are taken from documents that were presented to the Tribunal.

There can be no doubt that certain types of gas are used by the United States in South Vietnam. The only argument is about whether or not the effects are lethal. Here again we have a typical situation in which most Americans are vaguely aware that gas is being used— and are even proud that their democratic government and "free press" have not concealed this fact from them—but have absolutely no comprehension of the realities. In trying to present itself in the most favorable light, the United States has officially taken a position which is scientifically untenable: it describes the supposed effects of the gases it uses without describing the concentrations employed or the conditions under which they are used. Referring to occasions when mild doses of the same gases are used outside Vietnam without killing anyone, it argues that the employment of gas in Vietnam is clearly nonlethal. It is as if the murderer claimed that his victim could not possibly have died from an overdose of some barbiturate because the substance is widely used to combat insomnia.

Secretary of Defense Robert McNamara in a U.S.I.S. bulletin of March 24, 1965, described three "tear gases" in use in Vietnam, CN, CS, and DM. He stated that CN on the average makes the victim helpless "for a period of three minutes," CS "on the average makes one incapable of resistance for about 5 to 15 minutes," and DM incapacitates the victim during "a period of from half an hour to two hours."

For United States consumption, an article in the *New York Times* of March 23, 1965, reported:

> The United States disclosed today that it was giving the South Vietnamese some temporarily disabling "types of tear gas" for combat use. . . . [A] statement was also distributed by the Defense Department. It said: "In tactical situations in which the Vietcong intermingle with or take refuge among noncombatants, rather than use artillery or air-bombardment, Vietnamese troops have used a type of tear gas. It is a nonlethal gas which disables temporarily, making the enemy incapable of fighting. Its use in such situations is no different than the use of disabling gases in riot control."

Unfortunately these explanations were more effective in lulling public indignation in the West than in saving the lives of the Vietnamese. The reasons can be found in the following analysis by the Tribunal's Scientific Commission, which describes the chemical properties of the gases far more scientifically than Secretary McNamara did, for all his computers and university research teams:

> CN (choloracetophenone) in air suspension produces a temporary irritation of the cornea and the appearance of tears at the weak concentration of 1/10,000 mg. per litre of air; a serious irritation of the eyes and of the respiratory tracts at a concentration of 2/10,000 mg. per litre; and death, through acute pulmonary edema at strong concentrations of 10 to 15 mg. per litre of air.

Secretary McNamara admits that both CS and DM are significantly stronger in their effects than CN. The scientists who testified before the Tribunal pointed out that, as with CN, their effects vary in accord with the degree of concentration, with both becoming lethal in milder concentrations than CN. In laboratory tests conducted in Tokyo, Tribunal scientists found that when they exploded a single small grenade, captured in Vietnam, in an underground shelter measuring 50 square feet, the resulting concentration of gas was sufficient to kill a healthy monkey or cat within a few minutes.

At the Tribunal we saw captured U.S. films which showed gas being sprayed into underground tunnels and American soldiers pulling out the dead bodies of Vietnamese, including women and children. The spraying is carried out with typical American technological efficiency. The gas is forced into the tunnels by " 'Mighty Mite,' an air pump which sends out a jet of gas at about 200 m.p.h." (A.P. dispatch from Saigon, *Le Monde,* Paris, January 5, 1966). The same dispatch mentions "cylindrical grenades thrown by hand or fired from rifles." Sample grenades were presented in evidence at the Tribunal, together with the powder inside which turns into a highly concentrated gas when the grenade explodes. The use of the powder and grenades is not accidental. Brig. Gen. Jacquard Rothschild explains in his book *Tomorrow's Weapons* that higher concentrations of gas are achieved through the explosion of powder.

The *Wall Street Journal* reports:

> Most peasant houses have underground shelters designed to protect residents from typhoons and wars. Now when American troops are entering South Vietnamese villages, they generally throw grenades in the shelters. Of course there are innocent victims. (January 5, 1966.)

In more concrete terms, Dr. A. Behar reported to the Tribunal that on the 5th of September, 1965, in the village of Vinh Quang (Binh Dinh province):

> The spraying of forty-eight toxic gas containers into the shelters resulted in the death of thirty-five persons and seriously poisoned twenty-five others. (Out of the total of sixty it should be mentioned that twenty-eight were children and twenty-six women.)

Ex-G.I. Peter Martinsen, relating his experiences as a prisoner interrogator, testifies as follows:

> There were some people in a tunnel, and the Americans found the tunnel entrance. They looked inside the tunnel and found it was occupied. They immediately gassed the tunnel with tear gas. It might have been "antiriot gas." . . . The people came out the other end of the tunnel badly gassed and coughing. All of them sounded as if they had serious damage to their lungs. The prisoners were brought in to us. . . . Four or five of the prisoners were girls between the ages of sixteen and twenty. . . . They were coughing, wheezing and gasping. . . . I took one look and called the doctor [who] gave them all injections and dosages of adrenalin. . . . One girl grew more ill. . . . The doctor said "No, no, she'll get better," and she kept growing worse.

Later she was evacuated to a field hospital, where she died.

So powerful is the gas that Americans use gas masks four miles away. Thus:

> According to a North American adviser, a district seventy miles northwest of Saigon, May 10, 1966, received 72,000 pounds of tear gas, which were spread from helicopters in parcels of 80 pounds. According to this adviser, "members of the leadership of the operation who were staying four miles from the place had to put on their masks to protect themselves against the gas." (The *New York Times,* May 11, 1966.)

Despite precautions, even the executioner sometimes falls victim. On January 13, 1966, the *Brisbane* (Australia) *Courier Mail* reported that an Australian corporal, Robert William Botwell, 24, *who was wearing a gas mask,* "died of asphyxiation" when he was trapped in a tunnel into which the Australian forces had thrown "tear-gas grenades" and smoke bombs.

> Two other Australian soldiers were overcome by the gas when they attempted to rescue Botwell . . . ; four Australian engineers were overcome by carbon monoxide poisoning during the same operation. Army dogs brought in to help in the tunnel were also overcome.

In addition to inundating shelters and tunnels as we have seen, the U.S. forces drop the gas wholesale on enemy troops and suspected V.C. areas. In a dispatch from Washington, the *New York Times* for February 22, 1966 reported:

> Defense Department officials explained today that the new tactics of a helicopter-borne tear gas attack was designed to flush Vietcong troops out of the bunkers and tunnels before the attacks of B-52 bombers. . . . One of the past limitations of B-52 saturation bombing attacks was that little or no damage was done to the Vietcong troops unless a direct hit was made on a tunnel or bunker in which they were hiding. The purpose of the gas attack was to force the Vietcong troops to the surface where they would be vulnerable to the fragmentation effects of the bomb bursts.

The *New York Times* of February 23, 1966 prints a dispatch from Saigon which states that:

> Before the bombers struck the area, twelve miles southwest of Bongson, hundreds of tear-gas grenades were dropped from helicopters. The first soldiers to enter the area wore gas masks.

On August 17, 1967, a U.P.I. dispatch from Danang said that:

> Marine helicopter gunships dropped thousands of gallons of combination tear-nausea gas on a suspected Communist position last Thursday, the first use of gas this way in Vietnam. (*Asahi Evening News,* Tokyo, August 18, 1967.)

To add a footnote to the above, Dr. Wulff told of treating patients in the Hué hospital who were suffering from "vast burnings of a great degree, cramps and vomiting" after having been exposed to "tear gas" in the open air in the suppression of Buddhist demonstrations. "The South Vietnamese authorities themselves told me that the gas used was tear gas," he testified. "In a slight concentration it is tear gas, but in greater degrees of concentration it is lethal."

I have mentioned the impossibility of summing up the *evidence* given at Roskilde—but it is possible to sum up the *findings* and to spell out some of their implications for mankind. It was to this last task that the Tribunal asked me to devote the closing speech of the session, and I shall end here with some words from this "appeal of the Tribunal to world and American public opinion":

> The Nuremberg Tribunal asked for and secured the punishment of individuals. The International War Crimes Tribunal is asking the peoples of the world, the masses, to take action to stop the crimes. At Nuremberg the accused rested safely in jail, and the main focus was on the past; our Tribunal is quite different. Unless the masses act, and act successfully, we stand only at the beginning of war crimes and genocide—genocide that could bring down the cities and destroy the populations of the world. . . .
>
> Let us remind you that the history of the war in Vietnam is a history of continuous escalation. When the United States has found that it cannot defeat the enemy of the moment at the level of warfare of the moment, it continually redefines the enemy and expands the form of its aggression. I will not go into the history of this expansion, but I will remind you that it began with diplomatic warfare at Geneva and elsewhere; it went through the stages of political infiltration, the training of puppets, the organizing of counterinsurgency, the training and leading of massive Saigon troops, and, finally, the commitment of masses of U.S. troops.
>
> As the United States loses in its battle with one enemy, it takes on new enemies. And as it escalates its enemies, it escalates the weapons. Already, as the United States is losing at the present level of warfare and claims that as a "Great Power" it cannot admit defeat and cannot withdraw from this criminal enterprise, Secretary Rusk is raising fears of the "Yellow Peril" in China. The state of mind that affirms napalm and pellet bombs and poison gases as weapons is the state of mind that can affirm nuclear warfare.
>
> Many people in the countries of the world, especially the Western countries, are watching from the sidelines, as they watched Hitler. In the time of Hitler they said, "It can't happen here." And in the time of the U.S. aggression in Vietnam they are saying, "It can't happen to our cities; it can't happen to our populations." But already their countries are subjected to the diplomatic warfare that began the attack on

Vietnam. They are subject to pressures on their governments and their economies. The U.S. Special Forces are scattered throughout the world. The Vietnamese know that they have no choice, except to resist. In many other countries, particularly the Western countries, people think that they have a choice still. But they have none; they must resist.

Paradoxically, if Hitler announced his intention to wipe out the Jews, the photos and the reports of the atrocities did not appear in the daily newspapers or go into the living rooms on television. And if the democratic facade in the United States has prevented the American generals and presidents from announcing their intentions, perhaps even from comprehending them in their full intensity themselves, the same democratic facade allows some of the reports and some of the photos to appear in the American mass media. And the psychology becomes: it's all right to do these things because we are a democratic country, as shown by the fact that we tell about them in the press. And at a certain stage, the psychology becomes: because we admit that we are doing these things, we are not really doing them at all. In other words they do not call them by their proper name, and they do not present them in their proper perspective or intensity. But a democratic society *can* commit genocide, as is illustrated by the history of the United States. I need only remind you of what happened to the American Indians and the black people.

If the people in the Western countries in particular underestimate the total and genocidal nature of the United States' aggression, there is something else which they underestimate also. And that is the ability of the Vietnamese people to resist. If they underestimate the inhuman nature of U.S. actions, they also underestimate the human nature of the Vietnamese resistance.

The legitimacy of the Tribunal has sometimes been questioned. Its legitimacy will be determined by the answer given to its findings by the people of the world. The people of the world must refuse to commit the crimes that have been documented here. They must refuse to be accomplices in these crimes. But it is not enough to stop there. In addition they must take positive action to stop the crimes. The Tribunal appeals to the people of the United States to stop the monstrous aggression of the United States at its source. It appeals to the people of the United States to put an end to U.S. genocide. And finally, the Tribunal appeals to all the peoples of the world to act in the name of humanity and the name of solidarity with our Vietnamese brothers and with all other peoples whose lives and honor and integrity are threatened.

The New United States
Strategy in Vietnam

1969 I have a thesis about what is happening in Vietnam that runs counter to most of what is being said in this country, including in the antiwar movement. Briefly it is that *The United States has given up its attempt to win the war and has substituted a policy of unprecedented punishment from the air and sea, which is intended to force the Vietnamese to grant concessions in Paris that will cushion the international and domestic effects of America's military defeat.* According to the Vietnamese with whom I talked recently in Paris, "Search and Destroy" has been replaced by "Probe, Withdraw and Bomb." The TV networks have admitted that helicopter gunships on patrol duty in the countryside are shooting down anyone who runs— on the assumption that the fleeing peasant is a draft dodger or a "V.C." This brutal procedure is part of a drastic escalation of the war, not only after Johnson's dramatic April Fool's Eve speech but also after the late October cessation of bombing in the North. The crucial fact, however, is not simply that the war is being escalated but that the escalation, more in the air than on the ground, is not designed to win militarily or politically in Vietnam. Rather its aim is to strengthen America's bargaining power in Paris and in the post-war Third World.

In World War II, the United States refused to respond to Japanese peace feelers until it could first drop its terrifying new bomb on Hiroshima and Nagasaki, thus strengthening its power position at the peace table and in the post-war world. This time it is the United States which has lost the war, without, however, purging itself of its power drive. It is not considered politically profitable to bring in nuclear weapons, because of the negative effect this would have on world public opinion. But the U.S. has intensified non-nuclear bombing and shelling to previously inconceivable levels. It would be a mistake to refer to such bombing as "conventional" any longer, because of the extreme sophistication and cruelty of the bombs and shells—pellet bombs, shrike missiles, new "improved" napalm and phosphorus. In World War II, when the U.S. dropped a thousand tons of bombs in a single night on the city of Hamburg, a wave of public indignation swept the world, causing protests among those who had no reservations about Allied war aims. Beginning in January, the U.S. has repeatedly dropped between four and five thousand tons of bombs in single raids on small areas of Vietnam. Some of the new bombs are as large as 5,000 kilograms (nearly six tons), whereas "normal" bombing of the North was with 500 and 750 pound bombs and the largest bomb used was 2,500 kilograms. Naval shelling in the South is now four times higher than before the bombing halt in the North, and the use of pellet bombs has increased by about five hundred percent.

The decision to pursue this new policy was made in March 1968, after the military had demanded 206,000 additional soldiers, in order to "win the war." According to a lengthy analysis in the *New York Times,* one year later, "The gist of the Wheeler-Westmoreland report . . . was blunt: 'We've got to have a big infusion of troops or we can't achieve our objectives.'" The request caused consternation in high government circles. By then the clearest thinkers had begun to realize that even with another big infusion of troops, the prospects of achieving their objectives were grim. Moreover, "If tolerance of the war had worn thin, so had the nation's military resources—so thin, indeed, that there was almost nothing more to send to Vietnam without either mobilizing, enlarging draft calls, lengthening the twelve-month combat tour or sending Vietnam veterans back for second tours of duty—all extremely unappealing." (The *New York Times,* March 6, 1969.) (Who says that the antiwar teach-ins, protests and resistance activities have had no impact?)

The *Times* summarizes the alternative that was eventually adopted as a policy which "urged a less aggressive ground war, called for new efforts to open negotiations, and implicitly laid the groundwork for political compromise." The *Times* omits its most terrifying aspect—genocidal bombing and shelling.

The U.S. has come a cropper in Vietnam and has little time and few options left. There is no way for it to get out of the present debacle except through political compromise. What it is now trying to accomplish, pious rhetoric and rational pretenses aside, is to murder enough Vietnamese so that the N.L.F. and the D.R.V. will also be forced to accept political compromises. The logic of the new policy is that it continues one, at least, of the objectives of the old policy by other means. That objective was to discourage underdeveloped countries from following Vietnam's example of asserting its independence and sovereignty. Now it hopes to minimize the contagious effects of Vietnam's victory by withholding its full fruition and leaving that country in ruins when it finally withdraws.

Besides the devastation of the bombing, over half a million U.S. troops are trapped in Vietnam in increasingly vulnerable positions, and the U.S. refuses to move them out.

The new policy is part of a public relations effort by the Nixon administration in behalf of the American system of unrepresentative government under capitalism. It is designed to prevent the very thing this country needs most—politicization of the people through a searching analysis of the foreign policy of the last twenty years and of the nature of the economic and political institutions at home that have expressed themselves in such a policy. Defeated though they may be on the terrain and in the hearts and minds of the Vietnamese people, the military-industrial complex does not want itself exposed at home. The stubborn insistence of two administrations on flouting popular opposition has not only revealed the lack of meaningful decision-making in the U.S.—it has stimulated a process of radical analysis that the shadowy rulers of the country fear at least as much as they fear any foreign "enemy."

Many establishment liberals, fearful of a bitter right-wing reaction to the military disaster in Vietnam, are anxious to blur the hard fact of America's defeat. *We must not let them succeed in this.* We should not, through our own passivity, indulge their pretense that an ambiguous resolution of the war—such as "supervised self-determination"—is a satisfactory outcome which they had in mind all the while. If the government is able successfully to bludgeon the Vietnamese into face-saving concessions, it's going to be that much more difficult for us to demonstrate the continuing bankruptcy of U.S. policy.

The only issues for the United States to negotiate in Paris are the time it takes to get its troops out of Vietnam and the size and nature of the indemnity it pays that ravaged country.

At home this is no time for the serious left to dismiss the war as "an issue for liberals." The left cannot heighten political consciousness or lay the groundwork for an alternative society if it shows only perfunctory concern for the G.I. and Vietnamese victims of the U.S. juggernaut. We ought to step up our resistance to the war, while continually stressing the tie-in between the war and the class society we live in.

New Urgency on Vietnam*

I

1969   There are some signs that the United States, like a wounded beast, may be gradually moving to extricate itself from Vietnam, killing and clobbering as it goes. If so, this is a tentative policy which would be reversed any time there was a let-up in military pressures in Vietnam or in political pressures at home. It is accompanied by unprecedented military escalation (bombing and shelling beyond the limits of human comprehension plus active implementation of the Phoenix Plan for assassinating 80,000 village cadres of the N.L.F.) and is aimed at extorting in Paris the political concessions whch will keep a U.S. foothold in Vietnam. As the *New York Times* admits, "[both inside and outside the Nixon administration] the argument is over how many Americans can be withdrawn, how quickly, without defeating *the purpose for which they went to Vietnam in the first place*" (Sunday, June 22, *The Week in Review;* emphasis added). In other words, the tentative new policy reflects not the slightest lessening of U.S. determination to control Vietnam (and the rest of the world) in the interests of American capitalism and anti-Communism. Instead, it reflects a long delayed but ultimately unavoidable response

* *Condensed*

to the fact that the United States is losing the war on the terrain and in the arena of world and domestic politics. There are at least three basic reasons why it requires *more* rather than less antiwar action, both in the form of massive national protest and in grass-roots resistance activities.

1. Faced with the prospect of "going under" in the same crush of public opposition which made it impossible for Lyndon Johnson to run for re-election, Nixon is trying desperately to prevent active, catalytic expression of the country's underlying discontent. His strategy has been, first to ask for time to study the situation and formulate new policy; then to create a mood of false optimism by leaking dishonest reports of "secret talks," "progress in Paris," declining morale in the N.L.F. and the D.R.V., "improvement" in the morale and efficiency of the puppet troops (a truly ridiculous claim), and impending American military victory. Now he offers phony concessions, such as the withdrawal of 25,000 U.S. troops.

Phony for the sheer tokenism of it, as when a university admits 30 students from the ghetto or a union takes ten black apprentices. But phony also for a less obvious reason: American troops spend most of their time holed up in tiny enclaves, vulnerable to repeated mortar and rocket attacks. They venture out only in periodic savage actions which provide psychological reassurance for the generals and lifers (feeding their *machismo* and careerist ambitions) but are carried out at great cost in G.I. lives, thus adding to the discontent both in the armed forces and at home. Increasingly the major U.S. aggression is being carried out by genocidal bombing and strafing of the liberated zones, the activity which so far has the least political repercussions at home because of the resulting low American but high "Communist" death tolls. The U.S. has given up on conquering territory or pacifying the Vietnamese but hopes to terrorize the liberation forces into yielding major concessions at Paris. So this highly publicized "proof" of peaceful intent and military improvement is a bummer. It is Nixon's equivalent of Johnson's April Fools' Eve bombing halt north of the 19th parallel, where it was most costly and least effective, a move that Herman Kahn had recommended as a step toward greater military efficiency which could be presented to the public as a step toward peace.

As Richard Ward has pointed out in the *Guardian,* "The number of troops to be taken out is in the low range of what has been widely reported in the press as 'excess' or 'fat' within the U.S. command. Robert G. Kaiser of the *Washington Post,* for example, in a May 11 dispatch from Saigon stated that there was a widespread belief among American officers of all ranks in Vietnam 'that at least 50,000 U.S. troops could now be withdrawn without significantly affecting the allied war effort.' . . . During a Senate Foreign Relations Committee hearing on March 27, Senator Albert Gore (D-Tenn.) reported that according to an assistant to Secretary of State Rogers, a system of gradual withdrawal could prolong the war by two or three years. The official had asserted that 'the American people will be bought off with phased withdrawals.' " (*Guardian,* June 21.)

2. Inaction, apathy, allowing ourselves to be bought off, leaving it up to the government to phase out the war at its own pace could lead at the very least to an unnecessary extension of the war by months or even years. Yet every week that the war continues, thousands of Vietnamese and Americans are killed or wounded; others are tortured in prison or confined under inhuman conditions in military stockades. It may be boring to march down the streets in yet another antiwar parade; it may be frightening to face the Mace, clubs and handcuffs of the police; it may be irritating to take part in coalition activities at which some of the marchers or speakers portray life styles or political viewpoints contrary to one's own. But these are minor problems compared to the sufferings, sacrifices or deaths of those who are carrying out the struggle in Vietnam.

3. The establishment is on the run and it is necessary to keep it there. So far it has only taken steps which are intended to cool off the public while it continues to pursue its original war aims. The Sunday *Times* cynically sums up the establishment's objective: "Will the American public, offered for the first time a discernible, measurable reduction in the cost of the war in lives and dollars, relax its antiwar pressure and support a continued effort to win an 'honorable' peace?" (June 22)

But the U.S. can continue its dishonorable efforts to win a dishonorable peace only if the public does indeed relax its antiwar pressure. Caught in a desperate situation, the establishment has been forced to employ a strategy which will work, if the antiwar movement allows it to work, but will turn into an establishment disaster if an aroused and intelligent antiwar movement takes advantage of the openings created.

This strategy, which began under Johnson and continues under Nixon, attempts to convince the public of the administration's good faith in working for peace by offering a series of palliatives and promises which are not intended to interfere with prosecution of the war. In the short run, several of these gestures have been quite successful in deenergizing the antiwar movement, but as the war has continued and the movement has become more sophisticated and realistic about what is going on, the government has been forced to raise the ante in order to have any effect at all. First the opening of talks in Paris, then the end to bombing in the North, now the token troop withdrawal—all have aroused serious expectations of peace. In the first two instances the immediate result was a temporary diminution in public anger and protest, followed, however, by increased impatience. The Vietnamese were quick to see that by calling the U.S. bluff and appearing in Paris they had the opportunity to set up an irreversible dynamic which imposed on the United States a much-reduced time span in which it must either win the war or be forced to end it—*with or without having achieved its objectives*. Because they appear to have known more about the morale of U.S. troops than General Westmoreland and the Pentagon, they realized that the peace hopes generated by the Paris talks would immensely increase the Army's problems with its own troops, and that this would compensate for and ultimately overcome any temporary defections in civilian antiwar protest. It is worth noting that with characteristic ideological rigidity and practical stupidity, the Progressive Labor Party derided the Vietnamese as revisionists who, by going to Paris, had sold out the Vietnamese people, America's revolutionary working class and (worst of all) Progressive Labor. They failed to notice that the Vietnamese arrived with an unyielding line on fundamentals, a seductive flexibility on secondary matters, and a realistic appraisal of the political dynamics that were being created.

For the first several years of the war, the antiwar movement had the crucial but unrewarding task of preventing the building of a national consensus in support of the government. Those who complain that teach-ins, massive demonstrations and nonviolent resistance had no effect because they did not lead to a negotiated peace or the withdrawal of troops fail to realize the tremendous significance of what was accomplished, particularly against a background of political naïveté and noninvolvement, a tradition of righteous patriotism, and the Cold War legacy of anti-Communist brainwashing.

Now the government is in serious trouble. It can't win in Vietnam, either with its ground troops or in its attempts to establish a

South Vietnamese government that is both pro-American and politically respectable. For all practical purposes Ky has disappeared, Thieu is hated by all and trusted by no one, and the little clique of generals and landlords who have sold themselves in turn to the Japanese, the French and the Americans are checking their escape routes and filling their foreign bank accounts with American aid money. The United States is having difficulty bombing the patriots into submission. American money and technology are not all-powerful after all.

At home the war is immensely unpopular but lingers on, cushioned by the traditional passivity of the population, the lack of a tradition of direct action, the reluctance of most people to involve themselves in political matters (except in the treadmill of electoral politics). But there is a tremendous reservoir of disillusionment and discontent waiting to be tapped. The movement's job is to subordinate its tactical disagreements and doctrinal disputes to the need for highly visible and energizing public action. There are many possible formulas under which this can happen without causing any group or viewpoint to lose its separate identity or abandon its own program. For about two and a half years, from April of 1965 through October of 1967, groups which hated and distrusted one another's politics managed to work together to plan and carry out actions that transformed the political climate and forced the Johnson administration onto the defensive. In that case we were all pushed not only by our sense of outrage but by the rising minority tide of antiwar sentiment, as shown first by the thousands, then by the tens of thousands, ultimately by the hundreds of thousands who belonged to no organization but responded to coalition calls for action. Now there is an overwhelming majority out there, millions as a matter of fact, not pushing us and even reluctant to get involved, but fed up with the war, fed up with promises and delays, distrustful of Nixon and the Pentagon, anxious for the troops to come home and the war to be over. Our job is to find a way to build a sense of public outrage and urgency that will give Nixon this year no alternative but to end the war, just as Johnson last year had no alternative but to withdraw from the Presidential race, turn down the military's request for 206,000 troops, and send his negotiators to Paris.

One final observation: the way the war ends will have important repercussions in the coming years. Politically the U.S. is an underdeveloped country. One manifestation of this is the superstitious belief in the underlying decency of American institutions and the responsiveness of the government to the public will, as expressed in the normal electoral process and supplemented by lobbying and petitioning in Washington. This attitude underestimates the importance of the government behind the visible government—the power structure of American capitalism. There is indeed a huge reservoir of decency in the American people but normally that decency is frustrated and prostituted by corporate capitalism, which makes the drive for profits and power, at home and abroad, the dominating force in American policy.

As a concrete way of accelerating the transition already under way from narrowly antiwar activity to the broader struggle against the lethal structure of the military-industrial complex, it may be time for the antiwar movement to project mass actions against corporate as well as political targets. To date, the transition has been mostly in terms of platform rhetoric with here and there a misguided emphasis on creating Leninist vanguards which concentrate on ideological purity, sectarian infighting and a romantic idealization of the working class.

This is not the time to sketch out the details of possible efforts to impede the functioning of industries which are murdering people in Vietnam and simultaneously exploiting American consumers and workers, pandering to male chauvinism, and corrupting American education and politics. But a possible inside-outside strategy could combine careful organizing of workers within the corporate insulation with the outside pressure of demonstrators nonviolently interfering with the smooth operation of warfare capitalism. Firms which rely on precision technology and tight production schedules are highly vulnerable to such actions. The fact that telephone company employees in California openly joined consumer representatives in an attempt to defeat the company's bid for a rate increase indicates the possibility for worker-citizen action. Similarly, there is growing evidence that white-collar technicians are prepared to scrutinize the moral implications of their work as evidenced by the March 4 scientists' protest, at M.I.T. and elsewhere.

The energy released and political structures created by regional antiwar, anticorporate actions might help propel the movement into the post-Vietnam war period when it will have to focus on causes as well as symptoms—for the sake of preventing future Vietnams and in order to struggle for self-determination and economic brotherhood at home.

Part Three

Cuba and China

Cuba:
America's Lost Plantation[*]

In all my travels through Europe, America, and Africa, rarely have I come across peasants who existed in greater misery than the Cuban agricultural workers.

Dr. Jose Ignacio Iasaga, 1957
Bureau of Information and Propaganda
Catholic University Association

I cannot help it if the Cuban revolution sounds "too good to be true" to ignorant and biased outsiders. The present happy situation may not survive the American cold war of the next few months. But while it lasts it is the duty of the reporter to report it.
E. J. Hobsbawn
New Statesman (London), Nov. 5, 1960

1960 Not since I was in Spain in September 1936, six short weeks after the outbreak of the Franco rebellion, have I been in such a heady atmosphere as that of Revolutionary Cuba. For the second

* *Condensed*

time in my life I have seen man's cynical and self-destructive inhumanity to man being replaced by the spirit and practice of a kind of brotherhood that is unknown to those of us who live in a country whose idealism is behind it and where the "rights" of property override the rights of human beings.

In Spain the idealism was first corrupted from within and then destroyed from without in a brutalizing struggle for power between the Communists (backed by and eventually controlled from Moscow) and the Fascists (backed directly by Mussolini's Italy and Hitler's Germany and indirectly by the United States and England). As a reader of the American press (and as a life-long student of the deterioration and corruption of previous revolutions) I went to Cuba twenty-two months after the installation of the revolutionary regime, half expecting to find that I had gone "too late" and would see that once again the Revolution (and the people in whose name it had been made) was being sacrificed to the drives for power or the sectarian preoccupations of a handful of revolutionists. I knew that Herbert L. Matthews had written: "In my thirty years on the *New York Times* I have never seen a big story so misunderstood, so badly handled, and so misinterpreted as the Cuban Revolution." I knew that a wide range of non-Communist observers, including Carleton Beals, I. F. Stone, Leo Huberman, Robert Taber, Douglas Gorsline, Lyle Stuart, and Robert F. Williams, had brought back reports that were at variance with the published reports of Cuban emigrés and American diplomats, businessmen, and newspapermen. But I could not help being somewhat influenced by the persistent reports in American papers of growing dictatorship and "Communist control." Not only was I greatly reassured about these questions, but I found a whole series of breathtaking accomplishments that are bound to have a permanent impact on the imagination of future generations *even if* the United States should succeed in destroying them or if, in attempting to combat counterrevolutionary pressures, Cuba should fall gradually into the hands of the kind of "revolutionist" to whom human beings are less important than dogmatic ideas or political control.

In all I spent three weeks in Cuba, and traveled from Pinar del Río, in the west, to Santiago de Cuba, in the east, a distance of about 700 miles. I made a point of tracking down every kind of opposition to the regime (opponents are not hard to find) and spent hours at a time listening to religious, political, and economic objections to what is going on. Before analyzing these objections, however, I would like to summarize a few facts about pre-revolutionary Cuba. Most of these facts are available in the United States, but my experience is that they do not weigh very heavily in the thinking of the minority of Americans who have chanced upon them in some dull history book or low-circulation publication. They do not influence most American liberals as much, for instance, as do the charges that Cuba has gone Communist, communism being an evil with which they probably have had more directly disillusioning experience. But to the Cubans, who have suffered the indignities and abuses of American domination and Cuban poverty, they are the driving force for the present revolution. To talk to Cubans is to be convinced that the Cuban Revolution has *not* been fashioned after any foreign revolution or from any Marxist (or anti-Marxist) theory. It has been a native response to the ugly realities of day-to-day life under the grip of a nefarious combination of American financial interests and corrupt Cuban collaborationists.

In 1898, after Cuba had been fighting for the greater part of thirty years in what was rapidly becoming a successful attempt to gain its freedom from Spain, the United States stepped in and completed the military defeat of Spanish forces in the Western Hemisphere. The United States proceeded to seize both Cuba and Puerto Rico, against the wishes of the people of these two islands, who had already formed the Joint Republic of Puerto Rico and Cuba. Cuba was not even allowed to be present at the signing of the Peace Treaty in Paris, and American military forces occupied Cuba for the next three years. During the military occupation, American business interests intensified the process that had already been begun in the war-torn 1880s and 1890s of profiteering on Cuban misery, buying up the richest Cuban lands for a song. They also forced through their own version of a Cuban constitution and extorted the notorious Platt Amendment (first drawn up and passed by the United States Congress), under which the American government had the "right" to intervene militarily in order to protect American property and insure the stability of Cuban payments to American investors.

> Article III. The Government of Cuba consents that the United States may exercise the right to intervene for the preservation of Cuban independence [!], the maintenance of a government adequate for the protection of life, property

and individual liberty, and for discharging the obligations with respect to Cuba imposed by the Treaty of Paris on the United States, now to be assumed and undertaken by the Government of Cuba.

The troops came back again from 1906 to 1909, in 1912, and again in 1917. (They have never left Guantanamo, although it is clear that they have no legal right to be there.) After the last American military occupation, the pattern of American control was well established. For example, Ruby Hart Phillips, the *New York Times* correspondent in Cuba, tells in her recent book, *Cuba, Island of Paradox,* of how President Machado, one of the bloodiest of Cuban dictators, was kept in office long after he would otherwise have fallen because "the Chase National Bank, with its influence in Washington, was determined that President Machado should remain in office so long as he continued to make payments on the public works loans." (This did not even live up to the verbiage of the Platt Amendment, since American "property" was protected at the expense of Cuban "life . . . and individual liberty.") And writing of her experiences with Batista (that "charming" man with whom she and the American Ambassadors got along so well), she comments: "with Cuban officialdom trembling in their shoes as to the final action which would be taken by the United States, a word from the Ambassador was usually sufficient, and the memory of U.S. intervention in 1907 still gave an American Ambassador considerable prestige."

When Batista finally fell, on January 1, 1959, sixty years of this kind of American control had produced the following conditions: a corrupt and parasitical Cuban upper class lived in fabulous luxury, mostly in Havana, while in the rural areas, where the wealth of Cuba is produced, only 4 percent of the inhabitants were able to eat meat. (This and most of the following statistics are taken from a little pamphlet put out by the [anti-Castro] *Buro de Informacion y Propaganda, Agrupacion Catolica Universitaria, Havana.*) Only 2.12 percent were able to eat eggs, and less than one percent fish; only 11.22 percent drank milk, and 3.36 percent had bread. To put it simply, the Cuban agricultural worker and his family lived on beans and rice. In one of the richest farm lands in the world, capable of producing a variety of healthy foods, the interests of the big sugar producers (two-thirds of them American) forced through a one-crop culture under

which Cuba had to import 70 percent of the food she consumed—
and under which a majority of Cubans could not afford to buy the
kinds of food that are ordinarily considered necessary for the suste-
nance of life. Little-discussed aspects of the "philanthropic" sugar
quota (instituted in 1934 as part of Roosevelt's "Good Neighbor"
policy, a policy toward which the Cubans are less than enthusiastic)
are: 1) that the profits went to the big producers, not the Cuban people; 2) that this provided an automatic subsidy to American beet-
sugar producers who could not compete on the world market; and 3)
that in return for the quota, Cuba was forced to import foodstuffs
from the United States at preferential tariffs that paid off handsomely
to the American exporters.

Under this artificially induced one-crop, short-season culture,
the vast majority of Cuban agricultural workers were employed at
most four or five months a year. Under the Batista regime, the average
rate of unemployment was one man in four. This means that every
year unemployment was roughly equivalent to that of the United
States in the worst year of the depression of the 1930s. And there
was never any "relief" or unemployment insurance. In the Catholic
survey from which I have been quoting, 73.46 percent of those interviewed said that the thing they wanted more than anything else "in
order to improve their situation" was "work."

In rural Cuba before the Revolution, 48 percent of the adult
population was illiterate. Sixty-four percent of the people had *neither*
indoor toilets nor outdoor privies; only 2.08 percent had indoor toilets, and 3.24 percent running water. The average *per capita* income
in all of Cuba was $6.00 per week—which, of course, meant consid-
erably less for the poor, since this average included the income of the
urban upper classes.

I saw with my own eyes the miserable *bohios* in which most of
the rural population lived and in which many still live—wretched
huts made from the bark of palm trees, with roofs thatched from palm
leaves, and in many cases with dirt floors. Many an American dog
lives in greater comfort. Less than thirty miles from the pretentious
luxury of the Havana Hilton hotel (now renamed the *Habana Libre,*
and available to Cubans at rates approximately one-fifth the former
rates), even today I saw peasants tilling the soil with crude wooden
plows, women carrying pails of water down long dirt roads, and oxen
pulling homemade sledges or carts with homemade wooden wheels.

Under these conditions, and because of an almost complete absence of medical care of any kind, the death and disease rates were astronomical. In Latin America as a whole, according to a recent study made by the United Nations, 44 percent of the children die before they reach five years of age. In Cuba, after sixty years of lavish American profits, of those who survived, a disproportionate number of the girls found their way to the cities, where they became, at the ages of twelve and thirteen, whores for jaded American tourists. Meanwhile Batista and his henchmen grew rich from the "take" of both prostitution and gambling. The National Lottery alone earned a net profit of almost 215 million dollars during the last seven years of Batista's reign, besides supporting, at the time of his fall, 3,684 persons who rendered no useful service whatsoever. As the revolutionary government commented, in the preamble to its gambling reform law: "the contaminated millions of dollars of gambling profits had been used to maintain political parties, buy votes, and enrich Congressmen." Now the slot machines have been abolished, and most of the casinos are shut down. The profits from the remaining casinos "go to the support of the aged, the invalid, the blind, and for other welfare activities" (Article 8, Revolutionary Reform of Gambling). As a substitute for the National Lottery, bonds are issued by the National Institute for Savings and Housing (INAV) and weekly drawings are held to award prizes to the purchasers. The bonds rise in value from 40 percent in the first year to 110 percent after the fifth year, at which time they become interest-bearing. From the sale of such bonds alone, ten thousand new houses were constructed during the first year. (Cuba's population is about six and a half million.) This was two thousand more houses than had been built in the year of heaviest construction under Batista. I do not have statistics for the first ten months of this year, but I saw *bohíos* being replaced by INAV houses, all over Cuba. Under the new law, a house which would have cost $15,000 when built by private constructors under the dictatorship and would have required a $2,000 down payment and minimum monthly payments of $54 is now sold for $5,400, with no down payment and with monthly payments of $15.01. An interesting requirement is that the payments must be made from the earnings of one's own labor.

In 1952, Fidel Castro, one of a series of Cubans who resented the conditions and was determined to do something about them, ran for election to Congress. But the elections never came off. Batista used the army to seize control. Fidel filed a brief in court, protesting the violations of democratic procedure, but Washington had already recognized the Batista dictatorship as the "legitimate" government. When Castro's brief was thrown out of court (where was the American Ambassador, before whom Batista "trembled in his shoes"?) he turned to armed revolt. For the next seven years of growing rebellion, Batista was supplied with millions of dollars' worth of American arms, which had no purpose except to maintain his bloody regime. A permanent American military mission trained and supervised his forces. When the Batista air force bombed the city of Cienfuegos in September 1957, killing several thousand Cubans with American-made bombs, the United States Air Force officially decorated the Cuban general who had directed the bombings. He had been a good pupil.

Since I have been back in the United States, one of the questions I have been frequently asked is why Castro rants and raves so against the United States. I think that if people would take the trouble to read the full English texts of what he says (and to study the history of Cuba-United States relations), rather than get their impressions ready-made from the commentators and headline writers, they would find his statements remarkably restrained and accurate. But in any case, how many Americans realize the full fury of the assault that was levied against Castro by American-trained, American-supplied armies? When Batista made his last big attempt to wipe out the Castro forces, he sent 1,300 American-trained troops against Castro and his 300 men. First they dropped American napalm bombs in the mountains where the rebels were located; then they strafed them with American bullets from American guns. Then they advanced with American Sherman tanks and bazookas, and American machine guns. Castro survived because of the rugged mountain terrain—and because of the support of the overwhelming majority of the surrounding farmers. But is it any wonder that he has a somewhat different attitude toward the "free" and "peace-loving" American "democracy" than do most American liberals? Who are we to object if he now tells the truth about Cuba's poverty under American domination and about America's current attempts to overthrow him?

While I was in Cuba, the *Miami News* published accounts of airplanes that had left Florida to bomb Havana, but had failed to get through Cuba's anti-aircraft defenses. This made a somewhat different impression on me, in crowded Havana, than it might have if I had read it in New York as a half-buried item in the back section of an American paper whose front page was headlining charges that Castro had gone Communist because he had received a shipment of anti-aircraft guns from Czechoslovakia. In Havana I became acquainted with three different young men who had been put in prison in the United States, during the Batista dictatorship, for buying guns for Castro. Is it insolent of them to complain that anti-Castro forces are training today with impunity (and with the encouragement of President-elect Kennedy) and that a sizable force of counterrevolutionaries is receiving military training in Guatemala in a heavily guarded area that the Central Intelligence Agency recently purchased with a million-dollar expenditure of American tax money?

In December 1956, there were only twelve men in the mountains (sole survivors of a landing force of eighty-two) heading up the fight against Batista. But as the struggle progressed, Castro was joined by more and more persons from every walk of life. The intensity of the conflict ripped the mask off the Batista regime and revealed it to be so corrupt, bloody, and tyrannical that all decent Cubans gradually united against it, *whatever their political, religious, economic, or social ideas.* Castro had presented the main outlines of his program in 1953, in his famous "History will absolve me" speech, after the attack on Moncada Fortress (now an impressive school, which I visited), but it was inevitable that he was joined by many relatively honest politicians and just plain decent citizens who were less interested in economic revolution than in overthrowing the stinking Batista. The later defection of large numbers of these people was inevitable in the face of Castro's determination not just to sweeten and legitimize the old forms of exploitation but to replace them with revolutionary economic and social forms. Once the victory was accomplished, all of those whom the American press likes to call "original supporters of Castro" could not have united on *any* program—whether right, left, or center. The fact that Castro was more responsive to the needs of the peasants (who more than any other single group were responsible for his survival) and the poor than to the hopes of the middle-class politicians who expected to reap "legitimate" personal rewards was bound to lead to dissatisfactions among a considerable number of his early, liberal supporters.

As I saw the thorough-going nature of the Cuban Revolution, it seemed quite logical to me that it would be supported, as I found it was, by an overwhelming majority of the peasants and workers whom it has benefited, and that it would be opposed (as I also found it to be) by large numbers of conventionally honest but personally ambitious and overprivileged members of the middle and upper classes. (A study made by the Princeton University Institute for International Social Research, in April and May 1960, showed that "opponents were concentrated in Havana, and the opposition tended to grow in proportion to income and age." The *New York Times,* August 2, 1960.)

The thing that surprised and excited me was the number of former liberals who have grown with the Revolution and enthusiastically support it even though it means a lessening of the personal incomes and privileges they might otherwise have expected. (The Princeton study found that "even among upper-income groups, seven or eight out of every ten continued to speak favorably of the regime.") Typical of the spirit of idealism that has caught up so many of these people, a Cuban oil technician told me without any self-consciousness (when I asked him, as I asked almost everyone I talked with, how much money he was earning) that he had turned down a $200-a-month increase in salary, when he replaced a departing American engineer, because he thought that the government should use the money in its program to help the poor. Then there are the thousand teacher volunteers who went to the Sierras for six months' training in the rigorous mountain conditions—without pay, without comforts, and, according to the terms of Castro's invitation, with the knowledge that they would not always have enough to eat. (After the training period, they receive regular salaries, as teachers.) When I was on the edge of the Sierra Maestras, at the bumpy end of the last new road under construction, I saw a second lot of five hundred volunteers starting out, on foot and with packs, to get acquainted with the living conditions of the people whose children they were going to teach. The day I left Havana, a brilliant young career diplomat in the Cuban State Department told me that he had just volunteered to spend six months in the mountains, under similar conditions, while attending a special training school for diplomats. He said: "Castro wants the people who represent Cuba abroad to be personally acquainted with the conditions of the country we are representing."

The first revolutionary step taken by the new regime (which

hit Americans directly below the belt in their sensitive pocketbook area and led to speedy political reprisals) was the reform of agriculture. The Land Reform Law of May 17, 1959 pointed out that "1.5 percent of the owners possess more than 46 percent of all the farm land of the country" whereas "70 percent of the farms occupy less than 12 percent of the nation's farm land. . . . The existence of large leaseholdings . . . not only runs counter to the modern concept of social justice but constitutes one of the factors that shape the under-developed, dependent structure of the Cuban economy . . . [under which] national income depends on production for export."

Article I declared: "Large landholding is hereby prohibited. The maximum area of land that a natural or juridical person may own shall be thirty *caballerias* [990 acres]. Land owned . . . in excess of that limit will be expropriated for distribution among the peasants and agricultural workers who have no land." Certain exceptions were made, up to a maximum of 3,300 acres in the case of efficiently managed, unusually productive land, and in the case of cooperatives.

The law declared an area of sixty-six acres to be a "vital minimum" for a peasant family of five and provided that the land necessary to provide such a vital minimum be awarded "free of charge to tenant farmers, subtenant farmers, sharecroppers or squatters."

Provisions were made for the setting up of Agricultural Cooperatives "formed by peasants or agricultural workers for the purpose of utilizing the soil and harvesting its produce through the personal efforts of the members."

The expropriated lands were paid for in twenty-year bonds, backed by the national government and bearing 4.5 percent interest. The valuations were based on *the declarations made by the owners for tax purposes,* a basis which enraged the American corporations, which had been draining huge profits and dodging taxes for decades.

In my visits to cooperatives in Pinar del Río and Oriente, I found that there is a wide variety of forms and sizes, depending on the agricultural conditions of the locality and the desires of the members. In all cases, there is a fantastic contrast between the modern sanitary houses, with toilets, showers, refrigerators, and electric stoves (only 7.26 percent of rural Cuba had electricity before the Revolution), and the primitive, often dirt-floored *bohíos* of the surrounding countryside. No wonder observers have commented that for these people the Agricultural Reform leaped several centuries in a few months. I had serious questions in my mind, however, about the possible spiritual price—and loss of freedoms—involved in these material advances. Had the beneficiaries exchanged impoverished subservience to an absentee sugar baron for more sanitary and prosperous subservience to an all-powerful state?

After talking freely with dozens of members and several managers, and asking every relevant question I could think of, and especially after observing the exhilarating atmosphere of freedom, self-reliance, and individual initiative, I was convinced that there is no present evidence of overweening state control, thought control, or suppression of meaningful freedom.

Sometimes in the presence of a manager, and more often when alone with a member, I explicitly asked about the dangers of state control and probed the same area indirectly by asking how specific decisions were made, about freedom to join or leave (it was always an occasion for amazement that I even considered that anyone might not want to join or might want to leave), freedom to take a day off, freedom of movement, etc. I observed that the presence of a manager caused no more change in the member's conversation or pace of work than the presence of a member or relative. I found that even in a cooperative where ninety percent of the members had been unable to read or write eighteen months earlier, members were being given special technical training in order to take over the accounting, administration, and other special functions necessary to efficient self-management. I found a tremendous sense of participation, of people making their own revolution and running their own lives, a perplexity that I should even ask whether the managers lived in better houses, ate better food, or made more money than anyone else, or whether they exerted a disproportionate influence on such questions as distribution of the profits. I found that the books were open to all the members and were discussed at membership meetings.

I found that the present determination of both the members and the government is to develop diversity of form and local freedom of function. In the Mariana Lopez cooperative, in Oriente, when I asked the manager about the dangers of state control, as evidenced by the early experience of the Soviet Union, he answered: "You can ask any of these fellows what they think about anything. They will tell you." (He was right: I had already asked several of them, and they had spoken with a pride and enthusiasm exhibited by few, if any,

American workers.) "The trouble is that before they always looked to the big man. We got to teach them to look to themselves. Later on I go away. They have to learn to do it all by themselves." Before the Revolution, this farm had been owned by a Senator (most of the Batista politicians were businessmen-profiteers of one kind or another), who lived in a state of luxury which contrasted sharply with the squalid poverty of his workers. Now the manager is a gnarled worker who labors in the fields along with everyone else, and feels the same sense of participation in a great Revolution that the others do.

I found a similar freedom from the artificial distinctions of class and status wherever I went. In Santiago de Cuba, two Canadian TV men who were traveling all over the island making a documentary film confirmed my impression. They told me that they had visited an impressive fishing cooperative and found "the director" working waist-deep in muddy water. Being used to the ways of what we call "democracy," they were shocked to think that the *director* of a cooperative would be sharing in this type of work. When they expressed their surprise, they were further shocked to find that the man was the government director not of one cooperative or of one province but of the fishing industry for the whole of Cuba. After telling me this, one of the Canadians put his hands to his head and said: "This man is directing an eight-million-dollar program that has revolutionized the fishing industry and we couldn't tell him apart from the local fishermen. That's the way it is everywhere we have been."

I began early in my visit to seek out the beneath-the-surface realities which I knew must either counterbalance the inspiring achievements of the Revolution, or at least threaten their continued existence. My search brought me in contact with dozens and dozens of oppositionists, most of them open and outspoken but some of them members of a clandestine group who, to my amazement, went so far as to praise Batista, albeit cautiously. All the opponents fell under one of three general classifications: 1) Americans and a small group of Cubans who benefited from American hegemony (some pimps, bartenders, waiters, taxi-drivers, and owners of luxury shops catering to the tourist trade); 2) businessmen, landlords, and some professional men (who, prior to the Revolution, enjoyed special privileges far in excess of those enjoyed by their counterparts in the United States); and 3) certain Catholics.

Strangely enough, these people did not voice several of the objections most frequently raised in the United States—the summary executions, the failure to hold elections, deprivations of civil liberties, and the alleged lack of freedom of the press. Their objections boiled down to two: "You can't make money any more" and "Cuba has gone Communist." I want to evaluate each of these objections briefly.

1) *You can't make money any more.* The people who voiced this objection were largely right. It is impossible to make the amount of money formerly made by many owners of tenement houses, stores, factories, sugar mills, large farms, etc. (Not to mention whorehouses and gambling casinos, which were important sources of revenue under Batista.) Many of those who made this complaint were likable, sincere people who had "worked" all their lives to gain luxuries for themselves or their children. Many of them only wanted things which could rightfully be considered the "finer" things in life (or even, perhaps, in a technological society, necessities) except for the fact that some people got them by denying them to others who worked under them, rented, or bought from them. As typical examples, I will mention the former owner of two stores who felt a natural resentment because he had recently constructed a third merchandising center at a cost of $190,000, only to have the government limit him to ownership of one store; the daughter of a small-businessman who had been sent to the United States to college and then lived off the family income for twenty years but now feared that the business would be nationalized; the doctor who was legally prohibited from taking his money with him if he emigrated to the United States but who had worked out a system for supplying an American businessman with pesos on the black market in return for having money deposited to his credit in a bank in the United States; the owner of two apartment houses who in March 1959 saw his rents cut forty percent by government decree and then had to suffer the indignity of the Urban Reform law of October 1960, under which he receives a guaranteed income of $450 a month for life but loses title to the property, "ownership" of which is being transferred to the occupants of each apartment, in return for rent payments for the next ten years.

2) *Communism.* These people usually began by telling me that they had been for the Revolution at the beginning but are against it now "because it has become Communist." When I questioned them, no one was ever able to supply any tangible evidence of Communist

infiltration or control, but each, in his own way, told me a personal story similar to those above. To them the limitations on personal exploitation and gross inequality are communism, and who is to say that they are not right? But if so, it is a communism closer to the teachings of Jesus, Francis of Assisi, Tolstoy, and Gandhi than to the ideology of Stalin. As I saw the pragmatic attempts of the Revolution to feed the hungry, clothe the naked, care for the sick, and educate the illiterate, it seemed appropriate that one of the slogans I saw displayed most frequently was: *To betray the poor is to betray Christ*— Fidel Castro. To some of the upper- or middle-class "victims" of the Revolution, it is inconceivable that people like themselves should be deprived of their "right" to enjoy the surplus rewards of ownership, investment, and special training in order to assure "even the least" of their brethren the minimum-decency level of work, food, shelter, clothing, and medical care. Since most American liberals find real economic sharing similarly distasteful, it is perhaps correct for them to condemn the Cuban Revolution. But if so, they should at least realize what it is they are opposed to and not think that they are standing idealistically for the protection of the "little people" of Cuba against the encroachments of a tyrannical state.

There is no doubt that in the cities many "little people" *have* suffered economically because of the absence of the free-spending American tourist. I found some dissatisfaction and grumbling among such people but far less than I did among the more well-to-do. I talked at length with a taxi-driver who had tried to leave Cuba, in August, in a small boat because he found it so hard to support his family in the mildly privileged style to which they had been accustomed. He and his companions had been caught four or five miles off the coast, brought back, and charged with complicity in a plot to smuggle arms for counterrevolutionists. After two weeks in jail they had been tried, acquitted and released. He did not hesitate to complain freely or to say that he has applied for a visa to get to the United States. But when I asked him if the government is Communist, he laughed. "Listen," he said, "one thing the people don't want is Russian domination. They wouldn't stand for it. When I read in the New York papers what they say about Cuba I begin to wonder about other things they say in those papers."

"That's right," chimed in his friend. "This Revolution helps the family, and that is the opposite of communism. Don't forget that

England trades with Russia and China, and no one thinks England is Communist. If we hadn't bought from Russia, everything would be at a standstill. That is what the United States wanted to happen, but we would have been fools to let it happen."

As an example of what this man was talking about, I thought of how the American-owned oil refineries had tried first to put a squeeze on the Revolution by instituting a gradual slow-down in production and then to paralyze the economy altogether by refusing to process oil for the government. By May of 1960, the Texaco plant in Santiago de Cuba was refining only 4,500 barrels of oil per day in a plant whose capacity was 25,000 barrels. When the Castro government tried in desperation to buy crude oil on its own, all sources were shut to it except the United Arab Republic and the Soviet Union. Nonetheless, the first arrival of a Soviet oil tanker in Cuba was widely cited in the United States as conclusive proof that Cuba had become a Communist pawn. When Texaco continued its program of economic warfare by refusing to process the government oil, Cuba took over the plants. Everyone knows that modern society cannot operate without gas and other fuels, but few people stop to think of such things when a seemingly trustworthy statesman or news commentator cites *Red oil* and *Cuban expropriation of American property* as evidence of Cuba's communism. As a matter of fact, most Americans know, when they are reminded, that the oil trusts are vast octopuses which control governments, start local wars, stifle honest competition, and make millions of dollars by overcharging consumers. Still, it is considered somehow reprehensible to defend oneself from them. In Santiago de Cuba, Texaco had rigged its operations so that it did not have to pay taxes to the Cuban government. It managed to buy machinery, oil, and transportation from its subsidiaries, sister companies, or foreign branches at prices which made it possible for it to show a purely fictitious loss on paper on its Cuban operations.

Those who still think that Cuba revealed herself as Communist when she entered into trade agreements with Russia and China should recall how the United States and England allied themselves with Stalin when they were locked in conflict with Hitler. For five years American political leaders and publicists had nothing but praise for the newly discovered democracy and freedom in the Soviet Union. Today tiny Cuba is in a position similar to that of the United States and Britain during the war. The United States is admittedly trying to isolate and overthrow the Castro government. The more scandalous of its methods are withheld from the American people—and even from Congress—just as the facts of how the Central Intelligence Agency overthrew the democratically elected government of Guatemala in 1954 were denied at the time and have only recently been admitted, in part, in the heat and confusion of the presidential campaign. American policy leaves Cuba no alternatives except economic and political collapse or closer alliance with the Communist countries. This will make it harder for Cuba to maintain her independence and follow the revolutionary path she is trying to take.

The real threat to the United States is not communism—but humanism. The United States is not nearly so afraid that communism will spread from Russia to Cuba as that humanism will spread from Cuba to the rest of Latin America. In fact the United States seems determined to do everything it can to drive Cuba in a Soviet Communist direction, either to provide a pretext for suppressing Cuban humanism directly or because it is anxious to prove to the people of other Latin American countries that their only choice is between capitalism which starves them and, as Castro said in 1960, "the Communist state [which] by its totalitarian concept sacrifices the rights of man." Latin America is a vast, largely undeveloped region with rich resources in metals and oil (both sorely desired by the American military machine) and in agriculture (highly profitable to American investors and absentee owners so long as it is organized for the export market rather than to feed the people). Already American trade with Latin America is larger than with any other region of the world, and American investments are greater there than in any other area. The United States has the same stake in Latin America that France has in Algeria and Belgium had in the Congo. It is trying with similar desperation, dishonesty, and disregard for the natives to turn back the clock of history. It will not succeed, but if the American people continue to be duped by the lies and propaganda of their bipartisan press and government, it may succeed in suppressing revolutionary humanism and forcing Cuba and the rest of Latin America into a totalitarian form of socialism.

I found no interest in holding elections in the near future, among either supporters or opponents of the regime. Everyone was agreed that if elections were held Castro and the Revolution would win overwhelmingly. Obviously this means that elections have no appeal to the counterrevolutionaries, who find it more advantageous to concentrate on getting money and arms from the United States. The only possible gain for the revolutionists would be to palliate the United States, but so convinced are they of American hypocrisy—and so anxious are they to stand on their own feet—that they don't appear to be even considering such a step. They point to the experience of Guatemala, and feel that elections would not protect them from America's evil intentions. They have a strong sense of operational democracy and contrast their own day-to-day freedom in the midst of a revolution with the subservience of the average American, who can choose periodically between the candidates of two mammoth machines, but in most important questions is at the mercy of either the government or the corporations. They point out, as an example, that Americans can be fired at the whim of their employers but in Cuba there is a law against arbitrary dismissal. They stress that Cubans hold elections in their unions and cooperatives, and vote, in these organizations, on many of the important questions that affect their daily lives. They feel that the Revolution is in mid-passage, is under severe economic attack from the United States and is in imminent danger of military invasion. They feel that to hold governmental elections would be merely to set up a meaningless diversion from the tasks for which they already have too little time.

For all the force of these arguments, I was disappointed that there was more emphasis on pointing to the farcical nature of elections in the United States, and in the past in Cuba, than on thinking about ways in which elections could be reorganized to make effective supplements to the day-to-day democracy which is evolving so impressively. The people may be getting what they want, but politically Cuba is under the control of a small group of idealists who formulate the laws and broad policy (after unusually imaginative and conscientious consultation with the people involved). The history of politics makes it clear that it is dangerous for even "good" men to hold this kind of power for any length of time.

A 20th Century Revolution?

1962   The Cuban Revolution continues to confound both its critics and its well-wishers. Its achievements and its failings continue to be those of Cubans acting in the peculiar heritage and situation of contemporary Cuba; and they fail to fit into either of the frameworks assigned to it by its severest critics and its most mechanical admirers. That it has repudiated the 18th century framework of parliamentary democracy and domination by the propertied classes (a framework under which Cuba had been raped and despoiled by the United States, with the aid and to the profit of its own leaders) has been clear for some time. What has not been clear has been the extent to which this repudiation would force the Revolution into the essentially 19th century framework of centralized state socialism, which would in turn permit it to be exploited in the interests of Russia, with the aid and to the "glory" of its own commissars. Man is bound by his past and because of the economic power for life or death of the two 20th century states which have most successfully applied and perverted the revolutionary thrusts of the two preceding centuries, Cuba will undoubtedly show the influence for years to come of the United States or the Soviet Union. But by now it is clear that she will not succumb lightly to either.

The Cuban Revolution has made some unfortunate mistakes and is under bitter attack by both capitalism and communism, but at the grass-roots level it continues to exemplify human relationships that are far and away superior to those of either the Soviet Union or the United States. The political superstructure is faulty (as yet no 20th century framework has been developed for holding the government in check or making it responsible to those it governs), but the day-to-day relationships in the cooperatives and the factories express a revolutionary egalitarianism which is inspiring in itself and serves as a *de facto* check on any overriding ambitions of a political elite. Of what other country would a visiting sociologist be able to report, as Maurice Zeitin has done in his *Cuban Journal,* that there were no status differences of any kind (and only slight differences in salary) in the factories, that the managers of cooperatives dressed, lived, and worked like the other workers, that the floor sweeper was as important as the longshoreman or the steelworker? It is significant that neither the liberal democrats who condemn Cuba nor the Communists who praise it include such items in their analyses. (I once heard a Russian diplomat "boast," off the record: "We have millionaires in Russia.")

What has been disturbing in Cuba for some time has been the spirit of mob patriotism expressed in the press and in the speeches of secondary political figures. I am not speaking primarily of the content of much of what has been said—after all the United States has used every dirty trick in the book against Cuba, and the Cubans have a right to be indignant about this and to be proud of their accomplishments. But the tone has too often been a propagandistic and cliché-ridden one that stifles thought and is the opposite of the genuine fervor of individuals thrilled by their participation in a new life. By going to the Cubans at home, at work, and at play, Zeitlin has been able to show us that this individual fervor still exists. Fortunately for the completeness of the record, however, Zeitlin also held an interview with Ché Guevara which shows the existence of a frightening ambivalence within the 26th of July Movement. Perhaps the most distressing of Ché's comments was:

> You cannot be for the revolution and be against the Cuban Communist Party. The Revolution and the Communist Party march together. The Trotskyists say that they are

> against "Stalinism." But in the [1959] general strike, for in-
> stance, the Trotskyists refused to cooperate with the Com-
> munist Party.

This is a blatant and ominous rewriting of history. The Trotskyists, who were apparently too insignificant to make any difference
one way or another, are being blamed for not having cooperated with
the Communists in the general strike. Yet it was the failure of the
Communists (entrenched in the labor movement under Batista) to
support the general strike which led to its abysmal failure. The only
valid historical argument is over the extent of their perfidy.

In addition, Ché has this to say about the Soviet nuclear tests:

> I am also very enthusiastic—because I sincerely be-
> lieve that the Soviet Union wants peace . . . and if the Soviet
> Union should fall behind, the U.S. would start a war leaving
> the Soviet Union in a dangerously vulnerable position.

It is sad to see the Cuban people, whose glory is in their social
and economic relationships rather than in their military technology,
succumbing to the arms-race mania which permeates the United
States and the Soviet Union. Perhaps it is too much to hope otherwise: the Cuban Revolution was accomplished with the aid of violence, and was defended in April 1961 by military means. But it is
obvious that the total armed forces of Cuba were insignificant compared to those of the United States in April 1961, just as the 26th of
July Movement was far inferior in military technology to the United
States-supported Batista regime. In both cases it was the psychological
factors which inspired the revolutionists to great accomplishments
and which held back the United States. One might have hoped that
Cuba would inject a similar human factor into the Cold War discussions by reminding the Russians of the political significance of
the world-wide sigh of relief that would accompany a renunciation
by either power of the arms race. Since the Soviet Union benefits, in
any case, from the presence in the Western Hemisphere of a socialist
country which is not part of the American colonial system, it would
not have been in a position to break off trade with Cuba, had Cuba
asserted her political independence in this manner.

But the most significant political development of recent months
has been almost entirely overlooked or misinterpreted in this country.
Fidel Castro's speech of March 26, 1962 in which he announced the

expulsion of Anibal Escalante from the recently formed Integrated Revolutionary Organizations (O.R.I.) was a powerful attack on the old-style Communist drive for power, together with an appeal to those who had been operating within the Communist orbit to renounce their narrow political opportunism and become real revolutionists in "an association of free revolutionists." Escalante, who had been a member of the *Partido Socialista Popular* (pro-Moscow Communist Party) for over twenty years, was the organizational secretary of the O.R.I. Castro complained that instead of integrating the revolutionary masses into the new organization, Escalante was "forming an army of tamed and submissive revolutionists," of "unconditional followers."

> In every province the general secretary of the P.S.P. was made general secretary of the O.R.I.; in all the nuclei, the general secretary of the P.S.P. was made general secretary of the O.R.I.; in every municipality, the general secretary of the P.S.P. was made the general secretary of the O.R.I.; in every nucleus, the general secretary—the member of the P.S.P.—was made general secretary of the nucleus.

These methods were "leading to the creation not of a party . . . but rather of a tyranny." In fact, Fidel Pompa, O.R.I. secretary in Oriente, had "the mentality of a Nazi *Gauleiter*." Also, Fidel stated, "I ask myself . . . why have we been discussing a problem [the cult of personality] which was not our problem but the Soviet Union's?"

The expulsion of Escalante and the merciless public exposure of P.S.P. methods not only indicates the continued vitality of the Cuban Revolution but has great practical significance. The O.R.I., to quote Blas Roca, Cuba's leading Communist, is not a "united front" in which each group "conserves its structure and committees." The P.S.P. has been "definitely and permanently dissolved to make place for the new organization." Therefore it will not be easy for the Communists to fight back, and there is hope that a number of them will grow with the Revolution (just as many former liberals have grown with it) and become "free Revolutionists" in the new movement. In our own country, where the Communist Party seduced a high percentage of the incipient revolutionists of the thirties and forties, the failure of most to emerge from the experience capable of carrying their original idealistic drive into real revolutionary activity has helped debilitate the radical movement. By the time they realize how they have been betrayed by the squalid opportunism, the internal struggles for power, and the blind subservience to Russia, they seem incapable of resuming the struggle.

Nine former members of the P.S.P. remain in the directorate of the O.R.I. and it will be interesting to see, in the months ahead, to what extent they will continue the attempt of Escalante to capture and "tame" the Revolution and to what extent they will accept Fidel's invitation to move forward with it. Equally important for the future of the Revolution is whether or not those in this country who have decried the "Communist take-over" in Cuba and asserted that they favor a "genuine revolution" will now resist the continuing attempts of the United States to suppress the egalitarian practices which, if allowed to survive, may some day help inspire a similar revolution in this country.

Cuba: Seven Thousand Miles from Home[*]

1964 *I went to Cuba legally, with a valid American passport, and State Department permission granted me as a journalist on specific assignment from a regularly publishing non-Communist periodical. The shortest way was by Mexico City, the only city in the Western Hemisphere from which there are passenger flights to Cuba. Cubana Airlines is allowed to make two flights a week. They must get in and out of Mexico City on the same day, and they are not permitted to use airplanes purchased from the Soviet Union, but only those bought some years ago from Britain, heavy planes which are less practical than the Soviet ships for the special requirements of this flight. The combination of intense heat and low-pressure atmosphere frequently found in Mexico City makes it unsafe for them to take off on a hot day. (My flight was delayed eight hours by this factor, causing us to arrive in Havana long after midnight.)*

Because I had been warned that it is extremely difficult to get permission from the Mexican government to reenter Mexico from Cuba, I began applying for a reentry permit at the Mexican Consulate in New York, but was told that I must apply in Mexico City.

* Slightly condensed from June-July 1964 Liberation

In Mexico City I wasted a day going to three different offices but in the end was told that nothing could be done until I filed application at the Mexican Consulate in Havana. In Havana I wasted two more days going back and forth, along with two other stranded journalists, among the Mexican Consulate, the Mexican Embassy, and the Swiss Embassy (which represents Americans in Cuba). The Swiss were extremely courteous but explained that they could not do much to help us. In the end we were given a message from the Mexican Ambassador that the United States State Department had instructed the Mexican government not to issue reentry permits for Americans who go to Cuba. We were told that our only hope was to call the United States Embassy in Mexico City and ask them to instruct the Mexican government to send word to the Mexican Consulate in Havana to issue the permits. When we did this the repeated words of the American Embassy were: "There is nothing we can do to help you. We cannot interfere in the internal affairs of the Mexican government."

I accepted the offer of the Cuban government to pay the cost of transportation to New York by way of Czechoslovakia, a distance of over 10,000 miles and costing $662, economy fare. (Added to the distance from New York to Havana, by way of Mexico City, this made a round trip of approximately 14,000 miles; hence the title "Cuba: Seven Thousand Miles from Home.") When I flew to Prague the plane was loaded with Latin Americans (visitors from Chile, Argentina, Brazil, etc.) who also had been forced to take the long route home—from Havana to Gander, Newfoundland (where no one is allowed to leave), to Prague—and back to Paris and the "free world."

The good side to all this was that I got a chance to spend eight days in Czechoslovakia and compare its ethos and practices with what I had observed in Cuba. I know a lot less about Czechoslovakia than I do about Cuba, but I did have a number of good contacts there, and even without them I think the contrast would have been shocking. There is no question in my mind that the revolutionary euphoria that still exists in Cuba is totally absent from Czechoslovakia, and for that matter never existed there, even at the beginning of its "revolution," which after all came in with the assistance of the Soviet Army. The close two-way identification between the people and the government which is so evident in Cuba does not exist in Czechoslovakia. Without entering into a discussion, at this point, of the successes or failures of Czechoslovakian socialism, it is clear that the Czechoslovakians

*have a higher standard of material living and far less freedom than
the Cubans. There is no longer the kind of terror that there was in
the early fifties, and a process of intellectual ferment and liberalization is clearly underway. But the best people I talked with, both "men-
in-the-street" and Marxist intellectuals, were thoroughly disillusioned
with the rigid and bureaucratic authoritarianism which doggedly re-
sists the forces of enlightenment.*

There are people who believe in the Cuban Revolution on faith,
because it is socialist, much as they (or their predecessors) believed
in the Soviet Union all through the days of Stalinist terror and hypocrisy. And of course there are others who believe just as dogmatically
that the Cuban people cannot possibly be free or happy because they
do not have a parliamentary system of government, a two-party system, and presidential elections.

It seems more fruitful to examine the Cuban Revolution prag-
matically. To what extent is it succeeding in overcoming the poverty,
humiliation, and servitude which were the lot of most Cubans during
sixty years of highly profitable United States domination? Is it encouraging the intellectual, religious, and political liberty of the people,
or is it "merely" (as well-to-do Americans sometimes put it) improving their economic lot at the expense of their political freedom (freedom, by the way, which the people did not possess before the Revolution, when the United States was well satisfied with Cuba)? Now
that Cuba has become a Marxist-Leninist country and a member of
the Soviet bloc, is it being run or controlled by the Soviet Union?
Does it appear to be succumbing to the centralized authoritarianism
and stifling bureaucratism which continue to plague the European
socialist countries, even as they are being forced to yield ground slowly
and erratically to the post-Stalin forces of liberalization and relaxa-
tion? Does the system work in Cuba or is it a chaos of disorganization,
inefficiency, and shortages? The answer to these questions is more important than the name given to the system or the forms and formulas
under which it operates.

As I begin to deal with these questions, I am haunted by the
words of a journalist who visited Cuba late in 1962. The day he returned to the United States he said to me: "I don't know how I shall
ever write about what I saw. The truth about Cuba is so different
than the American people think that if I write the facts no one will
believe them." Faced with a similar problem after spending twenty-

three days in Cuba from April 29 through May 21, I find that I simply cannot adopt the role of a propagandist; that is, I cannot tone down the facts in order to make them believable—or palatable—to skeptical Americans. The history of man's attempts to abolish exploitation, selfish privilege, overweening political and military power—all too often only to see them reappear under different names, in different forms, or with different excuses—is too disheartening to allow me to pretend, in the interests of political or journalistic expediency, that the Cuban Revolution is any less triumphant than it is. For if the accomplishments of the last five years are anywhere near as impressive as I found them to be (despite the existence of unresolved problems and some danger signals), they carry a whole new message of desperately needed hope.

Perhaps most Americans are incapable of receiving this message, not just because of the propaganda of the press, the government, and the C.I.A.-sponsored exiles, but because of the lack of comparable experience in American life from which to extrapolate. The only thing I know in the United States that comes close to the everyday spirit of liberated Cuba is the surge of faith and hope and love that often occurs in a Negro mass rally or action for integration in the South. On the other hand, the unfulfilled and bitter mood that more frequently characterizes Northern rallies and demonstrations—and recently has begun to appear in the South as well—is completely foreign to the Cuban ethos. "We never dreamed that we would own a house like this or that life could be as wonderful as it is now," one family said to me in a *Granja de los Pueblos* (Peoples' Farm) in Matanzas—and this is the mood I found all over the island, in the fishing cooperatives, the factories, the new schools and housing projects, and even, surprisingly enough, among those who still live in wretched *bohios* (huts) or in the remaining slums of Havana, Santiago, and other cities. Those who still lack decent housing show other signs of enjoying a rising standard of living and of being caught up in the general enthusiasm. The first time I stopped to photograph some sordid dwellings, I was amazed to see the new and attractive clothes everyone from aged grandparents to small children was wearing. This turned out to be commonplace. "Come take a picture of my ugly house," one attractively dressed woman said. Far from expressing bitterness or despair (as one would expect from similar words in the United States), she seemed to be saying that her house was an anomaly left over from days that are fast disappearing.

The poorest people receive so many unprecedented benefits that they take in their stride whatever hardships or poverty remain (and by comparison with the material standard of living in the United States there are many). They have been taught to read and write. (Nearly one-fourth of the Cubans were illiterate in 1958.) Their children are getting a free education, and there are allowances for food and spending-money for secondary school and university students. For the first time in their lives there is regular work at an eight-hour-a-day job (often including time spent in the factory at classes, in subjects ranging from elementary Spanish or arithmetic to science and technology), money in their pockets, and a month's paid vacation, which can be enjoyed at the beach or in the mountains, at one of the new tourist centers or in one of the formerly exclusive resorts that have been opened to the public at greatly reduced rates. On my first visit three and a half years ago, all of the new housing was being put up by the government, in the form of projects for slum dwellers or units for the newly formed agricultural cooperatives. This type of building is being continued throughout the island. In addition, there is now a tremendous amount of new housing being put up by independent farmers and workers as a result of improved conditions of employment and the expanded domestic market for the farmers' products.

In Oriente alone, I saw hundreds of new houses in various stages of construction—anything from a pile of bricks in a yard to a neat new house of brick, cinder block or cement, that had recently replaced a primitive *bohio*. The only discontent I found was not among those whose lot is still hard, by United States standards, but among members of the middle class who complained of shortages, the inferior quality of consumer goods formerly imported from the United States but now made in new Cuban factories or imported from Socialist countries, and the fact that "under communism there is no chance to make big money." One college student, whose parents are in Miami, kept complaining to me that "The Revolution is no good." When I pressed him to explain in detail so that I could report his complaints on my return to the United States, he took hold of my shirt and said: "Is that an American shirt? It is much better than this one which was made in Cuba. Before the Revolution there were many more nice things in the stores." Although it was not hard to find opponents of the regime (especially in bars, hotels, and the more expensive restaurants), I was never able to find any whose objections were more searching than this. The most rigorous questions about the Revolution were raised by members and supporters of the government.

As a pacifist and decentralist, I was not predisposed to like the Cuban Revolution, either on my first trip in November 1960, when I spent three and a half weeks on the island, or this time. My first trip was so utterly different than I had expected that I realized it was impossible to predict what I would find on the second one. But I must confess that after being subjected to more than three years of false reports, invented facts, and devastating analyses by ex-Cubans and other experts who have not even seen Cuba during several years of swiftly moving developments, I half expected to be as disappointed and disillusioned this time as I had been inspired and exhilarated in 1960. Only after I had been back in Cuba for some time did I realize how much the constant propaganda had sapped my morale and clouded my vision.

Not even in Havana, the hangout of foreign correspondents, Communists-in-exile and the so-called middle bureaucracy, is one apt to understand the real depth of the Revolution. For the Revolution is a very tangible phenomenon that tends to elude intellectual analysis and sophisticated political discussion. Furthermore, the greatest changes are taking place outside Havana, where the greatest poverty, disease and illiteracy existed. Only by traveling the length and breadth of the island (as I did by automobile) can one begin to savor the amazing success of the Revolution in providing houses, schools, hospitals, food, clothing, socially useful work, dignity, freedom, and an atmosphere of social solidarity and brotherly love.

I do not want to give the impression that the Revolution has passed Havana by. In addition to everything else, prostitution, the gambling casinos, venality, gangsters, beggars, and the high-priced pampering of American tourists and local parasites have disappeared —and now flourish in other American outposts instead (such as San Juan). By contrast, Havana is flooded by *becarios* or scholarship students (over a hundred thousand secondary school students alone, mostly from poor families outside Havana, are now living in the abandoned homes of the bourgeoisie) and vacationing *obreros* and *campesinos* (workers and peasants) who never had the money to travel before but are now enjoying the hotels, beaches, and clubs formerly reserved for wealthy white people. And when on May 1 Fidel told the people of Havana that the first increases in food supply would go not to Havana but to the countryside, beginning with the poorest province, Oriente, because the need was greater there, a great roar of approval went up from the crowd—a sign both that the people of Havana are not exactly starving (as some Americans believe), and that they have developed during the Revolution a wonderful new spirit of humanism that has long since disappeared from American cities. Can anyone imagine any American politician daring to tell the people of his state that new government contracts would go to another section of the country first because other people needed them more? Would anyone dare predict a spontaneous ovation from the crowd if he did? Yet this is the kind of unrehearsed response that breaks through in countless unforeseen ways every day in Cuba, in individual conversations or in a crowd, among friends or strangers, and that tells more about what is actually happening than any of the learned analyses by people who have not been there.

As Herbert Matthews of the *New York Times* wrote, after visiting Cuba from October 24 to November 3, 1963:

> It is axiomatic in journalism that it is not possible to know what is happening anywhere unless you go there. . . . The freedom for Americans to know and to travel has been curtailed, so far as Cuba is concerned. For teachers and students this is frightening. As scholars they are not allowed by the United States Government to go to Cuba to study one of the most important political and social phenomena of modern times. As a result none of our leading Latin Americanists knows what is happening in Cuba; they cannot teach with authority on the subject of Cuba; they cannot even read the many books and articles on the Cuban Revolution now being published, with the ability to judge whether they are right or wrong, good or bad. . . . One of my overwhelming impressions of the trip is how little I really knew the situation in Cuba, although I had done my best to read everything I could get hold of and talk to everybody who had visited Cuba.

Later, Matthews adds:

> Cuba has been transformed. This should be obvious, although it seems impossible for Cuban exiles and most Americans to realize. Not only the Cuba of 1958 but *the Cuba that the exiles left has ceased to exist.* (Emphasis added.)

Incidentally, it would be a mistake to think that the American public was able to read Matthews' analysis in the *New York Times,* of which he is a senior editor. Perhaps the following sentence, in which he explains his long absence from Cuba (more than three years) also explains why the *Times* did not print any dispatches from him when he finally did go:

> The intensely hostile climate of opinion in the United States, some of which is directed towards me and the *New York Times,* and the difficulties placed in the way of all visitors by the United States and Mexican governments, made an earlier trip seem unwise.

Matthews' report cleared up many widely disseminated inaccuracies about Cuba, but it was not published in the *Times* or any other newspaper or mass circulation periodical. Instead, it appeared in the *Hispanic American Report,* a scholarly journal with a circulation of 2,200.

When I arrived at the airport in Havana, a representative of the Cuban Institute for Friendship with the People (I.C.A.P.) greeted me and offered me the use of a car with a driver and a guide-translator. Even before I had a chance to inform I.C.A.P. that I distrusted guided tours and did not want to get swallowed up in one, my guide said to me: "If you have any place you want me to take you or any appointments you would like me to try to make, I am at your disposal, but if you prefer at any time to be on your own all day or any part of the day, we understand that. We are here to help you, not to restrict you. Naturally you are free to go anywhere you want and speak to anyone about anything. I only tell you this because we know that Americans have been told a lot of strange things about Cuba."

It turned out to be an ideal arrangement. I did wander on my own or make my own contacts and appointments more than half the time, talking to people for hours in complete privacy; but through I.C.A.P. I was able to travel with a minimum of effort to out-of-the-way places and see a wide range of people whom I might otherwise have missed. As we drove through Cuba, when I saw anything that looked interesting, sometimes because it was out of the mainstream of the Revolution, such as a Seventh Day Adventist Seminary, a local headquarters of the Jehovah's Witnesses, a Baptist bookstore and publishing house, a town that looked poorer than most, I simply asked the driver to stop while I investigated. Always the guide would say: "Do you want me to come with you or do you prefer to go on your own?" If I went alone, as I did most of the time, he would arrange to meet me at whatever time I suggested or wait patiently by the side of the road for anything from five minutes to an hour or more.

Dozens, perhaps hundreds of times, I struck up conversations in bars, coffeehouses, parks, and on street corners, often pointing out at an appropriate juncture that "I am not a Communist but an American journalist who has come to try to find out the truth about Cuba." I raised all sorts of provocative, even insolent, questions: "How much money do you earn? How much did you earn before? Do you have more freedom now or did you have more before? Why is it necessary to have volunteer brigades to help with the sugarcane harvest? Are they really volunteer or are you put under pressure to join? By your boss? by the Party? the Union? Has Cuba won her freedom from the United States only to lose it to the Soviet Union? Why is it necessary to guard so many stores and public places? Who are they afraid of? I know that Fidel denounced political sectarianism in 1962, but if this type of thing happened once how do you know that it won't happen again? Is there any evidence that it is happening right now? Do you have any say at all in the government? Why is there not freedom of press and speech and political opposition? (The usual answer to this was that I had no idea how much freedom there actually was.)

No one ever seemed afraid to speak freely—though on two occasions I met critics who, after pouring out their complaints practically from the moment they met me, in such loud voices that it would have been hard for other people *not* to have heard them, made a show of dramatically lowering their voices and saying: "It's not safe to talk in Cuba."

By day and by night—often after midnight—I wandered and snooped, in residential and commercial areas, warehouse and factory districts, slums and wealthy neighborhoods, even around the docks of

Santiago. I was never asked to produce any identification or justification for being there. Once a Soviet technician got a little annoyed when I asked him if it was true that there was a lot less freedom in the Soviet Union than in Cuba and wanted to know who the hell I was. But this is the only occasion I can remember when anyone balked at any of my questions.

In looking at the Cuban Revolution, whose forms are so different from those which most Americans are accustomed to associate with democracy and freedom, it is important to remember that operational forms which are liberating at one stage of a people's development often outlive their usefulness and, if not replaced by new forms, can become in their turn instruments of coercion and repression. Something of this kind has happened in the United States, where the forms that once provided democracy and freedom have not evolved to keep pace with the changes in population, technology, industrial organization and financial control. As a result they have gradually lost their original content and become the forms of a constrictive pseudo-democracy and pseudo-freedom instead. Cuba's experience with U.S.-style Batista democracy was especially disillusioning. Be that as it may, it is both arrogant and provincial for residents of the United States to insist that the liberation of Cuba and other Latin American countries can only take place if they adopt the same forms of economic and political organization that liberated the eighteenth century white American colonists under vastly different technological, social and political conditions. As Herbert Marcuse has written in *One Dimensional Man:*

> The higher culture of the West—whose moral, aesthetic, and intellectual values industrial society still professes —was a pretechnological culture in a functional as well as a chronological sense. Its validity was derived from the experience of a world which no longer exists and cannot be recaptured.

Ironically, the "Popular Assemblies" that take place regularly (usually once a week) in the Cuban factories, *granjas,* cooperatives, schools, and housing projects fulfill a grass-roots, democratic function similar to that formerly provided in the United States by the New England town meeting. In conjunction with other institutions that are gradually evolving (but whose eventual character cannot be predicted with certainty) they constitute a far more effective and dynamic form of "democracy" or popular participation in decision-making than has existed in the United States for some time.

But conveniently overlooking these assemblies the American critics continue to insist that there will be no democracy in Cuba until something similar to our Presidential and Congressional sweepstakes takes place. Yet the Negro in Mississippi can't vote. The Negro in New York can vote but (token exceptions aside) his vote can't get him a house in a "white" neighborhood, an education, job, or salary equivalent to those of a white person with comparable abilities. That eliminates twenty million Americans (almost three times the population of Cuba) from real democracy. Most of the rest of us can live in whatever neighborhood we can afford and, in some states, can even rejoice in our right to vote for a socialist or other minority candidate, who, of course, has no chance of election since he inevitably lacks the financial-industrial and mass-media backing necessary to make him a valid candidate.

I watched Cubans stand in line waiting in the hot sun for buses which are in short supply because the U.S. State Department will not allow Americans to sell Cuba either buses or replacement parts for the prerevolutionary buses still on hand. Meanwhile buses are arriving from Poland, Czechoslovakia, Hungary, and Russia—and of course from England, despite the anguished protests of the United States—and I wonder if Dean Rusk and President Johnson think that this contrast between American and socialist attitudes will turn the Cubans toward "democratic" capitalism.

Is it any wonder that the Cubans, who feel free for the first time in their lives and have seen their freedom growing through five years of revolution, are not in the least responsive to calls from American liberals and social democrats to model their institutions after those prevalent in the United States? No wonder they prefer to work out their own indigenous forms of political and economic organization in accord with their own evolving experience. But this is the one item of democracy, the one aspect of the American heritage which neither the United States government nor most of the liberals and social democrats are willing for the Cubans to have: the right to carry out their own revolution in their own way.

When I attended the May Day celebration in Havana, the first minor surprise was that the ceremonies began exactly on time (quite different from the last time I heard Fidel speak in Havana) with the firing of a twenty-one gun salute and the release of an equal number of doves of peace. This was the closest thing to militarism that was to take place during the next two and a half to three hours. Only near the end of the parade was there a very brief display of anti-aircraft rockets and, later, the appearance of the first group of draftees under Cuba's new conscription law, marching hand in hand with their mothers. There might have been something else military that I missed, but if so it was completely dwarfed by the jubilant workers, male and female—most of them with the faces of the obviously honest and long-suffering poor, and many carrying their youngsters or leading them by the hand—and the eager scholarship students and other young people, whose joy and pride showed more in their exuberant smiles and gestures than in any highly trained or coordinated manner of walking.

The motif of the parade was the celebration of the first five years of the Revolution: the Year of Independence, the Year of Agricultural Reform, the Year of Education, the Year of Organization, and the Year of Economy. There was no mistaking that this was a day of heartfelt thanksgiving for the fruits of the Revolution, the kind of communal thanksgiving that never takes place any more in the United States, though we have a day officially set aside for that purpose. And it was a day of determination as well, determination, as Fidel expressed it, on the one hand to press ahead to new accomplishments and, on the other hand, never to surrender to the imperialists no matter how great the military odds in their favor might be. This is part of what he said:

> On a day like this, we can see how far we have advanced. . . . Does this mean that we are satisfied? No. That we have already accomplished enough? No. Quite the contrary. What we have already accomplished will help us to reach higher achievements. . . . Perhaps we will never feel proud, perhaps we will never be satisfied and the people will always have newer and newer aspirations, newer and newer things to be done. Fortunately life gives us this incentive, the incentive of having many things ahead to accomplish, many things to achieve. And if on one occasion our incentive was to end illiteracy, later it was to have every worker

reach the sixth grade, and after that it will be to have every citizen complete secondary education. And as often as we achieve a goal, new goals will appear.

We can say that we have not wasted time. Some people accused the Revolution of moving too fast. We were in a hurry because we had lost more than fifty years ... and therefore each year has to be multiplied. Every single year of the Revolution must represent several years of progress.

And, when he spoke on the nature and extent of the Cubans' determination never to surrender, he was interrupted many times by shouts and applause.

The imperialists are buying themselves the worst problem of their lives. I am not speaking of international problems. I don't want anyone to think that if we speak out clearly, that if we speak out with dignity, we are doing so because we have a feeling of impunity, that we are doing it at the expense of other peoples, at the expense of the friendship and solidarity of the Soviet Union. No, when we speak in this way we speak for Cuba, and we speak in the name of Cuba. We do not speak thinking in terms of intercontinental missiles, because if we spoke in this way backed by rockets, what meaning would our words have? How serious would our statements be? ...

When it comes to defending our sovereignty and our dignity we do not measure the strength of the enemy or our own strength. The only thing that we consider is that we have the duty to defend that right and that we know how to fulfill that duty and that we are ready to fulfill that duty. Because this is our right and our dignity. There is no doubt that the imperialists have more planes and more guns than we have, but they do not have more right and more reason, and they would never have more courage.

Courage is not an animal concept, not a biological concept, courage is a moral concept, a spiritual concept. Peoples with more courage than others really do not exist—or men with more courage than others. Courage as a moral and spiritual concept is born from reason, from the force that inspires it—from justice, law, from the legitimate aspirations of the peoples—and therefore those who attack us would never have even a shadow of our courage to fight against us. . . .

Let's imagine that the imperialists invade us. That by the strength of numbers and at a very high price they succeeded in occupying our territory. Would the struggle end there? No. Just a stage of it, and a second stage would begin in the cities, in the countryside, and everywhere. . . . A long drawnout struggle would begin in which they would have to face a real people. . . .

If the imperialists should invade this country, you would have to realize that the majority of the leaders of today would die in the struggle. But the people will remain, and the party would remain. There would be no need to ask for names or for men. Each one of us would do his duty in the way demanded of him and do it well. . . . That's why we say that we are an invincible people and we say this thinking only of our own strength. That's why our people deserve the utmost respect and that's why even our bitterest enemies will have to respect us. . . .

The rights that our people have won and defended are not rights that were inherited, they are not privileges granted to us, they are rights that were won in struggles, rights that were won fighting. We did not win our rights in a lottery nor in a game of chance. They are the result of history, the result of the whole life of a nation. And we will know how to defend the rights that we have won. . . .

If life offers us triumphs and successes, may the triumphs and successes that we win come with dignity and with honor. If life offers us sacrifice and struggle, may the sacrifice and struggle be welcome, because that is what life offers us, with dignity and honor.

That is why we may all go back to our homes calm, serene, happy, facing the future with courage and serenity, with joy and optimism, conscious of our strength, of the strength of our principles, of the prestige of our cause. . . .

Our Revolution has many things, many experiences interesting and useful to all people. But above all our nation has something wonderful. . . . Our country has these people and these people are the most admirable thing the Revolution has.

When Fidel said that "the majority of the leaders of today would die in the struggle," this was not rhetoric. Fidel himself nearly lost his life in a tank, helping repel the invaders at Playa Largo (Bay of Pigs) in 1961—and again last fall in rescue operations at the height of Hurricane Flora. Are such acts of personal involvement romantic? Irresponsible? They probably are by ordinary standards. But on the other hand, perhaps only the stimulus and contagion of this kind of leadership could have led to the rebirth of a whole country which is so manifest in Cuba, to the emergence of a nation of leaders, so that for all their distinction and value Fidel and the other veterans are less and less indispensable with each succeeding year of the Revolution.

In the early struggles of other revolutions, the leaders have been willing, at one point or another, to sacrifice the lives of their political opponents to ensure the triumph of their own ideas (or the advancement of their own power position). In Cuba, though opponents have been executed openly for specific acts of murder, torture, or sabotage (and I deplore this fact; as I told my Cuban friends it would have been more in keeping with the Revolution's humanism to have sent them to rehabilitation centers), so far as I have been able to find out no one has been bumped off, Stalinist fashion, for political deviation. In fact the whole idea is foreign to the Revolution's character and I mention it only because of the terrible history of the Communist International in this respect and the widely held misconceptions about Cuba in the United States.

It was against a background of this kind of personal commitment that Fidel posed his famous question to Senator Barry Goldwater when Goldwater urged that the Marines be sent in to turn the water back on for the Guantanamo Naval Base. Fidel asked Goldwater if he was prepared to lead the first wave of attack personally. No doubt many Americans thought of this as a cheap political rejoinder, and resented the suggestion that the life of one of our Senators should be risked in an engagement with a minor enemy. But to the Cubans Fidel's question dramatized the difference between the integrity of their leaders and the irresponsible antics of American politicians, who are more ready to risk other people's lives than their own. After spending some time in the heady atmosphere of Cuba, one wonders how long the Congress, the State Department, and the rest of the Executive branch would continue to push on with their war in Vietnam if President Johnson, Dean Rusk, and a random assortment of Senators and Representatives were expected to take their turn, Cuban style, fighting in the jungles and paddies. The Cubans are wiser than we are: no man should advocate a war he is not prepared to risk being the first to die in.

There is another contrast which was not lost on the Cubans. Most of the politicians whom the United States supports in Latin America keep big bank accounts in Switzerland and the United States —and an escape route ready in case of emergency. But every Cuban knows that Fidel and the other leaders operate from an entirely different set of principles and that the welfare of the people and the leaders is inseparable—in case of counterrevolutionary attack and, by the same token, in everyday affairs.

Finally, it is instructive to contrast Fidel's integrity with the cynical maneuverings of an administration which sends mercenaries to their almost certain death in coastal landings (several took place while I was there) which have no chance of succeeding and apparently are not even intended to succeed. Far from being a major part of United States policy—or even an admitted part of official policy at all—these suicide operations represent a minor ploy in the political "game" the administration is playing. They serve as a warning to the restless and impatient people of Latin America that the United States will fight every inch of the way against any attempts they might make, Cuban fashion, to secure land, food, and freedom.

Several times during the May Day parade and during Fidel's speech, I left the stands and went down to the street to look at the people more closely, in order to observe their facial expressions and gestures. It was as if the black people of Mississippi and Harlem (and the inhabitants of all the other slums, ghettoes, and Appalachias) were holding a great festival to celebrate five years of freedom and happiness. To understand the mood of this laughing, singing, exuberant crowd of 800,000 people (more than a tenth the population of Cuba), you would have to imagine that the Negroes had done far more than to break out of their ghettoes and desegregate the schools, restaurants, parks, and employment agencies. You would have to imagine that in the process of doing this they and their white allies had developed a spirit of brotherhood which made it impossible for them to be satisfied with integrating into the existing commercial culture and engaging in its selfish competition for personal profit and prestige. You would have to imagine that those who clung to capitalism as their ideal had emigrated and the rest of the population was engaged in the infinitely more exciting business of working out a whole new society in accord with their deepest yearnings for brother-hood. You would have to imagine, for instance, that rents had been abolished in the poorest sections of Harlem and that overcrowding, rats, and the *de facto* segregation of schools had been eliminated by building free housing in the suburbs, with the people who had lived in the worst conditions getting priority. You would have to imagine that huge estates like Ruleville (Senator Eastland's Mississippi plantation) had been turned into people's farms, with new houses, schools, hospitals and workshops, and with democratic assemblies in which all the people participate and elect their own representatives to other political bodies. You would have to imagine, sad to say, that Senator Eastland had objected to these "violations of (his) democracy and freedom," had refused to accept compensation for that part of his estate that had been expropriated, and had moved to Madrid (or Durban, South Africa), along with a number of disgruntled police chiefs, White Citizens Council leaders, bankers, and industrialists —and that after their departure, the mansions and remaining land that they abandoned had been converted into schools, hospitals, tourist centers, social and recreational clubs (open to the public for a nominal fee), and even rehabilitation and retraining centers for ex-prostitutes.

Even sadder still, to understand the mood of Cuba on May Day (and to a great extent every day), you would have to imagine that the people had found it necessary to repulse five years of guerrilla warfare, sabotage, raids, and attempted invasion by the expatriates— and that the Eastlands and Wallaces had been supported by a few members of the Negro bourgeoisie (who had wanted freedom for their people but thought the movement went too far) and by liberals and social democrats who were alienated when the new government abolished private ownership of large factories, corporation farms, department stores, and apartment houses.

Of course if our imagined Second American Revolution (for that is what it would be) followed the Cuban precedent, it would allow private owners to maintain ownership of three buildings: their place of residence, a second house for vacations and similar uses, and a place of business (in general, if it did not employ more than five persons). What is more, the Cuban government guarantees former landlords and owners of businesses or farms a monthly income for life equal to their former income, up to a maximum of $600 a month (which in Cuba is roughly double the monthly earnings of a skilled worker, and goes much further than it would in the United States).

Is all this too much to imagine? Are these developments outside the possibilities of the American dream? If they are, then those who are desperately defaming or trying to overthrow the Cuban Revolution can relax. For they need not fear that the Cuban example will awaken the American people from their torpor. And certainly they will never succeed in reconverting the Cuban people to capitalism.

The Revolution in Cuba is irreversible. Even if Cuba should suffer military defeat and American occupation, the people would never forget the glorious years they have had, the discovery they have made that human nature does not have to be selfish and cruel, and brotherhood an empty slogan frustrated by the economic and political realities of the system. But the real question remains. Who will take up the Cuban example and fashion a new life of brotherly relationships indigenous to their own culture and responsive to their own needs?

In Czechoslovakia, an intelligent and humane Marxist told me that for him and many of his countrymen the Cuban Revolution is the most exciting development of the last twenty-five or thirty years. "It may transform the whole socialist world, which has long since gone stale. For all its genuine idealism, socialism has been bogged down for years in a stultifying bureaucracy. And although the socialist countries have thrown off the worst aspects of Stalinist terror and Russian control, real freedom is still more of a hope than a reality. The stimulus of Cuba may speed up our liberation by years."

As I listened to this man speak, I wondered how many Americans are equally open to the message of Cuba. Are we too frightened by the words "Communist" and "Marxist-Leninist" to study the Cuban Revolution dispassionately, and perhaps introduce some of its concepts into the mainstream of American political discussion? Are we convinced that the backward-looking refugees and the State Department know, and are able to tell us, the truth about what is actually happening in Cuba, so that there is no need to upset the travel ban? Are we so satisfied, basically, with the American way of life, its affluence, its "free press," "democracy," and "Free World" alliances that we feel we don't need to find out for ourselves about the experiment the Cubans are engaged in?

Cuban Contradictions

1965 I am extremely grateful to David Wieck for his careful and intelligent analysis, which appeared under the title "Cuba: An Effort at Interpretation," in the May issue of *Liberation*. It is by far the most perceptive and challenging article that I know of that has been written by a person who has not had the benefit of observing the Cuban Revolution at firsthand—and indeed in many ways probes more deeply and humanistically than most of the analytical articles written by those who have been to Cuba since the Revolution. It stands in revealing contrast to those facile endorsements and condemnations alike which are based on narrow political partisanship, routine application of preconceived dogma to a living revolution, or some combination of the two. Life always eludes the rigidities and abstractions of party-line doctrine, whether that doctrine be Communist, mainstream American, democratic-socialist, anarchist, or pacifist.

"The easier way," Dave Wieck writes, "is a dogmatic statement that Marxism implies totalitarianism, violence begets greater violence. . . . By and large such propositions hold and tend to be instructive, but Iron Laws they are not." Being a complex and changing phenomenon that defies all blueprints and philosophical utopias, the Cuban Revolution did not develop according to my own conceptions of an ideal revolution: in particular it was not nonviolent—the Marx-ist-Leninist label came twenty-eight months later and did *not* imply totalitarianism, even though there were a few old-line Cuban Marx-ists who apparently thought that it did. I have always opposed some of the Revolution's features, both in this country and when I was in Cuba. Among other things, I find the executions appalling (but I am no less appalled by executions in the United States, where addition-ally they fall most heavily on racial minorities and the poor). Like David Wieck, "I am sick unto death, and more than that if there is more than that, of arrests, executions, missiles, soldiers, police, secret police, militias, assassins, informers, and anything similar which I have not named—wherever and whenever." I have been distressed at the low level of the Cuban newspapers (though not of the rest of the press), which were virtually monolithic, politically, for a time and have been improving only gradually the last two or three years. I de-plore the passage of military conscription in November 1963 and have never considered myself an apologist for that evil practice (which, of course exists in the United States as well) simply because I occasionally point out to Americans that most Cubans look upon conscription much as they look upon rationing, as a realistic method of equalizing burdens largely imposed on them by the United States.

The fact that violence tends to beget greater violence does not lead me to equate the defensive violence of Cuba (which in many ways is still akin to the spirit of the embattled farmers of Lexington and Concord) with that of the C.I.A. and the Pentagon. I would like for Americans who agree with Dave Wieck and myself in repudiat-ing *all* violence to concentrate on developing a nonviolent resistance in the United States that could stop American aggression *at its source,* rather than become pedantically hostile to the Cubans (or the National Liberation Front), who are not convinced that nonviolence could successfully stop American aggression *at its point of impact, after we have failed to stop it from being launched.*

In general, I think that it makes more sense for white Amer-icans to try to convert their more dark-skinned brothers to nonvio-lence by example (by demonstrating its effectiveness) than by ser-mons insensitively directed to persons who, after all, suffer because of our apathy or ineffectiveness. The ordinary complacent American may not think that some of us in the peace movement are apathetic, but the perspective is apt to be different to the North Vietnamese whose child is killed in an American bombing raid or the member of the N.L.F. who faces torture and death daily. I did speak on behalf of nonviolence all over Cuba, and warned of the pitfalls of both defensive and revolutionary violence, but I always spoke in the context of the nonviolent heroism of civil rights and peace workers (such as John Lewis, Bob Moses, Jim Peck and Eric Weinberger) and of thousands of anonymous Negroes. It is fascinating to me to notice how many pacifist critics of Cuba and the N.L.F. saw a vital distinction between Johnson and Goldwater that led them to campaign and vote for Johnson (who was carrying on an undeclared war at the time and had already attacked North Vietnam after the Gulf of Tonkin incident) but are horrified when a person like myself sees some moral distinctions between the violence of the N.L.F. or the Cubans and that of the United States.

Copies of the Wieck article are circulating in Cuba, and I have no doubt that they will make a significant contribution to the political discussions taking place there. David expresses some dismay that the questions he raises are hardly considered worth asking (let alone answering) these days, but he fails to realize that his strictures are far more applicable to some of Cuba's cold-war supporters in the United States than to most of the Cuban people. Dave writes:

> A fundamentally bureaucratic—shall I add: Statist and militaristic?—theory of socialism is so widely accepted . . . that hardly anyone even thinks that such questions are worth asking. . . . What evidence do we have of interest in decentralism, in strong communities possessing autonomy and initiative and effective power? What evidence do we have of a conception of socialism which is anything other than centralized planning? . . . All that I mean by "bureaucracy," a meaning in which I would expect [Dave Dellinger] to concur, is *the administration of the economy by a socially alienated officialdom.* [Italics in original.] When this alienation is more or less complete, state-capitalism has been achieved. I realize that in the present day the concept of workers' control (or direct popular control—I mean the same thing by it) has virtually disappeared from socialist currents of thought.

The fact is that questions revolving around the development

and preservation of de facto, grass-roots freedom concern the Cubans very much. Or perhaps it would be more accurate to say that the confidence of the vast majority of Cubans that such questions are being answered positively—and their insistence that this continue to be the case—is one of the most encouraging things about the Cuban ethos. Dave Wieck, after all, formulates his questions out of anxiety and disillusionment with past Marxist-Leninist revolutions, as well as out of a very exalted conception of freedom and human potentiality. By contrast, the Cubans have an almost maddening self-confidence in the future.

Let me quote from two American journalists who visited Cuba last July. Politically they are both opposed to the Revolution, as they make clear in sentences I will not quote here, but they have good enough journalistic eyes to convey some things that are not ordinarily understood in the United States. The first is Bob Considine:

> Like him or lump him, the guy [Castro] is going to be around for a long time. If he would permit an honest election tomorrow, which he won't, he would win by an overwhelming majority. He would win on his record, the only record a majority of the Cuban people care about, and that is that he has taken from the entrenched rich and given to the poor, has provided schooling for children who could never have had it under his predecessors, hospitals, roads and a sense of being important in the world. . . . The Castro revolution is unlike anything else in the Soviet sphere. Everybody is permitted to have a gun, all denominations are . . . wide open and well-attended. Ordinary people interrupt Castro in the middle of a speech and question him. He's as friendly to Red Chinese here as he is to Russians, though the Chinese give him nothing. He must be as much of a puzzle to Khrushchev as he is a pest to Johnson. (*New York Journal American,* July 27, 1964)

The second is Stephen Solarz, associate editor of *News Front,* Management's news magazine:

> The hard and undeniable fact is that for the formerly underprivileged, the Negroes and the young, the material accomplishments of the Revolution have been of such a sweeping character as to secure their enthusiastic support

for the regime. . . . What has taken place, in short, is a radical redistribution of the national income. . . . The extremes of great wealth and grinding poverty which once existed have been diminished. The regime is committed to a thorough egalitarianism which must pain the privileged as much as it pleases the deprived. The private clubs and beaches have all been opened for public use. An exceptionally tight control on wages has created an economy where the highest income is not significantly more than the lowest income. A graduated income tax and the easy availability of social services, from old-age pensions to vaccinations, have further reduced the disparities in wealth. . . . It is doubtful that the one-third of the nation which previously lived almost exclusively on rice, beans, bananas and root vegetables finds the limitations on its new consumption of meat, milk, eggs and fish a great inconvenience. These people regard rationing as a boon rather than a disaster. It represents a formula for equal distribution and, as such, has been hailed as one of the key political achievements of the Revolution. (*News Front,* September 1964.)

It is commonly assumed in this country that people are almost always ready to exchange political freedom for a full stomach. Perhaps this is the case when people are convinced of the absolute necessity for making such a choice, but my impression of Cuba is quite different. The Revolution made the lower classes somewhat heady. It stimulated and released a tremendous burst of creative energy, an euphoric sense of individual dignity, solidarity and idealism. Far from creating an atmosphere in which people felt they must choose *between* economic advancement and freedom, the main thrusts of the Revolution convinced the formerly underprivileged and harassed Cubans that they could have *both*. In general the mild reformist "revolution" desired by middle-class intellectuals, liberals and "democratic-socialist" office seekers (who sincerely opposed Batista's tyranny and corruption but were hardly either egalitarian or libertarian in outlook or program) was "betrayed" more by the thrust from below than by any doctrinaire conceptions on the part of Fidel. (As usual, and contrary to popular misconceptions, the Communists were urging Fidel to go slow rather than to extend the Revolution.) The

economic egalitarianism described in *News Front* encourages feelings
of equal worth rather than a tendency to be subservient or submissive.
The facts that "everybody is permitted to have a gun," and "ordinary
people interrupt Castro in the middle of a speech and question him"
(Considine) serve as brakes on the development of a socially alienated officialdom and encourage ideas of direct popular control. The
victory at Playa Giron (Bay of Pigs) reinforced and restimulated the
the sense of grass-roots dignity and power, though the attack and the
months of vicious sabotage and terrorism that led up to it also set in
motion a counterforce, the idea that it might be necessary to accept
some restrictions on freedom because counterrevolutionaries operate
most easily under the cloak of freedom. One sophisticated Cuban expressed the popular mood when he told me that Justice Holmes' dic-
tum, that the right to free speech does not cover the right to shout fire
in a crowded theater, justified restrictions on organized political opposition because people who consistently oppose the Revolution are offered guns and plasticos (and of course money) by C.I.A. agents.
Both moods are operative today, the one that insists on real, grass-roots
control and the one that is willing to accept, even ask for, restrictions
on freedom in order to protect the Revolution from the "clear and
present danger" of American-instigated invasion or counterrevolu-
tion. As a result of these counter-pulls, Cuba is neither a tyranny nor
fully free, and it is impossible to know, despite the general and unmistakable ethos of freedom, what abuses may have been committed from
time to time in the name of defense of the Revolution.

Let us look at a concrete example of the struggle between two
different attitudes toward revolution, attitudes which probably reflect
both the ambivalence and the experimental approach of many Cubans
(including Fidel) as much as they reflect any hard division of Cubans into good guys (Fidelistas) and bad guys (former Communists). I say this in part because one of the most noticeable phenomena in Cuba is the way in which a wide range of persons, including
former social parasites from the privileged classes (not all of them
have become refugees), old-line Communists, and politically indif-
ferent persons have grown in the invigorating atmosphere. David
Wieck writes:

> The Castro group, rightly perceiving "the Party" (any
> party) as an instrument of domination and power-struggle,

have rejected it as the leading instrument of social revolution (the Communist Party has been held in check); they
have deviated from Lenin, thereby avoiding the characteristic Communist trajectory.

Dave is close to the essence of what happened, but technically
is inaccurate. In actuality all existing political parties were dissolved
in the spring of 1961, just prior to the Bay of Pigs invasion, as part
of an agreement to build a totally new, all-inclusive party. Communists were eligible for membership in the new party, along with everyone else. At the time, this development was cited in the American
press and among opponents of the Revolution as conclusive proof
that the Communists had taken over (or would shortly take over)
the revolutionary apparatus. To anyone who had probed at all in
Cuba, this seemed extremely unlikely because of the very real distrust
of the Communists among the people and the top Fidelistas alike.
After all, the P.S.P. (Popular Socialist—or Communist—Party) had
been badly compromised under Batista and was generally thought to
have sabotaged the Fidelista's attempted general strike in June of
1958, six short months before Batista's overthrow. At the time that
plans for the new party were announced, Sidney Lens, who had been
in Cuba and was aware of realities there, wrote in *Liberation* that
this was probably the beginning of the end not for the Revolution
but for the Communists.

Apparently some of the Communists feared a similar outcome.
In any event they used the traditional tactics of the Old Left (in
which I include, from my experience in this country, a large section
of the anti-Communists as well as the Communists) to try to gain
control of the new party. They had considerable success, particularly
in some cities and provinces. Their success, combined with the atmosphere of suspicion created by C.I.A. and counterrevolutionary
sabotage and invasion, made this one of the most repressive periods in
the history of the Revolution, a period lasting roughly from April
1961 to April 1962. Many of the more libertarian exiles are from this
period. Lou Jones has written from Havana, summing up the first
experiment in organizing an all-inclusive political party as follows:

The first attempt at the creation of a political party in
1961, the short-lived O.R.I. (Integrated Revolutionary Organizations), was intended to fill the formal gap between

leadership and masses. As the O.R.I. was formed first at the top, the cadres were handpicked from above. It soon became evident that the party did not represent the masses, nor did they feel it to do so. With greater understanding of the problem of forming a truly representative and effective revolutionary party, it was decided to restructure the party completely (changing its name to P.U.R.S. [United Party of the Socialist Revolution] in the process). The revolutionary leaders decided to structure the new P.U.R.S. beginning with the smallest local unit and working upward, leaving only the National Direction to supervise the building of the party. (*Liberation,* June 1965.)

The change from O.R.I. to P.U.R.S. was signalled by a devastating speech by Fidel, on March 26, 1962, in which he exposed and attacked the attempt by *some* old-line Communists to gain control. It is sadly typical that neither the American press nor the doctrinaire American opponents of the Revolution paid much attention either to the speech or to its significance for the problem which ostensibly worried them: whether a genuine revolution would be taken over and perverted by repressive Communists. Since most of them had already made up their minds in accord with their political predilections, insofar as they referred to the event at all, they hailed it as evidence of the ruthless struggles for power to which Communists are addicted.

Fidel's tremendously popular speech was not just an attack on P.S.P. attempts to gain *political* power. It was also a denunciation of the alienation of officialdom from the ordinary people ("a socially alienated officialdom"). Fidel says:

> We went to Ambar Motors. . . . We went there to exchange a few opinions with the members of the nucleus [the party] and out came the head of personnel, in a work center like that one, which is filled with workers dressed in sweat shirts and overalls smeared with grease, a head of personnel wearing a "cute" shirt with loud colors and a pair of white pants. And he was a member of the nucleus! What the blazes! They were completely separated from the masses.

It is a well-known fact, which Americans don't know how to interpret because it is outside their political experience, that top Cuban officials participate in cane-cutting and share the risks of both man-made and natural danger. Fidel manned a tank against the Bay of Pigs invaders and nearly drowned while taking part in rescue operations during Hurricane Flora. For years Ché Guevara, at the same time that he was head of the National Bank and a member of the Council of Ministers, worked regularly one day a week in a factory. (He may still do so; I have no up-to-date information.) Adolfo Gilly in *Inside the Cuban Revolution* (Monthly Review Press) has pointed out that if in a specific area local officials shirk participation in volunteer cane-cutting, by making it merely *pro forma* and ceremonial (like an American politician's breaking ground for a new building), there is a sharp drop in the number of volunteers in that area. This is typical of the informal controls that Lou Jones refers to: they are not fool-proof, but then neither are constitutional guarantees, as American Negroes and nonconformists can testify. It helps to have both types of protection, but whereas most Americans seem to feel that Cuba should have adopted an American-style constitution and parliamentary democracy, the Cubans are trying to develop something more up to date that will evolve gradually under revolutionary conditions. Meanwhile, in the United States we are used to *de jure* democracy and feel politically impotent, whereas in Cuba there is a serious lack of constitutional guarantees but most Cubans feel free and act as if they are.

"How is the decision taken to fortify the island with missiles?" Dave Wieck wants to know, adding that "the reader may believe that the last question . . . is nothing short of ludicrous." In one sense, many Cubans probably think so too, since unfortunately they know very little about revolutionary nonviolence and therefore find it hard to believe that serious revolutionaries can question the use of missiles to ward off the threat of invasion. But Nikita Khrushchev and John Kennedy made a deal which, as near as we can tell, provided for removal of the missiles in exchange for a no-invasion pledge and United Nations inspection of the Island. When Fidel seemed to waver a little in his condemnations of the Russians for assuming that they could make decisions of this kind on behalf of Cuba, the Cuban people let Fidel know, in no uncertain terms, that they were opposed to such encroachments on their sovereignty. Jones writes of Fidel's having taken "the pulse of popular sentiment during the crisis," in "exchanges [that] were free-wheeling and frank." I was told that "indignant" would be a more appropriate word to describe the response of the Cubans in meetings at which officials tried to suggest that Russia knew best. The missiles were Russia's, so Cuba could not prevent her from removing them. But international inspection of the island was another matter. In the end, Mikoyan spent thirty-three days in Cuba without gaining the Soviet Union's objective of persuading the Cuban government to accept international inspection.

Like David Wieck, I am worried that in the end a debilitating split will occur between the people and the regime. Over and over I probed into the nature, function, and existential reality of the new revolutionary party, P.U.R.S., and warned Cubans, both in and out of the party, of the history of the Communist Party in the Soviet Union. I also spoke of the disastrous growth of a union bureaucracy in the United States despite the exhilarating growth of worker militance and class consciousness in the 30s. I did volunteer organizing for the Steel Workers Organizing Committee and remember the sit-ins of the autoworkers, in the militant days of the depression, yet have seen both unions degenerate into the present United Steel Workers and United Automobile Workers (A.F.L.-C.I.O.). I found out that in Cuba, as Jones points out:

> In each work center, elections are held under the close supervision of a member of an extremely small corps whose job is to ensure that there is full discussion of the candidates, an absence of internal politicking, and complete honesty. . . . The party is not given power to act on its own, but rather acts as adviser to the executive bodies and mobilizer of mass effort, creating a two-way flow of communication between the executive and the masses.

Of course all this can be abused, as it clearly has been abused in the Soviet Union and Eastern Europe. But again the *de facto* situation is reassuring. I cannot guarantee that the supervisory corps does not throw its weight around unfairly or, as seems more likely, that the local electors do not sometimes elect sectarian or statist candidates. But talking with a wide variety of "ordinary persons," and questioning members of the party, I concluded that for the present, at least, the party is in most places a genuine vanguard and the elections honest.

Another contrast with the past history of the Soviet Union and its satellites is pointed up in Fidel's speech against bureaucracy and sectarianism, from which I have already quoted. He says:

> What is the function of the party? To orient. It orients on all levels, it does not govern on all levels. . . . In any mass of workers one will find an infinite variety of intelligence, of talents, of merit . . . when a personnel manager is to be appointed, when an important post is to be filled, there is no need to go to the nucleus for it to pick him. He must be picked from among the masses; he must be promoted! . . . The personnel for the functioning of the state must be chosen from the masses themselves, and all work centers should choose their personnel from the masses of workers. . . . If not, it would become a problem of political chicanery, it would become a prize which someone could award. The nuclei would begin to be infested with flatterers and fawners, with position-seekers. That is not the function of the nucleus! The nucleus has other tasks. Its tasks are different from those of state administration.
>
> . . . A party of tamed and unconditional followers, of conceited individuals, of vain individuals can be built up.

I do not gather from this that the state has withered away or that the ideal of some anarchists has been realized, in that all positions of supervision and management are filled by direct election, but I do see a healthy concern to avoid an overriding, socially alienated, bureaucratic party.

From my observations, the labor unions have been more flawed in Cuba, from the point of view of popular or workers' control, than P.U.R.S. One must remember that the unions were well established under Batista and unfortunately had played a role somewhat similar to that played by the A.F.L.-C.I.O. in Johnson's United States. The unions were the center of political opportunism and conservatism, including Communist conservatism. (Americans often fail to realize how conservative the Communists generally are, since they push the doctrine of political realism to its extreme and try to pick up fringe benefits from the dominant sources of political power, whether Batistiano or Johnsonian.) Even before the new law which "established elected committees at the work center level to apply sanctions and deal with workers' grievances," I found in May of 1964 that workers in a number of plants had elected grievance committees independent of the unions. I was told a number of times that genuine democracy had been frustrated in the unions themselves (much as it tends to be in the United States, where bureaucratic machines and strong-arm methods tend to dominate). In Cuba there were signs that the workers (and P.U.R.S.) were beginning to work out ways of bypassing such unions and developing more meaningful representation. Jones' description of present election procedures corresponds to the pattern of worker-control (worker-influence might be more accurate) which I observed at other levels, and gives me hope that the workers are beginning to revitalize the unions:

> Elections of union officers are held annually in each work center. In a general assembly of workers, a slate is proposed by the outgoing executive committee and is thrown open to discussion. The workers make additional nominations, discuss each nominee, then by majority vote on each and every nominee determine if he should be placed on the ballot. On election day, . . . a nominee who gains a plurality of votes by secret ballot is winner. *Cuban labor union elections today have a marked absence of ballyhoo and politicking: such nonsense electioneering is repugnant in the extreme as it carries very strong emotional overtones of prerevolutionary political racketeering.* (Italics added.)

One has to savor the Cuban scene to appreciate the significance of the italicized section, which in effect makes the difference between real elections and degenerated ones, run by opportunistic political machines which dispense not only ballyhoo but patronage and deals. David Wieck writes:

> Part of the theory of early socialism was initiative from below, the delegation of responsibility by the working people themselves, and control over the persons to whom responsibility was delegated. . . . The principle of the election of politicians was irrelevant to this conception of society, but the principle of direct delegation and answerability, in all the affairs of the society, as opposed to carte blanche powers, was a fundamental principle of any socialism that was not authoritarian.

How true! In the United States, the common ideological battle over the Cuban Revolution has been waged over its failure to provide as yet for the election of politicians. Americans speak quite matter of factly about the absence of elections in Cuba. And yet, there are probably more elections in Cuba than in any other country in the world. Every important unit to which one is related—place of work, school, neighborhood, etc.—has its elections, as well as its grass-roots assemblies and discussions. Even the Committees for the Defense of the Revolution are elected, on a block-to-block level.

Most American accounts picture the C.D.R.'s as some sort of top-down Gestapo, instruments of statist repression and terror. How different it begins to appear when one realizes that these committees are elected by their neighbors, when one finds out that they work for community betterment and beautification (teaching former slum dwellers, for instance, the desirability of maintenance of lawns, grass, and physical facilities). I attended a party put on by one C.D.R., at which children were honored for having planted flowers in their block—corny for Americans, perhaps, but I found it very touching. When it comes to "spying," I really don't know what to say, but one cannot approach such questions abstractly: the Cubans have had their water pipes, power lines, crops and stores bombed or burned by C.I.A. agents and other counterrevolutionaries. Perhaps you or I might take suspicious persons aside and try to reason with them, but it is not *prima facie* evidence of totalitarian tyranny if Cubans try to head off sabotage in the normal manner, by reporting suspicious persons and events to local officials.

I have not been able to answer a number of David Wieck's questions, much as I wish I could. I know that there are two "completely autonomous" towns in Cuba, which supposedly operate independently of the National Council of Ministers and the National Direction of P.U.R.S., as experiments in decentralization and local autonomy. But I was unable to follow up on them. One can learn a lot about tone and attitude, in two visits totalling seven weeks, and can clear up many politically motivated distortions of fact that have come to be considered as data in the United States, and still have significant gaps in his knowledge. One can be reassured and inspired, and still not believe that Cuba is either utopian or about to become so.

Wieck writes that "For many Americans this Revolution presents a model." He says: "I have seen no evidence of a sense in which the existing Cuban society can be said to challenge the principle of authoritarianism, and I will not join Dave [Dellinger] in a call for missionaries from Cuba until I hear of this." I know of no society that presents an overall model to be followed exactly, but I believe that the Cubans have a great deal to teach us, particularly in their movement toward economic egalitarianism and social solidarity. My greatest bother is the limitations on freedom and organized dissent, which are not nearly as extensive as is commonly believed in the United States, but nonetheless are blots on the Revolution and are fraught with danger for the future. The Cuban people are making a serious and dynamic challenge to the principle of authoritarianism, though they have not demolished it. I would like to see the American people challenge the disgraceful authoritarianism of their own government, which prevents free travel to and from Cuba and imposes economic and military disabilities on the heroic Cuban people.

Cuba: The Revolutionary Society

1968 When I met with Fidel Castro recently in Havana, he said that he had been caught as unprepared for the development of a broad and vigorous protest movement in the United States as most Americans had been for the first Russian sputnik. Unfortunately, Cuban ignorance of the dynamics of social development in the United States is more than matched by American ignorance of Cuba.

Our own ignorance is based partly on a shortage of information, which is not surprising since the State Department forbids Americans to travel to Cuba without special permission. Permission is usually granted nowadays to full-time professional journalists, but we get some idea of the State Department's restrictiveness from the fact that Robert Lowell, Dwight Macdonald, Philip Rahv, Eric Bentley, and Susan Sontag, among others, were denied permission to attend the Congress of Intellectuals on the Problems of the Third World, held in Havana in January 1968.

Lowell was told that he did not qualify as a journalist, despite the fact that his projected visit was sponsored by *The New York Review of Books,* where his poems appear frequently. If Lowell's disqualification was that he writes poetry, Susan Sontag's was that she spends more time writing books than magazine articles. Thus, at one fell swoop, the commissars in the State Department both disallowed Plato's contention that poets are uniquely qualified to appraise a society's laws and customs and expressed disdain for the likes of Alexis de Tocqueville, James Bryce and Marco Polo. (None of these, to the best of my knowledge, would have been able to meet the State Department's requirements for a writer's visiting "controversial" lands: that he be a full-time employee of a regularly appearing newspaper or magazine.) Even those journalists who were "approved" by the U.S. government were forbidden to take part in the exchange of ideas at the conference, on pain of losing their passports.

To cap its performance in defense of Freedom, the government forbade others (including four distinguished scientists: Doctors Roy John of New York Medical College, Mark Ptashne of Harvard, Stephen Chorover of M.I.T. and Frank Morrell of Stanford) to go to Havana because it had ruled that the conference was not genuine but was a Communist propaganda show. It is beside the point that leading intellectuals from almost every country in the world (including Franco Spain) attended the Congress, and that discussion was free and uninhibited (the Soviet Union, for example, being both castigated and defended). What kind of society is it in which the state decides—not just for its leading intellectuals but, more importantly, for all its citizens—which countries they can visit, how much freedom of speech they can exercise while visiting, which intellectual conferences are legitimate and through which persons and agencies the news shall be filtered?

But the causes of our ignorance go deeper. I am reminded of the girl in John Dos Passos' early novel, *U.S.A.*, who "knew" that all men were alike even though she had always been too afraid of them to get to know any. She had learned from her mother that "they all want the same thing," to go to bed with you, and this knowledge dominated all her reactions. Whether we have neurotic fears of communism or, conversely, lust after it as the miraculous solution to all our problems, we have difficulty getting beyond one-dimensional stereotypes which interfere with our ability to interpret even those facts that are available. We overlook, for example, the uniqueness of Cuba's development and fit the facts into our confused preconceptions of what Communist countries are like. Most Americans identify every Communist country with an oversimplified image of Stalinist Russia and the Eastern European countries (where a Stalinist form of communism was forcibly installed by a combination of the Red armies, Moscow-trained commissars, and the little-known Churchill-Stalin pact of 1944).

Central to the process of distortion are reporters and editors who select not only what facts will become most readily available to us but also the context within which they are presented. Thus, Juan de Onis, the *New York Times'* man in Havana, began an article on the trial of forty old-line (pro-Moscow) Communists by referring not to the differences between Russian and Cuban communism but to "the familiar ritual touches of a Communist party purge." If you read carefully, you found that the men were accused of supplying information to the Soviet Union and urging that country to use its economic and political power to overthrow the Castro regime. The *Boston Herald-Traveler,* whose headline also characterized the arrests as a "purge," revealed on an inside page that the men were accused of stealing secret documents. Does any non-Communist country permit spying or conspiracy with a foreign government to overthrow the existing regime?

Perhaps it would have been possible, without putting the men in jail, to expose the plot publicly and to remove them from positions of political power and access to secret documents. I favor such an approach, because the power of an informed and liberated citizenry to distinguish between genuine and false revolution is a more secure base on which to build a new society than the police-power of the regime. Yet in fairness to Cuba it should be pointed out that this was the very step it took the first time round. In 1963, when Anibal Escalante, alleged mastermind of the present plot, was accused of conspiring to impose a Moscow-type regime on Cuba's fledgling Revolution, Fidel made a long and detailed speech on "sectarianism" and allowed Escalante to go to Russia and Czechoslovakia for a rest.

There is also, of course, the sticky fact that we are in no position to appraise the accuracy of the charges. The Soviet history of leveling similar but often false charges against political deviationists makes us all wary of being taken in. But in reading the *Times* one could easily forget—if indeed one ever learned—that the long-standing conflict between the Fidelistas and the Moscovites stems to a great extent from Cuba's opposition to the monolithic culture, heavy-handed bureaucracy and two-way alienation of people and government that have plagued the Soviet Union and the Eastern European countries. The struggle to combine communism and freedom is taking place throughout the Communist world, challenging the self-serving assumption of both Stalinists and bourgeois anti-Communists that freedom and communism are incompatible. But in Moscow and Warsaw it is students and intellectuals who are being put in jail, as the bureaucracy tries to stifle the rising popular pressures for freedom. In Havana, it is the allies of the Soviet and Polish bureaucracies who are accused, not of having written poems or articles but of stealing secret documents and, in the absence of popular support, appealing to a foreign power.

Communism has its stereotypes just as capitalism does, and Cuban impatience with them was expressed by Fidel Castro when he spoke at the televised closing session of the Congress of Intellectuals. He complained that at a time when many Latin American priests—and many intellectuals all over the world—are becoming progressive and revolutionary, some so-called Marxist parties (the orthodox Communist parties of Europe and Latin America) are becoming more ecclesiastical. "In actuality," he said, "there is nothing more anti-Marxist than dogma; nothing more anti-Marxist than stagnation. But there are many ideas in Marxism that appear today as fossils. Marxism has many brilliant thinkers, but it needs to develop in order to overcome stagnation and relate to the realities of the contemporary world. It must act as a revolutionary force and not as a church."

In private conversations a few days later, Fidel told me that what he admired in the revolutionary priests is their closeness to the people and their ability to put the needs and development of the people ahead of all abstract dogma. On the same day, Roberto Fernández Retamar, a Cuban poet who taught at Yale University before the Revolution, said:

> We knew what had happened to the European socialist countries and we have had a preoccupation with avoiding those things. A burning question in our minds has been whether or not Cuba could be an exception. We have intellectual freedom. Now it is important to develop political freedom as well. We are fighting for the success of the Revolution—for its freedom and its strength.

One should not overemphasize the opposition between the Soviet Union and Cuba. Cubans still remember that it was the Soviet

Union that came to Cuba's aid—with oil and other supplies, weapons, technical assistance, and purchases of sugar—when the United States first tried to strangle the Cuban Revolution through imposition of an economic blockade and by military subversion and intervention. But Cuba is fighting to maintain her cultural and political independence and to develop her own life styles. Equally important, she has not rejected communism but is trying to humanize it (in accord with its underlying *raison d'être*) and to make it more of a living reality, here and now, than it is in the Soviet Union.

Both countries speak of a necessary stage of transition from capitalism to communism by way of socialism. But the Soviet Union seems to be stalled in the "transitional period," with rigid control of art, literature and politics, on the one hand, and, on the other, greater concessions to man's heritage of selfishness—through "material incentives" that lead to substantial discrepancies in income and privileges.

In the Soviet Union it has been felt necessary to give "the managers and workers of an enterprise a 'material interest' in its profits by allowing them to participate in the profits through bonuses." (Edward Boorstein, summarizing the "reforms" instituted in accord with the proposals of the late Professor Y. C. Liberman.*) Professor Liberman argued that "What is profitable for society as a whole will also be so for each production collective, and on the other hand, what is uneconomic from the point of view of public interest will also be so in greater degree for all enterprises. In principle there should be no place in socialism for contradictions between the interests of society and those of any enterprise." (Similar statements may be found in the writings of other revisionist Marxist economists, e.g., Professor Ota Sik, of Czechoslovakia, explaining the "new system" in that country.)

Such arguments recall Adam Smith's contention—on which the U.S. economy was founded—that if everyone works for his own material advantage, the invisible hand of God will straighten everything out in the best interests of society as a whole. In the Soviet Union and Czechoslovakia, the selfish collective enterprise is substituted for the self-seeking individual and it is the all-too-visible hand

---

* *The quotations are from Boorstein's* The Economic Transformation of Cuba, *Monthly Review Press, 1968.*

of the Party and state bureaucracy that is supposed to straighten out the contradictions for the good of the whole. Smith developed his theory in *The Wealth of Nations,* which was published in the same year as our Declaration of Independence and helped undercut its idealism. In the fifties General Motors' Charles E. Wilson, an American Liberman, proclaimed that "What's good for General Motors is good for the country."

In Cuba there is far more emphasis on the reality of new, socialist man. The Cubans believe it is possible to create a general "communist consciousness" even during the transitional period, and have set up experimental outposts of pure communism—on the Isle of Youth (formerly the Isle of Pines) and at Pinares de Marari.

Material incentives have not been entirely eliminated in Cuba, but they are very much downgraded. They are applied mainly to holdover members of the old bourgeoisie, who are allowed to live not in the manner to which they were accustomed but at a level of wealth and material privilege higher than that of those technical and professional people who have been brought up in the ideals of service and egalitarianism. Members of the Cuban Communist Party and new governmental cadres do extra work—often including voluntary physical labor—and receive incomes either equal to ordinary workmen's wages or far closer to them than those of holdover professionals.

When I was in Cuba in 1964, there was a great debate going on over the relative merits of material and "moral" incentives, and it was difficult to predict which would win out. Basically this debate has been resolved in favor of the superiority of moral incentives and the importance of minimizing and gradually eliminating economic differentials. But the aspirations of Cuban revolutionists have not stopped at this level. In January 1968 I talked with a number of Cubans who stressed that not all so-called moral incentives are socially desirable either. One Cuban said: "The traditional socialist emphasis on vanguard workers and party membership can work out to be almost as destructive as the material incentives of capitalism and revisionist communism. It can produce a divisive emphasis on status and encourage social climbing." Another said, "We have gone beyond the debate between monetary rewards and moral recognition and are trying to build a society in which the operational moral incentives are the socially acceptable incentives of communism rather than dressed-up versions of the selfish incentives of capitalism. People are encouraged to work for self-fulfillment through the joy of the work and for social fulfillment through the satisfaction of being useful."

The remarkable thing about this "utopianism" is that it was not developed in the privileged sanctuary of a cloister or a college bull session but comes out of eight years of struggle with refractory human nature, "underdevelopment," shortages, miscalculations and confusion—not to mention the powerful pressures of the United States and the Soviet Union.

Fidel explained the philosophy behind these policies to K. S. Karol of *Le Nouvel Observateur* (Paris):

> I am against material incentives because I consider them incompatible with socialism. In the society which we are in the process of creating, a man's interest in his work should not depend on his being offered a greater or lesser amount of remuneration. You cannot imagine the barbarous inequalities in our society before 1959. We have already eliminated many special privileges and inequalities and our aim is to eliminate them all. But repressive measures don't serve any useful purpose. We need other methods whch we are in the act of developing. . . .
>
> The real problem is not to equalize salaries to place the emphasis on the redistribution of income. If one limits one-self to that, one has not broken yet with the conception of a society based on money. Money remains at the center of the social policies of China, which favor egalitarianism, as it does in the Soviet Union, which encourages differentiations in income. What we want is to do away with the mythology of money, not to rehabilitate it. We propose to abolish money altogether.

It is typical of the restless idealism of the Cuban revolutionaries that in a time when there are still serious material shortages and when productivity is not always as high as it should be, they are moving rapidly in the direction of supplying the basic necessities of life free. Medical care and education are traditionally provided free of charge in most socialist societies. Cuba also provides water, electricity, local telephone service, baseball games and funerals gratis. Medical care includes doctors, prescriptions and hospitals. Free education covers not only elementary and secondary schools but also neighborhood schools for adults, technical and professional schools, academies of the arts and universities. "Scholarship students," the bulk of those receiving advanced education, are given food and clothing plus spending allowances.

Housing is well on the way to being free; it is now free for many and at a minimum for everyone else. Persons displaced by slum-clearance housing are given new houses rent-free—in fact with titles of ownership. Others in the traditionally poorer classes live rent-free, while most other people pay approximately ten percent of their wages. This represents a steady progression from the first days of the Revolution, in 1959, when all rents were cut across the board—fifty percent for those paying less than 100 pesos (approximately 100 dollars) a month, and thirty to forty percent for those (presumably better off) who had been paying more.

Next on the list of free items, according to Fidel, are the remaining rents (the aim is to do away with all rents by 1970) and public transportation. "And we will continue until the day, not too far off, when all food and clothing will be free." Already bus fares in Havana have been reduced from ten cents to five.

I attended one of the free baseball games in Havana. Anyone who thinks that the drama of baseball, the quality of the play or the intense enjoyment of the crowd is dependent upon commercial exploitation (paid admissions, astronomical salaries for the superstars and a cut of the World Series gate for the top teams) should see a baseball game in Cuba, where professional athletics have been abolished and baseball is a sport rather than a big business.

The big league season begins in Cuba with several months of competition in each of the six provinces. During this period the players work half a day at their regular jobs and spend half a day practicing or playing. Beginning in November and lasting through March or April each province is represented in the national tournament by its winning team plus a second team of all-stars chosen from the losing teams. During this period, the players are on leave from their regular jobs. At both stages of the playing season, the players are paid at the regular rate for their normal jobs. It goes without saying that one of the freedoms baseball players have lost under communism is the freedom to prostitute themselves and confuse their young admirers by selling testimonials for cigarettes and other commercial products.

A similar system of remuneration exists for people whose "Communist consciousness" leads them to volunteer to leave their regular jobs during the cane-cutting season to do the hard but urgent work of cutting cane. They receive neither the lower pay that often accompanies the performance of back-breaking, "socially inferior" labor in the United States nor the higher pay which is often held out under capitalism as an inducement to lure people into areas where there is a shortage of skilled labor. Instead they are paid at their regular rates of pay for their nonseasonal jobs, to which they return at the end of the cane-cutting season. Before the Revolution most cane cutters were idle during the eight or nine months of the year between harvests, forming a reservoir of cheap labor for United Fruit and other sugar companies. During the idle season, the companies had no obligation to them. Profits from the sale of sugar supported the luxury of the upper classes in Havana or were drained out of the country to provide dividends for foreign investors. Now the earnings are used to finance free housing and other facilities, or for investment in native Cuban industry through the importing of machinery and equipment.

Not all Cubans have responded positively to the new society. This is hardly surprising. In the history of man's struggle to overcome institutions and customs that grant special privilege and power to some while condemning others to subservience and poverty, old ideas and attitudes have always died slowly. It takes time to outgrow the rationalizations and moral justifications associated with dying institutions, whether they be the divine right of kings, feudalism, chattel slavery, limited suffrage, or an economy based on private profit and personal aggrandizement. At the time of the American Revolution, thousands of Tories fled to Canada, while others aided the British.

Not all Cubans like living under an egalitarian system, especially those who feel that their skill, education or just plain native abilities or hard work entitle them to live with higher incomes than their fellows. Others were discouraged by the red tape and bureaucratic confusion which at one time threatened to engulf and dehumanize the Revolution. Bureaucracy remains a problem, although an antibureaucracy campaign has begun to simplify procedures and reverse the proliferation of clerks and forms. It is claimed that today there are 80,000 fewer people working in bureaucratic positions than there were two years ago. Rationing and shortages have become a persistent problem for those who had been accustomed to finding what they wanted in the stores whenever they wanted it. Now many luxury items are no longer imported and there are persistent (though diminishing) shortages of many staple items as well, since they have to be shared among the entire population—now that peasants and the traditionally unemployed or underpaid are able to buy meat, milk and shoes for the first time in their lives.

Even without a revolution, there is always a substantial migration from the underdeveloped nations to the more affluent ones, as is indicated by the number of Puerto Ricans living in the United States, despite U.S. claims that Puerto Rico is a showcase of the benefits of belonging to the "Free World." The lures of American prosperity and a philosophy of economic individualism largely account for the much-discussed "brain drain" toward this country. (The "brain drain" is really a subtle form of imperialism by which the United States sucks up the talents of scientists, physicians and other professionals trained at the expense of their native, "less advanced" countries—i.e., the rest of the world—and uses them to increase its lead while decreasing the other countries' abilities to catch up.)

The uniqueness of Communist Cuba lies not in the fact that some of its citizens want to emigrate, but that the regime permits them to do so. Unlike East Germany, which built the Berlin Wall to keep its discontented elements from emigrating to the West, Cuba permits 1,000 Cubans a week to leave for Florida and the "Free World." Many Americans consider this exodus to be proof of the failure of Communist Cuba to develop a viable economy and satisfying life. But it was evident, in January, that there are more goods on the market now than there were when I was last there, in 1964. Transportation is much improved, and everything seems to be better organized and more smoothly functioning.

Movies, concerts, dance groups, art galleries, theatres, cafés, pizza houses, night clubs, ice-cream parlors, vacation resorts, and sports are all flourishing. According to a young Cuban editor, more books were published in the single year of 1967 than there were during the entire quarter century preceding. During the eight years when the gap between Latin American poverty and North American affluence has steadily widened, and the Alliance for Progress has proven a dismal failure, Cuba has made significant advances in its overall standard of living and the quality of its daily life, despite the economic pressures of the U.S. boycott and the problems involved in a total reorganization of its economy.

Life is not at all drab; in fact there is a tremendous sense of excitement and *joie de vivre,* akin to the euphoria of 1959 and 1960, but based now less on the joys of having overthrown the oppressor and more on the daily satisfactions of the new society. Cubans speak freely of the errors and mistakes they have made, of their failure to accomplish some of the statistical advances predicted in their early plans. One gets the impression that they are so convinced of the obvious benefits of the new life that they do not need to be defensive or to cite endless statistics to prove their point.

In a conversation I had with Haydee Santamaria, veteran of the Moncada Assault and the guerrilla war, and currently director of the Casa de las Americas, she stressed that Cuba is concerned not only with the elimination of poverty, disease, and illiteracy, but with the development of opportunities for creative leisure:

> We hope one day to have the technical advantages of the developed countries, but we must find forms so that the human being is not mechanized and corrupted. If a man pushes a button two hours, he needs four hours to go to museums, concerts and parks, to take part in sports and to make love—to make love as a creative human being, not a machine. We are very much preoccupied with such problems. If a man performs eight hours of mechanical labor, he will be brutalized, made subhuman. With mechanization, we must have leisure—to paint, think, create.

I met a variety of impressive persons in Cuba, ranging from Fidel to a gnarled tobacco worker who did not know how to read or write before the Revolution but now not only is educated but has advanced to become administrator of his factory, after having been selected by his fellow workers to attend a training school for administrators. None impressed me more than the 18-to-25-year-olds who have grown up under the Revolution and are its finest products. Twenty-five hundred of Cuba's seven thousand prerevolutionary physicians left Cuba after the Revolution but a new generation of doctors has been trained, and they have no interest in leaving. They have responded to the challenge of the Revolution by developing a whole new sense of priorities and attitudes in which the welfare of one is indistinguishable from the welfare of all. Their own sense of worth and independence is enhanced by these attitudes.

One day, a senior medical student took me and a half dozen

others to visit a factory. After we had visited the various departments and talked with the workers, we sipped coffee in an office and talked with the administrator, the head of the union and the local secretary of the Communist Party. The party head began to give us a lecture on the merits of communism, the only time I remember having the impression that I was being subjected to a canned indoctrination lecture. After about two minutes, the young medical student interrupted, very politely but just as firmly: "I really don't think they're very interested in that," she said. "It would be much more valuable if you would tell them about the specific conditions of this factory."

This little incident was typical of the unself-conscious way in which the new generation of Cubans insists on translating all noble phrases and revolutionary aspirations into the concrete realities of everyday life—and on relating even the simplest daily events to the purposes for which the Revolution exists.

Report from
Revolutionary China

1967   After spending eleven days in China in late October and mid-November, on my way to and from North Vietnam, I feel only expert enough to disagree with most of the China experts, of both the left and the right, as to what is going on there.

In part I disagree because real life always defies the best efforts of those who study it from afar—no matter how fair and objective they may try to be. In part I disagree because most of our information comes from partisan sources in Hong Kong, Tokyo and Moscow and is just plain false—whether it happens to appear in the *New York Times* or in some less prestigious journal of public information. I might add that as near as I could tell most of the public information in Peking about Moscow is also false.

I don't know the truth about China. All I know is some truths which I can report with the authority of personal observation. How these particular truths fit into a general framework or how one weighs them and other evidence in developing a theory of what is happening and what is apt to emerge—all this is more speculative. Although I do not promise to avoid such speculation altogether, my main interest is to present some firsthand observations of facts that are generally overlooked in the United States today but which in one way or another form part of the total picture. They should be made part of any educated guesswork as to what is going on in China.

Most discussions overlook the extent to which the Red Guards are expressing an indigenous youth revolt against the educational and cultural institutions of their society. Intent on interpreting the Cultural Revolution as a gimmick in a grim Communist struggle for personal power or for factional political control of Chinese society, most commentators ignore the personal stake of the Red Guards in what they are doing. To understand their motivations and dynamics, one would do well to start with the similarity of the Red Guards to the American students who revolted against the "multiversity" at Berkeley or dropped out of college to take part in the civil rights movement or community organizing. Given the difference in the two economies and cultures, the analogy is far from exact. On the other hand, it provides a more useful initial frame of reference than to imagine that the Red Guards are narrow political demagogues or simply youthful shock troops at the service of adult politicians.

One of the things that disturbed me the most in China was the apparent idolization of Mao, but it is worth quoting what a student from Tientsin said to me when I complained of it and said that it went ill with the student attitudes which he had been describing to me. His reply was:

> I don't expect you, an American, to understand that for us Mao is the symbol of the masses in revolt against authoritarianism. For us, to study Chairman Mao's words means that we can cite them and our interpretation of them against any authorities above us. Chairman Mao wants to encourage young people to rebel so that no authoritarianism can suppress the individual and the spirit of rebellion.

I don't pretend to know what is going on in Mao's mind, with relation to the Red Guards or anything else. Nor am I privy to the internal conflicts within the Chinese Communist Party. But from talking to Red Guards and seeing them in action, I surmise that whatever Mao may have in mind, it is almost as inaccurate to think that Mao created or controls them as it was a few years ago to think that the civil rights agitators who invaded Mississippi and the South had been sent there by the American Communist Party and were acting in its behalf.

I found Red Guards with whom I could talk at length not only in the cities of Peking, Wuhan, and Nanning, but also among the stewardesses and fellow passengers on the planes that carried me twice from one end of China to the other. I also spent five hours in intense discussion with an extremely intelligent and open graduate student, who was en route from Peking to London, where he was going to continue his studies in English literature. Always the subjects most on their minds were the nature of their schooling and the role of intellectuals and trained technicians in society. Everyone complained that the established educational system placed too great an emphasis on abstract intellectualism and verbal achievement. They always presented the Cultural Revolution as concerned primarily with the gap between academic and "real" life, the failure of communism to extend its revolution into the areas of daily life that affected them most as students and prospective intellectuals. Most of them saw an interrelationship between the shortcomings of existing Communist pedagogy and the privileged economic status of brain workers in both China and the Soviet Union. In this way they reminded me of S.D.S. members who complain about the 2-S draft deferment for students—though (with the encouragement of Mao) up to the present time a lot more Chinese students than S.D.S. members have been ready to relinquish their privileges.

In Peking one of the Red Guards said to me:

> We hope that a new system of education will come from this [the Cultural Revolution], though we don't know just what it will be. Some kind of system which places a new emphasis on firsthand knowledge. After all, the Russians copied their educational system from the West and China copied ours from the Soviet Union. The fact is that the true spirit of communism has never been carried out in education, at least not on a large scale. Our schooling today is still based on secondhand knowledge. We want to find out what the function and limitations of the classroom are, the uses of travel, of seeing for oneself, of engaging in productive labor on the farms and in the factories. Then there is another question—what kind of education is good for all people, not just for those with a particular kind of talent who go on and on under the present system and become part of a privileged caste?

A student movement with such far-reaching concerns is bound

to be involved in a definite interaction with adult political figures even though its dominant mood and goals may stem from its own experiences. For one thing, many of the students refer to Mao's Yenan experiences, when some of the leaders of the present Communist Party dug out their own caves for living quarters, grew their own food, and held classes on the principles and strategy of revolutionary communism. There is a tendency to look to Yenan as an example of successful revolutionary education which provides cues for the present intended revisions. When I was in Peking there was a public exhibition on *kangta,* the form of education organized by Lin Piao at Yenan. I did not get to the exhibit but I was told it was thronged with Red Guards who were eagerly studying the displays and taking notes, in the manner that I saw them taking notes all over Peking and Nanning whenever new *tatzupao* (wall posters) were put up.

Part at least of Lin Piao's appeal to the youth is apparently based on the fact that he introduced into the army the sweeping egalitarian reforms and the kind of combined theoretical and practical education that the students want to see worked out, in somewhat different form, in the educational system. Americans have interpreted Lin Piao's recent prominence as evidence of the dangerous ascendancy of the professional military, but in China one hears the opposite. It is said that he has liberated the army from the traditional military clique and the military mentality and transformed it into a genuine "people's instrument," in line with China's belief not only in "people's wars" (of defense and self-liberation, I might add) but also in the necessity for gradually remodeling all institutions in accord with Communist ideology. Lin Piao's reform of the army is hailed as a prescursor of the present Cultural Revolution.

Recently I read an article in the American magazine *Dissent,* with the thesis that "Mao's revolution has nothing to do with the liberation of the people or, despite its continued use of Marxist language, with the class struggle and the emancipation of the proletariat." Writing in the name of democratic socialism, the author complains that "the army had to be transformed from top to bottom; its officers had to be placed under the supervision of political commissars; *privates were given political rights they have in no other army* [emphasis added]; insignia were abolished. In short, the army was remade into a militia. . . . China now has an army which is good for home use and perhaps for a quickie raid into India, but which is hardly equipped and organized for a conflict with one of the major powers . . . the professional officers were overruled on all three counts: organization, defense, and foreign policy." (Henry Pachter, "Mao vs. Marx in China," *Dissent*, Jan.-Feb. 1967.)

Although Pachter's description may be influenced by his displeasure with these innovations, his summary of the reorganization of the army was remarkably close to that which the students described to me with pleasure. Where Pachter concludes that the Chinese army "is hardly equipped and organized for a conflict with one of the major powers," the students had said, with obvious pride, that the Chinese army is not organized for foreign wars, not even for a foreign war of liberation—which, according to Lin Piao must be the responsibility of the native population—but only for a war of self-defense.

The students' actions have had a cumulative impact on all aspects of life in China. During my first week in Peking, there were an estimated million and a half Red Guards roaming the city. The majority of them had come to Peking from schools and universities all over China. Most of the ones I talked with had stories to tell about the ups and downs of student struggle and bureaucratic suppression by the university authorities, during 1964 and 1965, and especially in the spring of 1966. Then in June, after a student strike at Peita (Peking University) and administrative expulsion of some of the leaders, Mao intervened in behalf of the students. Public hearings were held, the students were reinstated, and the university was at least partially reorganized.

The student rebels at Peita had called themselves Red Guards and Mao received them at a public ceremony in Tien An Men Square, at which their girl leader pinned a red band, the group's symbol, on Mao's arm. From then on Red Guards and student agitation sprang up all over China, as faltering organizations took encouragement from this high-level intervention and blessing. Many of these organizations dropped their old names and began to call themselves Red Guards, after the Peking group.

A "victory" for the students at Peita did not herald automatic victories for the other student groups in their particular battles, but it increased the ferment. In July a large group of students at Tientsin University decided to walk to Peking to visit the university where students had successfully challenged the administration and, if possible, to present their own grievances directly to Mao. I was told that the Tientsin officials called out the police to stop them and that many of the Peking Communist Party officials sided with the Tientsin authorities. Mao, however, intervened again by sending a special train to meet them. Then, as one of the Tientsin students explained to me:

> We took over the train. We had it stop at all the stations along the way. We held meetings and exchanged ideas with the young people. Many of them decided to go to Peking too. After Chairman Mao's initial decision to send the train, everything happened spontaneously, without authorization from anyone, parents, school or government.

Student enthusiasm and ferment spread. So did opposition. I don't want to give the impression that I think I know all the steps and stages of the immensely complicated development that followed or the forms in which the conflict expressed itself in different parts of that vast land. I can only report a few things that I saw and interpretations that were made to me by Red Guards themselves or by other persons I talked with in China (not only Chinese, by the way, but also a Mongolian, an Indonesian, a French woman, several Russians, Japanese, Vietnamese, and East Europeans, as well as half a dozen Americans, most of whom have lived in China since World War II or before the triumph of Chinese communism in 1949).

By the time I first arrived in Peking (October 20), the universities and middle schools (high schools) had been closed for several months, so that students and faculty could engage in a searching reexamination of the educational process. Part of this reexamination was taking place through travel and the exchange of ideas with people from other sections of the country, part of it through meetings and manifestoes, principally the *tatzupao,* or wall posters. Every college student was guaranteed free public transportation on the trains and buses. Middle school students were encouraged to elect one representative for every twenty students, and this delegate was also provided free transportation. Food and accommodations were provided for those who came to Peking. (They may have been provided in other cities as well, but I realize now that I did not check this out, and clearly the reception varied from city to city according to the attitudes of those in power.)

Students spoke to me about stopping in communes along the way, helping in the work, being fed and sheltered, and engaging in an exciting process of exchanging ideas. I was told of several instances in which students had made arrangements for moving their schools to one of the communes they visited, with an idea of effecting a more meaningful combination of academic and productive work. I was not able to determine the likelihood that this would come about or if so, what this would mean in terms of "bureaucratic relationships"—with the academic administration or various political authorities. What was clear from the conversations was that some of the Red Guards and at least a few faculty were going through explorations similar to those that have led to experimental free universities and S.D.S. community organizing projects in the States.

One night when I was walking through Peking with a friend who was translating some of the wall posters for me, he said, "Here is one attacking the mayor of Peking." "Oh yes," I replied, "Peng Chen." "No," he responded, "the new one." According to most Western observers, Mao had used the Red Guards to get rid of Peng Chen, one of his political opponents—and perhaps he had. But the students had other things in mind. The *tatzupao* was criticizing the new mayor for having sent out "work teams" from Party headquarters to assist in local reorganizations. It complained that the outsiders 1) didn't really understand local situations, 2) brought the apparent authority and prestige of the Party into the local conflict, and 3) put local people in the position of seeming to attack the Party when they protested against its method of intervention. During the time I was in Peking, many of the manifestoes were making this same point, and the Party was definitely put on notice that the Red Guards were revolting in order to gain some control over their own lives and institutions rather than to exchange one set of bureaucratic administrators for another. They wanted the Party to intervene, if necessary, in order to open up or guarantee what we Westerners would call freedom of speech and the rights of dissenters but they wanted the speaking and reorganization to be done by local people..

As we discussed the opposition to the "work teams," which really were investigators from Regional or Central Party headquarters, my translator offered his version of what was taking place:

> The Central Party will remove or defend no one unless or until there has been full local debate. This must take place over an extended period of time so that the truth can grad-

ually emerge. The Central Party only insists on the right of Red Guards to make the charges and the right of the accused to defend themselves. Also it insists that there must be a "way out" for those found guilty. This is Mao's interpretation of Marx.

One of the things missed in the West is the fact that the wall posters are used as a means of public argumentation and debate and therefore express a wide range of opinions. At all hours of the day and night one could see students solemnly discussing the contents of posters, taking notes and, in many cases, preparing answers. Barbara Deming, who passed through China in late December 1966 and January 1967, told me that the same "fascinating process" was going on when she was there. She said that she just did not know how to relate what she had seen to the accounts of violence and intimidation and other "terrible things" that she read in the Western press as soon as she got back.

When I was in Peking, if a poster appeared attacking a public figure, soon there would appear another poster defending him. Western analysts have usually assumed that to be able to quote a poster which attacks a man by name is to prove that he has fallen from favor and been "purged." Or that to quote a poster which takes a certain ideological approach is to reveal what the "official line" is. Occasionally a contrary poster is quoted a few days later as an indication that the balance of power has shifted and a new group has got the upper hand (usually, it is assumed, as a result of violent combat or the cracking of skulls). Some of this confusion is undoubtedly innocent, and in particular I can understand how readers of the newspapers would fall into these traps, especially after years of being told that Chinese Communism is monolithic and totalitarian. On the other hand, those knowledgeable enough to supply the quotations in the first place should be in a position to provide more accurate information about the context in which they appear. We should never forget that most of the "facts" that we read about China in the American press have been supplied by Chiang Kai-shek Nationalists or American government agencies, such as the C.I.A. and the U.S.I.S. (United States Information Service). Both the Nationalists and the American agencies own or control newspapers, "research institutes" and other seemingly impartial sources of information in Hong Kong and other Asian cities.

Whatever else may be unclear about what is happening in China, there is no doubt in my mind as to the eagerness with which students have been exploring new ideas and formulating new programs. Most of the slogans that were painted in huge red letters on the upper walls of public buildings seemed to me as routine and devoid of content or imagination as most official exhortations to virtue in any culture: "Long Live the Glorious Cultural Revolution!" "Long Live the Proletarian Cultural Revolution!" "Down with Soviet Revisionism!" "Mao is our Helmsman!" etc. On the other hand, one could take them as endorsements of the whole process of exploration and revitalization that was reflected in the thousands of manifestoes that lined the walls at eye level. In any event, there was no doubt about the seriousness with which individual students and small groups of students went about composing their own posters to express their own thoughts and sentiments. One could see them kneeling on the sidewalks after midnight putting their thoughts on paper, discussing a particular turn of phrase, and then pasting their own views as close as possible to a poster with which they disagreed. The ground rules apparently didn't permit tearing down a poster you disagreed with or covering it over with your own.

All of this democracy of debate conflicts, of course, with the reports and photographs (undoubtedly genuine) of people being led through the streets in disgrace with dunce caps on their heads. How much of this has taken place I could not tell. I can only report what I saw and was told. I saw no such incidents myself but no one denied that some acts of violence had taken place. On the other hand, I talked with no one who had seen such things himself or justified them. Everyone seemed vague about where and when they had happened and no one thought they had been extensive or typical. One professor told me:

> Don't forget that this is a real revolution, not playacting. A revolution is very serious and very deep and is bound to arouse opposition from people whose special privileges are being taken away. At the beginning the Red Guards had no experience in how to do it. This is a revolution of the people and the leaders can't do it for them. Naturally some of the Red Guards got out of hand in the beginning but the leaders came out strongly against violence and most of that seems to be over now.
>
> In my university I sometimes felt bad. It was unpleas-

ant to see people being criticized so strongly by their students. Yet the vice-chairman really was arrogant and had assumed too much power. He was very lordly to his students and was acting as a member of a privileged class. It was better to stop it then, before it did more and more harm. He has lost his power but he will have a chance to remedy his ways.

A student said to me:

So far as I know no one has been put in prison or executed. That never has been our way of doing things. You must remember that for us a purge means that there is open criticism and discussion and if a person is found to be wrong he loses his position in the government, the university or wherever it is. No harm comes to him.

Destroying the "four olds" means destroying only the bad in the old, not all old things. There has been practically no old Chinese art destroyed, such as that Buddha there [referring to a photo in *Life* magazine that I had shown him]. Naturally some young people didn't understand at first and in some places things like that did take place, but Chairman Mao and Lin Piao and Chou En-lai—all the adult leaders— came out against such things.

Another person to whom I showed the *Life* account of violence rampant in the streets was an American who has been in China since 1946. He rubbed his head in disbelief.

"Some of those things must have happened," he said. "We know that things got a little out of hand in some places, but that gives a very false picture of what is going on. You've been here [Peking] for nearly a week. Have you seen anything like that?"

When I pressed him and said that many intelligent radicals in the United States thought of the Red Guards as bands of roving vigilantes he said:

You've seen them in the streets. You know how gentle they are. When did you see a group of vigilantes that was so lovable that the biggest problem is that you have to remember that you're not supposed to kiss them?

Of course the Red Guards are very serious about what they are doing. They get a big kick out of walking from town to town and when they get to Peking they gawk and stare like any farm boy his first time in the big city. The romance and the adventure is a very important part of their excitement. But at the same time, they are also walking because they want to go through a Long March that links them with their elders and toughens them up for the expected American invasion. Don't forget that they stop and harvest crops and talk about these things with peasants. The government provided free transportation for them but many of them prefer to walk in the manner of the Long March.

In Nanning, I talked at length on two different days with Huang Ji Zhu, a Red Guard in his early twenties who worked for the China International Travel Service and spoke excellent English. He translated the Nanning newspaper for me and various *tatzupao*. He said that he had seen no violence in his city and hadn't heard of any, but he made no claims that there couldn't have been some local violence that he didn't know about. Nor did he see any reason to turn against the Cultural Revolution if some of its enthusiasts had mistakenly attacked its enemies physically:

> People are very serious about the struggle to get rid of bourgeois institutions and ways of thinking. The Cultural Revolution is badly needed. I don't think there is much opposition to Mao but old ideas about special privileges die slowly. Also, we know about the American plans to attack us and we are getting ready. But the main thing is to get rid of our own revisionists and bureaucracies with capitalist ideas. Naturally some of the people who were used to living better than other people have wormed their way into the Party, in some places. We have to take their power away but it doesn't do any good to beat them or humiliate them by parading them through the streets. Our chairman, Chairman Mao, teaches us that you have to give them a way back. You have to change their ideas.

Huang insisted on translating for me sections of a speech by Lin Piao, which Lin had made at a rally of Red Guards in Peking on August 31. I already had an English version that I had picked up in Peking and I quote the key passage from it:

> We must carry out the struggle by reasoning and not by coercion or force. Don't hit people. This applies also to the struggle against those persons in authority who are taking the capitalist road as well as to the struggle against landlords, rich peasants, counterrevolutionaries, bad elements and rightists. Coercion or force in the struggle against them can only touch their skins. Only by reasoning is it possible to touch their souls. Only by reasoning, by exposing them fully and criticizing them profoundly, is it possible to expose their counterrevolutionary features thoroughly.

Similar sentiments have been expressed over and over again by Mao and Chou En-lai.

By stressing the concern of the Red Guards over the form, content and context of their education, I do not mean to minimize their concern with substantive political questions of economics and foreign policy. Most American student rebels tend to see the American educational system as both reflection and perpetuator of the larger dehumanized and undemocratic society. Such "Red Guard type" activities as sit-ins during draft-deferment exams or at university centers for chemical and biological research programs combine indignation at the passive role assigned students in university decison-making with revulsion from American foreign policy and war atrocities. Similarly the Chinese Red Guards move naturally from discussing the stupidity of exams and grading to the shallowness of the "bourgeois literature" they have been studying—with its "exaltation of capitalist virtues"—the "errors" of "Soviet Revisionism," and the necessity of combating those who are anxious to restore capitalism to China. As with a lot of the Chinese polemics, the language about "capitalism" is apt to be misleading for Americans. Talk about the persistence of capitalist attitudes and the dangers of a capitalist restoration has gladdened the hearts of U.S. Senators, editorial writers for the *New York Daily News,* and countless other Americans who believe that freedom and democracy cannot exist unless the ownership and control of the economy is in the hands of private individuals and corporations operating on the basis of the profit motive. Visions have been created of a China ready to welcome back Chiang Kai-shek and the big industrialists.

When I was in China, the people I spoke with talked as if something very difficult were involved—not the restoration of private corporations and the return to a system of vast private and corporate holdings in agriculture and industry, but rather the perpetuation and growth of excessive income differentials. The Chinese were having basically the same debate that the Cubans had been having when I visited Cuba in the spring of 1964, though the slogans and the methods of carrying it on were different. In Cuba they were arguing about the relative importance of "material" and "moral" incentives. Apart from questions of foreign policy, the debate in both countries and throughout the Communist world is essentially over how far and how fast to travel in the transition from socialism ("To each according to his work"—and those who won't work won't eat) to communism ("From each according to his abilities and to each according to his needs").

A complicating factor is the emergence of new economic conditions in the Soviet Union and Eastern Europe. So long as there was a shortage of consumer goods, everything that was produced was sold, but when the socialist countries achieved a substantial expansion of production, the buying public began to be more selective. If a factory produced items that were unattractive or of poor quality, no one bought them. So the various countries began to experiment with new methods of planning and marketing that would make output and quality more responsive to consumer demand. Poles, Romanians, Czechs, and Russians with whom I talked described the shift in economics as experimentation with decentralized contracts between producing organizations and marketing organizations. On the other hand if one listens to the American or Chinese critics, the more affluent socialist countries are reintroducing the capitalist free market and the profit motive and beginning a shift back toward capitalism.

In Cuba and China, where production is at a lower level than in the Soviet Union, the problems are different and revolve around the importance of increasing production while maintaining (or achieving) equitable distribution.

In Cuba, which had seen so many of its engineers, doctors and other trained professionals lured away by the capitalist "freedom" of the United States, there was a tendency in 1964 to increase slightly the emoluments and other privileges of the professionals who were holdovers from the old society, while at the same time appealing to the newly trained professionals to put their talents and training at the service of their fellows without demanding exorbitant rewards.

Different institutional opportunities were available to the old professionals than to the new, but both groups were exhorted and encouraged to follow the more egalitarian example of the Communist leaders. There was general agreement that the Communists had not succumbed to corruption and luxury but lived simply and inexpensively, close to the rural and urban poor. In 1964, I noticed that various governmental agencies had begun to operate a number of more expensive facilities (restaurants, hotels, night clubs) on the dual theory that they kept the bourgeoisie happier and served as a means of getting back from them some of the extra money they were allowed to earn.*

In China, Red Guards and Maoists said very little about the people who coveted special rewards and privileges and fled to Taiwan or Hong Kong (this was not a current issue) but rather complained about those who had looked after their selfish interests by entrenching themselves in certain sections of the Party and in other bureaucratic posts, where they were slowing down and even trying to reverse the progress toward communism. The educational system was faulted for perpetuating class divisions by preserving a curriculum and system of examinations that had been inherited from a class society and had never been thoroughly revolutionized. Not only were there natural privileges that inhered to the sons of intellectuals and the middle class under the present system, but it was charged that in certain universities special discrimination had been practiced against the sons of peasants and workers because of the snobbishness and "revisionist attitudes" of the professors and administrators. Certain magazines and other cultural institutions such as theatre groups and (until recently) the opera were charged with promoting bourgeois virtues such as individualism and philanthropy, rather than encouraging the ideologic and spiritual attitudes of communism.

I don't want to be misleading. The Chinese were very definite in stating that capitalism had been restored in the Soviet Union or

---

* *The theory was impeccable, from the point of view of the short-run defense of the revolution, but the question still to be answered is whether such "necessary" adjustments set up a dynamics of elitism. Of such an order are the problems involved in outgrowing the selfishness of capitalism. That is why on the one hand I try to be generous toward Stalinists but on the other hand scrupulously outspoken against Stalinism as it manifested itself in the Old Left and as it begins to settle in on the New Left. (1970.)*

(depending on whom I was talking to) that it was in the process of being restored. They also said that there were Revisionists in China, some of them within the Communist Party, who wanted to restore capitalism to China. But when I said that I had spent three weeks in the Soviet Union and was convinced that the Russians had not gone capitalist and from what I could see did not intend to, they answered by referring to exaggerated Russian differentials in wages and income. They told me that the maximum income differentials in China were about five to one. In the early days of the Revolution the gap was approximately ten to one, but this had been gradually reduced by a process of freezing the top levels and gradually raising the lower ones. By contrast they argued that the differentials were far greater in the Soviet Union—for movie stars, administrators, managers, famous intellectuals, etc. They argued that in contrast to China, the Soviet Union was widening the gap. This is what they called the restoration of capitalism. The main political conflict in China, they argued, was between those who wanted to reduce the five-to-one differential and a small minority who wanted to increase it.

The turmoil of the Cultural Revolution is generally interpreted in the United States, on both the left and the right, as evidence of weakness and failure in China. After watching this revolution for eleven short days and talking at length with some of those taking part, I tend to think that it is a sign of strength and vitality. Of course there are aspects that I find distasteful, including the sloganeering and the ritualistic study and praise of the writings of Mao. Will the pressures to conformism sap the strongly libertarian attitudes which are so noticeable in the Red Guards and (contrary to the assumptions of most Westerners) in Chinese society generally? One would have to spend much longer in China than I did to appraise the dynamics of this turbulent continuing revolution. But it is clear to me that many of the participants are striving to achieve an unprecedented combination of Communist solidarity and individual freedom, which would avoid both the stultifying conformism of the ant heap (communism at its worst) and capitalism's individualistic rat race for special privilege at the expense of one's fellows.

I especially deplore the humiliation of revisionists and other "sinners" by placing dunce caps on their heads and parading them through the streets. Who can judge whether robbing a man of his dignity in this manner is not both as cruel to the victim and as spiritually corrupting to the practitioners as shooting a man or sentencing him to prison? I have already said that I spoke to no one in China who justified such incidents and that the top Maoist leadership has condemned them, but I have no way of knowing how widespread this and similar practices have become. The Western press delights in presenting them as typical of what is going on in China but we may find out later that they represent but a few instances in which the hooligan spirit has taken over.

My impression was that the loudspeakers and mass rallies, the shouting of slogans and the beating of cymbals and drums, the public readings of the words of Mao on airplanes and trains—most of which I found offensive—were not as coercive as they sound secondhand. There were times when I was reminded of the singing of "The Star Spangled Banner" at baseball games or the group recitals of the pledge of allegiance in our schools and at P.T.A. meetings. There were other times when I wondered whether a more apt comparison might not be with the singing of "We Shall Overcome" at civil-rights rallies in preparation for an encounter with repressive authorities.

It is ironic that Americans condemn the turbulence and excesses of the Cultural Revolution as if they reflected an innate Communist (and/or Chinese) predisposition to violence. Americans should at least take care to place these activities in the context of China's expectations of an American attack. In the United States, the nuclear bomb tests of the fifties, the consciousness of omnipresent fallout, the sense of impending doom in a nuclear holocaust contributed to the end of student apathy and the emergence of a new mood. Similarly, the American invasion of Vietnam, with its million child victims (dead or mutilated) and its message that the United States will go to any extreme to prevent Asian self-determination and dignity, is a major factor in producing the present mood in China. The recent massacre of nearly a million Indonesians in a Washington-aided pro-Western coup was hardly noticed and quickly forgotten by the American people. At the same time, it was hailed in Washington as a triumph of American foreign policy. Not surprisingly, it helped produce a different psychology in China—a psychology in which the Chinese appear to be finding a new unity of purpose.

Part Four

Violence, Nonviolence,
and the Movement

Why Were the
Rosenbergs Killed?

*". . . And I prophesy to you who are my murderers that
immediately after my death, punishment far heavier than you
have inflicted on me will surely await you. . . . You have
killed me because you wanted to escape the accuser and not
to give an account of your lives. . . . If you think that by killing men you can prevent one from censuring your evil lives
you are mistaken."*

Socrates

I

1953 The long, cruel drama came to an end a little over a
month ago. Julius and Ethel Rosenberg were finally murdered by the
American government.

If you look at it the way the government wants us to look at it,
they were murdered because they were atom spies. But it is doubtful
if more than a dozen persons had any way of knowing whether or not
the charge was true. No matter. It is clear that their supposed guilt

was not the real reason why the Justice Department, Judge Kaufman, the Supreme Court majority, and President Eisenhower combined to murder them. And the damning facts from which we desperately want to hide are no less damning whether the dead couple was innocent or guilty.

In either case, the Rosenbergs were victims of the lusts and hates and ambitions of little, fearful men. In either case they were apparently ennobled by their long ordeal to the point where honest men and women should speak of them with respect and admiration. In either case, you and I and the rest of the American people contributed to their murder by the apathetic manner in which we have tolerated inquisitions, purges, and legal blackmail. We were all too disoriented by the anti-Communist war cries, too fearful of being misunderstood by our neighbors, or too enmeshed in our own petty endeavors to be concerned when a man and his wife were held in the death house for twenty-six long months of a shameful legal farce and finally killed in cold blood.

I can hear people saying: "Why are you getting so excited? There were many more being killed in Korea every day."

True. But there are some symbolic issues in which the larger battles of human decency are fought. The fact that the American people were more concerned with Arthur Godfrey's operation than with the fate of the Rosenbergs is in itself a terrifying critique of our American culture. But it also means that it will be easier for there to be more executions—and more Koreas.

It is significant that the greatest concern for the Rosenbergs was in Europe. For perhaps the first time since 1945, reactionaries, middle-of-the-roaders, and leftists rose above their political antagonisms to unite in pleading for the pair. Twenty years ago these same Europeans did not recognize the signs which led to Belsen and Buchenwald. Today they are chilled and fearful as they see the United States moving smugly along the same tragic path.

"It was only two Communists," we say. But in France, the right-wing paper, *Figaro,* fights desperately to forestall the monumental blunder. *Figaro Litteraire* publishes the heart-moving letters of the condemned couple, letters which all the fabled printing presses of Free America failed to make available to those who live across the Atlantic from the Iron Curtain.

"I believe your conduct . . . has already caused . . . the Communist aggression in Korea" solemnly intones Judge Kaufman. The *New York Daily News* smirks that "the mousy Julius went first," while the anti-McCarthy *New York Post* writes with apparent approval of the wisps of blue smoke that rose from the heads of the two traitors.

But in Paris, Paul Rivet, the beloved and moderate curator of Le Musee de l'Homme, whom one would have thought too old and wise to be moved by the fate of "a couple of spies," writes unashamedly:

> . . . The atrocious drama is over. Two singed corpses, side-by-side are the terrible witnesses—and two innocent orphans over whom hangs a terrifying curse. I have forced myself to wait a few hours, not that I might become calm but that a slight appeasement might temper the violence of my revolt. And now I believe that I can speak with a little more objectivity of an execution the news of which created amongst the people of France a unity which has not been seen for years in such a noble cause, and which produced throughout the whole of Europe a spontaneous reaction which didn't seem possible amongst peoples who had been so desensitized by the horrors of war.

The bitterly anti-Communist Jean-Jacques Bernard reacts to "The Tragedy" by writing straight from his heart in a paper which is normally considered to be Communist-controlled.

> Some of those who are so vehemently aroused on behalf of the Rosenbergs know that although I am in agreement with them in this case, I cannot countenance their silence about tragedies in certain other countries. [Nevertheless] what overcomes and revolts us is the ease with which in some countries human life is sacrificed, life on which we in France still place such a high value. . . .
>
> The most friendly explanation would be that President Eisenhower, in sacrificing these two lives, actually thought that he was protecting peace for millions of others. He said, and we should believe him, that he is sincere. But it is this very sincerity, shared by the majority of Americans, which so appalls us. Is it a crisis of chauvinism, or a phenomenon of collective fear? Or is it simply a superiority complex so dangerous amongst childish peoples?

II

Earlier, I stated that the significance of the Rosenberg case is almost completely unaffected by the question of the Rosenbergs' possible guilt or innocence. Whether or not they actually conspired to steal atomic secrets is something that I and most other persons are not in a position to know. But for anyone who takes the trouble to read even a few of the statements of the sentencing judge and the prosecuting attorneys, on the one hand, and of the Rosenbergs themselves and the Rosenberg Defense Committee, on the other hand, certain facts are indisputably clear.

Unfortunately, most Americans went peacefully to sleep the night the Rosenbergs were executed, without any suspicion of these facts. The American press and radio now manufacture public opinion with the same mechanical efficiency and brazen dishonesty with which American advertisers persuade people that one brand of soap or aspirin is vastly superior to its identical counterpart which sells under a different label. But it is far less harmful to smoke Chesterfields because we are told that Bing Crosby finds them good for his throat, than it is to allow (or even applaud) the murder of Julius and Ethel Rosenberg because we are told that they were Communist spies who had been given "the fullest measure of justice," under the fairest court system in the world.

There are many ways in which the trial in Judge Kaufman's court was a heartrending travesty of justice. When I read the remarks of Judge Kaufman and of prosecuting attorney Irving Saypol I can only feel a deep sadness, akin to the sadness one feels at reading of gas chambers and slave labor camps. Saypol has been "rewarded" by appointment to the Supreme Court of New York State, and we would do well to remember that a high percentage of our "impartial" Judges (including the two Supreme Court Justices who wrote the majority report which finally sent the Rosenbergs to the electric chair) are men who have been similarly rewarded for "successful" prosecutions. It used to be said that in an American court a man was innocent until proven guilty. Now the court is presided over by men who have earned their post by proving everyone guilty, even if innocent.

A fellow judge, Chief Justice of the Supreme Court of Utah, James H. Wolf, condemns Judge Kaufman's handling of the trial on three clear-cut grounds:

This conviction was obtained during a period of mounting hysteria by evidence of witnesses whom the law considers
unreliable because of the very hope of reward or mitigation.
Besides the general hysteria generated by fear and hate of
communism *which was injected into that trial* [emphasis
added] it appears that there may have been the influence of
anti-Semitism in a reverse sort of way. The trial judge was
Jewish and . . . there may have been unconsciously an effort
to lean over backward against the Jews who were accused . . .

When one considers the charity and diplomacy with which a
judge of one state criticizes the judge of another (if he ever goes so
far as to criticize at all) the significance of Chief Justice White's remarks becomes apparent. Hell hath no fury like that of a member of
an insecure minority who turns on his fellows in order to advance his
own ambitions.

I cannot go into the long and disgraceful list of transgressions
by Judge Kaufman, but I will cite two examples of his "fairminded-
ness," one of which also reveals the level at which Prosecutor (now
Chief Justice) Saypol conducted the prosecution.

1. Only a handful of material exhibits were introduced to try
to prove espionage. All of these were either so vague and circumstantial as to prove nothing, or have since been proven to be more in
support of the Rosenbergs than of their accusers. Yet Kaufman admitted into evidence:

a) a collection can for the Spanish Refugee Appeal, *licensed
by the City of New York.* (O sweet charity! In the United States we
dare not solicit food and clothing for the victims of a fascist dictator
or else the Judge will accept this as evidence that we are guilty of a
crime "worse than murder.")

b) a nominating petition for former New York City Councilman Peter V. Cacchione, signed by Ethel Rosenberg. Yet this petition
was signed by 50,000 other New Yorkers, and *Cacchione was actually
elected by the citizens of New York to the City Council.* The date was
1941, and it was during the period of international power politics
when both Franklin Roosevelt and General Eisenhower were praising
Soviet Russia in lavish terms.

2. In sentencing the Rosenbergs to death, Judge Kaufman said
that by placing the atomic secret in Russian hands, the Rosenbergs

had already caused the death of 50,000 in Korea, "and who knows but that millions more of innocent people must pay the price of your treason." Yet the top atomic officials in the country ridiculed the idea that any of the information the Rosenbergs were accused of passing could have been of any value at all. Even the Joint House-Senate Committee on Atomic Energy in a 222-page report on Soviet Atomic Espionage, written after the death sentence had been imposed, mentions the Rosenbergs only once and clearly states that the material they were accused of transmitting "must have counted for little." Finally the Atomic Energy Commission has "bared secret documentary proof that Russia has known the scientific secrets of atom-bomb manufacture since 1940" (International News Service, December 1949) but the Rosenbergs are not accused of having begun their activity until June 6, 1944.

When the government opened its case it promised to call 118 witnesses, including top nuclear physicists whom it identified by name. It actually called only twenty witnesses, and not a single one of the promised top scientists. *It used the prestige of such men as Lieut. Gen. Leslie Groves, head of the wartime atom bomb project, and Nobel Prize winner Dr. Harold C. Urey to help convict the Rosenbergs, but never dared call them to the stand.*

The reason for this can perhaps be seen in the following public statement by Dr. Urey when he cited five powerful points to show why "I cannot put to rest my doubts about the verdict":

> The government's case rests on the testimony of Ruth and David Greenglass . . . The Rosenbergs' testimony flatly contradicted that of the Greenglasses. I found the Rosenbergs' testimony more believable than that of the Greenglasses.

Perhaps one of the most telling points made to convince the American people of the fairness of the legal safeguards provided the Rosenbergs was the number of times their case was brought before the high courts. In the final tense day of the drama, when all eyes were on the Supreme Court, Justice Clark, speaking for the majority, emphasized: "Seven times now have the defendants been before this court." Surely, we are led to believe, they must have had a fair trial.

But the fact is that all of these complicated (and vastly expensive) appearances were only to try to get the Court to consider the case. *It never did.* As Justice Black, in dissenting from the majority decision, pointed out:

> It is not amiss to point out that this court has never reviewed this record and has never affirmed the fairness of the trial.

When the two orphaned Rosenberg boys—Robby, six and Michael, ten—grow up, it will undoubtedly be great consolation for them (after reading Judge Kaufman's shameful remarks) to know that the Supreme Court met on seven different occasions *in order to decide not to review* the fairness of their parents' trial. But meanwhile millions of Americans are convinced that we have the fairest system of justice ever conceived by man—and, if "necessary," we will drop atom bombs on the peoples of less just societies in order to defend it.

III

Since a government is inevitably composed of men who have been corrupted by power (or blinded or desensitized), we can never expect of it the highest human virtues—compassion and love. But at times governments have at least displayed "justice," a minor and sub-Christian virtue. One saddening, frightening aspect of the Rosenberg case is to discover how flagrantly the once proud American courts, about whom so many illusions still persist, now violate even the accepted canons of "justice."

But sadder and more frightening was the attitude of the people. If the hope of human evolution does not rest with even the most just legal system, it does stem from the ability of individuals to respond to their fellows with love and compassion. By using the magic smear word, "Communists," the government, press, and radio were able to transform the Rosenbergs, in the eyes of millions of people, from human beings toward whom it was possible to feel some sympathy or compassion or forgiveness or admiration (depending on your point of view as to what they had done or not done, and why) into some vague, hateful, subhuman species deserving of no consideration at all. (It is the sickness of communism that it encourages the same dehumanizing process toward those who are "fascists," "enemies of the people," etc.)

When we react in this way to the "worst" of "criminals," we are sick unto the death of all that is best in us. But when we are so degenerate as to be led into this error with respect to such fine persons as the Rosenbergs, it is grounds for despair.

After the cruel injustice of the trial and sentencing, the government offered a characteristic bargain: "Confess and implicate the Communists, and we will spare your lives." If you read the letters of the Rosenbergs (*Death House Letters*, National Committee to Secure Justice in the Rosenberg Case) you will, I believe, find the Rosenbergs to be lusty young idealists, with a love of life and with hearts full of love for their two young children. But for thirty months, Julius and Ethel sat in the death house, refusing to save their own lives by pointing the finger at anyone else. During all this time there is no record of any word or deed of violence or recrimination or hatred.

To the end Julius was comforting and strengthening Ethel:

> The greatest writers of all times have described love and explained the beauty and virtue of the complete acceptance of each other by husband and wife, but none of it can come near the painful and extreme satisfaction of what our relationship holds, even on the very threshold of death.
>
> I believe that because we have turned the great personal force of our love into working for the best interests of our children and humanity, we have given expression to the greatest single aspiration of mankind.

And Ethel was writing poems like the following:

IF WE DIE

You shall know, my sons, shall know
why we leave the song unsung,
the book unread, the work undone
to rest beneath the sod.

Mourn no more, my sons, no more
why the lies and smears were framed,
the tears we shed, the hurt we bore
to all shall be proclaimed.

Earth shall smile, my sons, shall smile,
and green above our resting place,

the killing end, the world rejoice
in brotherhood and peace.
Work and build, my sons, and build
a monument to love and joy,
to human worth, to faith we kept
for you, my sons, for you.

Ethel's last act was to embrace the prison matron, who left the room sobbing. Then, to quote the *New York Times,* " 'Mrs. Rosenberg sat in the electric chair with the most composed look you ever saw,' one witness said. She winced a bit as the electrode came in contact with her head, but her arms remained relaxed . . . Silent, she waited while the guards dropped a leather mask over her face."

The apathy of some, the blood-lust of others, the scornful acquiescence in murder by socialists and liberals were based on the feeling that the Rosenbergs were Communists. I believe that it is the tragic error of Communists to believe that they can advance the cause of human freedom, economic equality, and peace through the reluctant use of deceit, violence, and hatred—even as most liberal exponents of Western democracy reluctantly sanction the use of deceit, violence, and hatred by "our" side for similar goals. But who can read of the Rosenbergs—who, if not Communists, were at least Communist-oriented—and not realize that in the hearts of such as these is the love, the faith, and the idealism which makes it ridiculous for us to indulge in the current Red-baiting? To our unspeakable shame, we murdered the Rosenbergs—instead of finding ways to mingle the love that slumbers in our hearts with the love that was so nobly developed in theirs. Must we continue, on a larger scale, to stifle our love and stockpile our weapons of destruction toward Communists all over the world, thereby encouraging them to stifle their love and stockpile their atom bombs against us?

Communists in the
Antiwar Movement

1968 The McCarran Act is a "monstrous" law which disgraces the United States, with its once proud heritage of political freedom. It is perhaps indicative of a weakness in the peace movement that there is so much more opposition to the House Un-American Activities Committee than there is to the McCarran Act. H.U.A.C., which appears unable (or perhaps unwilling) to distinguish between Communists and a fairly wide range of non-Communist and even anti-Communist non-conformists, has aroused the ire of the entire liberal movement. But the opposition to the McCarran Act, which so far at least has been used only against real, "red-blooded" Reds, has been tempered by the distaste many socialists and pacifists feel for Communists. We hope that the opposition will grow and make enforcement unthinkable—not merely because "pacifists (or liberals or socialists) may be next," as the unfortunate phrase goes, but because tyranny is tyranny and can never be justified, no matter who the victim happens to be. To look the other way because the victim is a Communist ("who only believes in freedom for those on his side") is to succumb to the same double standard of values which does in fact characterize the Communist approach and must in the end keep all real humanists out of the Communist movement.

Many pacifists and socialists argue that it is intolerable for the government to police the peace movement, but that the peace movement does have an obligation to police itself, carefully screening its membership so as to eliminate Communists. In some organizations this is attempted directly by purges and loyalty oaths, and in others it is approached indirectly by what Paul Goodman calls the "Byzantine symmetry" with which they strain never to criticize the United States without being sure to lambaste the Soviet Union. I should like to offer three comments on this preoccupation with purging Communists from the peace movement.

Strange as it may seem, those most concerned with keeping Communists out of peace organizations are often those who, in one respect, are most like them—leaders who are more interested in selling a line to the public than stimulating individuals to develop their own independent thoughts and actions in the interests of peace. Communist infiltration is chiefly a threat to those who are themselves trying to develop and control a rather pliable membership. True nonviolence calls for an alert and responsible rank-and-file who know their own minds and are not easily manipulated by anyone, whether government leaders, peace leaders, or Communists. As Eugene Debs once remarked, "I would not be a Moses to lead you into the Promised Land, because if I could lead you into it, someone else could lead you out of it." What we need is a peace movement in which Communists (if they try to "infiltrate") will be heeded when they talk sense and ignored when they do not. If, as has happened so many times in the past, the party line shifts and peace is no longer "progressive," the Communists will drop out of such a movement but no one else will follow them. Or if their experience in the peace movement is vital enough, they will leave the party, not the peace movement. (Something of this kind appears to have happened, among fellow-travellers at least, when the Soviet Union resumed nuclear testing.) As Dagmar Wilson said at the H.U.A.C. hearings, unless we can win Communists, fascists, and everyone else to the cause of peace, goodby world.

Genuine nonviolence requires greater loyalty to the truth than to any partisan grouping of people. Gandhi called his autobiography *My Experiments with Truth*. Even so, his Indian successors were unable to disentangle themselves from the narrow confines of patriotism (something especially difficult for a recently subject people to do), with the present disastrous results. Unless the American peace movement thoroughly outgrows all partisanship toward *either* side in the Cold War, it will not develop the imagination and forthrightness to grapple with the root causes of war, anyway. Yet those within the peace movement who insist on rigid exclusion of Communists never argue for a similar exclusion of pro-Americans. On the contrary, their emphasis on excluding Communists is usually hard to separate from their attempts to prove their respectability as loyal oppositionists, oppositionists loyal, that is, to the American nation-state. Historically the peace movement, in this and most other countries, has suffered most, not from the unreliability of Communists but from the disaffection, in time of crisis, of those who had not thoroughly weaned themselves from loyalty to the country in which they lived. Mild criticisms of American foreign policy by American liberals no more constitute a genuinely independent attitude than do the belated criticisms of the abuses of the Stalin era by some Communists.

The power of a nonviolent movement stems from the actions it undertakes, not from its political statements or the private beliefs and associations of its participants. Most of those who praise Gandhi because of the campaigns he carried out would consider him a crank if they knew of him only through his writings on sex, diet, medicine, etc., or would consider him politically confused if they read some of his statements on economics or socialism. In the absence of purges, it is easy for fair-weather "pacifists" (including both Communists and liberals) to play leading roles in peace organizations whose stock-in-trade is geopolitical analyses, electoral campaigns, attempts to argue the government into turning in the general direction of peace, and devotion to future revolutions. They may indeed subvert the organization, but the organization is not apt seriously to challenge them. But when the unifying factor is the dynamic one of individual actions jointly undertaken, questions about political reliability and future loyalty recede into the background. It is not our business (any more than it is that of the government) to inquire into the motives or the outside associations of those who challenge American and Soviet tests, commit nonviolent civil disobedience against missile bases or Civilian Defense drills, refuse to pay income taxes for war or to perform war work, eschew economic and power relationships which involve living off the labor or subservience of their fellows. Radical personal actions carry their own power, and must always be the undergirding of an effective nonviolent movement.

Gandhi's Heirs

1962 The outbreak of fighting between China and India to-gether with India's requests for military aid from the United States have given a kind of perverse satisfaction to those who need to be-lieve that human beings are not *really* capable of peace on earth and goodwill to men. At the same time, these developments have caused considerable embarrassment to those advocates of nonviolence who have leaned too heavily on India's successful use of nonviolence many years ago under Gandhi and have not previously come to grips with the fact that the Indian government, however peaceful it may have seemed when compared with the United States or the Soviet Union, has turned its back on nonviolence for sixteen years now.

A.M. Rosenthal, reporting from New Delhi for the *New York Times,* put the case against nonviolence rather succinctly in the No-vember 18, 1962, issue:

> There was a time when India followed, or tried des-
> perately to follow, Gandhi down the road of nonviolence.
> But the important thing to remember is that although non-
> violence may have been a religious philosophy to Gandhi, to
> his followers it was essentially the best technique of shaming

and conquering the British. It worked more or less efficiently against the British, but Indians realize it could not have worked against other nations and peoples. . . . In the current crisis, nobody talks about destroying the invaders from the north by nonviolence.

To take the points in reverse order:

1) Nonviolence never calls for destroying an invader. It seeks to destroy his power to commit injustice, by using strikes, boycotts, civil disobedience and massive non-cooperation—unlike appeasement, which seeks to buy off a troublesome opponent by making concessions without regard for justice. It seeks to destroy his motivation (his patriotic justifications) by dealing fairly with him. In this it may be contrasted with violence, which characteristically refuses to grant any merit to the opponent and by its very nature unleashes its own injustice on the innocent and the guilty alike within the enemy country. Nonviolence is a method of love and looks forward to reconciliation based on adjustment of grievances through mutual respect rather than a selfish victory based on the power of one side to impose its will on the other. Gandhi sought no special privileges for himself or his countrymen (still less revenge) and always insisted that his fasts, which made the British Empire totter, were to help him and his cohorts purge themselves of their own shortcomings. Although all of India was inspired by Gandhi and millions followed him part way, he had to call off his campaigns many times because of the inability of his countrymen to understand his method. It is not surprising that with the birth of an Indian nation and the death of Gandhi, India, like every other nation-state, went further and further down the roads of appeasement and militarism. The Chinese attack was brutal and unjustified but, as Gandhi would have been the first to point out, justice is by no means all on India's side. The McMahon Line was loosely drawn up in 1914 by a greedy Britain and has never been accepted by *any* Chinese government—not even by the present Nationalist government on Taiwan, which makes approximately the same territorial claims against India that the Communists do. Ten months before the Chinese attack, Nehru put a new general, Lieutenant General Brij Kaul, in charge of one of the disputed border areas and publicly ordered him to drive out the Chinese. As *Time* magazine put it, "Before Kaul had a chance to try and 'clear out' the Chinese in N.E.F.A., the Chinese struck first."

2) The major reason why the Indians practiced nonviolence successfully in the past and are not able to do so today is to be found not in the differences between British and Chinese but in the difference between India at the time of Gandhi and India today. In the interim India has become a nation-state, with rigid boundaries, a centralized government, and "national interests." As Randolph Bourne said, "war is the health of the state," so a colonial people who win their independence by nonviolence must jump right over the obsolete nation-state stage into the future, into a status-free, egalitarian, human-scaled decentralism, if they are to remain nonviolent. Nonviolence is a person-to-person and people-to-people method, and once people begin to think of themselves and others as citizens of rival governments, they can hardly practice it. Nonviolence must be used to defend human rights, not national rights. The history of British rule in India had its savage aspects, from the Amritsar Massacre to the mowing down of Gandhian volunteers. To say that nonviolence worked because of the gentlemanliness of the British is like arguing that the nonviolence of the Montgomery bus boycott "worked" because of the Southern chivalry of the Ku Klux Klan and the White Citizens Councils. It is also to rewrite history and to imply, contrary to Gandhi, that nonviolence can be used to win or defend selfish privilege (provided the opponent is gentlemanly enough), but cannot be used to win basic human freedoms if the opponent is sufficiently cruel "by nature." (Members of other political blocs are usually thought to be more "cruel by nature" than ourselves and our allies.)

3) The genius of Gandhi and the basis for his remarkable success lay in his insistence that religion and politics could not be separated. Unfortunately his spiritual heirs have re-established the dichotomy. Nehru has become a traditional head of state who blesses the pacifists in their separate vocation, and Vinoba has concentrated more and more in recent years on religious and "constructive" work in the villages, without criticizing the Indian government as it became increasingly enmeshed in power politics. The logic of events has now carried each further along his chosen path. Nehru appears about to be engulfed in the Cold War and Vinoba has just issued a statement which says in part:

> As a *shanti sainik* my basic view that arms will do no good to the world or to anybody endures as ever. . . . But at the same time I do feel that India never thought of fighting

and was always prepared for peaceful negotiations. Even then China committed aggression. . . . My sympathies are with India. . . . I hope that the *shanti sainiks* will realize their true function at this hour and make their full contribution towards the maintenance of internal peace. This will be our special task and its fulfilment will lead to nonviolence and make the nation strong.

Perhaps we must learn today from the present Indian failures as in the past we have learned from their successes. To be viable, nonviolence must challenge both the militarism and the injustices of the society in which it operates. It must do this not only by pursuing its own long-range goals but by throwing up roadblocks against the worst abuses of its own government. Only then will it have the tradition and the experience to challenge outside aggressors.

The Black Rebellions

1967 One of the oldest laments in human history is directed against those who "cry 'peace, peace,' when there is no peace." Today, after the outbreaks of counterviolence in Newark, Detroit and a growing number of other cities, we hear the hurt cries of those who mistakenly think that there was peace in our society and that it has been broken by impatient or criminal individuals. Many persons who themselves managed to get educated, employed, adequately housed and socially accepted to some degree, are crying "violence and crime, crime and violence" against the rebellious acts of those who have been victimized all their lives by crime and violence, including the violence of the police.

Those who have never been bitten by a rat or beaten up in the precinct house fall rather easily into the trap of thinking that "law and order" is the framework within which justice is administered and progress takes place. Without going into the usual statistics of unemployment, disease, and poverty, we can observe the kind of justice and progress that was operative in the black American community of Newark, in the following excerpt from a report by Steve Block of the Newark Community Union Project (N-C.U.P.):

> Tensions in Newark have been rising all spring and summer, and have been centered around two issues. First the

mayor lured the New Jersey State School of Medicine and Dentistry to Newark, and a major part of the bait he used was the promise of 150 acres located in the heart of the Central Ward, the worst part of the ghetto. About 20,000 black people will be displaced as a result; and, as always, there are no real plans for finding or providing new homes for them. The black community has been furious and militant all spring and summer about this.

Second, the secretary of the Board of Education resigned. In appointing a successor the mayor and the other powers-that-be chose a white City Councilman . . . [with] no college education and no business experience. (The job consists mainly of handling the money.) The black community opposed him in favor of Wilbur Park, a black C.P.A. who works in a financial capacity. . . .

The spark that set off the . . . riot . . . came Wednesday night, July 12. Two cops beat up a black cab driver, with a crowd of people looking on. (Were they stupid, or did they want a riot?) . . . (*New Left Notes,* July 24)

When the camouflaged and orderly violence of established society is challenged by the crude and unpredictable violence of a forming—but as yet inchoate—countersociety, it is hard for idealists and humanitarians to keep a proper perspective. There is a temptation to condemn the newest recourse to violence—that of the rebels—or at least to equate the violence of the two sides in a way that precludes solidarity with those seeking liberation from the status quo.

This temptation is particularly seductive for those of us who advocate nonviolent methods of struggle but who do not experience in our own daily lives the unremitting violence of existing police and property relationships. Rather than face up to our failure to have taken the lead with a truly revolutionary nonviolence that is engaged in combat here and now, we are tempted to dissociate ourselves from the rebels and to end up, albeit reluctantly, on the side of those who invoke "law and order," "the democratic process," and the protection of the innocent as justification for the suppressive violence of the police and troops. Yet one of the factors that induces serious revolutionaries and discouraged ghetto-dwellers to conclude that nonviolence is incapable of being developed into a method adequate to their needs is this very tendency of pacifists to line up, in moments of conflict, with the status quo. Thus a vicious circle is set up in which the advocates of nonviolence stand aloof from—or even repudiate—the only live revolutions in the making (Cuba, Vietnam, the black American communities), and determined revolutionaries reject nonviolence out of hand because of the repeated defections from the revolutionary cause of those who champion it.

In this context I was saddened to see Martin Luther King, Jr. endorse the sending of federal troops into Detroit. One can only sympathize with him personally, given the pressures he has been under from all sides. But if there are occasions when those who act nonviolently themselves must become reluctant allies or critical supporters of those who resort to violence—as I believe there are—then at least there should be no doubt that we form our alliances on the side of the oppressed and exploited, not on the side of the establishment.

One can call for alternative, nonviolent methods of liberation and point out the dangers and shortcomings of the current form of rebellion, but it is contrary to the spirit of nonviolence to call for the punishment of those who have resorted to violence in their desperate search for a method of breaking out of the present intolerable situation. After all, nonviolence has ground to a halt in the area of black liberation, staggered by the depth of the problem and hesitating at the crossroads where one must move on from protest either to the illusions of liberal politics or to genuine revolution. The former means maintaining an uneasy alliance with the government but the latter requires solidarity with and loyalty to the people, even when they succumb to the temptations of violence.

The politics of Washington do not differ greatly from Saigon to Newark, from the Dominican Republic to Detroit. The current black revolts highlight both the hypocrisy and the futility of U.S. military intervention in Vietnam. How can a society in which millions of its own citizens fail to find jobs, housing, dignity, and meaningful democracy claim that its armed attacks on the towns and villages of Vietnam have the serious purpose of bringing the benefits of land reform, economic justice, and real democracy to the Vietnamese?

If slum-clearance housing in the United States enriches the real-estate operators and other commercial interests while frustrating the inhabitants of U.S. slums and ghettos, what chance is there that the expenditure of millions of dollars in high-sounding A.I.D. programs will do more than line the pockets of the tiny group of feudal landlords, war profiteers and generals who are the main collaborators of the United States in Vietnam? Those Americans who have taken seriously the Administration's claims of noble democratic purpose and ultimate success in Vietnam should re-examine their assumptions on the basis of the unmistakable message from the disillusioned black population of our own country.

There are some ghetto-dwellers who find it so oppressive in the United States that they are willingly in the armed forces, ready to settle for a regular paycheck, a degree of integration and the opportunity to wear a uniform which implies, however falsely, that they have become first-class citizens at last. But surely the revolts in Newark, Detroit and other cities, and the calloused attacks on the black population by police and national guardsmen should make them reconsider where their true loyalty lies.

All Americans who are shocked and appalled by the developing civil war in U.S. cities should redouble their efforts to bring about American military withdrawal from Vietnam. Not only the misdirection of funds and manpower but also the hardening of habits and attitudes contribute to the deterioration within the United States. Even as the U.S. armed forces often bomb, burn or shoot up Vietnamese villages suspected of harboring members of the N.L.F., or destroy a whole village from which there has been sniper fire, so there were instances in Newark, Detroit, and Spanish Harlem when police or other armed forces fired high-powered rifles indiscriminately into buildings that might hold snipers. As in Vietnam, a high percentage of the victims were women and children. Even as American troops and bombers feel frustrated and put upon by the successful resistance of the lowly Vietnamese and, quite naturally, resent the deaths of their buddies, so police and guardsmen were impelled to reassert their authority or revenge their slain cohorts by acts of senseless reprisal. Thus the Newark revolt, which had largely spent itself after two days of reaction to the arrest and beating of a cab driver, was transformed into a massacre on the third day, when the Newark police department, the New Jersey State Patrol and the National Guard decided to show the niggers who was boss.

An eyewitness reports:

> "We have got to kill somebody to show these black bastards that we mean business," said one of the Newark patrolmen. This is exactly what they proceeded to do. The people of the Central Ward were systematically insulted,

bludgeoned and killed after Friday morning. . . . Police were careful to cover their actions [as in Vietnam]. They haven't permitted newsmen to photograph the hundreds of bloody "casualties" which are being taken to the City Hospital. The death rate rose steadily after Friday morning even though the major portion of the rioting was over by that time. (*National Guardian,* July 22)

According to newspaper reports, forty percent of the Army troops sent to Detroit had been battle-hardened in Vietnam. Eyewitness accounts indicate that this meant, among other things, that some of them were able to shoot innocent people without the pangs of conscience that one might ordinarily expect. One of the prices France paid for her unsuccessful wars in Indochina and Algeria was the contempt for human life which many of the soldiers brought back with them. The longer the war continues in Vietnam the more casually will some of those who stick it out in the armed forces be able—whether as policemen, vigilantes or rebels—to take the lives of those who displease them at home.

Clearly the prospect is spiralling violence and a decline of humane values at home and abroad, unless U.S. troops can be withdrawn from Vietnam and kept out of America's troubled cities. But it is not enough to call for a simple redirection of federal funds from Vietnam to the United States. Massive freedom budgets at home can be as illusory as Washington-sponsored social reconstruction has been in Vietnam. Without local initiative and control by the people in whose interests the money is being spent, there can be no real dignity or self-determination. One of the characteristics of the ghetto-dwellers' present rebelliousness is resentment at having things done *for* them as well as *to* them by The Man.

The best way to combat violence is to work constructively against the cruelty and violence of the status quo. While remaining nonviolent ourselves, we must recognize and respond to the thrust for dignity of those who strike out, however blindly at times, against the system which oppresses them. Only those who have found a sense of dignity and worth in their own lives can believe enough in the dignity and worth of other human beings to become nonviolent. Others may be subservient or submissive—but that is not nonviolence, any more than the days without arson or sniping in our cities are days of peace.

The Assassination of
Martin Luther King, Jr.

1968 The assassination of Martin Luther King, Jr. released new forces in U.S. society whose long-run effects cannot be accurately predicted. But it is already clear that nonviolence as a method of social change did not die with Dr. King, despite what some opponents of nonviolence rushed to proclaim. Indeed there are indications that the opposite may turn out to be true: nonviolence may be made more militant—and therefore more relevant—by the impact of Dr. King's death on some of his closest associates and on others who never knew him but who share his hunger and thirst for righteousness.

One must consider in particular the effect of his assassination on the sixty or more poor people's leaders whom he gathered to serve as organizers of the Poor People's Campaign. They hunger and thirst not so much after righteousness as after food and drink, shelter and dignity and all the other necessities of life our society must provide before any real righteousness can exist. Coming as they do from communities of impatient blacks, Mexican-Americans, Puerto Ricans, American Indians and poor whites—communities totaling perhaps forty million persons—their potential power is undeniable. Ironically, King's assassination and the initial inspiration and political protection it provides for the crucial beginnings of the campaign assure a more dynamic and united beginning than probably would have been possible with him alive.

Not only are his nonviolent associates angry, with the anger of those who have been victimized once too often and much too personally for it to be easily assuaged, but his opponents are at a serious disadvantage. Who, for example, would have dared bar the march, in the name of law and order or under any other pretext, when it set out from the spot at the Lorraine Motel where he had been killed? Who would have dared break it up when it arrived in Marks, Mississippi, on its roundabout route from Memphis to Washington? What cabinet member could have afforded, a few days earlier, to deny an audience to King's successors and the advance contingent of poor people, who served indignant notice of their demands and of their determination to return in two weeks with thousands of supporters to insist on a redress of their grievances?

It is one of the strengths of nonviolence that those who disarm themselves are disarming their opponents. Those who voluntarily divest themselves of armaments but at the same time press forward in a just cause, making clear their willingness to die for it (as Martin Luther King certainly did), tend to rob their opponents of their weapons as well. For of what use is a machine gun or a tank if one dare not use it, because to do so is to expose oneself to the whole world as a tyrant? Even tyrants must maintain a façade of legitimacy and justice and must be able to characterize their opponents as evil men—or they gradually lose control. Those who combine nonviolence with intransigence transfer the battle from a contest of arms in which the soldier and the cop have the advantage, to a contest in which the advantage lies with those whose cause is just. If those who believe in the necessity of nonviolence in this age of technological warfare will take part in the Poor People's Campaign in the resolute spirit that Martin Luther King launched it, it is likely that the nonviolent movement will not only come back into its own but will emerge stronger than at any previous period in our country's history.

It is senseless, of course, to think that there will be no casualties. If there are no casualties then the battle is not joined. Either the demands are not far-reaching enough or a misinterpretation of nonviolence leads the protesters to call off the struggle too soon. But it is as ridiculous to dismiss nonviolence as a tactic because of the death of Martin Luther King as it would be automatically to rule out revolutionary violence as a tactic because of the murders of Malcolm X and Ché Guevara. The question is not which method of attempted revolution will avoid all casualties—because there is no such method—but which method can achieve the most far-reaching and cumulative results while minimizing the casualties on both sides. A strong case can be made that nonviolence can become the more successful of the two methods, but only if it is revolutionary enough in its aims and courageous enough in its application. A nonviolent movement for social revolution has the potential of mobilizing and strengthening the exploited (without turning them into tyrants in reverse), of weakening and demoralizing the Establishment (by robbing it of its pseudo-moral justifications) and of winning over or neutralizing the ambivalent middle (who, in a contest of violence, tend to side with the established order).

Oddly enough, whereas nonviolence is often condemned for being able to win concessions only in the early, reformist stages of social conflict and violence is credited with making a serious bid for power ("power comes from the barrel of a gun"), the opposite may well be true, at least in this country. Rioting, looting and the burning down of buildings win concessions from corporations—in order to save their profits. But at its best a nonviolent movement tends to revolutionize people, the only lasting power through which genuine revolution can take place.

The greatest danger to the Poor People's Campaign comes not from its outspoken opponents, the Southern senators who rail against it and would shortsightedly invoke the police and Army to keep it out of Washington, but from a motley combination of liberal politicians, civic and religious leaders, and nonrevolutionary well-wishers and do-gooders who are trying to embrace it in order to tame it. It is not that they are necessarily plotting to frustrate the Poor People's Campaign but that inevitably they are trying to limit King's program and the activities of his successors to their own limited visions of justice and timid conceptions of the democratic process.

For years, while King was still alive, such "moderates" tried to capture or contain him. Underestimating his potential for growth and mistaking his nonviolence for lack of revolutionary seriousness, they thought they could control him and pushed him to the fore as public leader of the movement. To an unfortunate extent they did succeed in slowing down his development and containing him, as in Birmingham, in Albany (Georgia), in Selma and in Chicago. These were campaigns which had their days of glory but in which King, under tremendous pressure from his financial backers and political advisers, abandoned his announced objectives without proper consultation with or regard for the people who had to remain and suffer after he and his more glamorous supporters withdrew. In the election year of 1964 the moderates succeeded with some difficulty in persuading King to adopt and promulgate a six-month moratorium on demonstrations in order to insure the election of President Johnson—a goal more in line with their own nonrevolutionary conceptions of how progress is made than with his own developing radicalism. But they never succeeded in capturing Martin Luther King or turning him into one of their own. He kept coming back to launch new campaigns based on the bedrock of his religiously motivated dissatisfaction with anything less than freedom and justice for all.

As long as these objectives remained unfulfilled he could not settle comfortably into the lecture circuit, where he could easily have traded on his fame as a Nobel Prize winner. With growing indignation he rejected the role of serving as a humanitarian adviser to a government which showed its true character by turning its back on the poor at home and waging war on the poor abroad. His fair-false liberal friends succeeded in slowing down his development as a revolutionary leader but not in stopping it—his moral integrity and drive for social justice were too great for that. Exactly a year before his death he served unmistakable notice of his emerging independence and deepening commitment to the American and foreign victims of our liberal society when he launched a belated but courageous campaign against the war in Vietnam. In the last months of his life he began to organize the Poor People's Campaign, an imaginative joining of black, white, brown, and red people in a program which relied for its strength on the aroused nonviolent actions of the disadvantaged rather than on the liberalism of the government. (A few months earlier he told me that his experience had convinced him that progress comes through militant, initially unpopular actions that have a shock effect on the participants and the general public, forcing people to face the need for previously undreamed-of solutions.)

Some people told him that it would not be safe to turn the poor people on, that it would not be safe to bring them to Washington, where he might not be able to control them. But he rejected the advice of Bayard Rustin, Roy Wilkins, Whitney Young and the liberal churchmen, labor leaders, philanthropists, senators, and congressmen

—men who are more afraid of the people than they are of the alliance of Big Business, Big Labor, and Big Government that dominates the economy and controls U.S. foreign policy.

In the last week of his life, King showed the new seriousness of his intentions by interrupting his schedule and journeying to Memphis to join the outcasts of that city, the striking, black garbage men. It was an explosive situation and he was warned that he could not control it, but that did not keep him away. On the first day violence broke out, and he was criticized for not being able to prevent it— warned to call off the poor people's march on Washington, which he would also not be able to control. But he had learned that his kind of nonviolence could no longer turn its back on those whose grievances were so great that they exploded into violence as an outlet for their legitimate anger and despair. He also knew that as usual the greatest acts of violence were committed by the police, who used the instances of looting as a cover for inexcusable brutality—clubbing and tear-gassing the marchers, dragging people out of their cars and beating them to the ground, shooting and killing a sixteen-year-old boy. He was aware that the teenagers who had broken store windows and taken some of the goods which a just society would have made available to them without looting had been provoked by the police. When they had sought to leave their schools to join the march they had been surrounded by police who tried to prevent them from doing so. He was faulted by many—myself included—for allowing himself to be whisked away to safety when the police attack began. But he demonstrated his commitment both to the poor and to the ultimate triumph of nonviolence when he prepared the scene for a second march, knowing full well that when he returned he might never leave Memphis alive.*

It remains to be seen whether the Poor People's Campaign will

---

* *At the time of the April 15 Spring Mobilization against the Vietnam War both Dr. King and I were informed by a police contact that a contract had been signed in the underworld to assassinate him. Besides our normal security measures, it was decided that King should not dally on the platform. The next day the press (anxious as always to drive a wedge between those who had won public acclaim and their revolutionary allies) made a great deal of King's short stay, erroneously attributing it to his distaste for the more militant speakers (Stokely Carmichael, Howard Zinn and I). In fact, when King left the platform, he said, "It's a fantastic success. Greater than the March on Washington. See you at Harry's [Harry Belafonte's] as soon as you can make it."*

be able to combine a radical commitment to justice with an imaginative and militant nonviolence or whether it can be seduced by token concessions from the liberal Establishment. Fortunately Ralph Abernathy, the new leader of the Southern Christian Leadership Conference, appears to be not only committed to the need for radical social change but also sensitive to the mood of impatience in the black and Spanish-speaking communities—both Mexican-American and Puerto Rican. (The mood of intransigence seems to cut less deeply into the Indian and poor-white communities, though the participation in the campaign of militant individuals from these communities is very important symbolically and may speed up the process of radicalization.) On April 29, in Washington, shortly after Abernathy first confronted government officials with an advance group of one hundred poor people and supporters, I heard him say, to a wildly cheering crowd of over two thousand black people:

> You know they thought that Martin Luther King was tough and rough and so they decided to assassinate him. But I got news for them. Under Martin Luther King's leadership we were just going to shake America a little, but now, under Ralph Abernathy's leadership we are going to turn America upside down.

I had the impression that he meant what he said. There is a good chance that he will keep on meaning it, not only because of the depth of his feelings about what U.S. society did to Martin Luther King but because he will be constantly pushed from below. He will lose his moral and political authority in the black community if he settles for much less.

This does not mean that we can expect a nonviolent conquest of the strongholds of racism and exploitation in the next few years. More important than the actual concessions that may be won from the government this year, in the form of Congressional bills and appropriations, is the potential effect of the campaign on the participants themselves—and on millions of others, both poor people and disillusioned members of the middle class, who will be observing it. However limited the Poor People's Campaign may be in its specific demands and its immediate gains, if it gives these people a new sense of strength and a new purpose it will have made an important contribution to the slowly developing dynamics of revolution in this country.

It is better that nonviolence is no longer a fad, winning the much-too-superficial acclaim of the partially committed and nonrevolutionary as it did in the early years of the civil rights movement. Certainly it is healthy that nonviolence is challenged and kept honest by the militancy and courage of comrades who share our revolutionary goals but believe, on the basis of their own experience as victims, that these goals can be achieved only through violence. But let us hope that we are also emerging from the more recent period in which the rhetoric of revolutionary violence became, in its turn, a fad. During this period, romantic and self-defeating excursions into violence (such as fighting the cops) have served as substitutes for serious programs, planning and organization, and nonviolence has been much too easily brushed aside on the theory that it is of necessity a method of caution and compromise. Martin Luther King contributed to the emergence of both fads—by the early dramatic successes of movements he led and eloquently interpreted, and by the vacillations and compromises he was subject to as he tried to work out a politics that gave expression to his drive for freedom and justice. The heroism of his last year, with his opposition to the war, his imaginative conception of and dedication to the Poor People's Campaign, his identification with the striking garbage men of Memphis and his resulting martyrdom, should contribute to the ending of both fads and the rebirth of a more vigorous and revolutionary nonviolence.

Obviously, the revolutionary struggle will be long and difficult, with many detours and defeats, whether it is carried on by nonviolence, violence or (as seems most likely today) a shifting combination of the two. But nonelectoral, nonviolent, direct action is far from dead. In fact it is on the move again, strengthened by the example of Martin Luther King, radicalized by the participation of militant poor people and deepened by the anti-Vietnam-war experience of the last few years.

The Warren Report

1965 The Warren Commission appears to have acted from the beginning as prosecuting attorneys against the dead Lee Harvey Oswald rather than as an independent body of investigation and inquiry. They seemed intent above all on wrapping up the case for a lone, nonpolitical killer, with a minimum of public debate and uneasiness. Contrary to the assumption made by some of the Commission's critics and supporters alike, one need not know even in the most general way—or think that the Commission knows—what the results of an uninhibited and objective inquiry would be, in order to be dismayed at the prejudicial nature of the Commission's conduct. They may simply have felt that given the explosive nature of the subject and the difficulty of determining conclusively just what did lie behind the assassination, their particular task was to concentrate on allaying public uncertainty and anxiety. C. L. Sulzberger, who accepts the Commission's findings, unwittingly states the considerations that may have led it to act as it did:

> "The commission dismisses the theory that Oswald must have received aid from one or more persons or political groups ranging from the far left to the far right of the political spectrum, or from a foreign government. . . . This con-

clusion is primordial. It was essential in these restless days to remove unfounded suspicions that could excite any latent jingo spirit. And it was necessary to reassure our allies that ours is a stable, reliable democracy." (The *New York Times,* September 28.)

Against this intended soporific, I am grateful for the efforts of Mark Lane and others who have refused to be stampeded into accepting the desperately promoted consensus and have tried to keep the question open by pointing out inconsistencies and contradictions in the accounts of the Dallas police, the F.B.I., the mass media, and the Warren Commission. But the official agencies have maintained a monopoly on much of the evidence that is needed for a satisfactory investigation. Inevitably much of the material brought forth to challenge the official version has been highly speculative or circumstantial; some of it has turned out to be inaccurate; unfortunately, some has reflected special pleading on the part of persons who, on their part, were as anxious as the Warren Commission to find supporting evidence for a predetermined viewpoint.

From the beginning, I have pointed out that the C.I.A. and other government groups think nothing of assassinating the political leaders (and laymen as well) of other countries. But I have not been in a position to play detective and come to even a tentative conclusion as to whether or not they had anything to do with the assassination of President Kennedy. Besides I am as deeply shocked by the political murder of a Negro, a civil rights worker, or a Vietnamese peasant as I am by the assassination of a President.

More than a year after the assassination of John F. Kennedy, I am still horrified by it; but I think that the worst imaginable reaction would be to close ranks behind the governmental consensus and public attitudes which sanction the continued murder of other people in other lands. Why is it so important to persuade the American people that the murder of Kennedy was the isolated act of a psychopath rather than a politically motivated act similar in nature to actions carried out in our name in Vietnam, Venezuela, the Congo, and all over the world? Is it perhaps time, rather, to face up to the fact that the United States is no longer a privileged sanctuary from which politicians can order acts of brutality abroad without reaping sooner or later a similar harvest at home—if not in retaliation, by avengers of the victims, then through the political acts of disgruntled accomplices or agents who have fallen out over policy or power? Did the terrible murder of President Kennedy perhaps rip the mask off an ugly aspect of our public morality that the American people prefer not to think about—and the government dare not allow us to? This particular assassination cannot be passed over lightly, because it struck down "one of us," a man of considerable charm and personal appeal who entered our homes and our hearts by television and represented the political aspirations of many. Is that why it was so important not to have a real investigation of the facts?

Haunted by these considerations, I think that my revered friend I. F. Stone misses the point when he rallies behind the Warren Commission and angrily attacks its left-wing critics in *I. F. Stone's Weekly*. His denunciation of "demonology" on the left is badly needed in these times, but hardly seems applicable to all those who have found the Warren Report less than convincing:

> Demonology is the notion that because a man disagrees with you politically, he must be impervious to honor, duty, patriotism, and mercy—in short a demon, i.e., all of one piece, black evil, and not a human being, i.e., full of contradictions. Demonology also implies that such a person is fair game for any libel or slander, since ipso facto beyond the pale of decency.

Stone says that people "belong in the booby hatch" if they believe that the Warren Commission ("chosen to provide a bipartisan body which could command the widest public respect") "and the vast network of the police, the F.B.I., the C.I.A. and the Secret Service all conspired to keep [a] secret." But is it really so inconceivable that they might have done so, so inconsistent with what has happened in other instances?

Probably a greater number of people "conspired" to keep the secret of the atom bomb until after the United States had incinerated Hiroshima and introduced that monstrosity into world affairs. Only Earl Warren, of the present Commission, approaches the stature of some of the outstanding "humanitarians" involved in that conspiracy against the public. They acted as they did, not because they were evil men, in the usual sense of the phrase, but because they thought that they were saving American lives and defending the democratic way of life. How many people lied to us (or acquiesced in the lie) by saying that the illegal U-2 plane shot down over Russia was an innocent weather plane that had wandered off its course? Cannot quite "decent" and conscientious persons argue that it would shake the foundations of democracy, disrupt the consensus, and lead to widespread disillusionment, as well as possible new acts of barbarism, if the American people even suspected that the C.I.A. or a political group from *either* the left or the right may have assassinated the President? (That is the real reason, I think, why the government moved so quickly to convince the public that Oswald was not really a leftist, despite powerful evidence to the contrary.)

Even if everyone involved in the investigation knew of an underlying conspiracy and was horrified by it, could they not feel it was imperative to handle the matter *behind the scenes* (as most crucial public matters are handled these days), taking steps to prevent a recurrence and at the same time soothing the public in order to preserve its faith in the stability of our internal affairs? There is a certain elitist *noblesse oblige* in times of crisis, a conscientious closing of the ranks to preserve the seeming security of "law and order," and the fragile facade of civilization. If it turns out later that the Warren Commission has been involved in this type of conspiracy, it will not mean that they are monstrous men—except perhaps in the sense that Harry Truman was monstrous when he ordered the bombing of Hiroshima, that Dwight Eisenhower was monstrous when he sent the U-2s into Russia and lied to us about them, that Kennedy himself was monstrous when he sanctioned the illicit Bay of Pigs invasion and sent paramilitary forces into Vietnam, that Lyndon Johnson and Robert McNamara are monstrous today concerning Vietnam.

The problem is that our civilization encourages us all to be *both* honest *and* deceitful, generous *and* selfish, kind *and* monstrously cruel. It will not do to deal with the assassination of President Kennedy by saying that it is beyond belief that it could have been the work of a politically dissident group, or that Earl Warren is a fine and honorable man and therefore would be incapable of being a party to a cover-up.

Many persons, as ignorant as we are as to the identity and purpose of the killers, would find it more soothing to allow the matter to die. It would be less challenging to their myths about the kind of freedom, decency, and democracy that exists in the United States, about the kind of future that is being prepared by our present actions. But the Warren Report leaves many unanswered questions that need to be faced up to.

The Assassination of
Robert F. Kennedy

1968 The assassination of Robert Kennedy, coming as it did hard on the heels of the assassination of Martin Luther King, Jr. and Bobby Hutton (of the California Black Panthers), affected me deeply. One does not have to agree with a man politically to be shocked by his premature and brutal death. Personally, I find it hard to disentangle the elements of genuine grief and self-serving hypocrisy in the public mourning for King and Kennedy. (There was little mourning for Bobby Hutton, except among his black comrades and a few others who understood that his murder was a vicious act of police power, white racism, and defense of the status quo.)

Because all genuine emotions tend to be manipulated in our society for selfish and commercial ends, it is easy to underestimate the extent to which most people, including some political figures, are moved and horrified by certain calamities that stem from the society to which they cling. One can expect no adequate repentance and rebirth on the part of the country's political leaders, who will continue to rely on the routine violence of "law and order," police, and armies to repress serious movements for social change, both at home and abroad. But there is no doubt that certain of the assassinations of the last few years (a Bobby Kennedy but not a Bobby Hutton; a Martin Luther King but not a Malcolm X; Schwerner, Chaney and Goodman but not the students of Orangeburg) have shocked and bewildered a lot of people who are not seriously upset by the ordinary violence of our society. Combined with the war in Vietnam and middle-class America's inability to co-opt its youth or pacify the cities, the dramatic deaths of a series of charismatic public figures have sapped the country's complacency and left it vulnerable to charges that the structure and working assumptions of society are neither as moral nor as practical as had been assumed.

The political morality of Bobby Kennedy is a case in point. I believe that the charges of ruthlessness and opportunism that haunted him in his campaign for the Presidential nomination were justified, on one level, by a series of actions he performed in the pursuit and exercise of political power, first in behalf of his brother and then in his own behalf. But Kennedy himself could not understand why people made these charges. He knew that he was only doing (with more flair, family connections, and financial resources) things which every successful politician does. He was aware of the extent to which feelings of love, human sympathy, and devotion to justice (within his understanding of them) were an important part of his motivation. But these are new times. The old political morality and customs are increasingly being called into question.

In a way Kennedy's dilemma was similar to that of President Johnson. Johnson has been surprised and perplexed by the domestic revolt against his Vietnam policies. He believes, quite correctly, that in the main he has been carrying out (in his case with a notable lack of flair and charisma) a foreign policy that virtually all of his predecessors, including Presidents Kennedy, Eisenhower, Truman* and Johnson's mentor, Franklin Roosevelt, pursued.

When Martin Luther King, Jr. was shot, Bobby Kennedy connected the deed with the institutional violence of our society—hunger, racial discrimination, poverty—that undermines our respect for human life. I have no reason to believe that he was not sincere—but his remedy was to make it more profitable for private industry to invest in the ghettos and slums, even though the profit motive and the established rights of wealthy corporations automatically express dis-

---

* *Dwight Macdonald and Dr. Spock to the contrary notwithstanding, there are few, if any, major differences between the issues in the Korean War and those in Vietnam.*

respect for human life. Moreover, it was Kennedy who had Martin Luther King's phones tapped. And it was while he was Attorney General that King's hotel rooms were bugged, though it is at least possible that Kennedy was not personally responsible for this invasion of privacy and the political blackmail that followed. At the very least, Kennedy was willing to allow these abuses to take place (if indeed he considered them abuses) rather than to take on the political risks involved in crossing J. Edgar Hoover.

Robert Kennedy's admirers cannot understand why he was accused of opportunism when he entered the Presidential race after Senator McCarthy's New Hampshire triumph. Indeed, in the terms in which the case is usually argued, the charge was unfair. After all, Kennedy seemed to have a chance of winning the nomination and McCarthy did not. From the point of view of achieving whatever social gains can be achieved by winning Presidential elections, McCarthy's failure to step aside and his acceptance of *sub rosa* pro-Humphrey aid in the primaries in order to advance his own ambitions are at least as unprincipled as Kennedy's invasion of the field.

But the real opportunism of both men goes deeper than these considerations and falls within the normal pattern of U.S. politics. It lies in their failure to oppose the war until draft resistance, mass demonstrations, defections within the Establishment, and military and political failure in Vietnam had made it safe to do so. Whether opposing the Administration and calling for peace in Vietnam (without calling for U.S. withdrawal or otherwise defining the issues clearly) would turn out to be politically advantageous or not was harder to estimate a few months ago and involved different considerations for McCarthy than for Kennedy. But there is nothing in the history of either man to suggest that he was willing at any time to risk his political career in order to shorten the war.

Americans demand far too little from their public figures in the way of principled dedication to the public interest. Opportunism, called "practical politics," is built into our political processes, as in the nominating procedures for Presidential candidates and the log-rolling and other debilitating techniques for getting bills passed. This opportunism is encouraged by the willingness of large sections of the "left" and the antiwar movement to participate in farcical election campaigns by backing the "lesser evil" or by succumbing to the illusion (promoted privately by some of the candidates) that Mr. X or

Mr. Y really thinks much as the left or antiwar forces do but cannot come right out and say so. Even if the claim were true, even if other aides were not simultaneously whispering similar messages into the ears of opposing groups, what kind of rebirth could come out of such deceptions?

It is convenient for antiwar figures who supported peace candidate Johnson in 1964 to accuse him of having betrayed his promises, but everything he did after the election was foreshadowed by his August 1964 bombing of North Vietnam, not to mention public promises and commitments that he made simultaneously with his promise not to widen the war. Neither Senator McCarthy nor Senator Kennedy before his death seriously distinguished himself in the 1968 campaign from the Johnson of 1964. For example, in the television debate that took place shortly before Kennedy's assassination, Senator McCarthy defended U.S. commitments abroad, including support for the Nationalist Chinese and participation in NATO. His criticism of Johnson was not that he has maintained American troops throughout the world but that he failed to handle de Gaulle properly and thus contributed to the expulsion of U.S. troops from France.

Neither McCarthy nor Kennedy made any bones about accepting the major assumptions of America's counterrevolutionary society. They both argued openly against resistance and civil disobedience. McCarthy said over and over that one of the main purposes of his campaign was to get people to express their grievances through the ballot box and not in draft resistance or in the streets.

Similarly, when Senator Kennedy was asked shortly before his death whether he favored amnesty for draft violators, he said no. When this got an unfavorable response from his youthful audience, he made a cheap and inaccurate appeal to white guilt, saying that black people bear the burdens of war without complaining and that white students must learn to accept their responsibilities with equal dedication.

Kennedy and McCarthy are not shoddy as our public figures go. In fact, both of them are clearly a cut above most of our country's political officeholders, men such as Johnson, Rusk, Eastland, Russell, Dirksen, or Ford. But neither represents a break with the fundamental economic or political assumptions of our society or with the accepted tactics of political expediency. In the short run a politician seems to get more done by playing according to the present rules and the rest of us seem to accomplish more by backing men like McCarthy and the late Robert Kennedy. But in the end the things that get done turn out to be tokenism. The series of reforms secured by such methods, from the New Deal of Franklin D. Roosevelt to the Alliance for Progress of John F. Kennedy and the Great Society of Lyndon B. Johnson, have left the cancerous core of our society untouched. The cumulative result is the kind of society we now have, with its blood sacrifices in Vietnam, its poverty and repression in the ghettos, and its lack of reverence for human life which is dramatically reflected in the recent assassinations.

It seems to me, then, that we need to face up to the implications of public violence in a far more meaningful way than concentrating on the passage of gun-control legislation or rallying behind Senator McCarthy. Our task is to analyze, expose, repudiate, and take direct action against the violent institutions that poison our society at home and find their natural extension and intensification in U.S. attempts to impose its way of life on the rest of the world.

There are no panaceas for eliminating man's inhumanity to man, but must we not begin to experiment with concrete ways of institutionalizing reverence for life? Must we not do this even if the new institutions conflict with our present institutionalized reverence for profit, property and privilege?

The Poor People's Campaign has gone beyond Senators McCarthy and Robert Kennedy in recognizing the necessity for extra-legal direct action by the victims of this society, but it has not gone nearly far enough in its institutional assessments and demands. Although it has paved the way for a more far-reaching program by its repeated insistence on the primacy of human needs over the established prerogatives of government bureaucracies and private corporations, it tends always to fall back into pressure for increased handouts rather than for the more basic institutional changes that are required. *Le Monde* (Paris) sums up this shortcoming as follows:

> The underlying thesis . . . is that poverty is functionally an error, perpetuated by prejudice and selfishness but rectifiable with a little goodwill and some judicious reapportionment of funds. How could one imagine, in effect,

that [poverty] can be the natural by-product of the most dynamic and prosperous system on earth? . . . Unfortunately, the problem is more complicated.

Perhaps it is not really all that complicated—at least in conception. One can reject the notion that superficial goodwill and reapportionment of funds can solve our problems (so long as private profit and corporate power continue to be the mainsprings of our society) and still propose alternatives which are so simple that any child (or uncorrupted adult) can grasp them. For example, I propose tackling the problem simultaneously with three complementary programs: 1) making a direct reduction of the income gap; 2) supplying the basic necessities of life free; and 3) introducing the principle of participatory democracy.

1. *Reducing the income gap.* There is no justification in an advanced technological money-society such as the United States for allowing anyone to have less money than that required for a basic standard of minimal decency. There is no justification for allowing some to spend tens of thousands on conspicuous consumption and luxury items while others cannot afford rat poison or milk. So long as we allow payments for welfare or wages that are below even the government's figures for minimal decency, we are insulting and wounding millions of persons. So long as we tolerate economic institutions and customs which encourage others to live in selfish privilege, we are depriving them of real self-respect and human solidarity. With the tremendous powers possessed by private corporations to rig prices, write off expenses and pad incomes, even an adequate minimum guaranteed annual income means little without a balancing maximum. As long ago as the late 1930s, Franklin Roosevelt suggested a maximum allowable income of $25,000. One of the signs of hope in the newer Communist countries (most notably Cuba and Vietnam) is that on the one hand they supply more basic items free than the older Communist countries and on the other hand they have kept the income gap smaller. For purposes of discussion, I propose a minimum income guarantee of $6,500 for a family of four, and a maximum income of $15,000, also for a family of four. As necessities are put on the free list, the amounts can be reduced accordingly.

2. *Supplying necessities free.* The principle could be established by starting with such obvious necessities as food, clothing,

housing, medical care, funerals, and education throughout life. These should be taken completely out of the money economy and furnished to every human being as a basic right of being (and staying) alive. The list could be extended gradually to include travel, recreation, electricity, telephone, etc.

3. *Participatory democracy.* As in the other two areas, this requires experimenting administratively, but it is clear that political democracy means little if it merely gives us the right to elect people to rule over us and make the decisions that control our lives. In practice huge areas of our lives are controlled by political appointees who are answerable only to government officials, who are themselves only remotely accountable to people through elections that are dominated by the power of the two established parties (patronage, government contracts, discriminatory election procedures, access to funds, etc.). Insofar as possible, grass-roots democracy should be introduced into the various functional groupings which affect the quality of our daily lives—the school, the university, the residential area, the economic enterprises, etc.

These programs represent up-to-date applications of the principles of democracy which are enshrined in our national rhetoric but are vitiated by our failure to apply them to the economic sphere. They restore the primacy of man over property. All three programs express reverence for life, putting a higher value on the life and development of each individual than on the entrenched rights of groups and classes who currently have disproportionate access to money, privilege and power.

These comments are not meant to minimize the responsibility of the left to search its own soul concerning tactics and methods of struggle. The left, too, is weakened and corrupted when it fails to extend reverence for life consistently to include the lives and dignity of all human beings, including those who profit from or defend the status quo. A distinction has to be made between the indefensible privileges of dehumanized society (such as power over the lives of others and the privilege of living in luxury while others starve) and the basic right of every human being to life, dignity and as much liberty and pursuit of happiness as does not interfere with the similar rights of anyone else.

An Integrated Peace Walk
Through Georgia

I

1964 On November 9, 1963, the Quebec-Washington-Guantanamo walkers were brutally assaulted by police officials and representatives of the Georgia Bureau of Investigation in Griffin, Georgia, for insisting on their right to give leaflets to Negroes. On November 19, they were arrested (but not otherwise abused) in Macon for distributing leaflets in violation of an unconstitutional and erratically enforced local ordinance against leafleting. On November 23, less than twenty-four hours after the assassination of President Kennedy, they were released from jail because local authorities felt that they could not be responsible for their continued safety, in view of the notion, current in Macon at the time, that both the assassin and the walkers were "pro-Castro Communists." Within a few hours of their release, the walkers left for Atlanta because of indications that their continued presence in Macon might provoke an attack on the church or home of the courageous black minister who had given them hospitality. The Walk was suspended for two weeks, in order to give the walkers a chance to take stock of the situation and the residents and officials of southwestern Georgia a chance to settle down.

During the two-week period of analysis and discussion, six of the twenty-two walkers decided to leave the project for a variety of personal and philosophical reasons. Differences in emphasis that would be minor under other circumstances loomed larger when every day brought the risk of brutality or death. As one of the departing members put it, "I am willing to face death for my views on peace, but I am not prepared to die just yet for insisting on my right to walk through the towns of Georgia with Negroes and carrying signs against racial discrimination."

"This is a new phase in the development of a realistic American pacifism," Brad Lyttle, coordinator of the Walk, told me on the phone. "This is the first peacetime project I know of which is losing participants because of the danger of death." Ominous as these words were, they carried a challenge to anyone interested in developing the kind of nonviolence which can both bring about and defend economic and social revolution. I had been planning to spend a few days with the Walk some time during its journey through the South, as a small gesture of solidarity and support, so I decided to join it for the resumption of activities in Macon and, if we made it that far, until the Walk got through Americus, the city which had vowed to "get any outsiders for anything [we] can get them for until they find out they're not wanted here."

As we walked along the highways and through the towns of southwest Georgia, I came to feel that we were engaged in a strange, nonviolent, guerrilla-type operation behind enemy lines and in territory that was occupied and technically controlled by the enemy but only partially hostile. And, as I shall point out, even our bitterest opponents seemed somewhat demoralized and unsure of themselves when confronted with our strongest weapons. Like the guerrillas and saboteurs of the Central Intelligence Agency, the Army's Special Forces, and other government agencies, our job was to destroy the enemies' defenses and weaken their will to resist. But instead of treachery, secrecy and deception, we relied on friendliness, openness and honesty. Instead of the assassin's knife, the sniper's bullet, and the kit of explosives and flammables, we carried our signs, our leaflets, and our obviously unarmed and vulnerable bodies. We did not know how to kill with our bare hands or paralyze with a sudden blow (as they teach in the armed forces). We had only been trained to cover our genitals, to go limp, or to fall on top of a prone comrade who was being kicked. Instead of lurking in the shadows and working at night, we walked into the main squares in the middle of the day. We sent advance teams to contact the police chiefs and mayors, the sheriffs, ministers and editors, not with money or offers of favors in the future, when the tables might be turned, but with sympathy for their dilemma and the message that although our integrated team might be beaten, shot or arrested (fates with which we were continually threatened), we would not turn back. We were only twenty men and women, inexperienced, poorly trained, and sometimes afraid. But one night when we attended a mass rally of Negroes for civil rights, we heard the speaker say that the twenty unarmed peace walkers had shaken the state of Georgia and unnerved and confounded the whole power structure. And our experiences had been such that we knew that what he said was at least partially true.

In Macon, I relearned the lesson that I had learned in Birmingham last spring: that though the South may be occupied and run by racial bigots, it is not entirely subjugated by them. There were only a few overtly friendly words by whites, but as I scanned the faces and studied the reactions of the noonday crowds, I could see that most of the people took us in their stride. To my surprise, I felt less hostility than I have felt, on occasion, on peace demonstrations in New York, Jersey City, New London, Chicago, or a half dozen other Northern cities. Of course there were some like the man who screamed at us in a near-apoplectic rage: "I hope you go to Americus, because if you do they will beat you to death." But his words and his obvious frustration seemed, in part at least, to indicate that he realized that in Macon the mood of the people was not one to tolerate such barbarism. Yet, as I glanced ahead of me in the line, I saw that our Walk was led by a Negro (Ray Robinson) and that directly between him and me were a white woman (Erica Enzer) and another Negro (Carl Arnold, a former S.N.C.C. worker who had joined the project in Atlanta).

In addition to this provocative arrangement, we carried signs with such comprehensive slogans as: "Demand Free Trade with Cuba," "Abolish All Racial Discrimination," "Freedom NOW," "We Advocate Unilateral Disarmament," etc. I thought of the difference between our approach and that advocated by some of my friends in peace groups which sometimes seem more concerned with maintaining a soothing public image than with presenting clear-cut and deeply challenging alternatives to present policies. I could almost hear them saying: "If you insist on advocating integration on a peace walk through the South, at least put it in a framework the people will understand. Say something like 'Be Patriotic: Extend Democratic Rights to All Citizens,' or 'Strengthen America's Image Abroad: Let Everyone Vote.'" Yet just behind me was Dennis Weeks, who is limping through the South on a bad foot (he couldn't even run away if he wanted to) and insisting each day on carrying a sign which said "Refuse to Serve in the Armed Forces." And from time to time there were indications that it was the very radical quality of our message (its purity, if you will) and our refusal to temporize or hedge which won us a strange kind of respect.

The greatest fear (and therefore the greatest hatred) often seems to come in response to the unknown, particularly when there is a suspicion that there are things being concealed or held back. (Through the years I have learned that rightists often have an uncanny understanding of the full implications of a liberal position, penetrating to meanings which liberals often nervously conceal from themselves: such as the fact that you can't integrate the schools and the churches without having interracial marriages follow as inevitably as rivers flow into the sea.) We got everything basic out into the open right away, in our signs, our literature, and our advance negotiations, and on a number of occasions we found that this gave people the feeling (as Americus Police Chief Ross W. Chamblis said to me) that we were "aboveboard" and therefore could be trusted. And who will listen to you if he feels he cannot trust your integrity? Instead of spending their time gossiping about our hidden beliefs— or triumphantly accusing us of holding views (such as refusal to serve in the armed forces) which, by implication at least, were so indefensible that even we were ashamed to acknowledge them publicly —they seemed baffled and, on occasion, even touched by the simplicity of our message and approach. What more could they accuse us of? Had we not volunteered the "worst"? And when our most extreme views were held up positively in the light of day (and without any troops or weapons to confuse matters), did they perhaps see some resemblance between what we were advocating and some of the words that are read to them in church, some of the ideals that are espoused, in an abstract way, in their newspapers, school books and civic gatherings?

More than once I saw a group of toughs advance menacingly toward us and become paralyzed, as it were, when Edie Snyder, Kit Havice, Barbara Deming, Yvonne Klein or Michele Gloor ran to

meet them with an unbelievably cheery and disarming greeting:
"Good morning, sir, would you like to read about our walk?" or
"Hello there. How are you this morning?" I couldn't help feeling
sorry for some of them. They started out all fire and brimstone, with
clenched fists and angry faces, but became utterly bewildered as our
line passed them cheerfully by, most of us with a friendly word or a
wave, and always with the friendly forward movement of our girls.
If we had hesitated in fright or snarled back at them, tried to escape
down a side street or told the girls not to cross the road to meet them,
they would have known what to do to us. But we never accepted their
choice of weapons or their mood, and a few times I saw grown men
run back to take shelter in their houses or in stores as the girls moved
relentlessly toward them.

Not everyone was transformed, of course. And no doubt the
fact that we were only passing through helped. A longer sojourn in
any one town might have given the extremists time to regroup their
forces, regain their nerve, and demolish us. And, of course, you could
never tell when it might happen anyway. Once I was struck sharply
by small stones thrown from a passing car that paused only long
enough to discharge its weapons. Others were hit with pecans. An
enraged man spat in Michele Gloor's face (though I think he would
rather have led a charge against the men, but could not rally his gang
to join in). Irving Klein, who came to visit his wife for a few days,
was kicked from behind. From time to time cars played chicken with
us on the highway, charging down the shoulder to see who would
move aside first, we or they. (The only time I was really frightened
was when one of the Sumter County sheriff's cronies, a man who had
been unable to provoke me into a fight outside the sheriff's office in
Americus and had stormed angrily away, returned on two later occasions to play chicken with us. One time he gunned the accelerator
and swerved sharply toward me. The car brushed my jacket and left
me shaking. Perhaps he was unnerved too, because he didn't come
back again.) But the fact remains that almost every day we were told
(by friend and foe alike) that we would never get through the next
town, the next county, or the next crossroad—and yet, unbelievably,
we did.

I have said that it was like operating behind enemy lines. Another analogy that came to mind as we walked along was that it was

as if we were walking through territory that had been mined. So much was pleasant, easy and inspiring, but we never knew at what point our next step might set off an explosion. (I had just been reflecting happily on the power of nonviolence when the sheriff's crony nearly ran me down.) As Barbara Deming said to me, "It's a strange situation. You have to be alert every moment. Every day when you start out you know that you may all come home triumphantly or that three or four people may be shot." I thought of what John Stephens had said to me the night before: "This afternoon I heard a ping in the bank beside me, and the sound of a rifle being fired." "Why in the world didn't you say something?" I asked. "It wouldn't have done any good," he replied. "Besides, if I had mentioned it a lot of people would have tried to take over my position at the end of the line. Most everyone tries to take the most dangerous spot."

I think that it was this sense of solidarity and mutual aid among the walkers, as well as the success of our experiments in nonviolence, that buoyed us up when the going got rough. But most inspiriting of all was the reaction of the Negroes.

If we were traveling behind enemy lines, we were nonetheless surrounded by friends. These friends held no offices, commanded no troops, and could not have lifted a finger, or even raised their voices, to protect us without running the risk of being shot. Many of them lived in wretched huts that seemed to defy the laws of physics by remaining upright, let alone housing so many occupants. Yet they had only to say a few words or to look at us, in the untranslatable language of love, to communicate a mysterious power that has eluded men who have conquered kingdoms or amassed fortunes, won elections or attained academic prestige.

The day before we entered Peach County, the sheriff told us that we would be arrested if we tried to hand out leaflets in what he called "my county." The same day we heard a story that was told to us repeatedly during the following days. Two weeks earlier, two white officials had been beating a Negro in the county jail. When he resisted, one of them shot and killed him. No charges were filed against the murderer, since it was decided that he had fired in self-defense.

We distributed our leaflets for two days in Peach County and were not arrested. There were times when cars filled with white men drove out to meet us, and then drove back and forth beside us, at a snail's pace, ominously glaring and never uttering a word. The sheriff kept close to us all the way,* screaming imprecations, harassing our drivers and angrily honking his horn and waving his arms in attempts to frighten away anyone who might speak to us or take leaflets. Yet, amazingly, Negroes *did* take leaflets and call friendly greetings as they emerged from their shacks or paused in their work. Others looked at our black and white group, read our signs, and stood transfixed, as if they were seeing a miracle in Peach County. Once two Negro women in a car stopped and with great dignity handed a dollar bill to one of the walkers. Later, when we were passing through Fort Valley, chief metropolis of the county, they returned and threw another half dollar to us in full view of the assembled populace. I think everyone in Fort Valley stopped what he was doing to watch us. Many Negroes took leaflets or came forward to offer words of encouragement. A few whites—some friendly, others noncommittal—took leaflets; many cursed. The police department was both polite and cooperative.

Just south of Peach County lies the small town of Marshallville, which we walked through on a Sunday morning. When we came to the main intersection, fifteen or twenty angry men eluded close contact with our leafleters by standing in front of the corner filling station-store while the owner, backed by two policemen, ordered the girls to stay off his property. Barbara and Yvonne advanced gingerly and with their usual friendliness but could not break down the men's defenses. But two Negroes (out of a group of half a dozen) courageously took leaflets a few feet away.

Then we turned onto a magnificent avenue lined with stately Southern mansions, huge trees and well-kept lawns. A police car and an official county car accompanied us. We came to a church, with a couple of white men standing outside. The police ordered Barbara to "keep moving," but she walked toward the men, holding out a leaflet, until they beat a frantic retreat toward the church, where they apparently felt they would achieve greater peace of mind. (Later, four open-faced and friendly white teenagers from the church drove out to see us, asked for leaflets, and came back two more times. I reflected on

---

* *Was it my imagination or did he soften a little during the three days —two of walking and one of advance negotiations—we confronted each other? There was no question that his words and manner became less violent, but was he impressed or simply exhausted?*

the fact that several of us had been turned in a radical direction by taking the teachings of Jesus seriously when exposed to them in church at an early age. I wondered if our leaflets and signs would help these boys to see new meanings in the scriptures.)

At the very end of the luxurious avenue, perched precariously on top of a mud bank, was a wretched shack, outpost of an impoverished Negro settlement and the only Negro house to front on the highway. Standing together on the ramshackle steps, erect, motionless, and in rags, were seven or eight Negroes, apparently a mother and her children, mostly teenagers. The police car drove ahead and, characteristically, stopped directly in front of the house. As Michele turned to mount the bank, one of the policemen jumped out to restrain her and then, thinking better of it, drew back. "Don't go up there," he said. (The line of march stopped, as it generally did in such situations.) The Negroes remained motionless, like an inspired statuary. "This is those people's property," Michele replied gently, "and if they want a leaflet, I want to give them one." "If they wanted a leaflet, they would have come down to get one," the policeman replied. Michele hesitated, advanced slightly, hesitated again. For a long time no one moved or spoke, not the Negroes (who had not moved perceptibly since we first saw them), not Michele, the policeman, or the silent walkers. Then there was a slight movement, and with infinite grace a girl of perhaps fourteen slowly detached herself from the group, walked down the bank, and took a leaflet. A moment later, a slightly older girl did the same. We moved on.

After we had walked ahead a short distance, we realized that the police car had not left the house and that the county car had joined it. We stopped walking and turned back to face the house. After several minutes, the cops' car drove toward us and we resumed walking. Soon it turned around and went back to the house. Once again we stopped, but now we were too far away to observe clearly. A third car and then a fourth pulled up in front of the house. What should we do? To go back unnecessarily might endanger the courageous Negroes by precipitating a riot. Yet we could not abandon them either. We kept facing in their direction, and edged slightly toward them. We thought we could see that the family group was still standing in place, that no one had gotten out of the cars. Were the whites after all just watching us from a good vantage point, or were they lecturing the Negroes? Were they waiting for us to leave before seizing or attacking them? Did we have a right to subject the Negroes to such perils by inviting them to take our leaflets?

After a seemingly interminable five or ten minutes, two cars came out of the Negro section, passed the little group, and drove out to meet us. The police car followed them and parked adjacent to them. Two well-dressed Negroes got out of each car. They were neighbors of the first family, had observed the scene, and had come out to get leaflets themselves. They assured us that no one had been arrested or attacked. We gave them the phone number where we would be staying that night and urged them to call us if there was any trouble so that we could come back to picket, as well as rally outside help. After warm words of mutual friendship, they drove back and we went on. We never heard anything further from them.

Brad Lyttle and I went to see the authorities in Americus a week before the Walk was due to arrive there. Local integrationists warned that we might be attacked or arrested as soon as we were recognized. We stopped at a supermarket to buy some bread and fruit. (The Walk makes it a practice not to patronize segregated establishments; all the restaurants in downtown Americus are segregated.) As we were leaving, an elderly man approached us, asked a few preliminary questions, and then started shouting at the top of his voice: "There's gonna be a big KLAN meeting Tuesday; are you going?" We said that we were not planning to. "Why not?" he thundered triumphantly. "We don't usually attend Klan meetings," Brad replied, somewhat lamely, and added: "We don't support the Klan." "There's gonna be an N.A.A.P.C. *(sic)* meeting Monday. I suppose you're going to that," the man roared, obviously trying to attract as much attention as possible. There were not many people in the streets, but those who did pass within earshot during perhaps fifteen minutes of loud and provocative discussion ignored us.

There were many indications that the average white Southerner is no more anxious to take part in mob violence than most people, that the majority of them are distressed by the brutality that has been exacerbated by the demagogy of traditionalist politicians, the inevitable and long delayed upsurge of the Negro, and the employment by the authorities of the methods by which police have traditionally resisted law-breakers and determined opponents of the *status quo.* On the Walk, and in other demonstrations in the South, we have learned that violence is more apt to be instigated or carried out by the police than allayed or prevented by them. When the authorities decide that they will not tolerate violence, it usually does not occur. But there is a moral vacuum created by the reluctance of the "decent" people to come out positively for integration, to identify with the exploited and persecuted, to open themselves to charges of being "nigger-lovers" and "Communists."

These people are in the unpleasant position of having either to embrace new ideas and make personal sacrifices for them (primarily loss of prestige and of economic or political advancement) or abandon the Negro to the brutalities of the fanatics, with god-knows-what ultimate outcome. (I was constantly reminded of my visits to Germany in the thirties, when the silent, decent people had no idea that Nazism would attain the momentum that it did—and I thought back to how decent Americans had also kept silent, until it was too late, and had refused to do away with the immigration quotas that kept most Jews from finding asylum here.) Our group visited white ministers who expressed sympathy for our project but lowered their voices when they heard the sound of approaching footsteps. After listening to our overtures, one civic leader sighed: "I came from Indiana twenty-three years ago," which was, in the context, clearly an indirect way of indicating his disapproval of "Southern" attitudes. But he would hardly utter a word beyond that. Americus and Albany, Marshallville and Fort Valley, reminded me not only of Munich and Berlin in the thirties, but also of universities I have attended and towns I have lived in, in the North. The social customs and the issues—and the extent of the violence—vary from place to place, but the moral climate is not that different. How many in the North are ready to risk advancement or jeopardize their freedom in order to take on the crushing burdens of economic inferiority and ghettoization off the Negro—or for that matter to resist the country's reliance on nuclear annihilation? And when from time to time I saw members of our own group wilt a little under pressure—or when I nervously dodged a potentially embarrassing question myself, after I had left the group and was alone and afraid in Atlanta—I realized that the utter lack of self-righteousness with which we must seek to build bridges of understanding with our confused and beleaguered white Southern brothers is more than good tactics. It is a simple recognition of the facts. But it would be a mistake to think that the way to be nonviolent—i.e., the way to avoid pharisaism and to reach out in the deepest kind of friendship—is to pretend, under pressure, that one doesn't believe that the Negro is as abused as he is, or to accept tokenism.

It took us a long time to communicate to Police Chief Ross Chamblis that we stood unequivocally for integration, nonviolence, and the right of the Walk to parade and leaflet in Americus, and yet did not fall into the Southerner's stereotype of Northern agitators who condemn all white Southerners out of hand and are more interested in stirring up trouble than in helping solve problems. If the chief had been a lesser man, we might not have succeeded. And I suppose we would not have made it at all a year or two earlier, before the terrible sacrifices made by the S.N.C.C. organizers and the local Negroes, and the rising pressures from outside sources (belated and inadequate as the outside response has been). At the beginning, the chief made it emphatically clear that we would be arrested: 1) if we marched with signs, with more than two persons in a city block; 2) if we tried to hand out leaflets in the "fire zone" (the entire business district of Americus); and 3) if we "allowed" any local Negroes to join us. When we left an hour and a half later, it seemed that we might be able to parade with signs, but that the last two prohibitions were absolute and final. More importantly, we had come to like the chief, and he did not seem as frightened of us as he had been at the beginning.

We had two more conferences with Chief Chamblis before the Walk arrived in Americus, as well as a number of discussions with civic and religious leaders. (We walked only twelve to fifteen miles a day, using the rest of the time to plan or prepare our attack.) The chief's final statement to us was that he could not permit us to hand out leaflets in the "fire zone" but that we appeared to be upright men and he thought we might be able to get through Americus without serious trouble. There was no way of telling what the outcome of these enigmatic words would be.

Meanwhile we had made two visits to the Sumter County sheriff's office, which appeared to be a hangout for local toughs. The sheriff emphasized that he did not want to hear anything about the Walk, that he would not protect us, and (addressing himself more to the local men than to us) that he didn't care what anyone would do to us when we got into Sumter County: he would make it a point to be elsewhere. We quickly pointed out that we did not want protection. "You yellow-livered Communist," a big man shouted at me, at this point. "You got no guts." When I turned to address him, he screamed indignantly: "Take your eyes off me!" During the approximately ten minutes we managed to stay in the office without being arrested or mobbed (and another five minutes of jostling and threats outside), we did our best to convince them, by holding our ground as firmly and gently as we could, that we would indeed be glad to accept their invitation to meet them when we crossed the county line.

We crossed the Sumter County line about ten miles outside Americus. After a while there began the procession of slowly moving cars and silent occupants that was always more foreboding than threats and gestures. At least one of the cars was full of men from the sheriff's office. But the day ended without incident. The following morning, we walked into Americus, accompanied by a heavy contingent of policemen who stopped automobile traffic for us and did not interfere with our leafleting. Most of the whites glared at us from behind glass doors and windows, as if we were carriers of some dread contagious disease. But I was surprised at the number of whites, even here, who managed to wave pleasantly or take leaflets. At a garage, two whites refused leaflets and the Negro grease monkey accepted one. As I looked back out of the corner of my eye, I saw one of the whites walk over to the Negro, take the leaflet from his unresisting hands, and tear it up. I smarted at the indignity. But we knew that virtually every Negro in the vicinity of Americus had already received our leaflet, through the good agencies of the Sumter County Movement.

As we reached the city limits, I crossed the highway, shook hands with Chief Chamblis, and exchanged words of mutual respect with him. At the end of the day, as I was packing my bags to go home, I asked Clarence Jordan (at nearby Koinonia Farm, which had provided us with heartwarming hospitality) if he thought that the chief would suffer politically from having dealt with us as he did. "I don't think so," Clarence replied. "A lot of white people are fed up with the way things have been going, but they don't know how to make a fresh start. I think that they will applaud him for having acted intelligently."

II

After the Walk proceeded safely through Americus, where we had expected the worst trouble, I returned North to my job. A few days later, the walkers were arrested in Albany (Georgia) for trying to carry signs and distribute leaflets in the downtown area. The arrest was met with a hunger strike on the part of the imprisoned walkers. The hunger strike lasted twenty-eight days before the walkers were released from jail (with no assurances as to whether or not they would be allowed to carry out their original plan of walking through downtown Albany with signs and leaflets).

Midway through this first Albany imprisonment, I flew back to Georgia, where I worked outside jail for a week trying to rally outside support. Then I picketed the jail, was roughed up, arrested and spent eight days in jail, fasting with the others. After a week's recuperation, the walkers tried to continue on their original route and were arrested a second time, with most of them resuming their hunger strike. I returned to Albany to assist them again. This time I was joined by A. J. Muste and together we worked to rally white and black support among the residents of Albany. It is from this perspective that the following analysis was written, shortly after an agreement was reached that led to the release of the walkers. Permission was secured to parade and leaflet the contested areas, but with the compromise arrangement that only the first four marchers would carry signs, though everyone leafleted.

No victory, such as the very real victory of the peace walkers in Albany, Georgia, can be properly assessed without considering its psychological effects on the community, not just the impact of the breakthrough itself, but the psychological changes that took place as a result of the way in which the day-to-day struggle was carried on. The first lesson of Albany is that nonviolence has the power to win tangible victories against seemingly overwhelming odds, if its practitioners are prepared to make almost limitless sacrifices. Not a pretty picture—that one must be prepared to go to the lengths the peace walkers did in order to make a concrete breakthrough. But the daily cruelties that the Negro suffers are not pretty either, and tangible victories have been all too rare, at any price. So this aspect of the struggle at Albany is rightly being celebrated, and I myself cannot say enough for the determination and courage of those who carried through the struggle in jail or for the significance of the breakthrough they finally achieved. A black leader of the Albany Movement asserted that "the actions of the peace walkers restored my wavering faith in man." Marion Page, executive secretary of the Movement, said, "This is the first crack in the rock of Gibraltar and I have always understood that the first crack is the important one." C. B. King, brilliant and courageous Negro attorney, said, "The city yielded far more than I ever thought possible."

The lessons to be learned from the daily conduct of the struggle are obviously more complicated and subject to a variety of interpretations. Personally, I came away from Albany newly aware of the fact that it would be possible to carry on such a struggle, use all the techniques of nonviolence that were employed (civil disobedience, refusal to pay bond, long-term fasting, supporting demonstrations, publicity, mailings, and negotiations), perhaps even win a substantial "victory"—and yet leave the situation worse than at the beginning. For despite the importance of making the first hole in the dike which had kept all demonstrators south of Oglethorpe Avenue, the key questions for the future are the readiness of others to pour through that hole and the willingness of the more enlightened members of the white community to prevent its being forcibly closed again. And behind the symbolic hole in the dike are the actual changes that must be made in the structure and relationships of Albany. Unless at least a partial breakthrough in human understanding accompanies whatever tangible breakthroughs are made, progress will be very short-lived.

The greatest danger, I think, is that of approaching the conflict in terms of a stereotyped struggle between the forces of righteousness and the forces of evil, with insufficient recognition of the complexity of motives and rationalizations on both sides. It has been said that the difference between the method of violence and that of nonviolence is that violence shoots the opponent and nonviolence converts him. But our understanding of life is too limited to justify the presumption that the goal of nonviolence is to convert our opponent, at least to our exact way of thinking. Let me give two examples from relations not with an opponent but with an ally.

Once, during the brief period I was in jail, I woke up from a nap to hear a conversation between one of the white walkers, in an adjoining cell, and C. B. King, visiting Negro attorney, which made me wonder at first if I was not having a nightmare. The walker was saying: "The greatest evil in Albany is the Air Force base. Militarism threatens far more people than segregation." Statistically, no doubt he was correct. But, as King pointed out, "When you are down in a ditch with someone's foot on your neck, you can't respond to some other evil the same way you might if you were free. You are more apt to say, 'Help me get this man's foot off my neck, and then we can face up to the other evil together.' "

Later, one of the walkers, in an excess of enthusiasm, sent a note from jail to A. J. Muste and me, saying that we must tell the Negro leaders that the time had come for them to take action. "Tell them they must be prepared to be arrested, to refuse to pay bond, and to fast while in jail." A. J. said to me (only half facetiously, I think), "Burn that note before it falls into the wrong hands." Anyway, we never issued the prophetic call to righteousness, since the Negroes, who have to live with the white problem every day of their lives and have displayed unparalleled perseverance and courage, had only recently recovered from the feeling that a few of the walkers were trying to push them into a conflict neither the time nor the terms of which were in accord with their own timetable and agenda.

If the intensity of one's feelings, in the midst of a protracted and painful struggle, can lead one to become insensitive to the complexity of the situation in which one's allies find themselves, how much easier it is to turn one's opponents into cardboard representations of evil, and thus approach them with a maddening self-righteousness that merely stiffens their resistance and blocks their openness to new understanding. I don't think that one should equivocate about the extent of the evils—in this case segregation and the police state—but one must try to understand the position in which the liberal white finds himself. In a struggle like that at Albany, I think it was virtually impossible to communicate with some of the officials, though it was important to keep trying and perhaps to make some minor dents in their psychological defenses. Anything honorable that we did was bound to be anathema to them, and their chief frustration was that politics and the threat of publicity made it impossible for them to shoot us or beat us to death, as they would have done in the good old days—and as they still do to Negroes when there is a plausible excuse, such as in the case of "suspected" criminals fleeing from the scene of a crime, or "resisting arrest." But it was both possible and of crucial importance to reach some of the other people in the community on whose support (or at least on whose silence) the officials depend for their continuation in office or for the continuation of repressive policies. And the only way we could reach these key people was to sit down with them as reasonable men, prepared to learn as well as teach, ready to acknowledge the many mistakes we had made in the course of the conflict as well as to point out some of the unpleasant realities about Albany justice that they might have preferred not to have to face up to.

It is clear that the fast has no automatic power to reach these people, no matter how long or courageously it is carried on. If they can dismiss the fast as "self-imposed," or the fasters as "fanatics," they can go about their business with a clear conscience while the fasters suffer indefinitely, perhaps even die. This is what happened in Albany for many, many weeks. During this time the white community was filled with stories that convinced almost everyone that the walkers were self-seeking, unreasonable, or worse. Many of these stories originated with the police and were made up out of whole cloth. Others stemmed from some error in judgment on the part of one or more of the prisoners, such as the ruckus some of them raised on several occasions (at least once at 3 A.M.) to demand that a doctor be summoned for an ailing faster, who, when the doctor finally arrived, refused, "as a matter of principle," to cooperate with him. But whether true or false these stories have to be faced up to and discussed as honestly as possible with that important part of the white community that is trying to operate on the basis of conscience and enlightened community interest. It is a terrible mistake to dismiss the entire white community, in Albany or any other Southern city, as monolithic, thereby reducing the struggle to a nonviolent power play, relieved only by moralistic attempts to bring about a few dramatic conversions from among the forces of evil.* Perhaps the beginning of the real breakthrough at Albany took place when Barbara Deming made an enlightened plea for understanding, in court, and her statement, along with a letter by Kit Havice which showed obvious common sense and compassion, was circulated in the white community. Circulation of these statements, combined with community visita-

---

* *I found a tendency on the part of some to interpret occasional acts of kindness by police and other authorities as striking proofs of "conversions." I think this indicated a failure to recognize that these men, in their own minds, had moral justifications for almost everything they did, and, just as they were capable of unbearable cruelty when they considered it justified, were also capable, under other circumstances, of showing genuine sympathy and kindness. In any case, some of the men who were thought to have been "converted" later returned to their former actions.*

tions by A. J. Muste, Arthur Evans, James Bristol, and others, made it more difficult for conscientious white leaders to evade the fundamental challenge which the peace walkers had been raising all along but which had been largely obscured.

It's hard to call for understanding of the white community without seeming to call for weakness and compromise. I am sure that what normally passes for such understanding will accomplish little unless it is accompanied by an equally perceptive understanding of the desperate plight of the Negro community. In other words, the understanding that is needed must be accompanied by action, not become a substitute for it. In the end, it was the accomplishment of the peace walkers in Albany to combine resolute action with humility and openness to human interchange. And it is my view that the ferocity of their fast and the efficiency of their techniques would have gone for naught but for the gentleness of spirit which, for the most part, went along with these things.

Ten Days in Jail

The law, in its majestic equality, forbids the rich as well as the poor to sleep under bridges, to beg, and to steal bread.

Anatole France

I

1961 People generally laugh when I mention that I went from Yale to jail and that I got a more vital education from three years in jail than from six years at Yale. The laugh always makes me a little uneasy (even apart from the feebleness of the play on words) because I am afraid it implies that far from being dead serious I am merely indulging in a humorous exaggeration, since one wouldn't really expect to learn more in prison than in a university. A little reflection should convince most persons that one can learn more about the nature of our society by sharing in a small way the life of its victims than by interacting intellectually with its privileged academicians. Be that as it may, I spent ten days in jail recently and had my complacency jolted once again (nonconformists can be more complacent than we realize) and my imagination quickened by this little refresher course in the realities that lie behind the facade of our society.

I have never forgotten my first experience of arrest and imprisonment many years ago: how inexorably the transitions took place from being treated as "saints ahead of our time" (a comment by a member of the grand jury that indicted eight of us for our refusal, as pacifists, to register for the draft); to misguided and stubborn idealists (the attitude of the judge); to criminals with "no rights of any kind" who had better wise up if we wanted to stay in one piece (as we were told by a guard five minutes after being ushered out of the polite and superficially civil-libertarian atmosphere of the courtroom into the prison world into which no visitors are admitted and from which no uncensored letters are released). If the details varied slightly this time, the pattern was similar: only when we were safely out of sight of judge and spectators were the realities of the prison system revealed to us.

My recent arrest grew out of a "vigil" outside the Central Intelligence Agency headquarters in Washington, D.C.* where ten of us picketed, handed out leaflets, and began a two-week fast (taking only water) in protest against the invasion of Cuba and to help forestall future invasions. About a hundred persons joined us for a brief supporting stint the first afternoon and nearly two hundred and fifty were on hand the final day, but in between, when the numbers were less, we soon found that some of the police were not above a selective enforcement of the law. When Bob Steed, of the *Catholic Worker,* sat down to rest a few hundred feet from the vigil line on some concrete steps that led to a nearby Veteran's Hospital, one of the policemen hurried over and ordered him to move, under threat of arrest. When Bob pointed out that other people were sitting on the steps, the policeman retorted: "It doesn't matter. As long as you are connected with that project *you* can't sit here." Another time, when some of us sat in a parked car for a few minutes we were told that we must drive away or be arrested for vagrancy. On this occasion the police failed to follow through on their threat, but the next day we were not so fortunate. After three days of fasting, seven of us decided to sit for a while on a narrow grass strip between the sidewalk and the wire fence that encloses the C.I.A. buildings. We chose this spot not

* *C.I.A. headquarters have since been moved to Langley, Va.*

only because of its strategic location but also because we had seen passersby sit there without interference. No matter, we were ordered to move, and arrested when we refused to do so.

Those who engage in nonviolent demonstrations are not always allowed to decide for themselves whether or not the project will include civil disobedience. As the police become increasingly uncivil, the demonstrators are forced to become increasingly disobedient if they want the project to accomplish its objectives. On this occasion the object of the police was clearly to keep us as nearly invisible as possible. We were told that we could sit on the grass around the corner (where there were not so many passersby and where the relationship of our action to the C.I.A. would have been obscured) but we were arrested for sitting where we could engage in "free speech" most effectively. In court, the police admitted that we would not have been arrested for sitting around the corner and that we had been completely nonviolent, but we were convicted of disorderly conduct on the grounds that our demonstration *might have provoked other persons to violence against us.* The judge offered us a suspended sentence if we would promise not to repeat the action, but since our objective was not to preserve our own private liberty (we could have done this by staying home in the first place) but to protest public evils, we were unable to make such a deal. We chose instead to express our conviction that Americans must set aside their own personal convenience in order to act as counterweights to America's criminal foreign policy which, in Cuba, included not only economic boycott and indirect military aggression but having its spokesmen lie in their teeth about it at the United Nations.

To make clear the pattern of police dishonesty and abuse of power, even outside the prisons (in prison democratic restraints on the officials are at a minimum), let me tell what happened the day we were released from jail. We informed the police of our intention to have a poster walk the following day, with several hundred persons marching from the C.I.A. headquarters through the streets of Washington, past the White House and to the site of a mass rally. Several officials, including the acting Chief of Police, told me that we could not do this because 1) parades are not allowed without a permit (on previous occasions I had learned that permits are not usually granted for *such* parades); 2) no one is allowed to parade past the White House; and 3) our route went past several foreign embassies and no one is allowed to carry a sign within five hundred feet of an embassy. The reasons sound plausible and on a number of previous occasions peace walkers have yielded because on the one hand they believed what they were told, and on the other hand they lacked a united conviction that the seriousness of the occasion justified the disregard of local ordinances and the risk of arrest. Nonetheless I had also participated in poster walks and leaflet distributions, both in Washington and other cities, where the police had backed down when the demonstrators refused to be intimidated. I knew that earlier that very day the San Francisco-to-Moscow Peace Walkers had carried signs over part of the same route without a permit and that a thousand Quakers had been allowed to do the same, a few months earlier. After consultation with the rest of the planning committee I informed the police that we knew of these precedents and that in any case we felt that the immorality of the intervention in Cuba made it imperative for us to speak out publicly in this way, even if it meant another arrest. The police not only yielded but provided an impressive (if undesired) official escort for our "illegal" procession. Perhaps the noble old slogan "Eternal Vigilance Is the Price of Liberty" should be replaced by a more earthy, and paradoxical one, something like this: "Being ready to go to jail is the only way of remaining free."

II

> *The best prison community is no more than an extreme totalitarian society, and the most it can produce is a good convict who is quite different than a good citizen. . . . Reformation of convicts must be attained chiefly outside any penal institution.*
>
> *Encyclopaedia Britannica,*
> Article on "Prison"

Most convicts would rather serve time in an old-fashioned jail or pen than in a liberal "correctional" institution. The basic prerequisite for a decent life—freedom—is lacking in either case, but in the "reformed" institutions the prisoner finds that he is subjected, in addition, to a kind of manipulation and psychological assault that the old-fashioned warden and keepers had no interest in. I remember a Christmas at Danbury (Connecticut) "Federal Correctional Institution" when the Christmas party consisted of an exhibition of dancing and singing by the warden's young children and their classmates. When the performance was over, the warden mounted the platform and made a speech in which he kept reminding the prisoners that if they hadn't broken the law they could have been with their wives and children on Christmas Eve, as he was. Perhaps only those who have been deprived for a lengthy period of the company of wives, children, and loved ones can appreciate how cruel this little sermon was and how it embittered rather than enlightened the men. Never did I receive a half-hour visit (we were allowed a total of one hour of visits a month) without having my parents or fiancée subjected to a prior interview with the warden or a social service worker in which they were treated to a lengthy analysis of my various character defects. Wives were often told, on the basis of "scientific" case-studies, that they should divorce their husbands, or stop visiting them, because they were "no good." Censorship of reading material, "to help rehabilitate the convict," was so extreme that at one time only one New York newspaper (the *New York Times,* which appealed to the warden but not to many of the inmates) was allowed to circulate and copies of it were distributed only after every news story that dealt with crime had been cut out. When a friend sent me a copy of *The World's Great Letters,* the censorship department passed it on to me only after having deleted a letter by Benjamin Franklin which was considered "salacious." Did they really think that the inmates would have learned more about the perverse glories of crime from the *New York Times* than from their fellow inmates with whom they were joined in the common, embittering experience of living in an "extreme totalitarian society" and with whom they united in a thousand imaginative ways of "beating the system" (everything from stealing food and manufacturing a powerful prison brew to smuggling tobacco, at great personal risk, to men in the "hole")? Did they think that sexual abuse and insensitivity were more apt to result from reading a letter by Ben Franklin than from being locked up for years without contact with loved ones? If anyone had interrupted one of the jailhouse bull sessions on sex to read out loud the offending passages from Franklin he would have been hooted down for boring the audience.

The Washington, D.C. jail was an uneasy compromise between the old-fashioned jail in which confinement and the prevention of escape are almost the only concerns, and the modern paternalistic institution which tries, unrealistically, to combine confinement with rehabilitation. In the main, it succeeded in combining, in slightly modified form, the shortcomings of both types of institution and the virtues of neither. On the one hand, we were subject to classification interviews with social service workers whose sheltered, conformist lives had so limited their ability to grasp the realities of the system that it is hard to imagine their ever understanding a criminal or establishing any significant human contact with him—even if they had any interest in considering him as anything but a "case." (In the first information-gathering my name was somehow transcribed as David Dillings and a series of interviewers insisted that I must sign my name in this fashion if I did not want to go to the "hole." I suppose that in some future court appearance I shall be accused of having used an alias.) On the other hand, the daily routine was such as to encourage utter boredom, and physical and mental deterioration. We were awakened at 4:30 A.M. and spent the entire day sitting in the overcrowded chapel, without reading material, work, exercise, or diversion of any kind. The windows were even frosted to prevent looking outside. The only breaks were the three daily meals and the periodic "counts." In our case, we were continuing to fast, so benefited from the mealtimes only by having a brief respite from living in a dense crowd. There were 160 beds in my dormitory, arranged in doubledeckers so close together that if anyone lying in his bed (we were only allowed on the bed between 9:30 at night and 4:30 the next morning) stretched his arms out, he would touch the beds on both sides. I am told that the prisoners are allowed to go to the stockade for two hours on Sundays, but since it rained we watched television instead. As beautiful women and expensive status symbols were flashed on the screen, I looked at the men around me and thought that the crime of many of them was to have been hypnotized by the lures of our society and to have sought to attain them by methods which were outside the law (the ground rules of capitalist society) but not necessarily more antisocial than the accepted legal ones. In varying degrees they lacked the education, the contacts, the pigmentation, the patience, the inherited capital, or the hypocrisy to attain their goals by accepted methods of living off the labor of others—collecting rents, profits, dividends, interest or the excessive salaries of the professional and managerial classes; buying or hiring cheap and selling dear; excelling in the attractive packaging or psychologically effective advertising of an inferior product, etc. The man who pockets a cool million by speculating in slum-clearance housing or installing inadequate air-conditioning in fancy apartment houses becomes a public hero by setting up a scholarship fund or contributing to charity, but the man who sat beside me, his eyes glued to the TV screen, had "lost all his rights" because he had stolen some jewelry.

The question is, does a person ever lose his rights as a human being? Both kinds of prison operate on the assumption that he does. As I entered the D.C. jail I was greeted with the words, so familiar to me from previous experiences: "You have no rights." (In liberal institutions the advances of modern penology are summed up in the fuller phrasing: "You have no rights, only privileges.") A "good convict" is one who acquiesces in this defamation of character until he finally explodes in resentful violence or becomes a shadow of a man who is made a trusty or is considered safe to release on parole. I have seen men put in the "hole" for "silent insolence," because the system cannot function without breaking the spirit of its victims, and the light of independence in a man's eye is more frightening to the authorities than occasional violations of administrative regulations.

As pacifists we revealed at least a few signs of inner-directedness and this caused immediate tensions with the authorities. But we also tried to go out of our way to be sensitive to their human qualities, and the more contact we had with individual guards the more willing they were to overlook our minor transgressions, in apparent (if somewhat bewildered) appreciation for being treated, for a change, as fellow human beings. They were more used to opportunistic subservience, without personal respect, than to foolhardy resistance combined with respect. Traditionally tough guards who had gotten to know us pretended not to notice our idiosyncratic violations of prison routine, but whenever we entered a strange part of the prison and encountered new guards we were in danger. On one occasion, when we had been escorted to a new area and were waiting to see what would happen (prisoners are seldom told where they are going or why), two of us were excoriated for looking out a partially open window. When I asked, as gently as I could, what harm there was in looking at the grass, the guard became nervous and felt the need to assert his authority. He ordered me to take off some paper button-holes with which we managed to keep our shirts from being constantly unbuttoned because of the oversized buttonholes. His manner was so arbitrary (and the practice of wearing the buttonholes so well established) that I felt it necessary to explain that I was chilly, that the shirt would not stay buttoned otherwise, and then, in response to his shouted "You are in prison now; shut up and do as I say," that even prisoners had the right to be treated civilly.

When, as a result, I was thrown into the "hole," the modern prison's equivalent of the medieval dungeon, I found that the approximately five-by-six-foot damp strip cell, part of which was taken up by a toilet which could only be flushed from the outside, was already occupied by two other prisoners. There was not room for all of us to lie down at one time, but we managed by having two of us put our feet and legs up the wall while the third put his on the toilet. One of the prisoners was upbraiding the other for being a damn fool. "It don't make no difference that you're innocent," he said. "They don't want you to plead not guilty. You would've got off with thirty days. Now you'll get six months." "I know," said the other, "but it was a matter of principle with me."

The seasoned, guilty man had been in the "hole" a week, for having a fight. The principled "damn fool" had been taken to the barber shop earlier that day, in anticipation of his appearance in court the following morning. He had an attractive pompadour hair style and had balked when told that he would have to have it cut another way. "Just don't give me no haircut at all," he had said, "'cause when I appear in court I wants to be mine own self." But for this act of self-assertion he had been thrown in the "hole." It wouldn't have been right under any circumstances, but I couldn't help thinking that here was a man who apparently was innocent, and who, in any event, was supposed to be presumed innocent until proven guilty. Because he could not afford bail, however, he had already lost all his rights.

When I walked out of jail after my ten days were up, I couldn't tell whether I felt more elated at having my "freedom" or depressed at the thought of those whom I had left inside. I know, from previous experience, that I shall never forget some of them and that I shall never meet any finer persons out of jail than some of the friends I made inside. But I also know how easy it is to get caught up in other routines, and how hard it is to convince people that the only way to reform jails is to abolish them. For jails are necessary for the preservation of "law and order" in a society where there are rich and poor, overprivileged and underprivileged.

The 1964 Elections—
A Trap

1964 I don't have to spend much time demonstrating that Goldwater is not a desirable choice for the presidency. Nor is there much point in trying to determine whether he is in fact as innocent, incorruptible, and dedicated to his own understanding of the people's welfare as a number of observers and even some of his opponents have testified. Personally I find him likable—but I found Police Chief Laurie Pritchett quite likable too, when I was in jail in Albany, Georgia, and still would have preferred to deal with someone with a less attractive personality and a more enlightened attitude toward blacks and dissenters. In the case of Goldwater, I must add that I find it hard to believe that his Right hand (the one busy protecting welfare recipients, the medically ill, and blacks from the Federal government) does not have some inkling of what the other, Farther Right hand is doing (calling for violence in the streets and in the jails, so long as it is directed against the victims and critics of society rather than against their attackers). In any case it is not unusual for a man to fail to make a connection between a gracious "personal" charm and the sordid realities of his business, military, or political policies. Anyone who does make the connection is not apt to represent either major party on the ballot.

The biggest problem is that Goldwaterism, like the mythical Greek monster Hydra, has many heads. I am not referring to Barry's peculiar limitations of intellect or memory which prevent him from integrating his off-the-cuff remarks and the various books and speeches that are written for him. ("I think that some of the ideas in it are mine," he is reported to have said of *The Conscience of a Conservative.*) I mean that he is only the current spokesman for powerful economic and political interests that once backed Senator Joseph McCarthy—the new and therefore insecure and impulsive rich, who lack the finesse and indirection of long established wealth; the political boors who carry to a crude and consistent conclusion the intermittent preachments of the New Frontier that communism is the root of all evil and any act of violence, treachery, or ruthless suppression of human rights is justified if needed to contain it. Helen Mears has pointed out that "it is much easier to create a climate of hate and fear than to control it once it is generated."

Unfortunately Goldwater represents a far greater, more pervasive danger (and requires a far more drastic opposition) than is imagined by those who are urging a moratorium on radical action and a centrist closing of the ranks to ensure a Democratic victory this fall. I sympathize with those who are calling for a vote *against* Goldwater. But the most that even a smashing Johnson victory can do is to eliminate the man Goldwater from the forefront of politics. It will not attack the economic and political roots (intertwined as they are with the roots of Eisenhower, Kennedy, and Johnson) from which Goldwater has grown as an unlovely flower and from which new and probably more dangerous McCarthys and Goldwaters are bound to develop in the future.

It is perilous to make specific political predictions. (Thank goodness for the mysterious elements in human nature which make both commercial pollsters and more serious analysts turn out so often to be wrong.) But there are solid reasons for believing that Goldwater will be decisively defeated in November and that, before many more national elections, a representative of the far right will become President. This could come about in any of three ways: 1) by the election of a man like Lyndon Johnson, Hubert Humphrey or Bobby Kennedy, who subsequently responds to "grave national emergency" and "shocking betrayal," at home or abroad, by speeding up the present drift to the right (all three men have shown an aptitude for doing this when it serves their own political ambitions, as I shall bring out specifically in the case of the most "liberal" of them all, Hubert Humphrey); 2) through the election of a man who is more forthright than Johnson or Humphrey and more astute or charismatic than Goldwater; or 3) through a *coup d'état*.

This is the first time in my life that a *coup* has seemed seriously possible in the United States. Apparently conditions have not deteriorated that far yet, though the Kennedy assassination and cover-up, the growth of the C.I.A. (which specializes in assassinations and *coups*) and the willingness of the public to tolerate known lies and manipulations of the news (as in the U-2 incidents, the Bay of Pigs invasion, and the prevarications about Vietnam) are not encouraging. But such a development is no longer out of the question and will become progressively less so, if present trends continue—as apparently it is necessary to remind ourselves they *will* continue under Johnson.

Let us not forget that the Third Republic collapsed in France in the wake of the frustration and failure in Indochina and Algeria. The real struggle against the development of rightism in the United States is the struggle to achieve an about-face in America's relationship to the struggle of the underdeveloped and colored peoples of the world for independence, dignity, and material progress. Unless, of course, the United States can persuade the Vietnamese, Africans, Latin Americans, etc., to accept merely token concessions in order to prevent a vicious American "backlash." But that appears to be historically impossible as well as morally indefensible, as might be clearer to the liberal supporters of Johnson if they lived in one of the villages of Vietnam which the New Frontier-Great Society is incinerating in the name of a measured and responsible anti-communism. (It is only possible to "oppose" such acts and at the same time vote for the President who orders them, if it is someone else who is being tortured and killed.) If those who support the aspirations of America's economic and political vassals push the panic button and support Johnsonism against Goldwaterism, they will be delaying the development of an imaginative and independent left, with a program and sense of values entirely different from those of either Johnson or Goldwater.

Johnson may be a master at manipulating Congress and the American public but fortunately he is less successful with the people of Vietnam, Cuba, and the Congo. Only a master prestidigitator could convince so many peace people to vote for him while he is carrying on a losing war of aggression, but the people of Vietnam are not so easily fooled or brought under control. We were told that the "firm reply" in the Gulf of Tonkin constituted a great morale-building, moral (sic) victory, but only the Americans got this message, not the Southeast Asians. No white, "Christian," Western, capitalist nation is going to be able to dominate Southeast Asia for long under any circumstances.

Sooner or later the stench of American actions in Vietnam is going to be too great for the deodorizers in the Pentagon and the White House to cope with—and then the public will be ready to move drastically in one direction or the other. We should be preparing for that day right now by developing and consolidating the peace forces in vigorous action against Johnson's war and his aim of preserving America's foreign hegemony. We should be calling for fundamental solutions to fundamental problems instead of implying that somehow United States aims and methods in Vietnam can't be as bad as we sometimes say they are, since we are willing to endorse them, even indirectly, in order to defeat Goldwater. Desperate "remedies" are brought forth in desperate situations, and the situation in Southeast Asia is going to become increasingly desperate under either Johnson or Goldwater. In the absence of a sufficiently powerful opposition from the left, the domestically soothing and superficially "responsible" militarism of Johnson will merge with the frank and "irresponsible" militarism called for by Goldwater—as it has already begun to do without adopting Goldwater's hysterical style. It won't make a lot of difference whether a Lyndon Johnson, a Barry Goldwater, or a Bobby Kennedy is the head man at the time.

A lot of worried people are saying that Hitler triumphed in Germany because the "good" people didn't take him seriously enough; so we must all turn out on November 3 to cast a vote in what has become a gigantic referendum on extremism. I take extremism far too seriously to think that it can be defeated in a referendum that will do nothing to solve the problems that give rise to it. As a matter of fact, Hitler was frequently repudiated at the polls in Germany, but the people who were elected to forestall his rise to power were unable to solve the underlying problems, so he kept right on rising. In a time of desperation, there was a vacuum on the left and only the discredited "lesser evil" of moderation to stand as an alternative to Hitlerism.

There is talk of the beneficial psychological effects of a Gold-water defeat. In the absence of a strong "Neither Johnson nor Gold-water" movement, one of the effects will undoubtedly be a period of soporific self-congratulation on this further "proof" that the United States is decent, liberal, and peacefully inclined. Let Johnson make one minor turn toward peace and there will be a mood of public re-laxation (which won't extend to the Pentagon, State Department, or C.I.A.) similar to that which followed the Test Ban Treaty. We are probably in greater danger of losing our remaining liberties and whatever restraints there are on American militarism to a sweet-talk-ing promoter of the "national consensus" than to the thugs associated with the Minute Men and similar groups. I wonder what the psycho-logical effects of a Goldwater defeat will be on Johnson. Do we really think that he will say: "All those people weren't really voting for me; they were only voting against Goldwater. Now that I have been elected I must reverse my policies." I see no way in which Johnson's election will be a mandate for him to get out of Southeast Asia, stop engineering *coups* and suppressions of democracy and freedom in Latin America, admit China to the United Nations, lift the boycott of Cuba, take the issues of unemployment, poverty, and automation seriously.

Finally, there has been too little discussion of the psychological effects of left-wing electioneering on present and potential radicals. We can say, "Vote for Johnson, but don't be fooled by him," but the very suggestion reveals that we have been fooled into accepting a false formulation of the choices. According to the *New York Times,* Hubert Humphrey "declared that the main question before the elec-torate was: 'which [candidate] do you want to have his hand on the nuclear trigger?' "

It is immoral and politically self-defeating to vote in such a ref-erendum—just as it would be immoral and ultimately self-defeating to vote in a referendum on whether or not Negroes should be segre-gated. Or, to make the parallel more exact, to vote on who should have his hand on the weapons that keep them from breaking out of the ghetto. Of course one can be sophisticated and say: Vote *and* en-gage in direct action. But it seems to me that any advocacy of a vote for Johnson encourages the illusion that there is some real sense in which Johnson is not so dangerous as we sometimes claim and that the mild and ineffective demonstrations we have been having are way-out methods to supplement electoral politics rather than paltry beginnings at direct action. Moreover, what about practical considerations? As everyone knows, it is a big job to get people out to the polls—and a bigger job to organize and energize direct action. I am afraid we would be squandering our limited resources as well as blurring our message.

There are some striking indications that those who say "Vote for Johnson but only as a vote against Goldwater" have been pretty badly fooled themselves. For example, the word is out that Johnson did a noble thing by appointing Hubert Humphrey as the Democratic nominee for Vice-President, instead of undermining Goldwater's appeal by bringing forth a conservative candidate. But I am with those who think that Johnson knew what he was doing, which is a way of saying that it was dirty pool. Let me give you an example. The delegations of nine states had pledged to wage a floor fight at the Democratic convention for seating the delegates of Mississippi's Freedom Democratic Party. This would have helped crystallize an important issue and would have helped the Negro struggle get out in the open where it deserves to be. But it would have embarrassed President Johnson, who finds it easier to represent *all* the people (Negroes and Southern racists, pacifists and militarists, poor people and big corporations) if he can keep the issues fuzzy. So Humphrey was given the job of persuading the nine delegations that the best way to help the Mississippi Negroes was to go back on their promised support. Do you think that Senator Richard Russell of Georgia or Senator Thomas Dodd of Connecticut or any other known conservative could have done the job? Possibly, if he had been willing to use the pressures that Humphrey is reported to have used: threats to conscientious dissenters that they would lose out in federal patronage and contracts for their states. But politically, liberals and Negroes would have been badly alienated if anyone but a liberal had done the job. There are going to be a lot of jobs like that for Hubert Humphrey to perform in the next few years, and his record indicates that he won't be squeamish about performing them.

Humphrey is making a lot these days of the fact that Goldwater voted against Senate censure of Joseph McCarthy. This was deplorable on Goldwater's part. But how did Hubert Humphrey champion the cause of freedom during the McCarthy period? Not only did he vote for the Communist Control Act, but he offered an amendment to outlaw the Communist Party completely, making it illegal even to be a member. His amendment was too McCarthyite for his more experienced colleagues and was rejected, but he was more successful with an amendment to the McCarran Act, which was accepted and became part of the law. It provided for the erection of concentration camps (they have been built and are ready for use) and gave the Attorney General power in time of "National Emergency" to apprehend and detain, indefinitely and without trial, "persons as to whom there are reasonable grounds to believe [that they] probably will conspire with others to engage in acts of espionage or sabotage."

After the mood of flagrant McCarthyism had passed, Humphrey's friends explained these amendments by saying that Humphrey had been poorly advised by a member of his staff, and later regretted them.

Humphrey had his eyes on the White House way back in 1956 and as part of his campaign introduced into the *Congressional Record* the "extraordinary" articles of "the distinguished American editor" William Randolph Hearst Jr. on conditions in the Soviet Union. All nine Hearst papers have endorsed Humphrey and Johnson in the present election. Liberals consider it revolting that Goldwater equivocated for two weeks on the endorsement of the Ku Klux Klan but apparently think it is smart politics for Humphrey and Johnson to represent Hearst and Faubus along with Negroes and civil libertarians.

We are told that Humphrey has demonstrated his "courage" and "persistent liberalism" by continuing his membership in Americans for Democratic Action. It is worth quoting at length from the television program "Face the Nation" of September 16:

> *Sen. Humphrey:* ... A.D.A. has asked for the restoration of free government in Cuba, supports this government's policies of economic sanctions in Cuba, but has said—and I think somewhat idealistically—that if Cuba could arrive at a position of nonalignment, if it would quit its program of subversion, that then it should be admitted to the Organization of American States. Well, I don't think Cuba is going to quit its program of subversion.
> *Martin Agronsky (C.B.S. News):* If they did, would you agree with that objective?

Sen. Humphrey: No, I would not. I do not believe in including in the Organization of American States a Communist country.

Paul Niven (C.B.S. News): . . . I am sure you don't agree also with its suggestion that we consider the *de facto* recognition of East Germany. I know that you do not agree with it on negotiations leading to U.N. admission of China because you belong also to the Committee of One Million whose whole purpose is against that.

Sen. Humphrey: You are surely right.

Niven: But the question arises—if you disagree with A.D.A. on so many fundamental points . . . why have you stayed in the organization all these years?

Sen. Humphrey: Well, first of all . . . it was an anti-Communist organization that helped clean out, in some of what we call the liberal forces of America, Communist infiltration.

Niven: Didn't that function disappear about fifteen years ago?

Sen. Humphrey: No, I think that you have to be ever on guard, Mr. Niven . . .

John Steele (Time, Inc.): You wrote recently—and I want to quote you directly—that "our direct involvement in Southeast Asia should be gradually curtailed, and in the Far East our military-oriented program should be gradually scaled down." Does this mean that you favor a policy of pull-out or a negotiated settlement or what there?

Sen. Humphrey: It surely does not. It means exactly what it says: that the *ultimate objective* [emphasis added] of American foreign policy is stability and independence and freedom. . . . We have no imperial design. But we have no intention of pulling out of South Vietnam. We are in there at the invitation of a government that is friendly.

Humphrey neglected to add that whatever government is in there at the moment is in power because it has convinced his running mate that it is friendly.

After listening to such a colloquy and looking at the record, we should not be surprised to read in the *New York Times* that although it took some time for Humphrey to overcome the fears of wealthy businessmen and bankers that he might be a little too radical, he has come in recent years to command their respect and support.

Having been lectured by some of our more "realistic" comrades on the necessity for using our heads so that we can become *really* revolutionary, let us make an effort to understand what is going on. Should we perhaps conclude that Hubert Humphrey is cleverly fooling the businessmen and bankers, the militarists and anti-Communists, in our behalf? If he seems to work so much against us, that only shows how much he is on our side. He is so much opposed to the John Birch Society that he has to support William Randolph Hearst and the Pentagon, form an alliance with Governor Faubus, beef up the Communist Control and McCarran acts. That's the way political realism works. If we stick with Hubert, some one of these days he may be able to appoint his own attorney general and put all our enemies and the enemies of A.D.A. in those concentration camps without a trial. That would be a clever blow for freedom. But I'm new to this kind of thing. And I find myself wondering if instead of fooling *them* in our behalf he might turn out to be fooling *us* in their behalf. Or is it perhaps that he is trying to fool everyone in his own behalf? Really, I don't know, and the trouble with the whole approach is that by now Hubert probably doesn't know either. And that's just what I am afraid will happen to the radical movement if it begins to try to fight Goldwater by Johnson's methods, Johnson by Humphrey's methods, and Humphrey by the methods of the Communist Party. I find it a little hard to believe that the Communist Party is permanently in love with Humphrey and Johnson, but it's doing its best to get out the vote for them because we have to be intelligent about these things, and even though the Communist Party in Germany didn't succeed in stopping Hitlerism by these methods, everyone knows that we've got to stop Goldwater by them. It's our only chance. Or is it?

Not Enough Love

I went to the Garden of Love.
And saw what I never had seen:
A Chapel was built in the midst,
Where I used to play on the green.
And the gates of this Chapel were shut,
And Thou shalt not, writ over the door;
So I turned to the Garden of Love,
That so many sweet flowers bore,
And I saw it was filled with graves,
And tomb-stones where flowers should be:
And Priests in black gowns, were walking their rounds,
And binding with briars, my joys and desires.

William Blake

"Religion is that I Love you"   Kenneth Patchen

1958 When sex is a gimmick in selling everything from tooth-
paste to life in the modern army, it may not seem revolutionary to
come out in favor of sexual love. But partly because sex is overstimu-

lated and undervalued, asceticism has a way of rearing its sickly head wherever people are considering ways of combating the evils of society more effectively. Gandhi renounced sex for the last forty-two years of his life, and it is often assumed that this renunciation stemmed from, and in turn contributed to, his extraordinary power. Similarly, it is generally believed that Christianity was conceived by Jesus, whose great insights and virtues were at least partly derived from his sexual abstinence—though there is no conclusive evidence that he either opposed or personally abstained from the sexual expression of love.

Not many persons actually practice sexual continence today (at least not voluntarily) because most of us are moral hypochondriacs who consider ourselves incapable of carrying out any great idea in our lives. But the feeling that asceticism is the "better way," the way of the saints, prevents many an idealist from becoming fully alive. Too many are afraid to enjoy what they are also afraid to renounce, and so they end up in a dreary desert of indulgence without creation and of restraint without purpose. One has only to attend a pacifist conference to see how dull and unattractive even a good cause can become when it is linked psychologically with asceticism.

The attitude involved extends beyond sex. Robert Granat, in "Not by Sex Alone" (*Liberation,* June 1958), refers to "the sublimation of . . . every passion the flesh is heir to" and speaks specifically of "sex, family, food, possessions, and financial security." His very list reveals the muddled thinking that often characterizes those who advocate renunciation as a step toward "life" (even those of such obvious sensitivity and intelligence as Granat): *food,* for example, is a material object which can be beneficial to human beings. *Financial security* and *possessions* refer to status relationships which have little meaning unless some persons have more power over material objects than others do. If everyone has lots of money, for instance, money loses its value and no one has the kind of financial security sought in the present society; i.e., power to commandeer the labor or goods of others. *Food* becomes detrimental in human relationships precisely when it becomes a *possession:* i.e., something which we appropriate and have dominion over without regard to the needs of others. It is not very helpful to lump together "renunciation of food" and "renunciation of financial security."

Similarly, *sex* and *family* are not entities of fixed moral value (or disvalue) in isolation from the context of human relationships involved. Even to look at a woman with lust (that is, to regard her as a commodity rather than as a person) is to perpetuate in personal relationships the ethics which capitalism and communism express in economic and military relationships, whether one decides to use *or* to renounce her. But to be sensitive to her as an autonomous fellow human, with all her rights and mysterious complexities, is a revolutionary act, in our present society, whether such sensitivity leads to sexual intercourse or not.

When two persons unite in order to produce a family, it makes all the difference whether they are using each other with the aim of producing a future president or whether they have some feeling for the mysteries of sex, birth, and personality; whether they are using each other and their prospective offspring to gratify their own ends or whether they love each other as persons and are willing to greet their child as a person with his own rights and freedoms.

Because Jesus and the early Christians had no "possessions," but rather shared material goods according to need, they are often thought to have been ascetic. The fact is that Jesus, far from being an ascetic, was accused, during his lifetime, of being "a wine-bibber and a glutton." This charge shows not that Jesus was a glutton but that there were religionists in his day, as there are in ours, who viewed all wining and feasting as identical, without regard to the circumstances. The early Christians were so little ascetic that it was sometimes hard to tell whether they were drunk with the spirit or drunk with new wine. But they were sufficiently "nonattached" to suffer imprisonment and death rather than bear arms or swear loyalty to the State.

Gandhi was a different kettle of fish. Anyone who takes the trouble to read his autobiography can see the pathetic, adolescent guilt feelings which left their scars on him as an adult long after he had outgrown the emotional uncertainty of his early life. Thrown by Indian custom into marriage with a child bride whom he did not love and apparently was unsuited to temperamentally, he had ambivalent feelings about the sexual orgies they shared. Although he was (unfortunately) what one can call a "loyal and devoted" son to a rather rigid and authoritarian father, he left his sick father's bedside after hours of patient care and was engaging in sexual relations when his father died unexpectedly. To pile guilt on guilt, he had been postponing for some days a confession to his father that he had secretly eaten meat, in a youthful escapade, contrary to the rigid vegetarianism of his parents' religion. One can only sympathize with the young Gandhi who, back in 1888, was overwhelmed with remorse after having been victimized by these coincidences. But his ultimate escape into asceticism hardly seems a suitable basis for believing that those who today refuse participation in war, the wage economy, and the power state must love without sexual expression and must avoid all pleasure in food and drink.

Gandhi was a man of deep religious conviction, but he was also a showman and politician who never made a seemingly personal move without carefully calculating the political effects. We cannot fathom the complex of his motivations but it is worth remembering that he could not have moved the Indian masses to blind obedience except as one of India's "holy" men who practiced *brachmacharya* (total chastity). Also, India was suffering from underfertility of the soil and overfertility of the people. We can never know to what extent his rigorous renunciation of sex and of all but the simplest food was a dramatic political gesture calculated to help the Indians tackle their perennial problems of overpopulation and famine.

My intention in bringing out these considerations is not to pretend to know the exact circumstances under which Jesus enjoyed or renounced sensual delight or to what extent Gandhi's asceticism was motivated by adolescent guilt or adult opportunism. It is enough to cast some doubt on the ideas that Jesus and Gandhi are authoritative witnesses to the special virtue of "sublimating every desire the flesh is heir to."

Those who emphasize either renunciation or curtailment of bodily pleasures usually make several assumptions:

1) *It is generally assumed that there is a conflict between the body and the "soul."* There is a widespread belief, even among non-ascetics, that the pleasures of the spirit are somehow separate from and "higher" than the enjoyments of the senses. To me, such distinctions are highly artificial and lead to disastrous social results. I can think of few acts with a higher "spiritual" potential than treating the wounds of the injured (or having one's own wounds treated); helping the naked, the cold, the homeless (whether oneself or one's neighbors) to secure clothing, fuel or shelter; kissing a child or having sexual intercourse with a beloved. The list is endless. On the other hand, our society is rotten because so many persons crowd into churches and intellectual centers to experience feelings of love or en-

lightenment which do not extend to sharing the physical burdens of society's necessary labor or the physical fruits of society's production.

How can one say that food which is grown in the ground and goes into the mouth is strictly physical, but music which comes from the physical manipulation of a physical instrument and goes into the ears is spiritual?

Just as one can become a "glutton" with food or a drunkard with alcohol, to the neglect of one's other capacities and without regard for the hungry and thirsty, so one can become a glutton with art and music and intellectual pursuits to the neglect of one's fuller development and without concern for those who become society's drones. Our society is suffering from a disastrous class division not only between owners and employees but also between intellectuals and workers.

If a man eats less in order to share his food with the hungry or because his income is reduced by his unwillingness to be a "corporation man," his physical act is "spiritual"—but he is not an ascetic. If he eats less in order to deny his body and improve his own "virtue," he is an ascetic—but hardly to be admired or emulated. He is rather a case of one who seeks to save his own life and thereby loses it through atrophy.

2) *Closely related is the assumption that our sexual drives can be sublimated into higher purposes—the pursuit of truth or the service of humanity.* In almost anything we do, we can get more done for a short time if we don't stop to eat, sleep, read, think or relax. But the toll becomes obvious fairly soon, as our powers decline with fatigue and staleness. In the same way, we can get more done, in work or study, if we renounce sex, family, and all outside pleasures. The quantitative benefits may pile up through a whole lifetime. But I am convinced that the qualitative results suffer from the crippling of our insights and understanding attendant upon the accompanying limitation of our experience. Disuse is not the answer to misuse.

Like the Catholic boys who speculated that their new neighbor might be a Father because he didn't have any children, the ascetic hopes he may learn more about love and humanity by cutting himself off from a whole area of the most intimate and enriching human relations.

It is probably truer to say that no one can love people—or penetrate the mysteries of human meaning—who does not love at least one person deeply. Idealistic movements—whether religious or political—have always suffered from persons who can love humanity in the abstract or in future generations but are blind to the immediate needs and rights of individuals here and now.

3) *It is assumed that ascetic self-denial helps us gain freedom from passion (which will help us avoid being distracted from noble purposes) and "nonattachment" (which will help us avoid compromising with the powers of wealth or government).*

No doubt some persons succeed in crippling their sexual drives just as others manage, in a competitive society, to suppress their attitudes of human solidarity with their neighbors. But an unnatural suppression seems likely to lead to an unnatural preoccupation, whether it takes the form of interference with the freedom of others or a tense austerity.

The Puritans reacted to the corrupt self-indulgence of the clergy by an exaggerated emphasis on self-denial of pleasure. It can be argued that it was their pent-up sexual energy which was redirected into material acquisitiveness and witch-hunting. They suppressed their love, for fear that it would become lust, and ended with a love of money and a lust for power. They set out to find God by chastising their own flesh, and ended by flailing, imprisoning, or burning the flesh of their neighbors, in whom they had found the Devil. Their negative preoccupation with conquering their own sins turned into a preoccupation with suppressing the "sins" of their fellowmen.

Gandhi and Francis of Assisi seem to have succeeded in growing in gentleness during the years in which they renounced their sexuality. But after forty years of self-denial, Gandhi was so preoccupied with sex that he used to go through a rigmarole of sleeping naked with one of his women disciples, in order to prove that he had conquered his physical passions. You can draw your own conclusions as to what he proved by this. But one of his closest associates has testified privately that Gandhi was so absorbed in this concern during the last few years of his life that he failed to respond to the communal antagonisms with his former creativity.

My own experience in prison and on at least a dozen fasts, ranging from one week to more than a month, has been that those who emphasize austerity as an aid to either physical or spiritual health have been more apt to fold under the pressure of privation or punishment than those who don't mind "living it up" a little when there is no reason not to do so. In case after case, the happiness boys have surprised me by continuing undaunted after our more ascetic comrades had compromised with such explanations as: "God told me to eat," or "I don't believe in self-torture." Those who have learned to enjoy life seem to be able to go on enjoying it even under conditions of enforced privation. They seem to have better balanced personalities which are capable of holding together under pressure. On the other hand, those who are self-conscious about rationing their pleasures tend to ration their discomforts also.

4) *Two final assumptions I want to refer to are the assumptions that the more difficult course is always the morally superior one and that it is more difficult (and therefore morally superior) to set aside sex, marriage, and feasting rather than to participate in a creative family and social life.*

Actually it is easier to build walls between one's self and other persons than it is to enter into creative relations with them. The roué and the ascetic both try to escape from the problems of intimacy. Asceticism is merely self-indulgence stood on its head. As George Orwell has pointed out, the main motive is "to escape from the pain of living, and above all from love, which, sexual or nonsexual, is hard work." Having felt the force of sexual desire, some persons panic and renounce sex altogether rather than make the effort involved in finding its proper expression. Frightened by the difficulty of human relationships, the ascetic repudiates human love in order to concentrate on God. But how can one love God whom we have not seen if we do not love our brother whom we have seen?

Everyone is in danger of being a slave to his own pleasure, and of making other persons slaves to it also. Self-control is necessary if we are to avoid gratifying our own desires (whether physical, intellectual, or aesthetic) at the expense of others. But self-control is a derivative of love, a by-product of some greater work in life than restricting one's desires in order to save one's own soul.

In a world of selfish indulgence without regard for the rights and needs of others, the ascetic and the "saint" appeal to us for a moment, because of their repudiation of the grosser sins. But too often they have repudiated the greater virtues also. They have fled from the problem instead of solving it, and, in the process, they have cast a shadow between many an idealist and the sources of vitality. Not many today follow the ascetic all the way but too many are haunted by him and end up only half alive. True "nonattachment" consists in being able both to enjoy and to give up sensual delight and human intimacy according to the overall human relationships involved.

Toward Revolutionary Humanism

1969 To the best of my memory it was Countée Cullen, a sensitive black poet who later committed suicide, who wrote in the thirties that the reason black people laughed so much was because when they opened their mouths they had to laugh so that they wouldn't cry.

For different reasons, those of us who advocate nonviolent revolution find it hard these days to know whether to exult or to weep. On the positive side, conflict and confrontation are growing more intense every day, in the ghetto, on the campus, in the streets and public places of the country. There is a growing consciousness on the part of nonwhites, young people, welfare recipients, women, draftees, and others that the present society denies them their heritage of dignity, economic well-being, and egalitarian control over their own lives. Moreover, a growing number of these people-in-revolt now perceive that the cause of their privation is not personal inadequacy, bad rulers, or the temporary malfunctioning of a desirable system. Rather it is the nature and purpose of capitalism to create a class society, both nationally and internationally, with vast inequalities in wealth, power, and privilege. If Randolph Bourne discovered, during World War I, that war is the health of the state, the youth of our country know in their bones today that inequality is the health of capitalism. And in their bones they reject this inequality, even when (especially when) they find themselves being channeled into privileged positions, either as apprentices to the ruling class or as trainees (both white and black) for the role of "house niggers."

Along with this growing rejection of a society of class divisions and delegated democracy is a rejection of the channels for social change within this society. It's not so much a question of "lacking patience," as is sometimes charged, but rather of realizing that the traditional methods do not lead in the right direction. The most that can be accomplished through electoral politics, lobbying, governmental commissions, polite negotiations with the authorities, or nonviolent demonstrations within the framework of law and order, is to shake loose a few benefits around the edges. These benefits may have immediate practical value for the recipients, but they are a small part of what is their legitimate birthright and leave them in the position of second- or third-class citizens. At best a few beneficiaries are raised to a slightly more privileged position within the established pecking order. This is what happened to skilled workers under the reforms of the thirties, which legitimized labor unions and divided the working class, making business unionism a co-optive substitute for the liberating goal of worker-control.

The movement has not yet discovered how to challenge the existing power centers effectively, but the built-in assumptions of the present society are gradually losing their legitimacy in the eyes of its victims, including many who would normally be expected to become its future rulers. At least there is heightened consciousness of what the real issues are, and the first experimental steps toward raising the level of the debate, both in the rhetoric of the demands and in the methods of raising them. The movement has discovered that in the absence of forceful confrontation (brought about by the seizure of buildings, strikes, the destruction of draft files and induction notices, or other direct disruptions of established procedures) the "rational discourse" so lauded by university authorities, editorial writers and other addicts of the status quo is slow, superficial and for the most part irrelevant.

All of this represents tremendous growth in a few short years, a growth for which the country owes a debt of gratitude to the Cuban revolutionaries, the incredibly heroic Vietnamese, and the black insurgency within our own country. Currently the Black Panthers and the Black Conference for Economic Development, together with the student revolutionaries of S.D.S., are continuing to transform the context within which the movement as a whole frames its questions and examines its tactics.

But history has taught that being anti-capitalist, courageous, and militant are not sufficient guarantees for contributing to the birth of a liberated and humanistic society. If the U.S. persistence in its aggression in Vietnam is an historical fact which is contributing to the deepening anti-capitalist consciousness, the Soviet invasions of Hungary and Czechoslovakia and the continued post-Stalin repression of individuals and groups advocating alternative forms and tactics for the building of communism make clear that non-capitalist societies can be brutal and dehumanizing as well.

Even without the warnings of history, one can look around and see a distressing recrudescence of Old Leftist tendencies and attitudes in the once New Left. The discovery that the forces of oppression are deep, deceitful and brutal, and cannot be dislodged by polite debate, has led some people to conclude that *all* debate is futile, except perhaps within the secret confines of a theoretically democratic and assuredly centralist vanguard party. In practice such self-elected vanguards rarely level with other revolutionary groups or with that vast reservoir of potential revolutionaries who must be won over (not just manipulated) if the revolution is to succeed. Some movement people have inferred from the reformist nature of the nonviolent movement of the late fifties and early sixties that smashing windows, beating up police, and roughing up our antagonists are necessarily part of becoming a serious revolutionary.

But these are bad ways to educate people and win them to the real freedom and universal solidarity of our cause. If, as the saying goes, we are what we eat, a potentially revolutionary movement becomes what it does. Today people are still being won to the movement because they are revolted by what the system does to Vietnamese, G.I.'s, nonwhites, students, and the poor; and, conversely, because they are attracted to the fraternal, humanistic, and liberating goals and style of the insurgents. But if the rhetoric and practice of some of the present advocates of "by any means necessary" becomes the dominant reality, the new recruits will include more and more persons who enjoy street-fighting for its own sake or get a neurotic kick out of beating up other people. If the movement succumbs to the notion that there is one vanguard party which has *the* correct ideology, tactic, and style and that all deviation is counterrevolutionary, it will attract and encourage those who are doctrinaire and repressive. Instead of becoming a family of revolutionaries who are united in some concepts and activities but have family differences about other matters, we will become a group of feuding sects, incapable of learning from our allies or of mounting a genuine united front. Already S.D.S. was treated to the spectacle of a caucus of about 200 members who refused to join in the applause, at the National Council meeting in Austin, when it was announced that the Oakland Seven had been acquitted of the conspiracy charges brought against them for their activities in Stop the Draft Week. Already some of the articles in movement publications which purport to describe the positions of rival groups are as grossly inaccurate as the statements of the government which led to the well-known credibility gap.

On the one hand, it is unfortunate that some of the criticisms of the type that are appearing in *Liberation* are also being made by people who do not share either the movement's revolutionary goals or its awareness of the need for increased militance. It is absurd that both the privileged elite and the timid moderates have become spokesmen these days for "nonviolence." University presidents and government officials condemn the seizure of buildings as "violent," but have no words of condemnation for the real violence of R.O.T.C., police and court repression, or university complicity in war and counter-insurgency. The authorities who frame the Black Panthers on imaginary plots to bomb department stores are themselves engaged in blowing up every store, home, church, and village in liberated Vietnam. In the general debasement that the word "nonviolence" has suffered, it may be necessary for those of us who are anxious to preserve the humanistic sensitivity and content of the revolution to find another word to sum up what we are advocating.

On the other hand, there is substantial evidence that the police and the government send infiltrators into the movement not only to spy but to advocate harebrained schemes of violence which will discredit the movement and obscure what the revolution is genuinely about. There have been repeated instances when the guy who shouted "Kill the pigs," or "Charge the barricades," turned out to be a cop himself. The authorities would love to make the struggle a conflict of violence rather than of rival institutions and ways of life.

Clearly the movement must feel its way through the present period, continuing to deepen its anti-capitalist and anti-militarist consciousness, experimenting with militant ways of disrupting the smooth functioning of the system. It must refuse to retreat either into liberalism or into the pseudo-revolutionary "infantile leftism" which plays at revolution while leaving the movement bereft of allies and credibility, because of the gap between its goals and its methods. In the long run the dynamics of the movement will be determined not by the words we use but by the tactics we develop. To be truly liberating the tactics must combine the newly developed anti-capitalist consciousness and the socialist humanism we are seeking to nourish and make real.

Escalation in the
Antiwar Movement*

1965 There are no adequate responses to what is happening in Vietnam. Whatever partial elation I felt at the relative success of the Washington Assembly of Unrepresented People, from August 6 through 9, 1965, was dissipated, shortly after getting out of jail, when I read the following headline in the *New York Times:*

U.S. MARINES KILL

600 GUERRILLAS

IN 2-DAY BATTLE

As if that were not depressing enough, a companion story, entitled "Death Overtakes a U.S. Supply Unit," contained these harrowing sentences:

> Under a sweltering midday sun, United States Marine Supply Column 21 lumbered to its death yesterday in the morass of a Vietnamese rice paddy. . . . Some of the column's 30 marines survived the withering Vietcong attack, but none escaped unmarked. . . . The marines ripped at the Vietcong with machine-gun and rifle fire from the vehicles, but still

* *Condensed*

> the Vietcong kept coming. . . . Suddenly, a young corporal
> shouted: "Okay men, we're Marines. Let's do the job." He
> started to climb out, but a bullet hit him between the eyes
> before he could raise his rifle. (The *New York Times,* Au-
> gust 20, 1965.)

Quite possibly, the unfortunate corporal, a not untypical product of jingoism and boot-camp training, was role-playing in the style
of the TV dramas that end in a blaze of triumphant commercials and
with real-life resurrection for the fallen actors. But neither the triumphs of science nor the catch in President Johnson's throat as he
speaks of his love of peace will ever bring back to life this misguided
hero or any of the six hundred Vietnamese who were slaughtered in
that two-day battle.

Words fail me when I think of such things, but I wonder if
there is not some terrible sense in which the American peace movement is also in danger of role-playing, as we go through the motions
of meetings, protests, and the necessary debates over strategy and
tactics without quite believing in the primacy of ending the war. The
victims become abstract, the day-to-day obscenity of events in Vietnam affects us only remotely, and we overestimate the intensity of our
commitment by comparing it with the relative placidity of life-as-
usual in temporarily sheltered middle-class white America.

"Will things get out of hand?" we anxiously ask each other.
They are already out of hand for thirty-one and a half million Vietnamese, and quite possibly for a hundred and twenty-five thousand
American troops as well, not to mention those whose lives are being
disrupted by the draft. "Will escalation lead to World War III?" Is it
so far wrong to reply that although World War III can magnify the
quantity of what is happening and extend it to other countries, it cannot alter the basic nature of what is already taking place? There is
something peculiarly insensitive about the way in which we tend to
tolerate "little" wars and distant deaths, as if they were not quite real,
so long as the deaths are spread out in time and total hundreds of
thousands instead of millions.

These are not natural disasters that are ravaging Vietnam. They
stem from the uses to which American tax money is put, from American munitions, American soldiers, American politicians, and therefore from the support (active or passive, enthusiastic or begrudging)

of the American people. If each of us knew that he and his closest circle of family and friends would be wiped out a month from now, if the war continued that long—or that every month that the war continued, just one of the thousands of bombers that raid North and South Vietnam would unload its death and destruction on a nearby American town—would we be satisfied with the present level of antiwar activities? There's something a little gauche about asking such a question, but I don't know how else to get at the problem: the lack of basic seriousness with which we go about trying to end the war.

There are many reasons why it is very difficult for us to progress from personal tokenism to existential involvement in a serious political effort to end the war. Obviously, some of them go pretty deep, if not into "human nature" then into a cultural environment that fragments the human family, minimizes human solidarity, and takes for granted vast differentials in human welfare. If we can tolerate ghettoes, prisons, hundred-to-one income differentials, and American investments in South Africa, there is a limit to how much indignation we can sustain over the fate of distant and recalcitrant Vietnamese peasants (who insolently refuse to negotiate and may, after all, be Communists). But more interesting, for the moment, is the profound sense of powerlessness that stems from the atrophied state of American democracy. At the very moment when the only "respectable" argument for American intervention is faith in the democratic way of life—that's what we're saving (killing) them for—there is little evidence of the vitality of that faith within the United States. It seems to be part of the American culture to believe that this is a democratic country, but also to feel that we cannot affect the major decisions of our time; to believe, in the present instance, that the American people are incapable of banding together and forcing the government to give up a war that has been publicly exposed as a brutal and intolerable fraud.

Oddly enough, there is considerable evidence that the war could be stopped, if even a small percentage of those who disapprove of it could get past their sense of hopelessness and focus actively on that objective.

We sometimes forget that it was not so much the military defeat of the French at Dienbienphu that caused the French withdrawal from Indochina in 1954 as the refusal of large sections of the French populace to tolerate the continued senseless destruction of human life in behalf of obsolete and meaningless conceptions of national prestige. More striking still, the French withdrew from Algeria, in 1961, *after* the French armies had virtually won the war and "successfully" crushed the military aspects of the rebellion. France's moral (and therefore political) position had been irreparably damaged, in Algeria, in France, and throughout the world, by the ferocity of their military campaign. Is it not possible that what the French, aided by world opinion, were able to do, Americans, assisted by world opinion, can accomplish also?

The Washington Assembly of Unrepresented People made a small but significant beginning at providing a framework in which persons with a wide variety of philosophies and political attitudes could discuss and debate their differences and also unite in common parapolitical action against continuation of the war. It is worth remembering that the Assembly took place on less than six weeks' notice, with a minimum of advance publicity, with no "big-name" endorsement or support, without the assistance of any labor union or other mass organization (in fact against the active opposition of N.A.A.C.P. and the Urban League), and on a shoestring budget that totalled less than the cost of a full-page ad in the *New York Times*. Students, who form the largest single constituency for mass demonstrations of an anti-administration character, were scattered for the summer, and Students for a Democratic Society provided almost no assistance. A bulletin from the S.D.S. national office even advised students to stay away from Monday's attempted assembly on the Capitol steps (though the same memorandum supported the workshops scheduled for the two previous days). The final civil disobedience took place on a working day, after hundreds of persons had left Washington to return to their jobs, on completion of a full weekend of workshops and demonstrations. (Understandably, at least half of the eighty persons who deliberately risked arrest on Friday, by sitting down at the main entrance to the White House, were among those who had left.) Thirty-six sit-downers were arrested on Saturday, and the psychology of these events in the past has almost invariably been that persons who have been arrested once rarely risk another arrest right away.

Despite all these factors, 356 persons were arrested on the Capitol grounds on August 9, by far the largest number ever arrested in any Washington demonstration. The heterogeneous composition of the group suggests that for every person who traveled to Washington and underwent arrest, there must have been thousands (quite possibly hundreds of thousands) of others scattered throughout the country who applauded the action. Considering the reluctance of most Americans to make "public spectacles" of themselves, let alone face police brutality and the repercussions of arrest, there must be millions of others who will not join in street demonstrations or civil disobedience but are acutely dissatisfied with Administration policy.

The Fort Hood Three

The G.I. should be reached somehow. He doesn't want to fight. He has no reason to risk his life. Yet he doesn't realize that the peace movement is dedicated to his safety.

Private David Samas

1966 The struggle against the war in Vietnam entered a new phase on June 30, (1966) when three brave soldiers announced their refusal to obey army orders to go to Vietnam. The three men, Private David Samas, Private First Class James Johnson and Private Dennis Mora, were on a thirty-day pre-embarkation leave, after having received their orders.

Significantly, the soldiers made their announcement at a press conference in New York City, called by the Fifth Avenue Vietnam Peace Parade Committee, a coalition of ninety-three local and national peace groups, and were supported in person by Stokely Carmichael, chairman of S.N.C.C., and Lincoln Lynch, public relations director of C.O.R.E., both of whom expressed their hope that other soldiers and potential draftees would follow the example of the three refusers. Badly needed muscle was added to the peace movement, not only by the soldiers' action but also by this coming together of three important groups: the traditional (if expanded) peace movement, the militant Afro-American movement for civil rights, and the soldiers themselves. In the past, the peace movement has been surprisingly slow to carry its message to soldiers, the men on whose unquestioning obedience the government relies to be able to thwart the democratic will in time of unpopular war. But then, in our lifetime no other war has been so clearly unpopular as the American aggression in Vietnam.

The three soldiers told the press that after seven months in the army it was their opinion that a majority of the soldiers do not believe in the war but feel trapped and helpless. Our democracy is not vital enough for its citizens to believe that they can decide for themselves such an important matter as whether or not to risk their lives killing Vietnamese peasants who are in search of their independence. After the press conference, Michael Armstrong, an ex-Marine who served ten months in Vietnam, told me that in his view as many as eighty percent of the military in Vietnam are disillusioned and disgusted by the war and want out.

These figures may be exaggerated. What is more, soldiers are notoriously brave under combat conditions, even when they are frankly cynical about the motives and trustworthiness of the home-front politicians. But clearly the men in the armed forces must learn that they are not alone, that it is both possible and honorable to resist, and that in the spirit of Nuremberg, large sectors of the American public will support those who refuse to commit atrocities against their fellow human beings.

There is no reason why any Americans, including those in the armed forces, should be cut off from their inalienable human rights. We have assumed too long that draftees and other soldiers can be separated from their constitutional rights of freedom of speech, press, assembly, and meaningful political expression, without harm to them or the democratic process—even as during most of our country's history it has been assumed that men with black skins could be excluded without making democracy a lie.

We can make an important beginning at opening up a vital new channel of democratic reawakening by getting the public statements of Samas, Johnson and Mora into the hands of friends and relatives in the armed forces—and of young men subject to the draft. Peace and civil rights groups can distribute these and other antiwar materials to the men in the armed forces—at bus and train stations, in front of U.S.O.'s, and at army gates. New York groups that have been doing this have found an encouraging amount of support from the soldiers themselves, especially those who have already been in Vietnam. In line with Samas' statement, they are skeptical about the peace movement but in many cases are even more skeptical about the war and the administration's good faith.

Today the militant wing of the civil rights movement is moving away from reliance on the inadequate and extremely unreliable charity of the political establishment, as negotiated by well-motivated middlemen who seek to liberalize the status quo without repudiating its main assumptions. Surely this is the major thrust of the emphasis on "black power." It is no accident that an integral part of the new, more revolutionary orientation is a more serious challenging of the war. Most "Gandhians" in the civil rights movement have been handicapped by loyalty to existing institutions, including the primacy of the electoral process.

A similar coming of age is important for the peace movement, which must learn to develop and use its muscle seriously. We must create a power base which is not beholden to the established power structure, mentally, morally, or politically. It may seem odd, but one of the ways for the peace movement to build its own independent constituency is to reach out directly to the soldiers and to other young people who are subject to the draft but presently lack the "religious training and belief" associated with the privilege of exemption as "legitimate" conscientious objectors. Soldiers and young people whose cultural position does not lead to draft deferment should be brought into the dialogue so that a badly needed cross-fertilization can take place between them and the peacemakers. Soldiers ready to take a stand similar to that of Mora, Johnson, and Samas should be given help in finding lawyers and gaining the support of broadly based defense committees.

In part it was a coincidence that the three soldiers announced their stand in the same week that U.S. flyers extended their country's murderous air bombardment into the densely populated industrial complex of the Hanoi-Haiphong area and simultaneously began to nibble away at the life-sustaining, life-protecting dikes of North Vietnam. Even so, the new bombings served to emphasize the logic of the three men's refusal to take part in a war which they characterized as "immoral, illegal, and unjust." In their joint statement they said: "[in the army] we have been told that many times we may face

a Vietnamese woman and child and that we will have to kill them."
Extending the bombing shocked and horrified most of the world.
(Only Americans are sufficiently insulated and blindly enough pro-
American to be relatively immune to the horror.) But this new act
of terror was only the latest of many immoral escalations in the illegal
commitment of more and more American conscripts to the killing of
more and more Vietnamese, including women and children, in an
unjust war for American domination of Southeast Asia.

A second coincidence took place about a week later when Hanoi
began to talk about trying the offending airmen and American military authorities announced that the three soldiers would be brought
before military courts-martial. The soldier-prisoners in Hanoi were
shot down while raining death on people below, but the three soldier-
prisoners at Fort Dix were seized illegally on the streets of New York
while on their way to address a peace meeting at the Community
Church.

Two days after the press conference, the Pentagon announced,
in its best public-relations manner, that the three men "had exercised
their right of free speech and had not—as yet—violated military discipline." (*New York Times,* July 3.) But in the same interview there
was an ominous note: "A senior legal expert at the Defense Department indicated today that members of the armed forces who refused
to fight in Vietnam might be prosecuted under existing laws and
regulations and, in extreme cases, might be sentenced to death." As
usual, the government gave lip service to America's high ideals but
issued a thinly veiled threat to those who might take them seriously.
After the men had made clear their refusal to succumb to bribery by
retracting their statements* and had agreed to speak at a series of

---

* The following is the text of a telegram sent July 7 to Attorney Gen-
eral Katzenbach and Secretary of Defense McNamara from A. J. Muste, Dave
Dellinger, and Norma Becker, respectively chairman and co-ordinators of the
Fifth Avenue Vietnam Peace Parade Committee.

*We strongly condemn harassment by Federal agents of servicemen such
as PFC James Johnson, Pvt. Dennis Mora and Pvt. David Samas, who have
filed injunction in Federal Court against shipment to Vietnam on grounds of
immorality and illegality of that war.*

*We are reliably informed that on July 4 an officer of the Modesto, Cali-
fornia, police force visited the parents of Pvt. Samas. The officer said he had
been contacted by "higher authorities" and that if Pvt. Samas would rescind
his action and his statement against the war, and in effect abandon his fellows,
he would not be prosecuted and would receive an Army discharge. The officer*

public meetings in their remaining days of leave, the government forgot its profound devotion to free speech and kidnapped them.

For humanitarian reasons, the lives of the prisoners in Hanoi should be spared. But Americans who are pleading for their safety should remember that all appeals to the humanitarianism of Washington have fallen so far on deaf ears. It is a sign of the corruption of American public life that even the eighteen "dove" Senators who have been criticizing the war felt compelled to say to Hanoi that reprisals against the captured airmen would turn the war into "a raging inferno, burning away the last barriers of restraint." Senator Richard Russell of Georgia threatened that the United States, if provoked, would turn all of Vietnam into "a desert." Clearly there is no time to be lost if our government officials are so close to total madness— or if the most sane of them estimate that the President and his advisers are. Already the blood of too many Americans and Vietnamese is on our hands.

In any event we must press for exonerations for James Johnson, David Samas and Dennis Mora. We should hail them as the heroes they are, make it possible for them to put their courage and devotion to humane and humanitarian tasks, and encourage others to follow their example.

The power of their action lies in the possibility that others will take a similar stand. Otherwise it becomes another in a series of isolated, idealistic acts, which typifies the traditional weakness of the historic peace movement. There can be no beginning without such acts but they must come to fruition in widespread, politically effective actions by "ordinary" people.

Today the peace movement has an historic opportunity to move from its perpetually repeated "beginnings" to a new stage of historic relevance. Close alliance with the black-power militants and the draftees is a necessary prerequisite.

---

obviously acted under instructions of Federal agents in proposing such a bribe.

Such acts show desperation in attempt to stem growing opposition to the war among young men facing the draft or already in military service. The peace movement will continue to aid in every possible lawful way anyone, civilian, soldier, sailor or Marine, who opposes this illegal and immoral war. The young men in the armed services are entitled to know the truth about the war and to engage in discussions about it. Citizens are likewise entitled to communicate the truth about the war to servicemen and the peace movement is determined to exercise that right.

Gandhi and Guerrilla—
The Protest at the Pentagon*

1967   Stewart Meacham, an American Quaker recently returned from South Vietnam, reports that on Saturday, August 26, while he was in Saigon, members of the National Liberation Front entered four movie houses, turned off the projectors, turned up the lights and spoke with the people. When they had finished they left as unobtrusively as they came.

    The incident belies American propaganda claims that the N.L.F. relies on terror to extort support and protection from a hostile populace. It never did make much sense, even on the face of it, to believe that the "V.C." could both terrorize the people and at the same time entrust their own lives to them, as they moved in and out of crowded areas or advanced without detection through the villages adjacent to U.S. army camps.

    In fact, the N.L.F. bases its tactics on the assumption that, given half a chance, all but a rapidly diminishing handful of generals and profiteers will recognize that their true interests lie with the indigenous resistance rather than with the foreign invaders. The new political program of the N.L.F. (September 1967) seeks to "afford conditions for puppet officers and puppet officials to come back to the just

* *Condensed*

cause and join the people's fight against U.S. aggression to save and build the country. . . . Those in the puppet army and the puppet administration at any level, who have committed crimes against the people but are now sincerely repentant will be pardoned."

The N.L.F.'s confrontations in the Saigon movie houses fit in with some of the conclusions that seem to flow from our own experience in Washington on October 21 and 22, when antiwar activists confronted the soldiers who had been assigned to guard the Pentagon.

In essence, we learned the importance of approaching the soldiers not as enemies to be "terrorized" (spat on, derided as "dirty fascists," or physically assaulted) but as potential allies whose true interests lie with the American resistance movement. That is, their true interests lie with this movement if it merits their support by developing a humanistic practice and program that appeal to their self-respect and human solidarity in contrast to the degrading rule and partisan hostilities which dominate their lives in the armed forces.

To some extent, appeals to the fraternal instincts and political interests of the soldiers are made more difficult by being combined with militant resistance activities, such as acts of blockage and disruption. But in my mind the greatest problem revolves around our ability to attain the psychological maturity and political seriousness necessary to combine methods of disruption and persuasion (acts of resistance to the system and acts of human solidarity with the people). As a matter of fact, our teach-in to the soldiers at the Pentagon would have been far less effective if it had consisted merely of a series of verbal preachments by docile instructors. If we had limited ourselves to actions permitted under the ground rules laid down by the government or, if after having advanced into forbidden territory we had retreated under pressure, our proud words would not have meant much —if indeed we could have uttered them at all. It was the existential unity between words and deeds that gave reality to both. We appealed to the soldiers to act as self-respecting individuals and at the same time we acted as such ourselves. It appeared to me that the soldiers, many of whom were in a mess because they had obeyed orders (first from the draft board and then from their officers) were challenged by the very fact that we refused to obey orders and refused to back down, even when physically attacked.

In the confrontation on the west flank of the Pentagon, I proposed to the soldiers that, in the spirit of the democracy they are supposed to be defending, they take turns with us on the portable loudspeaker. I was a little worried that this might seem self-righteous or like a cruel jibe, but I wanted to dramatize the contrast between their own subservient position as soldiers and ours as free men.

Contrary to the understanding of some, the mixture of Gandhi and guerrilla was planned in advance, although it was not adequately spelled out—in part because we found it hard to concretize, since there were so many variables in the government's likely actions and so many gradations in the experience and attitudes of the protesters. At the very least there was bound to be a juxtaposition of Gandhi and guerrilla, given the presence of both schools of thought and the permissiveness of the coalition. But juxtaposition is not the same as creative synthesis, which was the Mobilization's goal.

Not surprisingly, the government tried to force us to eliminate direct action altogether, by threatening on October 6 that otherwise it would withhold permits for the rally and march and for our buses to unload passengers. When this failed, they tried to persuade us to set up a purely formal and ritualistic civil disobedience: "those who want to be arrested" would cross an agreed-upon boundary line, sit down and tamely wait for arrest or removal from the area. We wanted something with far more teeth in it, a real confrontation instead of a legitimatized one. We refused to negotiate the terms of the civil disobedience or direct action at all. The furthest we went was to take steps to try to minimize government brutality—by warning in advance that we would not abide by their rules (in the hope that knowledge of this would reduce the likelihood of panic on their part and would eliminate the possibility of their crying "foul"), by making it clear that we would not retreat before violence, by letting them know that we would have trained observers on the spot (lawyers, photographers, and so on).

It was easier to reject the government's hollow ritual than to work out specific plans for acting in a more dynamic fashion. Since it was impossible to know where the government's line of defense would be drawn, we could only suggest a general program of nonviolent militancy, which would express itself through a number of flexible probes and thrusts. Different groups would seek to reach strategic areas where meaningful blockage and disruption could take place. We thought that we might have to concentrate at the last minute on roads and bridges, possibly even on strategic areas in Washington. Fortunately, this did not prove necessary.

It was not until the 21st itself, at a meeting of the steering committee which lasted until 4:30 A.M., that we finally stumbled on an idea which seems very simple in retrospect—that of combining active resistance with a teach-in for the troops. The massiveness of the expected turnout, together with our announced intention of disrupting the Pentagon, had prompted the government to import thousands and thousands of troops. Gradually it became clear to us that the government was going to supply us with a captive audience of the very men on whose blind servility it must rely to carry out its criminal aggression.

We have been saying for a long time that all strata of society are honeycombed with doubt and dissent. There is a lot of evidence that these include the armed forces. Further, we believe in participatory democracy—the right of those who carry out a policy to have a say in decision making. Obviously the soldiers have profound stakes in the policy in question—their lives and consciences. So why not make a determined appeal to the soldiers to discover the truth about the war and to act accordingly? To follow their own consciences rather than to accept unquestioningly the directives of the Pentagon and the White House? Why should it be assumed that American youth can be deprived of their "inalienable rights" simply because the government decides to conscript them? Conscription itself is a prima facie denial of democracy.

Because of the vast numbers involved on both sides, the number of separate but interacting scenes, and the lack of precedents, no one should be judged harshly. It was a fast-moving, turbulent affair in which people often had to make split-second decisions. But it is important to analyze dispassionately the relevance and effectiveness of various types of actions, in order to rid ourselves of stereotypes and prepare for future activities.

One of the lessons of the weekend was that it is indeed practical to forge a creative synthesis of Gandhi and guerrilla, although the exact forms are still hard to define and must be worked out through a process of trial and error. As the scene was played out on the 21st, some of the initial actions were crude guerrilla, such as the occasional heaping of abuse on the soldiers. In the concrete situation this was a caricature of revolutionary militancy, not being grounded in either the political or military realities. Others were static, semi-Gandhian gestures, such as a few self-conscious attempts to be arrested and led away without regard for the dynamics of the drama that was being acted out between the resisters and the troops. This, in turn, was a caricature of revolutionary nonviolence. But gradually a more positive pattern emerged as a revolutionary élan developed among the resisters. It was an élan based on the shared experience of holding firm and making do against the menace of all those troops and all that weaponry, a menace made real by spasmodic arrests, brutality and use of tear gas. It was also based on the discovery that the soldiers were our brothers. A community grew up that reached out to embrace first the resisters and then the soldiers as well. After all, soldiers are the first to lose their freedom and their lives. They, too, are victims and potential revolutionaries.

We didn't make many converts on the spot—nor should we expect to in most public confrontations. But like the Vietnamese we are engaged in a long struggle for liberation. We cannot afford to give up on everyone the military-industrial complex succeeds in drafting or seducing into its service. We too must make clear our determination to "afford conditions" for them to "join the people's fight against U.S. aggression [and] to save and build the country."

In the prolonged confrontation at the Mall entrance, two and possibly three soldiers did lay down their arms and attempt to cross over to our side. Two others—paratroopers—showed up at one of our Washington offices on Monday and said that they and large numbers of their fellows were "on your side." Despite the real and inexcusable brutality of marshals and police, and despite the shortsighted actions of a few "superrevolutionaries" in our own ranks who vilified the soldiers and made it more difficult for them to empathize with us, most of us either experienced or witnessed incidents in which soldiers were clearly moved by our combination of militant resistance and appeals to their political and personal interests. Cigarettes, coffee and friendly words were exchanged. Most of the resisters refused to be enemies and many of the soldiers discovered that they could not be.

In the series of encounters on the west flank, in which I and others were kicked, beaten and eventually arrested, not more than a half dozen soldiers out of perhaps a hundred who came into direct contact with us actually took part in the violence, although they were all egged on at one time or another by some of the sergeants, who in turn were in radio contact with higher officials inside the Pentagon. I do not imagine that we will always get off so lightly, but my own experience in a number of more violent situations—in the South, in prison, and in antiwar demonstrations—convinces me that a firm but nonviolent response to brutality is both the best defense and the most effective way of forcing the assailants to reexamine their prejudices and their roles. From the few words the soldiers uttered and the looks on the faces of those who kicked so gently that it did no damage (or refrained altogether), there was no doubt in our minds that our non-violent actions and appeals were having a profound effect on them. They were clearly caught in the middle, between their "military duty" on the one hand and their humane instinct and doubts about the war on the other. Their attitudes seemed to range from active sympa-thy and disillusionment with their situation to bewilderment and confusion.

Only time will determine the effect of this and subsequent confrontations. Certainly our plans must call for further attempts to confront the men in uniform—in everything from leafleting and dis-cussing to large-scale confrontations. It would be a serious error in tactics to adopt only one part of the activities that made October 21 and 22 so significant. Besides attempting blockage and disruption, we should continue to appeal to soldiers (and others who are called out against us) to act as free and responsible individuals. There is a great deal of satisfaction in achieving visible victories—gaining a few square feet of forbidden territory at the Pentagon, shutting down an induction center for at least a few hours, or stopping recruiters for the C.I.A., Dow Chemical or the State Department from doing their dirty work on the campus. But there are times when we may have to choose between temporarily capturing an outpost and cap-turing the minds and hearts of those who man it. Like "moral wit-ness" and dissent, resistance can degenerate into self-expressionism and personal catharsis unless we keep our objective goals in mind.

There is another aspect of the events in Washington that must not be overlooked. The Mobilization had a maximum impact because it combined massive action with the cutting edge of resistance. To begin with, we forced the government's representatives into a corner by insisting on our legal right to hold a march and rally. They got off on the wrong foot when they first stalled negotiations concerning permits and then tried to violate the constitutional rights of oppo-nents of the war by threatening to deny the permits altogether. As a result, many who had not been planning to travel long distances to

Washington decided to come in order to meet the challenge. Others came in a more militant spirit.

Without the direct action (which was badly needed in its own right), many of the young and the militant of all ages would not have bothered to take time off from their other involvements. On the other hand, thousands of others would not have come without the conventional march and rally and the assurance that the first rally would be sufficiently separated from the direct action to safeguard people against getting entrapped in activities that did not appeal to them. In addition, having a range of activities of different intensities made it possible for many who were ambivalent to come, savor the scene, and decide at the last minute how far they would go. Instead of weighing the merits of resistance amid the artificial seductions of middle-class affluence, they were enabled to decide in a more realistic context. They felt a sense of urgency and the strength that comes from community.

Without the massive numbers made possible by the presence of all these types, the day would have had far less impact and the resistance phase itself would have been less successful. In jail I talked with many persons who previously had not felt the need for resistance but had come to feel it that day. Others came to Washington and did not participate in the direct action but added the strength of numbers. They became part of a force of thousands of honest witnesses who went back to their local communities and counteracted the efforts of the press and the President to give a distorted impression of what happened in Washington. As with the soldiers, only the future will reveal the overall effect that day had on them.

Late at night, on the steps of the Mall entrance to the Pentagon, the Army drove a wedge of soldiers between the resisters. In this way they made it easier for the marshals to beat and arrest many resisters by twos and threes. The administration would like nothing better than to drive a political wedge between the dissenters and the resisters. They would like the antiwar movement to be as fragmented as possible. Those of us who are enthusiastic about new tactics must not do the government's job for it by plunging into the new phase self-righteously or with a short-sighted adoption of divisive and sectarian tactics.

As we all know, in South Vietnam the guerrillas are like fish and the masses of people constitute the friendly ocean which provides protection and support. If we are serious about the need for an American resistance, we must not cut ourselves off from the millions who are just beginning to oppose the war, the millions who are ambivalent and those who are prepared to dissent but not to rebel. On the steps of the Pentagon our cry to the soldiers was "Join us! Join us!" This cry must be reflected both in the working out of our tactics and in the heat of the actual confrontations.

In a time when an old and dehumanized society is breaking down there is a natural pathway for honest men that leads through dissent and protest to resistance, and from resistance to rebellion and revolution. Let us move forward as rapidly as we can, while preserving the humanistic values that led us to dissent in the first place. And let us keep the pathway open for those who may lag behind us today but may very well move ahead of us tomorrow.

The Future of Nonviolence

1965   The theory and practice of active nonviolence are roughly at the stage of development today as those of electricity in the early days of Marconi and Edison. A new source of power has been discovered and crudely utilized in certain specialized situations, but our experience is so limited and our knowledge so primitive that there is legitimate dispute about its applicability to a wide range of complicated and critical tasks. One often hears it said that nonviolent resistance was powerful enough to drive the British out of India but would have been suicidal against the Nazis. Or that Negroes can desegregate a restaurant or bus by nonviolence but can hardly solve the problem of jobs or getting rid of the Northern ghettos, since both of these attempts require major assaults on the very structure of society and run head-on into the opposition of entrenched interests in the fields of business, finance, and public information. Finally, most of those who urge nonviolent methods on the Negro hesitate to claim that the United States should do away with its entire military force and prepare to defend itself in the jungle of international politics by nonviolent methods.

There is no doubt in my mind that nonviolence is currently incapable of resolving some of the problems that must be solved if the human race is to survive—let alone create a society in which all persons have a realistic opportunity to achieve material fulfillment and personal dignity. Those who are convinced that nonviolence can be used in *all* conflict situations have a responsibility to devise concrete methods by which it can be made effective. For example, can we urge the Negroes of Harlem or the *obreros* and *campesinos* (workers and peasants) of Latin America to refrain from violence if we offer them no positive method of breaking out of the slums, poverty, and cultural privation that blight their lives and condemn their children to a similar fate? It is contrary to the best tradition of nonviolence to do so. Gandhi often made the point that it is better to resist injustice by violent methods than not to resist at all. He staked his own life on his theory that nonviolent resistance was the superior method, but he never counselled appeasement or passive nonresistance.

The major advances in nonviolence have not come from people who have approached nonviolence as an end in itself, but from persons who were passionately striving to free themselves from social injustice. Gandhi discovered the method almost by accident when he went to South Africa as a young, British-trained lawyer in search of a career, but was "sidetracked" by the shock of experiencing galling racial segregation. Back in India, the humiliations of foreign rule turned him again to nonviolence, not as an act of religious withdrawal and personal perfectionism, but, in line with his South African experience, as the most practical method Indians could use in fighting for their independence. During World War I, not yet convinced that the method of nonviolence could be used successfully in such a large-scale international conflict, he actually helped recruit Indians for the British Army. By contrast, during World War II, after twenty more years of experimentation with nonviolence, he counselled nonviolent resistance to the Nazis and actually evolved a plan for nonviolent opposition to the Japanese should they invade and occupy India.

In 1958 the Negroes of Montgomery, Alabama, catapulted nonviolence into the limelight in the United States, not out of conversion to pacifism or love for their oppressors, but because they had reached a point where they could no longer tolerate certain racial injustices. Martin Luther King, Jr., who later became a pacifist, employed an armed defense guard to protect his home and family during one stage of the Montgomery conflict. In 1963, one of the leaders of the mass demonstrations in Birmingham said to me: "You might as well say that we never heard of Gandhi or nonviolence, but we were determined to get our freedom, and in the course of struggling for it we came upon nonviolence like gold in the ground."

There is not much point in preaching the virtues of nonviolence to a Negro in Harlem or Mississippi except as a method for winning his freedom. For one thing, the built-in institutional violence imposed on him every day of his life looms too large. He can rightly say that he wants no part of a nonviolence that condemns his spasmodic rock-throwing or desperate and often knowingly unrealistic talk of armed self-defense, but mounts no alternative campaign. It is all too easy for those with jobs, adequate educational opportunities, and decent housing to insist that Negroes remain nonviolent—to rally to the defense of "law and order." "Law and order is the Negro's best friend," Mayor Robert Wagner announced in the midst of the 1964 riots in Harlem. But nonviolence and a repressive law and order have nothing in common. The most destructive violence in Harlem is not the bottle-throwing, looting, or muggings of frustrated and demoralized Negroes. Nor is it the frequent shootings of juvenile delinquents and suspected criminals by white policemen, who often reflect both the racial prejudices of society and the personal propensity to violence that led them to choose a job whose tools are the club and the revolver. The basic violence in Harlem is the vast, impersonal violation of bodies and souls by an unemployment rate four times that of white New Yorkers, a median family income between half and two thirds that of white families, an infant mortality rate of 45.3 per thousand compared to 26.3 for New York as a whole, and inhuman crowding into subhuman housing. (It has been estimated that if the entire population of the United States were forced to live in equally congested conditions, it would fit into three of New York City's five boroughs.) Many white Americans are thrilled by the emotional catharsis of a law-abiding March on Washington (or even a fling at civil disobedience), in which they work off their guilt feelings, conscious and unconscious, by "identifying" for a day with the black victims of society. But when the project is over the whites do not return home anxious to know whether any of their children have been bitten by a rat, shot by a cop, or victimized by a pimp or dope peddler.

Commitment to nonviolence must not be based on patient acquiescence in intolerable conditions. Rather, it stems from a deeper knowledge of the self-defeating, self-corrupting effect of lapses into violence. On the one hand, Gandhi did not ally himself with those who profit from injustice and conveniently condemn others who violently fight oppression. On the other hand, he temporarily suspended several of his own nonviolent campaigns because some of his followers had succumbed to the temptations of violent reprisal. In perfecting methods of nonviolence, he gradually crystallized certain attitudes toward the nature of man (even oppressive, exploitative, foreign-invader man), which he formulated in the terminology of his native religion and which he considered indispensable for true nonviolence. These basic insights have been translated by religious Western pacifists (including Martin Luther King) from their original language to that of Christianity. Similarly, they can be retranslated into the secular humanist terminology which is more natural to large numbers of Northern Negroes and white civil-rights activists.

The key attitudes stem from a feeling for the solidarity of all human beings, even those who find themselves in deep conflict. George Meredith once said that a truly cultivated man is one who realizes that the things which seem to separate him from his fellows are as nothing compared with those which unite him with all humanity. Nonviolence may start, as it did with the young Gandhi and has with many an American Negro, as a technique for wresting gains from an unloved and unlovely oppressor. But somewhere along the line, if a nonviolent movement is to cope with deep-seated fears and privileges, its strategy must flow from a sense of the underlying unity of all human beings. So must the crucial, semi-spontaneous, inventive actions that emerge (for good or ill) in the midst of crisis.

This does not mean that Negroes, for example, must "love" in a sentimental or emotional way those who are imprisoning, shooting, beating, or impoverishing them. Nor need they feel personal affection for complacent white liberals. But it is not enough to abandon the use of fists, clubs, Molotov cocktails, and guns. Real nonviolence requires an awareness that white oppressors and black victims are mutually entrapped in a set of relationships that violate the submerged better instincts of everyone. A way has to be found to open the trap and free both sets of victims. Appeals to reason or decency have little effect (except in isolated instances) unless they are accompanied by tangible pressures—on the pocketbook, for example—or the inconveniences associated with sit-ins, move-ins, strikes, boycotts, or nonviolent obstructionism. But for any lasting gain to take place the struggle must appeal to the whole man, including his encrusted sense of decency and solidarity, his yearnings to recapture the lost innocence when human beings were persons to be loved, not objects to rule, obey, or exploit.

This reaching out to the oppressor has nothing to do with tokenism, which tends to creep into any movement, including a non-violent one. In fact, tokenism is a double violation of the attitude of solidarity, because it permits the oppressor to make, and the oppressed to accept, a gesture which leaves intact the institutional barriers that separate them. One can gain a token victory or make a political deal without needing to have any invigorating personal contact with the "enemy," certainly without bothering to imagine oneself in his place so as to understand his needs, fears and aspirations. But the more revolutionary a movement's demands, the more imperative it is to understand what is necessary for the legitimate fulfillment of the persons who make up the opposition.

"We're going to win our freedom," a Negro leader said at a mass meeting in Birmingham last year, "and as we do it we're going to set our white brothers free." A short while later, when the Negroes faced a barricade of police dogs, clubs and fire hoses, they "became spiritually intoxicated," as another leader described it. "This was sensed by the police and firemen and it began to have an effect on them. . . . I don't know what happened to me. I got up from my knees and said to the cops: 'We're not turning back. We haven't done anything wrong. All we want is our freedom. How do you feel doing these things?'" The Negroes started advancing and Bull Connor shouted: "Turn on the water!" But the firemen did not respond. Again he gave the order and nothing happened. Some observers claim they saw firemen crying. Whatever happened, the Negroes went through the lines. The next day, Bull Connor was reported by the press to have said: "I didn't want to mess their Sunday clothes, all those people from church." Until now this mood of outgoing empathetic nonviolence has been rarely achieved in this country. It was only part of the story in Birmingham, where in the end a more cautious tokenism gripped the top leaders. But it is the clue to the potential power of nonviolence.

Vinoba Bhave indicates something of the same interaction on the level of international conflict when he says: "Russia says America has dangerous ideas so she has to increase her armaments. America says exactly the same thing about Russia. . . . The image in the mirror is your own image; the sword in its hand is your own sword. And when we grasp our own sword in fear of what we see, the image in the mirror does the same. What we see in front of us is nothing but a reflection of ourselves. If India could find courage to reduce her army to the minimum, it would demonstrate to the world her moral strength. But we are cowards and cowards have no imagination."

The potential uses of nonviolent power are tremendous and as yet virtually unrealized. But it is important to understand that non-violence can never be "developed" in such a way as to carry out some of the tasks assigned to it by its more naïve converts—any more than God (or the greatest scientist) could draw a square circle. It would be impossible, for instance, to defend the United States of America, as we know it, nonviolently. This is not because of any inherent defect in the nonviolent method but because of a very important strength: nonviolence cannot be used successfully to protect special privileges that have been won by violence. The British could not have continued to rule India by taking a leaf out of Gandhi's book and becoming "nonviolent." Nor would the United States be able to maintain its dominant position in Latin America if it got rid of its armies, navies, "special forces," C.I.A.-guerrillas, etc. Does anyone think that a majority of the natives work for a few cents a day, live in rural or urban slums, and allow forty-four percent of their children to die before the age of five because they love us? Or that they are content to have American business drain away $500 million a year in interest and dividends, on the theory that the shareholders of United Fruit Company or the Chase Manhattan Bank are more needy or deserving than themselves?

It follows that advocates of nonviolence are overly optimistic when they argue from the unthinkability of nuclear war and the partially proven power of nonviolence (in India and the civil rights struggle) to the position that simple common sense will lead the United States (the richest, most powerful nation in the world, on whose business investments and armed forces the sun never sets) to substitute nonviolent for violent national defense. In recent years a number of well-intentioned peace groups have tried to convince the government and members of the power elite that the Pentagon should sponsor studies with this end in view. But nonviolent defense requires not only willingness to risk one's life (as any good soldier, rich or poor, will do). It requires renunciation of all claims to special privileges and power at the expense of other people. In our society most people find it more difficult to face economic loss while alive than death itself. Surrender of special privilege is certainly foreign to the psychology of those who supply, command, and rely on the military. Nonviolence is supremely the weapon of the dispossessed, the underprivileged, and the egalitarian, not of those who are still addicted to private profit, commercial values, and great wealth.

Nonviolence simply cannot defend property rights over human rights. The primacy of human rights would have to be established within the United States and in all of its dealings with other peoples before nonviolence could defend this country successfully. Nonviolence could defend what is worth defending in the United States, but a badly needed social revolution would have to take place in the process. Guerrilla warfare cannot be carried on successfully without the active support and cooperation of the surrounding population, which must identify justice (or at least its own welfare) with the triumph of the guerrillas. Nonviolence must rely even more heavily than guerrilla warfare on the justice of its cause. It has no chance of succeeding unless it can win supporters from previously hostile or neutral sections of the populace. It must do this by the fairness of its goals. Its objectives and methods are intimately interrelated and must be equally nonviolent.

The followers of Gandhi were imprisoned, beaten and, on more than one occasion, shot by the British during the Indian independence campaign. Today, some Americans consider the death of a nonviolent campaigner as conclusive evidence that "nonviolence won't work" and call for substitution of a violent campaign—in which people will also be killed and the original aims tend to be lost in an orgy of violence. But instead of allowing the British in effect to arm them, thereby giving the British the choice of weapons, the Gandhians kept right on fighting nonviolently and in the end succeeded in "disarming" the British. In the case of a number of nonviolent marches, the first row of advancing Indians was shot, but a second and a third row kept moving forward until the British soldiers became psychologically incapable of killing any more, even risking death at the hands of their superiors by disobeying orders to keep on firing. Eventually it became politically impossible for the commanders and the Prime Ministers to issue such orders. Need I add that if the Indians had been shot while trying to invade England and carry off its wealth, it would not have mattered how courageously nonviolent they had been; they could not have aroused this response.

If a practitioner of nonviolence is killed fighting for a cause that is considered unjust, he is quickly dismissed as a fanatic. Indeed, at this stage of the struggle that is exactly what many white Southerners have tried to do in the cases of Medgar Evers, James Chaney, Michael Schwerner, and Andrew Goodman. But if the nonviolent warriors freely risk death in devotion to a cause that people recognize, even against their wills, as legitimate, the act has a tremendous effect. Willingness to sacrifice by undergoing imprisonment, physical punishment or, if need be, death itself, without retaliation, will not always dislodge deeply engrained prejudice or fear, but its general effect is always to work in that direction. By contrast, infliction of such penalties at best intimidates the opposition and at worst strengthens resistance, but in any case does not encourage psychological openness to a creative resolution of the underlying conflict of views or values.

Perhaps we can paraphrase Karl von Clausewitz's well-known observation that war is but the continuation of the politics of peace by other means, and say that the social attitudes of nonviolent defense must be a continuation of the social attitudes of the society it is defending. A little thought should convince us of the impossibility of keeping Negroes and colonial peoples in their present positions of inferiority once privileged white America is unable to rely on overt or covert violence. Secondly, it is ludicrous to expect such persons to join their oppressors in the uncoerced defense of the society that has treated them so poorly. (Even with the power of the draft at its disposal—backed by the threat of imprisonment and ultimately the firing squad—the United States found it necessary to make unprecedented concessions and promises to Negroes during World War II in order to keep up black morale.) Finally, there is the crucial question of how we can expect to treat our enemies nonviolently if we do not treat our friends and allies so.

On the crudest level, as long as we are willing to condemn two out of five children in Latin America to early death, in order to increase our material comforts and prosperity, by what newly found awareness of human brotherhood will we be able to resist the temptation to wipe out two out of five, three out of five, or even five out of five of the children of China in overt warfare if it is dinned into us that this is necessary to preserve our freedom, or the lives of ourselves and our own children? If we cannot respect our neighbors more than to keep large numbers of them penned up in rat-infested slum ghettos, how will we develop the sense of human solidarity with our opponents without which nonviolence becomes an empty technicality and loses its power to undermine and sap enemy hostility and aggressiveness? How will we reach across the propaganda-induced barriers of hate, fear, and self-righteousness (belief in the superiority of one's country, race or system) to disarm ourselves and our enemies?

Part Five

The Chicago Convention
and After

The Aims

1968 Every four years the country holds a presidential election, and for opponents of the status quo the question becomes what to do about it. Usually the antiwar movement is divided between those who support a candidate (whether enthusiastically or as a "lesser evil") and those who argue, as *Liberation* has done in the last three presidential elections, that to give serious support to any of the candidates is to divert energy and attention away from the primary tasks of movement building and direct action into the sideshow of electoral politics, where the establishment holds the trump cards. These cards consist of the power of big money and big government to control the obviously undemocratic nominating and vote-getting procedures and the power of these forces, plus the entrenched military, to circumscribe or overpower any recalcitrant officials who may have slipped through the electoral net. It is *Liberation*'s contention that the power of the establishment can be eroded and replaced only through the development of an active resistance movement and the building of countercommunities and counterinstitutions.

Of the three candidates supported by those in the Movement who disagreed with the *Liberation* position, Adlai Stevenson ended up as the official liar for the Kennedy and Johnson administrations at the U.N. (Bay of Pigs invasion, Vietnam, the Congo, etc.). Undoubt-edly this was an immense personal tragedy, which demonstrates not that all candidates are evil but that the system shares one character-istic with most violent revolutions: an insatiable appetite which prompts it to devour its own more idealistic offspring. John Kennedy was also devoured—in one quick gulp, at Dallas—even though, as Hans Morgenthau has pointed out:

> while he lived as president he achieved little of substance. His domestic program was hopelessly stymied in Congress. In foreign policy he was responsible for the fiasco of the Bay of Pigs; the Alliance for Progress never got off the ground; he achieved a tactical success and suffered a strategic defeat in the Cuban missile crisis; he started our serious involve-ment in Vietnam by increasing the number of military advis-ers from 500 to 10,000; he endeavored to counter the disinte-gration of the Atlantic alliance with the stillborn multilateral seaborne nuclear force. Only the limited test-ban treaty and the development of mobile conventional military forces can be counted real successes. [One is tempted to ask where the development of mobile military forces was a success. In Vietnam? The Dominican Republic? Detroit and Newark, last summer? On October 21 and 22 at the Pentagon?] The rest was rhetoric—well-chosen, forward-looking words— from which no action followed. (*New York Review of Books,* August 1, 1968.)

The third "peace candidate" for the presidency, during *Libera-tion*'s lifetime, was Lyndon Baines Johnson.

This year the fundamental tactical choices remain the same. The debate goes on in antiwar circles as to whether a McCarthy or a McGovern will turn out to be an improvement over any or all of Stevenson, Kennedy, or Johnson. As always there are many secondary debates too: what Senator McCarthy's "real" views and program are; whether or not he has a chance of winning either the nomination or the election unless he comes to terms with key sectors of the repressive establishment; whether, in fact, he needs to come to such terms or is already there; whether "liberalism" has anything to offer, even as a rearguard action, in this sick and rapidly polarizing society; whether as an alternative to a McCarthy campaign to run an "educational" campaign in behalf of a candidate such as Eldridge Cleaver or Dick Gregory whose lack of financial resources, media support and establishment machinery dooms him to electoral failure.

It might also be worth raising another matter, one which does not relate directly to the question of whether or not to support McCarthy but helps suggest where things are at in the summer of 1968: how long would the forces that did away with the two Kennedys, Martin Luther King, Jr., and Malcolm X—and are striving to put away Rap Brown, Huey Newton, Eldridge Cleaver, Dr. Spock, and others—be willing to let Eugene McCarthy stay alive if he did win the election and continued to maintain his unconventional style or his liberal politics?

Despite all the similarities between 1968 and previous presidential election years, something new has been added this time. It stems from the greater militancy of the movement and the growth of resistance and street tactics in the past few years, even among those groups and individuals who are not ready to abandon electoral tactics altogether. Eugene McCarthy may be making a determined effort to move people out of the streets and into the polling booths, but many of his supporters are obviously unwilling to confine their activities to lobbying and vote-gathering. A lot of students who wear McCarthy buttons took part in the occupation of buildings at Columbia. Others showed up in Washington to take part in the Poor People's Campaign during that brief period at the beginning when it appeared that the campaign's organizers were serious about wanting to develop a militant program of nonviolent direct action.

The National Mobilization Committee to End the War in Vietnam has developed imaginative plans for actions at the Democratic convention in Chicago which should unite both the more militant McCarthy supporters and thousands of opponents of the war and black repression who have no faith in present electoral procedures (or any possible refinement of these procedures, such as the so-called open convention) under the present economic system. For six days, from August 24 to 29, a combination of movement workshops, decentralized actions and massive rallies, marches and street protests has been scheduled. The decentralized actions are to be planned in Movement Centers, with likely targets being draft boards and induction centers, urban-renewal headquarters, police stations, research centers for chemical and biological warfare. There is even to be a special un-

birthday party on August 27 to counter the official Democratic celebration of L.B.J.'s birthday.

In these and other events, the Mobilization is asking tens of
thousands of Americans to:

> *demonstrate that the politicians do not speak for us;*
> *encourage and help discontented Democrats to seek new and*
>   *independent forms of protest and resistance;*
> *build a framework of continuing action for the postconven-*
>   *tion period;*
> *demonstrate our determination to stay in the streets of*
>   *America,* whoever the candidate or whatever the plat-
>   form, *until every G.I. is home from Vietnam.*

Not surprisingly, questions about the political feasibility of
this program have been raised from opposite ends of the movement
spectrum:

> 1) Does it not hurt McCarthy's chances by making it
> possible for his opponents to identify him with an unruly
> and "alienated" constituency?
>
> 2) Does it not foster the illusion that the electoral
> process offers people the opportunity to have a say in the
> decisions that affect their lives? Even if we are not coöpted
> directly by McCarthy or McGovern, do we not contribute
> indirectly to the overemphasis on the electoral process just
> by showing up at the convention, even in a protest capacity?

In relation to the McCarthy candidacy, it is doubtful that
McCarthy would have adopted his mildly antiwar position, would
have entered the New Hampshire primaries or would have received
sufficient support to have kept his candidacy somewhat viable, except
for the turmoil and pressures created by teach-ins, street demonstrations and active resistance. To abandon these tactics now would cut
down the movement's leverage and weaken McCarthy's bargaining
power. If McCarthy receives the support from within the establishment without which a successful candidacy is impossible, such support would come as a concession not to the movement's respectability
but to its power. The movement's power comes from those who refuse to be drafted, refuse to pay war taxes, desert or refuse orders in
the army, fill the streets, occupy buildings at Columbia, etc. Any can-

didate who is worthy of support had better have plenty of such "troops" visible if he is to be taken seriously before or after election. Given the history of previous peace candidates, we shall need *more* troops. The future will determine whether we need them to support a McCarthy, to keep him honest or to combat him.

As to the second question, the eyes of the world are on Chicago as the Democratic machine acts out its ritual of pretending to consult the people while escalating its aggression in Vietnam and the concomitant poverty and largely racist repression at home. What better place to demonstrate our determination to stay in the streets and not to be distracted from our major tasks by promises and candidates? We are presenting our more far-reaching programs and alternative methods at the very altars of the electoral ritual. The contrast is clear; the message will not be missed. Unlike most organizers of demonstrations at previous conventions, we are not concerning ourselves with the selection of candidates or the wording of the platform (that perennial document of hypocrisy and irrelevance). Our main targets are not the convention but institutions of militarism and racism in the convention city at convention time.

Naturally, many of the demonstrators are concerned with candidates and platforms. Movement workshops provide ample opportunity to discuss the pros and cons of electoral politics, the strengths and weaknesses of the candidates, the opportunities and limitations of public office under the present system. The Mobilization invites everyone—from delegates to the convention to those who are disillusioned with electoral politics—to take part in the discussions and the issue-oriented protests.

The Lessons

1968 When police dogs were photographed biting little children in Birmingham, Alabama, during the 1963 nonviolent civil-rights demonstrations, Police Chief Bull Connor complained of the press coverage. He said that in the face of similar provocation the solid citizens and police of Northern cities would respond in the same way. Now, some Chicago residents are defending the reputation of their city by saying that the events during convention week could have happened in any city in the country. This is a poor excuse, but unfortunately a fairly accurate description of where things are heading, give or take a few months, if the war continues. To zero in on Richard Daley as an atypical villain is as false as to lay exclusive blame for the war in Vietnam on Lyndon Johnson, an error in analysis which was laid bare last March, when the people who run the country fired L.B.J. in a holding action aimed at robbing the opposition of a tangible enemy. Daley may be the last of the old bosses, but unless the American people find a way to repudiate not just his methods but also the society he is defending, he may turn out to be the first of the new "realists," every bit as prophetic as Connor was.

The levels of tolerance and the managerial skills of the authorities vary considerably from city to city, but the basic power relationships remain pretty much the same. The veneer of democracy and respect for human rights tends to crack when the power elite is threatened with a clear and present danger to the continuation of its political power, foreign-policy prerogatives, or property rights. I refer not only to police riots against unarmed antiwar demonstrators in Los Angeles, Oakland, New York, and other cities in recent months. More basic to an understanding of the dynamics of our society, the prisons of every city and state are filled to overflowing with persons who have lost all their human rights because they violated existing property fetishes. These property relationships exalt private and corporate property over life, liberty and human community. They deny the essentials of human dignity (adequate food, housing and medical care; meaningful work and egalitarian relationships) to millions of persons in the midst of an era of technological abundance and democratic rhetoric. Let anyone who knows that the deck is stacked against him try to introduce a few wild cards of his own and society puts him away, if he isn't killed trying to avoid arrest.

The police know how our society deals with serious dissenters. One can understand their confusion and resentment when they are criticized for using these methods against the sons and daughters of the middle class who have begun to engage in active resistance. But I am glad for the revulsion against the use of police-state methods in Chicago and against the Humphrey-Daley suppression of constitutional rights by these methods. What the country needs is not a cynical acceptance of such barbaric methods on the theory that clergymen, newsmen, Yippies and white antiwar protesters must stay in line or accept the treatment routinely accorded the lower classes when they get out of line. Rather we need to extend the revulsion to include rejection of the use of such methods wherever they are used—against blacks, Puerto Ricans, Vietnamese, Latin Americans; against the native populations of countries which the decision makers covet for their corporate empire. After all, one reason demonstrators were clubbed and gassed in Chicago was that they had begun to identify with the other victims. With touching irony, Mayor Daley called the demonstrators "terrorists" and "Communists," employing the same distorted fear-words that his cronies use to justify U.S. actions in Vietnam. (In Czechslovakia, the Russians call people like us "counterrevolutionaries.")

George Wallace's alliance with H. L. Hunt and the oil-, space-, and war-industry millionaires on the one hand, and with large numbers of your local police on the other, is merely bringing out into the open some of the longtime relationships of our society. The better-established members of the power elite would prefer to preserve the liberal facade. It makes them feel better, confuses the opposition, and does not interfere with their power or privileges. But times are changing, the natives are getting restless, and possibly Wallace reads the situation more accurately than his betters. He demands a clear rejection of the liberalism which has soothed the consciences and protected the life-styles of the cultured middle and upper classes but has seldom prevented the decision makers from making ugly decisions or the lower class from being victims. In the decade of the credibility gap, Wallace is the only candidate who is credible because he openly embraces the realities that lie beneath the surface of our society.

Lester Maddox, Georgia's pickhandle-wielding governor, made a belated national sally into the same rich pastures when he announced, wistfully, after the battle of Chicago that he would like to run for president with Daley as his running mate. But historically Daley has always been a Kennedy man, just as he was the choice of both Jack and Bobby. "It should be recalled," says *Ramparts* in its September 28, 1968 issue, "that the Chicago mayor both backed John Kennedy in 1960 and—by all recent studies—stole the election for him by juggling the vote in Chicago precincts to give Kennedy his hair-breadth win in Illinois and the electoral edge." "Daley's the ball game," declared Robert F. Kennedy last spring, as he set out to prove himself worthy of the mayor's support. And while Daley's police were cracking the heads of demonstrators, Daley himself was trying to put together a draft for Teddy—one last try at the old supervised slaughter in which your fighter is clean-cut and boyish but lets you tape a lead pipe inside his gloves.

The old alliance of liberals who deliver the speeches and political realists who do the gut-fighting has been cracking for ten years now under pressure from Cubans, Vietnamese, blacks, students, and the antiwar movement. Either the humane rhetoric must become a reality for the first time (with the profound changes in economic and other power relationships that implies) or the contempt for human life which has always existed just below the surface will become increasingly naked and brutal. Today, as it relies more openly on the Bomb, napalm, C.I.A.-style assassinations, and Chicago police actions, the power system multiplies its own difficulties both at home and abroad. Richard Daley reflected in Chicago the same paranoia, the same bewildered self-righteousness, the same faulty intelligence (both of information and interpretation), the same irrational reliance on violence which have driven the United States deeper and deeper into the quagmire in Vietnam. Insanity is not too strong a word for the neuroses which have got this country bogged down in a hopeless land war in Asia without any "decent respect for the opinions of mankind" or honest regard for the lives of hundreds of Americans and thousands of Vietnamese who are being killed every week. It's not so much that a computer which was fed the data on Vietnam and asked to provide an answer in line with America's professed ideals of democracy, justice, and human rights would prescribe the withdrawal of U.S. troops. More to the point, you'd get the same answer if you asked a computer to resolve the problem in line with America's real foreign policy goals: maximum possible preservation of the U.S. empire, with the American people seduced by prosperity and domestic civil liberties while the native populations are held in check through a discreet combination of foreign aid, C.I.A. subversion and military power.

One of the most basic problems in the United States is the way packaging, public relations mentality and computer programming are replacing durable human values—love, friendship, human warmth and sensitivity, and respect for those who differ from us politically or in the countless ways that define an individual—self-reliance, self-respect, and creativity as opposed to routine work performed for money and status. As a current tune asks:

> *Did you see your children growing up today*
> *And did you hear the music of their laughter*
> * as they settled out to play?*
> *Did you catch the fragrance of the roses in your*
> * garden?*
> *Did the morning sunlight warm your soul . . .*
> *Do you qualify to be alive?*

But in the last analysis U.S. politics seems incapable of responding to the current crises with even the intelligence of a public relations firm. Perhaps it's because behind the computers and the public relations' packaging lies the drive for profits. But there seems to be something more apocalyptic at work—the breakdown of intelligence which comes in the last suicidal stages of every attempt to dominate the world. "Whom the gods would destroy they first make mad." We see it in Imperial Rome, in Alexander the Great, the fifteenth century Popes, Louis XIV, Napoleon, and Hitler. But it's harder to face up to in one's own society.

Our more intelligent imperialists—men like Senators Fulbright, McGovern, Morse, McCarthy and the Kennedys, men who accept the profit motive and America's right to be the richest, most powerful nation in the world, with spheres of domination in those sections of the world it can still control—are being denied the opportunity to do for our selfish foreign policy what an earlier generation of enlightened businessmen and politicians did for our selfish domestic economy.

For several years after the stock market crash in 1929 and the ensuing collapse of the business economy, official voices proclaimed regularly that the tide had turned and prosperity was just around the corner, if only the American people would have faith in their leaders. Then, after years of needless suffering, the country gradually accepted the minimal reforms that had been denounced for years as un-American and immoral. The New Deal embraced (and coöpted) liberal reformers and union organizers, patching up the system without altering its basic characteristics. Now in a repetition of the thirties, we have been told for five years that the tide of battle in Vietnam has turned in our favor, victory is just around the corner, and—if we do not waver—the troops may start coming home "next year." Similarly, it is claimed that life has never been better for black people and the remaining inequities can be resolved by a program of investments by private capital in the ghetto (with government-guaranteed profits) and black capitalism. The problem is that none of this is true.

What is more, the system shows little interest in reforming itself. The Alliance for Progress in Latin America, the Poverty Program, the "other war" in Vietnam (by which the United States woos the hearts and minds of the people while moving them out of their villages into concentration camps, executing their patriots, arming and subsidizing their oppressors) were all minimal gestures, doomed to failure before they began. Instead of a choice between a Franklin Roosevelt and a Herbert Hoover, we are offered a Humphrey-Nixon, with George Wallace and the John Birch Society waiting in the wings. It's hard to imagine men whose personalities more clearly mirror the ugly and hypocritical policies they serve than Johnson, Humphrey and Nixon. One begins to believe in the literal reality of the Dorian Gray story in American political life.

This inability of the system to produce a smooth and enlightened administrator of the American empire is beyond ordinary, rational explanation. So is the symptomatic failure of the Democratic bigwigs to find a way of saving face vis-à-vis the demonstrators and antiwar delegates who came to Chicago. It's hard to believe that some smooth operator could not have sold the decision makers on a sensible plan for containing the demonstrators and minimizing both their own radicalization and their impact on the television public. Lincoln Park could have been made available for a mammoth Be-In, the rocking Festival of Life projected by the Yippies. Even without the bread which an ambitious Lindsay administration makes available occasionally to Abbie Hoffman and others, a groovy rock circus would have pacified many people who were ambivalent about a direct confrontation with clubs, guns, and tear gas or had reservations about the Mobilization's political style. But the authorities gave them no choice. The Yippies were not allowed to bring into the park a flat-bed truck or sound system for their rock bands, not even on a Sunday afternoon. And the police clubbed, Maced, gassed and drove into the streets anyone who tried to stay in the park after eleven—including 150 clergymen, Quakers, and religious pacifists who, after the first night of brutality, tried to hold an all-night prayer vigil, aided and abetted by such international figures as Jean Genêt, William Burroughs, Terry Southern, and Allen Ginsberg.

A smart politician could have threatened and harassed for months—as Daley did with his shoot-to-kill statements and his stockpiling of tanks, Mace and guns—and then, after thousands of potential demonstrators had been frightened away, handled the rest with kid gloves. (Conversely, if Daley had not threatened, harassed and denied permits, the bulk of the arriving demonstrators would have been older, calmer, less ready to resist physically.) He could have given the Mobilization eleventh-hour permits to march to the Amphitheatre, picket and hold public hearings nearby, while an impenetrable wall of fences, troops and weapons kept us out of the Amphitheatre itself. It was never the Mobilization's aim to invade the Amphitheatre or disrupt the convention. If a few individuals had tried (or for that matter, the whole body of demonstrators because they were enraged by the treatment they had received earlier) they could have been stopped without the indiscriminate and brutal assaults that were launched by the police as much as seven miles from the convention site. But to the guilt-ridden who see their power challenged, their credibility shattered and their authority slipping away, there are no allowable forms of opposition and no rational ways of dealing with dissent.

It's not as if there hadn't been a dress rehearsal in which Daley and the national Democratic Party could have learned the pitfalls of the path they eventually followed. They didn't stumble unwarned or unawares into the events of convention week. On April 27 the Chicago Mobilization and the Chicago Peace Council held an antiwar parade of about 6,500 persons and attempted to hold a rally in the Civic Plaza. As with the August mobilization, the organizers gave advance notification, applied for permits and made every effort to ensure public safety. But the city displayed the same contempt for constitutional process and human rights that characterized its performance on convention week. An investigation into the events of April 27 was conducted by an impartial citizens' committee, headed by Dr. Edward J. Sparling, President Emeritus of Roosevelt College and composed of distinguished civic leaders, none of whom had been close to the Chicago Peace Council or had taken part in the demonstration.*

After six weeks of investigation, the commission spoke of "the ostentatious brutality of the police. . . . This brutality, of which the Commission has more than adequate proof, was inexcusable. The circumstances of this brutality indicate police ineptitude as well as hostility." The report warned of the implications for the August demonstrations and summed up its findings as follows:

---

* *In addition to the chairman, Dr. Sparling, the members of the commission were Warren Cabon, vice-president of Inland Steel Corporation and member of the Chicago Board of Education; Dr Edgar H. Chandler, executive director of the Church Federation of Greater Chicago; Earl B. Dickerson, president of the Supreme Life Insurance Company of America and former alderman of the City of Chicago; Monsignor John J. Egan, pastor of Presentation Church; Dr. Joseph P. Evans, professor of neurological surgery at the University of Chicago; Professor Harry Kalven, Jr., University of Chicago Law School; Rev. E. Spencer Parsons, dean of Rockefeller Chapel; and Rabbi Edgar E. Siskin, president of the Chicago Board of Rabbis and North Shore Congregation Israel.*

On April 27, at the peace parade of the Chicago Peace Council, the police badly mishandled their task. Brutalizing demonstrators without provocation, they failed to live up to that difficult professionalism which we demand.

Yet to place primary blame on the police would, in our view, be inappropriate. The April 27 stage had been prepared by the Mayor's designated officials weeks before. Administrative actions concerning the April 27 Parade were designed by City officials to communicate that "these people have no right to demonstrate or express their views. . . ."

The political system of Chicago, not merely individual officers, was at work that Saturday. (*Dissent and Disorder, a report to the citizens of Chicago on the April 27 Peace Parade,* pp. 30-31.)

In August it was not just the political system of Chicago, but the political system of the entire country at work. The Democratic Party, its national committee and all the candidates, from Humphrey to McCarthy, had an obvious stake in what would happen in Chicago —not only on the convention floor but in the handling of the protesters as well. It's not hard to imagine the president—humiliated, forced into premature retirement, not even daring to show his face in the Amphitheatre—rubbing his hands in glee at the reception prepared for his tormentors. It's not hard to believe that Hubert and the party tacticians planned to rob Nixon of the "law and order" issue by cracking down on the demonstrators. At the same time this would serve as a warning to the demonstrators that they should take McCarthy's advice and abandon street demonstrations and resistance activities in favor of working through the "normal" democratic processes. Some of the party leaders and federal authorities were clearly involved in planning or approving the broad strategy that was employed. Others, like McCarthy, were probably excluded from the advance planning but had a moral and political responsibility to speak out when the plans were made public* and again when the pattern of brutal attack

---

* *On Friday, August 23, Brigadier General Richard T. Dunn, commander of the more than 5,500 National Guard troops, said that his men would "shoot to kill . . . if there is no other way of preventing the commission of a forcible felony. The troops will be carrying ammunition. We use .30-caliber ball ammunition. This kind of ammunition is made to kill."* (Chicago Daily News)

was established as early as Sunday night, August 25. For four days and nights of indescribable brutality, McCarthy had nothing to say. Not until his own campaign headquarters had been invaded and his workers clubbed did he speak at all. He came late and moderately into the struggle against the war in Vietnam and spoke out late and moderately against the Chicago police state. To think that we complain because the German Social Democrats held their silence so long while Hitler's Brown Shirts took over the streets of Germany!

Inside the convention hall itself Mayor Daley played a heavy hand, with his signals to the chair, his "overreaction" to Senator Ribicoff (who did have the courage to speak clearly about what was happening outside), his packing of the galleries with stooges. But the arrangements and security were handled by federal agents. Presumably certain delegates were bullied and slugged not by Daley's police but by thugs from the Secret Service and F.B.I. The proceedings were under the control of the national Democratic Party. "It was that Congressional crowd," Washington newsman Jack Anderson said to me the day the convention adjourned. "They ran the convention the same way they run the Congress of the United States." Congressman Don Rumsfeld of Illinois, also present at the time, said, "That's right. They ran it just like they run Congress." (This exchange took place during a break for commercials, when we were taping a TV show the day after the convention adjourned.) To complete the unholy trinity of reactionary Congressmen, the Daley machine and the White House, the executive director of the convention was John B. Criswell, treasurer of the Democratic National Committee and a Johnson man. A direct wire connected him with Daley and with Postmaster General Marvin Watson at L.B.J.'s secret command post on the twenty-first floor of the Conrad Hilton, which was staffed by such Johnson commandos as Jack Valenti, Joseph Califano and Bill McSweeney. As *Ramparts* described it, "When Criswell had a question about what to do next, he called Marvin Watson who, if a higher decision was necessary, called Johnson in Texas."

In the case of both Roosevelt and Truman, rising unemployment and growing opposition were turned into prosperity and the sweet smell of patriotic unity by World War II and the Korean war. The growing irrationality of the establishment's policies at home and abroad may culminate in a similar plunge into the unknown. Recently on the same day that Hubert Humphrey visited Harry Truman to ask him the secret of his success at the polls, a former Truman cabinet officer, Harry Sawyer, said that "The Bomb could solve the problem and probably will."

> The possibility of bombing Red China's missile bases has been suggested [Sawyer said] and this could well happen as a development of our current war in Vietnam. Our worry there seems to be that we will blunder into a war with China. If we have committed no blunders up to this time we should perhaps commit one now and blunder into a war with China. (*New York Daily News,* September 22)

Perhaps the problem is that it is later than our rulers think. Or perhaps, on the contrary, it is that they know how late it is and, like Samson, would rather bring the whole temple down on everyone rather than be mocked by their enemies.

II—FOR THE MOVEMENT

At one stage of the Battle of Chicago, we spoke of the objective of the day as being survival without surrender. Thus, when faced with vicious attacks we held our ground as long as we could, retreated, regrouped, and advanced again. Sometimes we returned in small groups and by circuitous routes to the area just vacated. Sometimes we moved into new areas, such as the streets or parks near the Conrad Hilton, where our impact would be greater or the furor of the police would be, if not restrained, at least recorded for the whole world to see. The triumph of Chicago was the triumph of street protesters who displayed courage, imagination, flexibility, and fraternal solidarity as they refused to knuckle under to the police. The role of centralized, formal leadership was minimal in these events. A crude but creative kind of participatory democracy was at work. The organic needs of the occasion, the interacting but spontaneous reactions of the participants, set the tone. Naturally these interacting reactions were based in large part on experiences at previous protests (including what had happened a few hours or minutes earlier) and on the myriad analyses and interpretations that make up the intellectual life of the movement.

The tone was also influenced by which sections of the movement came to Chicago and by which stayed away. I wish that there had been a greater turnout of people experienced in militant nonviolence

—more, for example, who do not think it is revolutionary to taunt the police by screaming "oink, oink" or "pig" at them and more who also are willing to experiment with the new mobile tactics which are developing in response to the movement's greater militancy and sense of urgency. Despite the claims of Mayor Daley and some of the movement's romantic guerrillas, the violence of our side was minimal, defensive and discriminating. It was aimed at slowing down the advancing cops, holding liberated territory and protecting our people. If our aim had been to create indiscriminate havoc by burning, destroying or looting, does anyone think that we could not have done a better job of it? As Julius Lester wrote in the *Guardian* for September 7, "The demonstrations are also a testimony to the impact that nonviolent demonstrations can have. And anyone who criticizes the demonstrations for being nonviolent is foolishly romantic. The easiest thing to have done in Chicago would have been to commit suicide."

But the problem of having an increasingly cruel and irrational enemy that has contempt for human life and makes a cynical mockery of the democratic values it claims to believe in is the danger of becoming cruel and irrational oneself in the act of combatting that enemy. Because "they" are vicious and wrong and "we" are humane and right, it is easy to conclude that whatever we do is justified. For the most part this did not happen in Chicago, but it has happened more than once in the history of revolutionary movements. And some of the conclusions people are drawing from the battle of Chicago point dangerously in that direction. One has only to talk to some of the participants—and to read some of the reports in the underground press which exaggerate and extol the violence of our side while forgetting to mention the reasons for our being there—to realize that it can happen here.

There is a heady sense of manhood that comes from advancing from apathy to commitment, from timidity to courage, from passivity to aggressiveness. Anyone who has been forced to yield ground or surrender his rights in the face of the superior force and legal backing of the occupying armies of the state would surely be thrilled to stand side by side with an aroused body of comrades in resisting the police assaults. Anyone who has stood helplessly by in a poor neighborhood while the police abused a suspect, or anywhere when his comrades in the movement were being taken off to kangaroo courts and jails could not but respond favorably to the occasions in Chicago when the police were denied their intended victims.

There is an intoxication that comes from standing up to the police at last. There is an even greater sense of satisfaction that comes from feeling oneself a functioning part of a larger whole whose members act together not only to protect one another but to serve a larger purpose as well. All the things that William James wrote about in his famous essay on the need for a moral equivalent to war were at work among the resisters in Chicago. Ordinarily, a society which has frustrated the natural community of mankind and deprived its citizens of a more social purpose than money-grubbing, offers them a counterfeit sense of community and national purpose in a holy war against a foreign enemy. In Chicago, for once, a generation which sees through the false idealism and ugly purposes of the U.S. aggression in Vietnam found alternate, more meaningful satisfaction in a heroic battle in which righteousness was clearly on their side. Now it is our responsibility to see that righteousness continues to be on our side, both in the objectives for which we continue to struggle and in the spirit and activities by which we carry on that struggle. This will not be achieved by moving backwards into the old-style nonviolence, which seemed content with symbolic actions and token victories even when war and oppression continued undiminished. But neither will it be achieved by falsely concluding that the need of the movement is to stockpile weapons and increase the violence in the next encounter.

Some people are saying that the time has come when we must fight "by any means necessary." But some means that seem necessary at the moment end by degrading and corrupting the movement. Tactically they provide the enemy with ready-made excuses for its most repressive actions. They confuse and alienate people whose eyes are just being opened to the viciousness of the system and who should be providing not just cover and support but recruits for the movement. We came off well in Chicago. It was a clear-cut victory because the police acted abominably and our people showed courage, aggressiveness and a proper sense of values. But if street fighting breaks out when the police are restrained and if we act contemptuously of other people's rights, the sentiments of those who should be our allies could turn against us. More important, we will begin to lose sight of our objectives and develop a movement style which attracts lovers of violence rather than lovers of justice and brotherhood.

"The future of our struggle is the future of crime in the streets," says a September 16 article in *New Left Notes* by people intoxicated by the Chicago victory and eschewing a sober analysis of aims and tactics. "A new manifesto: there are no limits to our lawlessness." But there must be limits. Limits imposed not by the authorities but by our own political goals, our own respect for human life, our own sense of effective tactics. "Crime in the streets," but against what and as defined by whom? Against the rigged and repressive laws of an imperialist society which insists on the right of six percent of the world's population to control sixty-six percent of the world's wealth and natural resources? *Of course!* As defined by those who napalm people, rig elections, imprison those who refuse to commit war crimes? *Naturally!* But against the persons and rights of those who have been brainwashed by the system into various stages of support, acquiescence, or apathy? These include large numbers of victims who have been hoodwinked into supporting the monster that oppresses them. Our job is to win them to a true understanding of their plight, not to trample on their few remaining rights or clobber them. "The streets belong to the people." Of course. But the streets—like the factories, airwaves, the immense resources of the universe—belong to *all* the people, not just those who would seize them for their elitist clique, as the corporation magnates have seized them in this country and the Party bureaucrats have seized them in the Soviet Union and as some movement groups would do for their own indiscriminate self-expression. To stop a doctor on his way to the hospital or a worker on the way to his job or family, to overturn or burn the cars of those who chance by when a protest is in process—this is not to take over the streets for the people.

There is of course a delicate line to be drawn here. The war makers would like nothing better than to carry on "business as usual," challenged only by token dissent and static demonstrations, while draft boards go on drafting people, U.S. armies go on pillaging Vietnam, universities continue military research and war manufacturers go on drawing huge profits from the murder of G.I.'s and Vietnamese. But to be effective, disruption and disorder must be discriminating and purposeful. Thus the Mobilization Committee called for disruption of the Pentagon on October 21, 1967 and supports disruption of the draft and other military institutions. But we were not aiming to disrupt the convention and are not calling for disruption of the polls on election day.

After Chicago, as we continue the long struggle, the objective is not so much your survival or mine (though of course that remains a consideration) but survival and growth of the humane values and attitudes which made us resisters in the first place. In contrast to the establishment, we must become more and more life-centered and love-directed, not death-oriented or hatred-motivated. This means a clear-cut campaign of opposition to the capitalist economic institutions and authority patterns that squeeze life and love out of the people in an insane drive for status, power and profits. It also means creating alternative life-styles and counterinstitutions which operate in every field of life as communities of sharing and participatory democracy. Unlike some sections of the Old Left we do not seek to seize power on some magical day on the theory that we will gradually turn it over to the people and meanwhile wield it fairly. Our aim is to destroy power, dissipate it, decentralize it, democratize it if you will. This process must begin here and now in the organizations, institutions and activities which we set up as training centers and pilot projects for the new society.

After Chicago, the movement has taken to the offensive. For the moment at least, the problem is not to avoid surrendering to threats and intimidations (as Senator McCarthy and Allard Lowenstein did when they told their followers to stay away from Chicago) but to mount an offensive without mimicking the self-righteous disregard for free speech, human rights and life itself which characterizes the power elite. It is one thing to have a justifiable contempt for the "law and order" which the establishment attempts to use as a noose around our necks. As Dick Gregory has said: "Law and order is a new word for nigger"; it is a device for strangling the creative energies of the movement and restricting our activities to token actions which the establishment can handle quite nicely, thank you. But it is another thing to have contempt for human beings and their rights, even if they oppose us.

Even the concept of "free speech" becomes suspect, because meaningful access to the mass media is by no means free. The economic resources of the power elite, the domination of the public's airwaves by multimillion dollar corporations (both the networks and the sponsors), the power of the government to coöpt prime time (directly and indirectly) put us in a position comparable to that of a David with a slingshot who is engaged in a "fair fight" with a modern army of tanks, flame-throwers and heavy artillery. In the present society a revolutionist's right to effective free speech is as meaningless as a Mississippi sharecropper's right to buy a $60,000 home in the suburbs. But we will not prepare a revolution which makes free speech a reality by arrogating to ourselves the right to deny it to others, even to hypocrites, oppressors and illegitimate candidates (Humphrey-Nixon-Wallace). The Soviet Union, under extreme pressures from the military attacks and internal subversion of the imperialist countries, decided many years ago that free speech was a luxury it could not grant to counterrevolutionaries. Soon even fellow revolutionists who advocated "incorrect" policies were denied the opportunity to argue their cause. The recent imprisonment of Yuri Daniel and other Soviet intellectuals, the shocking invasion of Czechoslovakia, illustrate how hard it is to climb back from that downhill road, even in a period when millions of convinced Communists want to combine communism and freedom. Our fraternity is with the students, workers and intellectuals who are fighting for free speech in the Soviet Union and Eastern Europe, not with the rulers of the Soviet Union and the United States who are partners in a repressive tango, one in the name of an unrealized communism and the other in the name of an equally unreal democracy.

When the illegitimate candidates speak, we can confront them with a massive presence, with leaflets, signs and chants of "Stop the War." When they begin to speak, we can leave the auditorium and picket and leaflet outside. Let them wallow in their credibility gaps without being able to pose as martyrs, without being able to point to us as people who do not believe in freedom.

When people go to the polls, some will be going to vote for the phonies, some to vote for honorable countercandidates (Cleaver, Gregory, Halstead, et al.), some to vote for local antiwar candidates of their choice (O'Dwyer, Ribicoff, etc.). We should not try to impede them, any more than we should have tried to disrupt the Republican or Democratic conventions. The conventions revealed their own irrelevance, with their boss-controlled selection of discredited candidates. By house-to-house canvassing, by leaflets, speeches and public demonstrations on election day we can expose the candidates for what they are. (We will be aided and abetted of course by the candidates themselves.) We can attack their policies and interfere with the prosecution of their war by other means—as was demonstrated recently by the priests and other war objectors who burned the draft files in Catonsville, Maryland, and Milwaukee, as is demonstrated by the growing numbers of draft resisters, deserters and other protesters. Contrary to U.S. claims, the N.L.F. did not try to prevent people from voting in the rigged elections in Vietnam. They didn't want the people to lose their food-rationing coupons, which were voided if not stamped at the polls. They knew that the Vietnamese people would know the true character of the elections and would not obey the illegitimate authorities so elected. We're not quite so far along yet in this country, either in the pressure on people to vote or in the people's understanding of the irrelevance of our mock elections. But people are learning fast. Meanwhile let them make their own decision as to whether or not they want to vote—rather than turning them into enemies by trying to deny them one of the few freedoms, one of the few relics of democracy, which they think they still have left. We can make our own position unmistakable by organizing boycotts of Nixon-Humphrey-Wallace, by massive protests at the Inauguration, by refusing to be bound by the laws and directives of the illegitimate authorities.

To return to Chicago again, what if Mayor Daley's charge of unbearable insults and physical assaults by the demonstrators with cruel and unusual weapons had been true? That would not have justified the wanton savagery of the police. By the same token, the very real brutality of the police (of which we have not seen the last) and the underlying violence of the system do not mean that we will advance the cause of social justice and respect for human dignity by letting street fighting become a substitute for political education, community organizing, and the creation of counterinstitutions. If achieving political effectiveness is our goal, we had better not translate the new, heady mood into the illusion that we can defeat the police and the Army in a contest of violence. No one quite thinks that we can, at least when the question is raised that bluntly. But some of the loose talk about violence doesn't make much sense unless one assumes that we can.

"We had complete control of the streets. The streets were ours. There was nothing they could do about it." So proclaimed a Mobilization associate after a successful afternoon march from Lincoln Park to Grant Park. Later that evening, when the police delayed their nightly invasion of Lincoln Park, a Yippie leader announced, "We've won; we've won. They don't dare come into the park. Tell everyone to come to the park. Bring your sleeping bags and make love." At

Grant Park the next day, when the flag was lowered to half mast and a small group of policemen moved into the crowd, clubbing and Macing as they went, there were people who thought we should charge and beat up the police because we outnumbered them. In the first place this would have obscured the nature of our protest, revealing us to be as capable of brutality as Daley's cops. In the second place there were thousands of heavily armed cops and soldiers only a few seconds away. A week later, my associate who had proclaimed our complete control of the streets and had advocated charging the cops in Grant Park gave me his estimate of where things stand now. "We have won a complete victory at Chicago. The day of nonviolence is dead. I've already got my gun." Such paroxysms of overconfidence and romanticism do little to help the movement develop a sound strategy. What good would his gun have done him or anyone else in Chicago? A few encounters based on such illusions would cause an over-reaction the other way: an unfortunate retreat into caution and passivity.

One of the healthy new emphases of the Movement is its growing sense of identification with the G.I.'s. Not just "Bring the troops home now," crucial as that slogan is, but fraternize with them, support them, treat them as comrades who have a natural aversion to war and injustice and can be moved to "join us." But let's not have any illusions about the overall role of the U.S. armed forces if we turn the confrontation into one of violence rather than devotion to peace, civil liberties and genuine democracy.

Some of the people who are now arguing for a turn to violence were taunting the soldiers a few years ago, calling them fascists and robots. It was during this period that I first visited North Vietnam and discovered that Ho Chi Minh had more compassion for the U.S. soldiers, more comprehension of the social pressures and cultural brainwashing that had led them to commit war crimes, more hope for their conversion to "decent human beings" than was displayed by some of our own "clenched fist" revolutionists. In recent weeks, one of the reactions of the Vietnamese to current developments has been to ask, "What is the political content of the slogan 'Up against the wall, motherfucker'?" A good question if one is more interested in social revolution than self-indulgence.

The old nonviolence was weak in its overemphasis on converting the enemy and its underemphasis on the built-in violence of the system. This was especially true of that section of the nonviolent movement which focused unrealistically on the "decision makers" and usually came out second best in the encounter, adopting more of the system's anti-communism and economic reformism than it ever persuaded the decision makers to adopt of its nonviolence. One should try to win powerful people over to our side, when the opportunity presents itself, without neglecting more important tasks. But, converted, they would automatically have to abandon their roles as decision makers and officeholders (or policemen) within the establishment and take on decent functions and respectable jobs. And speaking truth to powerful men was never a proper substitute for joining the revolutionary movement, though Quakers and churchmen have often eschewed the advocacy of revolution in order to keep their "channels" open. Too often, nonviolence has seemed to bring out the "best" in its opponents only because it failed to offer a serious challenge to their power.

By contrast, the temptation of the new mood of violence is to stage situations which are calculated to bring out the worst in one's opponents. Once again Mayor Daley is wrong in charging that this was our purpose in Chicago. But there is a minority, post-Chicago, who speak as if this should become our objective. There is a sharp distinction between causing a guilty, fear-ridden establishment to bring out into the open the troops and weaponry on which it relies and baiting the police and troops once they are called out. We will come closer to achieving our goals of subverting an inhuman system and undermining its ability to rely on fascist methods when we conduct teach-ins for the police and soldiers and fraternize with them rather than insulting them by calling them "pigs" or raising their wrath by stoning them. We must make a distinction, both philosophical and tactical, between institutions and the people who have been misled into serving them. As the Panthers say, the police are not the enemy; they are tools of the enemy. The traditional pacifist has been misled by the gentility and gentleness of the men who order out armies, napalm, bombs and Mace. The unthinking revolutionist is misled by the crudity of the actions that police and soldiers can be conditioned into performing.

Even a dictator is only as strong as the willingness of his subjects to acquiesce in his rule (prompted in large part, of course, by their recognition of the willingness of armies and police forces to

inflict terror and violence unquestioningly on those who fail to acquiesce). The same holds true in a pseudo-democracy like the United
States. Here the rhetoric of democracy and a tradition of partial civil
liberties give us important leverage in our attempts to win over large
numbers of the population, including members of the police forces
and National Guard. We should do our best to educate members of
the police and military, raising doubts in their minds, and cutting
them off from community support when they indulge the more sadis-
tic side of their ambivalent impulses. This is not a substitute for
active resistance in the form of draft refusal, tax refusal, aid to deserters, strikes, boycotts, noncooperation and the disruption of repressive institutions. But it provides a proper context within which
to carry on such activities.

Where Things Stand Now

I

Someone who has enjoyed . . . a reprieve, however brief, from the inhibition on love and trust this society enforces—is never the same again.

Susan Sontag, *Trip to Hanoi*

Effective power, as Eisenhower once said, belongs to the "military-industrial complex." The monopoly of decision making and of information lies with the bureaucracies of the leading corporations and of the state. Modern capitalism has thus evolved a system of domination in which people have no democratic control over their political parties, their elected assemblies, or their labor unions; in which "democracy" is but a method of manipulating the atomized masses into accepting decisions they do not share in making, of preventing citizens from organizing themselves, from shaping, expressing, and exerting their will collectively.

André Gorz, *Strategy for Labor*

1969 The Battle of Chicago was an episode in a continuing war between people who take seriously the ideals (equality, justice, solidarity, love) on which this country was supposed to have been founded, but never was, and a government which fears and distrusts any movement which tries to organize itself outside the controls of electoral politics.

For some people, what happened in Chicago began in the South six, eight, or ten years earlier, and the Atlantic City Democratic Convention of 1964 was a way station. At Atlantic City, Hubert Humphrey secured appointment to the vice-presidential nomination by helping arrange a disastrous shotgun marriage between the leaders of the civil rights movement and the Democratic officeholders and politicians. The preliminary procuring took place a year earlier, under President Kennedy, during preparations for the 1963 civil rights March on Washington. At Chicago the scenario was different but the objective of the people who run the country was the same: to get rid of a protest movement which was not beholden to either major party, which had more faith in street demonstrations and nonviolent direct action than in lobbying or balloting, and which was developing an independent body of experience and counterculture known as "the movement." As we shall see, the threat of such a movement consists only partly in its disruption of the "orderly society," a state of surface tranquility which insures the perpetuation of the *status quo* (no matter how unjust). It also consists in the creation of a whole new ethos and attitude among its members, as a result of their experiences in the confrontations, in jails, and in their day-to-day relationships.

Years ago Ignazio Silone wrote of the terror created in the heart of a fascist government when a single opponent dared to scrawl "NO" in the dark of night on a city wall. There are periods in the life of a totalitarian government when any slight hole in the dike of conformity could all too easily lead to a flood, sweeping away the oppressive government. By contrast, capitalist democracy thrives on the existence of writers, speakers, candidates and parties that say "No." Their existence encourages the illusion that there is freedom of choice, though the actual choices are kept within narrow limits by the power of great wealth to dominate the normative institutions of the Free Society: the press, the job market, the allocation of capital resources, the universities, the political parties, the police, and the government.

The Free World allows bitter in-fighting between rival elites for political power or financial gain. The conflict between two schools of government—the liberals, who would be kind to the people, and the right-wingers, who would rely on the stick more than the carrot—spills over into the public press and the political campaigns (though often the differences are more in style and rhetoric than in substance). What the present system will not tolerate is the continued functioning and growth of a protest movement which relies not on speeches and articles, not on candidates and legislation, but on direct confrontation, either between the oppressed and their oppressors, or between an aroused and disillusioned people and the government. Beyond the problems created by the conflict and pressures of the confrontations is the danger of the human solidarity, the faith in oneself and one's fellow, the sharing of resources and raising of social vision that the protesters develop if they act together over a period of time and become a movement. A society based on cynicism and selfishness, on technology and money, on the kind of power that grows out of the barrel of a gun, cannot tolerate the growth in its midst of such a counterculture.

Whether such a movement should be coöpted or crushed—to be more precise, how far the government should go in trying to coöpt it before deciding to crush it—sometimes becomes a burning issue of partisan politics. But in general there is a bipartisan realization that one way or another it must be eliminated. Capitalism cannot survive unless it succeeds in "preventing (its) citizens from organizing themselves, from shaping, expressing, and exerting their will collectively." (Gorz) They must be kept atomized so that they can be manipuated "into accepting decisions they do not share in making."

In 1963, Democratic National Committeeman and Birmingham's (Alabama) police chief Bull Connor complained of the press coverage when police dogs were shown biting little children during nonviolent civil rights demonstrations. He said that when Northern cities were faced with similar situations they would respond in the same way. Richard Daley fulfilled Bull Connor's prophecy at the Democratic convention, but he did so not primarily in his role as mayor of Chicago, but rather as agent of the party in power in Washington. He, in turn, complained of the press coverage and said that any other city in which the convention might have taken place would have acted in the same way.

Was there a "police riot" in Chicago, as claimed by the Federal government's Walker Commission? Yes, if by that you mean hundreds of policemen charging, gassing and clubbing demonstrators, bystanders, clergymen, and medics. But it was not a police riot if you mean that what happened was caused by poor police training or by the police acting on their own initiative; nor if you mean that they were merely giving vent to the personal antagonisms of police officials or the private politics of Mayor Daley.

To blame either the police or Mayor Daley for the events in Chicago is like blaming the G.I.'s or the Pentagon for the war against Vietnam. Yes, it would be better for the police and the G.I.'s to resign or revolt. Yes, Mayor Daley and the generals in the Pentagon are particularly unlovely representatives of American reality who wield great power harshly. But wars and police assaults do not take place in a vacuum. They reflect the policies, written and unwritten, of the society. As a matter of fact, Chicago demonstrators got but a very small taste of the ugly violence that black people, Vietnamese, and Latin Americans have experienced for years from the same society. "These were our children," gasped the *New York Times'* Tom Wicker in disbelief.

It is true that many Americans, though by no means all, were outraged by the police brutality as revealed on television. Mayor Daley has become a dirty word in liberal circles, where it is seldom mentioned that he was John F. Kennedy's best friend in the 1960 elections, or that he was busy trying to engineer a draft for Edward Kennedy in Chicago while the police were bashing in demonstrators' heads. Few people like to think that "their" city would have accorded the demonstrators the same treatment. But Americans are also outraged when they see pictures of napalm strikes on Vietnamese villages, the torture of prisoners, or the broken bodies of little children. Yet the war has continued for years after the first widespread public revulsion because capitalist democracy has many devices to soothe and distract public indignation. The gap between public concern and government policy is not quickly or easily bridged when government policy is carrying out the long-run objectives of the military-industrial complex.

Mayor Daley was hoisted with his own petard in Chicago not because he acted contrary to the wishes and plans of the Democratic administration or the bipartisan forces which finance and dominate both parties. He failed because feelings against the war, against the

continued racist reality (twelve years after the Montgomery bus boycott, three years after Watts), against the rigged conventions, and the
joyless consumer culture ran so deep that a hard core of 8,000 to
10,000 demonstrators showed up at Chicago determined to voice
their protests and affirm an alternate type of human relationship, no
matter what happened to them. The mayors of some other cities might
have brought things off a little better, from the point of view of
style and public relations, just as J.F.K. clearly outclassed L.B.J. in carrying out the same basic policies. But given the determination of the
demonstrators to be seen and heard, the reality would not have been
much different wherever the convention might have taken place.

There are times when capitalist democracy can no longer tolerate the repeated presence of large numbers of protesters in the streets,
even if they are nonviolent. One of those times is when they both
reflect and stimulate widespread public uneasiness and "alienation";
that is, when they are growing sufficiently in numbers and militancy
to raise thoughts of a "clear and present danger" to the status quo.
The danger may remain in the future, but if its outlines become clear
enough to excite people and to arouse hope, the time has come to
divert or destroy the movement. Let the people register, vote, run
hopeless candidacies, even elect a symbolic figure or two (who can
easily be brought to his senses by the realities of campaign financing
and governmental procedure). But *keep them out of the streets!*
Especially outside the political conventions that are supposed to fulfill the people's democratic needs and provide them with acceptable
channels for the redress of grievances.

With the advent of national television, the nominating conventions have become a weak point in the public facade of democracy.
It is here that the deals are made, that naked power comes into play
when it proves necessary, that one way or another the candidates who
require curbing are either brought under control or dropped. Even
the delegates, most of whom are appointed by party bosses and only a
handful of whom can be claimed to represent the people, are alter-
nately cajoled and bullied, outmaneuvered and overpowered.

Only a small part of this is portrayed on television, but enough
comes through to suggest that the conventions are hardly models of
democracy or a genuine reflection of the popular will. They never
have been, and for years anyone who has taken the trouble to follow
them closely was aware of cynical deals, crude power plays, and minor-

ity control. But today's pictures on TV in 20 or 30 million homes have a potentially more unsettling public impact than generations of news accounts and political analyses. If the public comes to realize emotionally what it now half suspects intellectually—that the candidates are not democratically chosen and enter the campaign indebted to sinister figures like Strom Thurmond, Charles Engelhard, and Richard Daley—then it may conclude that the elections, the very hallmark of democracy, are a fraud and that there is no democracy.

Thus the political establishment is presented with a serious crisis in public relations at convention time. In 1968 the crisis was intensified by the clear contradiction between public will and government policy on Vietnam, and by public concern over a number of volcanic problems, including the ghettoes, youth alienation, and rising inequitable taxation, for which the government had no solution. That is why the establishment felt that it could not tolerate on top of everything else the presence outside the convention of thousands of protesters who voiced extremely popular demands, rejected the convention process, and offered the seductive alternative of a non-electoral movement in which joy and camaraderie, love and sharing were intertwined with action in the streets.

In order to understand the forces that came into conflict in Chicago, let us take a brief look at some of their early encounters in the Southern-based civil rights movement and at the Atlantic City convention of 1964. On the one hand, the movement that mounted the Chicago demonstrations grew out of and was profoundly influenced by the civil rights movement, both by virtue of the direct experience of many of its participants in the earlier movement and because its history forms an important part of the folklore of the New Left. On the other hand, the power structure that resisted and co-opted the civil rights movement without yielding any major ground is the same power structure that has both resisted and tried to defuse and divert the antiwar movement without abandoning its aggression in Vietnam or yielding any major changes in foreign policy.

History rarely repeats itself in identical ways, so there are certain obvious differences between what happened in Atlantic City and what happened in Chicago. It is useful to study the parallels and contrasts in order to probe the reasons for them and to consider what they portend for the future. After a brief interpretation of the decline and fall of the civil rights movement and the role of the Federal government in helping to destroy it (Section II), we will look at some of the changes in the movement that resulted from these defeats and from the war in Vietnam, with a side excursion into President Johnson's attempt to get off the hook in Vietnam by working out a deal with Russia, and the blow that was dealt this plan by the Soviet invasion of Czechoslovakia, five days before the convention (Section III). Finally, we will consider events in Chicago and a few post-Chicago developments (Section IV). In looking at Chicago and comparing it with Atlantic City, I will focus on three major areas in which the similarities and differences of approach, either by the establishment or the movement, are instructive in preparing for the future. They are: 1) The different roles and treatment of antiwar demonstrators; 2) the pressures to get the demonstrators out of the streets and into conventional politics; and 3) the attempts of the Federal government to pass itself off as being above partisan politics and interested only in freedom and justice under an impartially administered system of law and order. Throughout the whole essay I will be concerned with the complex and unresolved problem of the uses of violence and nonviolence as instruments of social change.

II

One of the first lessons the civil rights movement learned in the South was that none of the state or municipal governments onto whose turf it ventured could be trusted politically. It was not so much that they were biased in favor of our enemies and therefore could be won over to our side by presentations of the facts or appeals to democratic enlightenment. They *were* the enemy. Individuals in the governments of Birmingham or Atlanta or Washington could have their eyes opened or their consciences quickened, but if they did their new enlightenment came into conflict with the overall context of governmental policy and practice, within which they had either to operate or resign. To use the example of the war in Vietnam again, individual G.I.'s may have the friendliest attitude toward the Vietnamese and can even be disillusioned with U.S. foreign policy, but as long as they continue to operate in Vietnam as loyal members of the U.S. armed forces they are enemies of the Vietnamese liberation movement. The army may boast that "Peace is our Profession," and the Federal government may endorse racial equality and pass laws that are titled Civil Rights Acts, but anyone in the front lines of the struggle for peace or racial equality knows better. It came as no surprise to me that the statute under which the government is trying to put eight of us in jail for ten years, for our determined advocacy of peace and racial equality in Chicago, is the Civil Rights Act of 1968.

At the height of the civil rights movement, Northern supporters often complained that Southern officials violated the impartiality of the law or that the police departed from good police practice by lapsing into brutality. Why did they allow the mob to attack demonstrators? Why did the courts convict those who were exercising their democratic rights and acquit murderers? But people on the spot, whose lives and freedom were at stake, quickly learned what black people had known all along: public officials made up a "mob" of their own. Sometimes they merged with or used the mob in the streets; later they increasingly repudiated it, in the interests of less troubled public relations in the era of television and national press coverage. But the judge's robes and the policeman's uniform provided more effective cover for violence than the klansman's hood. We were safer in the streets than in the courtroom or jail.

Most of the residents of "niggertown" did not need to get hit over the head or taken for a ride to experience the violence of society. It came to them in the form of being restricted to menial work at starvation wages and having to live in miserable shacks without electricity, paved roads, street lights, or plumbing. The overt terror of cattle prods, clubs and prison was mainly a way of ensuring continuation of the daily violence that is built into the economy. Its purpose was preservation of the status quo "by preventing (black) citizens from organizing themselves."

Liberal mythology and government rhetoric aside, the Federal government also turned out to be the enemy. It gave some temporary protection to distinguished visitors-for-a-day: the clergymen, union officials, and other concerned liberals who flew down for symbolic national events. Occasionally it tossed the restless blacks a bone, but the bone was pretty well cleaned of meat and the purpose was to keep them away from the feast at the table. President Kennedy appointed racist judges, and the F.B.I. worked hand-in-glove with state and local police. It did so not just because it depended on the cooperation of local authorities in its other work, but because that was its politics. After the lengthy demonstrations in Albany, Georgia, in November and December 1961, which were met with mass arrests and brutality, the Justice Department secured indictments not of the guilty authorities but of the leaders of the nonviolent Albany movement. In a characteristic pretense at preserving the "impartiality" of government procedures from partisan pressures, it indicted them for picketing a grocer who had served on a federal jury.

The Federal government was willing to tamper here and there with Southern culture in order to reduce gross national and international scandal and in order to stabilize the status quo by updating it ever so slightly. But stabilization, not justice, was the goal. The Civil Rights Act of 1964 barred discrimination in public accommodations. The Civil Rights Act of 1965 was a voting rights bill. As everyone knows, Washington is dedicated to the preservation of capitalist democracy, in the South as well as in Vietnam and Venezuela. And capitalist democracy unashamedly divides people into classes: rich and poor, owners and employers, managers and workers, people who select the candidates and people who mark X on the ballot, a minority of decision-makers (only a few of them elected and none of them subject to any but the most remote, periodic controls) and a majority who lack control over their own lives. The government could not openly oppose the slogan "Freedom Now" in the South, any more than it could come out against the ideas of land reform and self-determination for Vietnam and Venezuela. But it was bound to oppose the growth of any movement which took these ideas seriously enough to become a threat to established power relationships and profitable private enterprise. The government saw the similarity between S.N.C.C. and the N.L.F. before most of the movement did.

More frightening than the specific demands and program of the movement (which tended to remain minimal and reformist) was the growth of a body of aroused blacks and supportive whites who began to develop a sense of their own dignity and worth, their own power as a movement. As the Southern-based civil rights movement gathered momentum and self-confidence, as it began to involve larger and larger sections of the black population and won increasing sympathy from the general public, Washington reacted to it with the same distrust it felt toward the N.L.F. in Vietnam and the *Fidelistas* in Latin America. The tactics of suppression had to be different against the internal colony, particularly because the movement was nonviolent and therefore provided few if any credible pretexts for the Federal government to crush it militarily, but the objective was the same. If the movement could not be crushed physically, it must be coöpted and contained within the prescribed limits of the existing hierarchical society. These included representative rather than participatory democracy, and lobbying, voting, and court challenges rather than confrontation politics. As Joanne Grant points out in *Black Protest, History, Documents and Analyses* (Fawcett Publications), "Much of the flurry of activity by the federal government was aimed, in the words of President Kennedy, at getting the demonstrators out of the streets and into the courts."

Sections of the movement that resisted domestication and continued to organize grass-roots, militant actions were subject to legal prosecution (often initiated by the Federal government, as in the draft and other prosecutions of the S.N.C.C. leadership) and reduced protection against state and local authorities. In addition, they found themselves deprived of funds for court costs and organizing. The convenience (for the capitalists) of capitalist economic realities—with the financial power for life or death of the foundations, wealthy private donors, and organizations like the A.F.L.-C.I.O. and the National Council of Churches—is that the process of strangling the unacceptable left can take place informally, without any new laws or unpopular state interventions. The tendency of liberals to look upon the government not as the enemy but as an ambivalent ally through which all realistic social change will take place in the end makes them particularly susceptible to governmental influence. Thus the present chairman of the National Council of Churches is Arthur Fleming, who was a former cabinet officer under Eisenhower. An organization which considers such leadership a feather in its cap and hardly notices the price it pays in reduced vision and militancy, naturally tends to subsidize civil rights organizations that are playing an "effective" role, as indicated by their access to the White House, rather than organizations like S.N.C.C., which are on bad terms with the decision-makers. This is exactly what happened in 1963 and 1964, the watershed years.

In the spring of 1963, President Kennedy himself, alarmed by the continued strength and independence of the civil rights movement, arranged for the tractable organizations to get huge grants from the Taconic Foundation and other groups, to which both his family and the C.I.A. contributed funds. In return, the organizations concentrated on voter-registration campaigns and abandoned the tactics of across-the-board demands backed by populations in the street, that had come to the fore in Birmingham. As part of the betrothal arrangement, the Civil Rights Leadership Conference, which had gone to Kennedy to get his informal assistance for the forthcoming civil rights March on Washington, made clear that it would not tolerate sit-ins and the tactics of disruption in Washington. The original idea behind the March had been to bring Southern tactics to Washington, in recognition of the fact that organizers in the field had discovered that the Federal government was indeed the enemy. By the time the March itself rolled around, not even free speech was permitted. A few hours before the event, John Lewis, Chairman of S.N.C.C., was pressured by the March's coordinator, Bayard Rustin, to change his speech, under the threat that if he did not do so, Archbishop Boyle (a Kennedy contribution), Walter Reuther, and other speakers or co-sponsors would drop out. Among other changes, the statement, "In good conscience, we cannot support the administration's civil rights bill," was altered to say: "True, we support the administration's civil rights bill but this bill will not protect young children and old women from police dogs and fire hoses."

For blacks, fulfillment was now to be postponed until the distant day when new voters would elect new officials, and the demands could then be filtered through established procedures and safeguards, including the inevitable indebtedness of the new officials to their financial backers and other establishment allies. For blacks and radical whites, the growth of a self-aware and self-reliant movement, with dynamics of its own beyond the easy control of the government, was to be halted by eliminating street demonstrators and direct confrontations between the oppressed and their oppressors.

In the next twelve months, the process of domesticating the movement continued. Bayard Rustin pleaded for the new realism in an influential article entitled "From Protest to Politics" (*Commentary*, February 1964). Shortly before the Atlantic City nominating convention, the Leadership Conference on Civil Rights announced a moratorium on all demonstrations, at the convention and during the presidential campaign. The agreement was signed by Martin Luther King, Jr., Roy Wilkins, Bayard Rustin, Whitney Young, Dorothy Haight, James Farmer, and John Lewis, although Lewis repudiated it the next day. Its purpose was to "prevent a white backlash," as if any dynamic movement for social change will not provoke a re-action—and in cases like the American Colonies in 1776 and Cuba today, an exodus—of those who cling to their selfish privileges. The answer, of course, is to build a movement strong enough to overcome the reactionaries, while at the same time paying careful attention to building bridges of communication to the ambivalent middle. The answer does not lie in becoming so inoffensive that the reactionaries know that they have nothing to fear. But instead of placing their faith in the movement, the signers were anxious to guarantee the election of Lyndon Baines Johnson, successor to John F. Kennedy as the Negro's best friend, and first President in history to intone "We shall overcome" on national television.

The result of the moratorium was to weaken seriously the more radical wing of the movement, including C.O.F.O. (that summer's Confederation of Federated Organizations, organizers of the Mississippi Summer) and its ally the Mississippi Freedom Democratic Party. C.O.F.O. had been advocating militant demonstrations at Atlantic City, including sit-ins, sit-downs or whatever tactics from the South could be adapted to the convention. Such actions had the potential of attracting thousands of black and white participants from the heavily populated Eastern seaboard, with supporters pouring in within a matter of hours in response to dramatic confrontations. Hundreds of college students had experienced firsthand the realities of Mississippi justice and Federal complicity. The brutal murders of James Chaney, Andrew Goodman, and Michael Schwirner (together with the discovery of numerous mutilated black bodies in the search for the three missing C.O.F.O. volunteers) had shocked the country and could have provided the emotional undergirding and moral support for militant actions. A dramatic confrontation could have electrified the country, revived the sagging civil rights movement, and materially altered the power relationships between the government and the movement. Instead of dutifully herding a passive electorate into the polling booths to cast their vote for the "lesser evils" of Johnson and Humphrey, the movement could have got back onto an independent course, building its own strength and not relying on unreliable friends in high places.

But at Atlantic City, Hubert Humphrey, Walter Reuther, King, Rustin, Wilkins, and Joseph L. Rauh, Jr. (Washington attorney for Americans for Democratic Action, who argued the M.F.D.P.'s case before the credentials committee) pushed the strictly "legal challenge" to the credentials committee, supplemented by a mild public vigil outside, in the form of petitioners loyally waiting outside for the monarch's decision. The decision that came down on the first day of the convention was engineered by Humphrey (working closely with the others named) in order to keep the convention untainted by protest demonstrations. It gained the M.F.D.P. two token (at-large) seats at the convention and promised to seat an integrated delegation in 1968. The M.F.D.P. rejected the compromise but was badly divided and disillusioned. It abandoned further protest. Humphrey was rewarded with the vice-presidential nomination.

Atlantic City marked the end of an era. The movement had been turned over by its nonviolent, moderate leadership and prestigious liberal friends to its enemies, the "statesmen" and politicians. Of course some demonstrations did take place, both during the campaign and afterwards. But the insurgents had lost the initiative and the movement as a whole suffered an incalculable loss in morale and growing power. It had surrendered its most valuable weapon, the one that had aroused the politicians' fear and interest in the first place: the energizing and radicalizing dynamics of masses in motion in direct confrontation with their enemies.

Not surprisingly, the resulting disillusionment and frustration in black communities contributed significantly to the eruption of politically unfocused and largely self-defeating explosions in Watts, Newark, Detroit, and other cities. These rebellions were hailed by some white radicals as the beginning of the black man's liberation through armed struggle. But most of the black residents of the cities where riots took place knew better. Joanne Grant sums up the opinion of ordinary black citizens and movement organizers as follows:

> The other mode of protest in Negro ghettoes—riots—
> provided a fleeting emotional outlet but little else. (*Black
> Protest,* Part VI, "The Birth of a Movement," page 260.)

It is true that by 1966 most of the black movement was disillusioned with nonviolence, since the nonviolent movement of the last decade had ended in frustration and failure. The drama of nonviolent confrontation and direct action had been turned into accommodation and compromise at the negotiating table, and self-defeating alliances with the enemy. To make the pill more bitter, King, the last major spokesman for nonviolence, had defended the use of police power to suppress the riots. (Did he think that the police and national guard were nonviolent?)

When the black movement rejected the idea of "nonviolence," they spat out moderation, compromise, and reliance on national leaders who hobnobbed with the mighty but failed to produce adequate results. At the same time they rejected the nonviolent tactic of refusing to defend themselves against violent attack. There was a logic to these simultaneous rejections. After all, failure to defend oneself and one's friends (except by such devices as coiling up into a ball or interposing one's own body between an attacker and his intended victim) calls for extreme self-control and group discipline. For most people such discipline is possible only in a period of upsurge and hope, a period when they can see some direct connection between accepting abuse nonviolently and gaining their objectives.

That most people need to see a clear relationship between nonviolent defense and the attainment of urgent political goals is demonstrated by the failure of the conventional pacifist movement (the Fellowship of Reconciliation, the War Resisters League, and the Quakers) to win over (even for a short time) followers in the numbers that adopted nonviolence in India under Gandhi, or in the South under S.N.C.C. and Martin Luther King. Partly because of its religious and moralistic preoccupations, and partly because it has been a movement ahead of its time (with its early advocacy of racial equality and its pre-nuclear-bomb opposition to all war), the rewards it offered tended to be symbolic and religious (moral witness and personal ennoblement) rather than directly political. Very few people are interested in undergoing imprisonment or physical punishment in order to gain symbolic victories.

The Southern civil rights movement thrived on nonviolence as long as its objectives were urgent and peripheral, like the desegregation of buses, restaurants, and other public accommodations; such objectives are at least partially attainable. As long as the movement was new and young and filled with naïve expectations that these peripheral advances would cause the walls of Jericho to come tumbling down, it displayed tremendous discipline in facing violence without striking or shooting back. But, even during this most optimistic period, when the tactics were nonviolent at demonstrations and in aggressive encounters organized by the movement, armed guards were commonplace in situations where it was hard for people to see any tactical purpose in nonviolence, as at the homes where civil rights workers congregated or held meetings. King himself had an armed patrol guard his home during the Montgomery bus boy-cott, until one night when a guard came within a hair of shoot-ing a shadowy figure who turned out to be a Western Union boy delivering a telegram. King then decided that the disadvantages out-weighed the advantages.

Nonviolent tactics began to lose their appeal when the people taking the headwhippings and seeing their ranks thinned out by murder came to realize how entrenched and institutionalized were the evils they fought. In a period of declining morale and losing bat-tles, after a series of bloody events in which the national leadership compromised their objectives behind closed doors or trafficked un-successfully with Washington, few people retained their enthusiasm for absorbing the physical punishment associated with strictly non-violent defense. If nonviolence is to make a comeback, as I tend to think it will, it will be in a new period of rising morale and move-ment solidarity. It will also be after militants have experienced some of the disadvantages of the recourse to fist-fights and guns—such as the already evident tendency, for example, of those militants who rely on these methods to turn their fists and guns on one another, and the greater ease with which the police, when their opponents are armed or violent, can claim justification for their own violence.

Despite the alarums of the establishment and the wish fantasies of romantic white anti-racists whose isolation, impotence, and gen-uine sense of urgency contributed to their infatuation with black violence, no city where there had been a major riot ever exploded a second time. Here and there, shoot-outs might have taken place, in self-defense or in response to unbearable provocation. Perhaps they provided fulfillment for some blacks who had reached the breaking point after years of humiliation and brutality. If so, all too often they provided it at the price of death or long years of imprisonment. What white person has the right or experience to judge the necessity or long-range effects of such acts? To measure the degrees of revenge, warning, or simple heroic assertion of personal dignity involved?

Most serious black revolutionists tried to avoid shoot-outs, riots and street-fighting, since they were disastrously out-armed. After all, their opponents have the arsenals and manpower of the police and the U.S. Armed Forces at their disposal. They might use violence in situations where the encounters were brief and clear-cut: forcing a barricade, ousting a scab or hostile administrator. They might speed up the process of arming and training themselves for self-defense. The psychological effect of such a speed-up might be to recapture a sense of their stolen manhood; the political effect, to try to develop some needed protection against police harassment and abuse in cities, or against nightriders and vigilantes in rural areas. But however militant the rhetoric and determined the self-defense forces, the black community remained uncertain about the possibilities of liberating itself through armed struggle. It did not set about the task of seriously preparing itself for armed warfare. Like its counterparts in the white antiwar and anti-imperialist movements, it found it easier to see the limitations of traditional methods and leadership than to develop a consistent, viable alternative.

Undoubtedly some of the leaders were pushed by community desperation and their own recognition of the failure of what had gone before into an uneasy acceptance of violent forms of action that they were not fully committed to or prepared to carry through on indefinitely. If so, there was a certain parallel with what had happened to Martin Luther King ten years earlier. In Montgomery and in the ferment associated with the student sit-ins, he allowed himself to be pushed by the new militancy and his own recognition that something more drastic than sermons and court action was required into forms of activity with which he was never fully at home.

King once told me that bringing people into the streets was a dangerous act that initially horrified all public officials and most of his liberal supporters. But he added that it was necessary in order to raise the level of public debate and to have any impact on public policy. It was clear that mass confrontations made him nervous. (I confess that they make me nervous, too, but not so much as the evils they attack or reliance on the slippery electoral method for which they substitute.) Even after his espousal of such a tactic, he remained more at home preaching at mass meetings (whether in churches or at the Lincoln Memorial), leading a march whose limits had been carefully worked out in advance, or personally confronting the White House with his own sense of moral imperatives. It was his S.N.C.C.-trained lieutenants and the S.N.C.C. regulars who revealed a gift for creative improvisation and nonviolent leadership in unpredictable encounters with the white establishment and the police. The more famous King became, the more he relied on static situations and prestigious supporters, and the more he curbed his lieutenants and S.N.C.C. He usually called people in from confrontations before they had achieved their maximum impact or developed a full sense of their own power and creativity.

The result was that he tended to use demonstrators as counters to increase his and the other leaders' bargaining power with local, state, or federal authorities, rather than to encourage their development and fusion into a continuing, independent, and self-reliant force. Writing in the *New York Times Magazine,* he said: "We must develop, from strength, a situation in which the government finds it wise and prudent to collaborate with us." (June 11, 1967) As it turned out, collaboration between the government and the movement proved more wise and prudent for the government than for the movement.

When the black community finally rejected this unproductive political collaboration, it was to a great extent rejecting not just the leaders who had presided over it, but an important part of its own past. When King fell into the trap of White House politics, he was acting out one of the persistent fantasies of the black community of that period: that there had to be a benevolent power at some higher level who actually believed in the noble sentiments that dignify the country's public utterances. As with the Communists of the thirties, who had deep psychological needs to believe in the transcendent virtue of Moscow even after the evidence had piled up to the contrary, so running through the black community was a deep need to believe that sooner or later (with the aid of a little prodding and explaining and proper voting) the White House would turn out to be occupied by a President who would lift their burdens and ease their way into the panacea of American democracy. In the 1960 elections, 77.7 percent of the vote in Harlem was for Kennedy. It was 80 percent in the black wards of Chicago, 82 percent in Philadelphia.

Since most liberals shared the illusion, and controlled the only potentially sympathetic press and the only large sources of money that could conceivably be made available to the movement, it is not surprising that the movement ended up half pushing and half following King into this trap. For all the movement's heroism in the field, and all the lessons it was gradually learning about the interconnectedness of the power structure and the domination of the Federal government by the very forces it was fighting, it was pretty close to a historical necessity that the civil rights movement end by being diverted in this way. Given the moral and political underdevelopment of the country and the power of entrenched privilege, there was no way it could change the racist institutions of the country in ten short years or suddenly lift itself (its own consciousness and political sophistication) by its own bootstraps. As a result much was tragically lost and some of the unsung heroes drifted away. But they left more than a heritage of failure. They had shattered the complacency and quickened the consciences of millions of people. They had routed the fears and false formulations of the McCarthy period. They had swept away student apathy and conformism. They had set up a living contrast in values between human relationships derived from commerce, property, race, and fear and those based on love, sharing, dignity, and courage.

Martin Luther King was a man of deep personal integrity and moral courage. If he had not been, he never would have got involved in leading a movement for which he was in many ways unsuited temperamentally and unprepared politically. This meant that although his political position was weakened in the black community by its growing alienation from nonviolence and reliance on the White House (two tactics that go ill together but were artificially linked from 1963 through 1965), he continued to be held in respect and viewed with affection by sections of the community that were going through the growing pains of trying to forge a more realistic combination of tactics. It also meant that although he could be trapped temporarily by White House politics, he could not be permanently contained by it. In the long run he could tell a thief and liar from an honest friend, an aggressor against Vietnam from a man of peace.

During the last year and a half of his life, King began to move, painfully and against the pressure of some of his liberal financers, toward reliance on the power of the people as an independent force more conscientious and trustworthy than the politicians in Washington. He did this first in his active support of the National Mobilization Committee and the Clergy and Laymen Concerned about Vietnam, in their demonstrations against the war in Vietnam. Then he went a step further in his visualization and preliminary organization of a Poor People's Campaign. Finally, he interrupted his other activities to go to Memphis to take part in the thoroughly unpredictable protests of the striking sanitation workers.

There is no telling what role King might have played in helping reconstitute a more independent, more aggressive nonviolent movement, if he had lived. There is no doubt that his disillusionment with the enervating alliance with the White House and the shock of the explosions in Watts and in other cities had caused him to rethink many questions of both tactics and strategy, though he remained wedded to nonviolence. During the last months of his life, he was responding not only to these events themselves, but also to the changes in mood and consciousness that they had crystallized in the black community. For if the elitist betrayals and subsequent withering away of the civil rights movement, followed by the crushing defeats at Watts, Newark, and Detroit, had put an end to two early thrusts toward black liberation, they had paradoxically strengthened and made more sophisticated the blacks' sense of urgency and alienation from the white society. As Joanne Grant observed in 1968 in *Black History:*

> Today the situation for the majority of Negroes has
> not changed, except in this all-important aspect: a major
> aim of the current movement, with all of its changes and
> floundering and periods of inactivity during which direction
> and goals seem to have been lost sight of, has been fulfilled.
> The masses of Negroes have been stirred, there is a wide-
> spread will to fight, a new-found ability to organize and a
> substantial decrease in fear.

Confrontations are springing up piecemeal around demands for community control of the schools and colleges, community curbing and control of the police and courts, welfare rights, job opportunities, adequate housing, etc. The government and the liberal wing of the power elite are trying to parry these thrusts by making money available for black capitalism—as earlier they made funds available for voter registration and as even earlier they cultivated house slaves to oversee and control the field slaves. They are continuing their efforts to persuade black people to focus on legislation, courts, candidates, and elections as substitutes for direct confrontations. This time the black community is backing black candidates, but is by no means turning the entire struggle over to them. Undoubtedly black capitalists and black mayors will succeed in diverting some of the energies of the black community away from confrontation politics and the dream of liberation for the entire community. But the patience of the community is thinner, its political sophistication far greater than in 1964.

Since 1965, the attitude of black groups toward national antiwar demonstrations has been cautious but friendly. Those groups and individuals who have worked off and on, formally and informally, with the shifting antiwar coalitions (the Mobilization Committee, the Conspiracy, and regional coalitions such as New York's Fifth Avenue Vietnam Peace Parade Committee) have rather consistently advocated a combination of revolutionary demands and analysis with tactical nonviolence. On the one hand, they have no illusions about the good intentions of the Democratic Party or the Nixon administration, or the ability of white, racist capitalism to reform itself at home or abroad. Nor do they have any illusions about the "impartiality" of the police. On the other hand, they have no desire to lose physical battles on enemy terrain and against superior military force. They have consistently opposed police-baiting, street-fighting, and physical assaults on government buildings.

At the Pentagon demonstrations in October 1967, about half the black participants dropped out at the termination of the activities at the Lincoln Memorial, when the main body of demonstrators headed for the Pentagon. As one of the black leaders expressed it ahead of time, "We do not want to be slaughtered playing Indian outside the White Man's fort." Those who went to the Pentagon avoided the supermilitant charge of the tiny Committee to Aid the N.L.F., with its barehanded assault on the individual troops assigned to guard the stronghold. They joined the teach-in for the troops, a tactic which they had helped devise in last-minute planning sessions a few hours earlier. It was a technique which anticipated and threw the movement's weight behind the growing opposition to the war within the armed forces. They took part in the nonviolent resistance to attempts to dislodge the protesters.

At Chicago, the black participants played a similar role. Ahead of time they helped formulate and consistently supported the nonviolent, nondisruptive tactics around which the coalition activities were organized. Only the police infiltrators and a handful of romantic adventurers who lacked the realistic experience of the black cadres ever urged anything different. When the police attacked the demonstrators, many blacks provided valuable on-the-spot assistance in the arts of physical survival without surrender.

III

The distance from Atlantic City to Chicago is only 750 miles and the interval on the calendar between the two nominating conventions was only four years, but the changes that had taken place in the attitudes of the American people were out of all proportion to these statistics. The foreign policy remained the same; the economic and political systems still operated on the same basic principles; but it is doubtful if even the massive depression of the thirties had produced such a deep-seated alienation of so many people from these governing principles. Criticism of concrete policies (the war, racism, poverty, urban blight, the impacted political processes) had grown from a whisper to a shout, while the most active sections of the movement had gone from criticism of specific evils to condemnation of the entire system of government and values that had produced them. They no longer looked on the war as a mistake, nor did they see racial injustice and the continued poverty of thirty million Americans as carry-overs from the past that were in the process of being rectified. They identified these offenses more and more with the drive for selfish power and profits that forms the mainspring of the American system of free enterprise. They argued with increasing passion and logic that the evils could not be eliminated until the system was changed. From being antiwar, virtually the entire movement had become anti-imperialist and was rapidly becoming anti-capitalist. From demanding integration into the existing society, black spokesmen were increasingly asking "out," demanding separation or the building of a totally new society or both. Unless something could be done to reverse the trend, there was no telling what troubles lay ahead for the power elite and the system of capitalist democracy which served as its figleaf.

A prime source of the growing disaffection was the incredible failure of the society to respond to fourteen years of black upsurge and militance with any significant alteration in the pattern of racist institutions and practices. The 1963 and 1964 alliances of Presidents Kennedy and Johnson with the civil rights movement had bought the government a little time. But now they were being used (along with the Alliance for Progress in Latin America, the Peace Corps and the Anti-Poverty program) as proof that even the gaudiest plans and promises were a decoy to camouflage the establishment's lack of desire or ability (it didn't matter which) to solve the problems.

After roughly ten years of civil rights demonstrations and sacrifices, after four years marked by riots and insurgencies in hundreds of cities and the growth of black power; after fourteen years of promises, court decisions, presidential commissions, foundation grants, church resolutions, and civil rights legislation, the conditions of black people were, if anything, worse than before it all began with the Montgomery bus boycott, the student sit-ins, and the Freedom Rides. To quote the devil to prove scripture, Bayard Rustin (who had helped engineer the disastrous political coalition with the Democrats and had drafted the moratorium on demonstrations) wrote in the fall of 1966:

> *Negroes today are in worse economic shape, live in worse slums, and attend more highly segregated schools than in 1954.* [Emphasis in original.] Thus—to recite the appalling and appallingly familiar statistical litany once again— more Negroes are unemployed today than in 1954; the gap between the wages of the Negro worker and the white worker is wider; while the unemployment rate among white youths is decreasing, the rate among Negro youths has increased to *thirty-two percent*. . . . Even the one gain which has been registered, a decrease in the unemployment rate among Negro adults, is deceptive. . . . To put all this in the simplest and most concrete terms: the day-to-day lot of the ghetto Negro has not been improved by the various judicial and legislative measures of the past decade. ("Black Power and Coalition Politics," *Commentary,* September 1966.)

Not surprisingly, an increasing number of persons who were familiar with this appalling litany were not about to put their faith in convention platforms or in the campaign pledges of anyone who could get the party bosses to nominate him.

A second source of disaffection that threatened the rulers gathered in Chicago was the disillusionment of millions of young people not only with the "failures" of capitalism but with its "successes."

They looked at the fabled material accomplishments and found them stifling. Some of society's technological accomplishments, such as television (but not the programs),* computers (but not the uses to which they were put), and air travel, they admired and considered the rightful property of all human beings. But in general the proliferation of consumer goods for which young people were supposed to surrender their initiative, their daily freedoms, and their human solidarity, they considered a bore. Those that were not adulterated or schmaltzy were inferior to rock, grass, sex, sleeping on the ground, be-ins, love-ins, and the fabulous world of inner consciousness and human relatedness. They dropped out of the plastic society and developed a youth culture of their own.

But the straight world would not let them alone. There were marijuana busts, obscenity arrests, vagrancy busts when hitchhiking, panhandling, or just walking down the street, enforced haircuts in the schools and jails, suppressions of the underground press, police and vigilante attacks, and of course the universal intrusion of the draft. For their part, whereas they rejected the values and routines, the customs and clothes, the hypocrisies and regimentations of established society, many young people were not content to leave society alone either. They marched and rallied against the war, burned money on the stock exchange and draft cards at antiwar demonstrations, put on guerrilla theater at public events, and entertained or rapped at coffee houses set up in army towns by the antiwar movement. They tried to levitate the Pentagon and called a Yippie Festival of Life in Chicago to exorcise the Democrats' Convention of Death. They announced that they would nominate a pig for president, as the only fit companion to the other candidates. As Abbie Hoffman, Yippie product of the idealism and failure of the civil rights movement, explained it, "We're dancing on the grave of the dying American Empire."

Originally a largely middle-class phenomenon, restricted to a

---

* *"While people today simply watch television as a surrogate for the lives they have ceased to live, in the new society they will use it as a means of widening their experience, of mastering the environment and of keeping in touch with the real lives of other people. If television programs were to be put on for their social value and not solely because they induce the maximum hypnosis on the greatest numbers, they would enable us to extend the real democracy to the entire population."* (*Daniel and Gabriel Cohn-Bendit*, Obsolete Communism the Left Wing Alternative [*McGraw-Hill*], p. 105.)

minority of college students and college dropouts, the youth revolt proved contagious. The evils it pilloried were real; the love and freedom and expanded consciousness it offered (but did not always succeed in attaining) appealed to many people of all ages and classes. Like the student antiwar movement, the cultural revolt spread to the sons and daughters of generals, senators, Wall Street financiers and corporation executives. Between the political rebels and the hippies, and with the considerable amount of cross fertilization that was taking place between the two, the ruling class was faced with an inheritance crisis. It could no longer count on its own sons and daughters to carry on the family's or the nation's capitalist traditions. The youth revolt moved into the high schools, then into the grade schools, into the armed forces (of all places), and finally began to make inroads into the ranks of the sons and daughters of the working class. The movement might not be in a position to overpower the establishment, but with the aid of the Yippies it was threatening to undermine its legitimacy by exposing to ridicule its pretentiousness and its fratricidal tendencies.

The catalyst that accelerated these changes in mood and attitude was the war against Vietnam. The antiwar movement began as a simple, humanitarian response to the horror of napalm, torture, concentration camps, pellet (fragmentation) bombs, corruption and dictatorship in Saigon, and the official lies that caused the credibility gap. It grew into an awareness that was far more threatening to the continued stability of the status quo. The government's insistence on continuing the war long after it had lost all semblance of political justification or popular support told us something about the absence of democratic decision-making in the country, despite the existence of an elaborate facade of democracy. It also suggested how much of a stake someone pretty powerful had in continuing the war. It pinpointed both the power and the contempt for human life of the military-industrial complex, with its secret drives that flow from the profit system, and its stranglehold on decision-making that results from its private ownership of the accumulated productive capital of society.

The type of lesson we learned can be summed up in the following analysis by André Gorz:

> The people do not have the choice between two (or several) fundamentally distinct sets of policies or programs

[in the present case, whether to continue or stop the aggression against Vietnam]; their choice is only to have one of several sets of politicians apply policies which, except for some marginal differences, are basically the same. How has this situation arisen? It springs from the concentration of power in the hands of a small number of private corporations whose decisions have a national and even an international scope. No government can afford to antagonize Big Business. . . . It must keep Big Business prosperous or the whole nation will suffer from the corporation's ill will, and so will the government's popularity. The prosperity of Big Business depends on constant intervention to keep the profit rates attractive and investment booming. In the guise of bringing corporate interests into line with the general interest, the general interest, conversely, must be brought into line with the interest of Big Business.

This constant mutual adjustment of business and governmental policies explains the strengthening of the power wielded by the State, and the weakening of the influence held by representative assemblies. Such "serious matters" as the military budget, the rate and the taxation of profits, the volume and location of new investments, diplomatic or military intervention abroad must not be discussed by "irresponsible" delegates of the people, since these might question, rather than understand and cooperate with, the leading corporations' aims.

Or, making the connection from the opposite direction, Rennie Davis and Tom Hayden wrote in a Mobilization position paper in preparation for the Chicago convention demonstrations:

We can accelerate the breakdown of confidence in the government and military by stressing that the decisions which led to the Vietnam war were rigged in the same way and by the same people who are rigging the conventions and the elections in 1968.

Ordinarily much of this knowledge of how capitalist democracy actually works is half recognized but repressed. After all, American capitalism has produced the highest standard of living and the most freedom from governmental control anywhere in the world. Or so we were continually told and half believed, given the repressive nature of the Soviet regime, which we had been led by capitalists and Communists alike to believe was the only conceivable alternative to what we had. Besides, what can ordinary citizens do to replace the present system with anything better? You can't fight City Hall or General Motors. In the present instance, in addition to the obvious horrors in both Vietnam and the ghetto that flowed from the monopoly of the military-industrial complex on decision-making, and the outrage people felt at the war's undemocratic prolongation, there was the invigorating factor of the successful David vs. Goliath role of the Vietnamese. Coming on the heels of Cuba's resistance, which had played a role in stimulating the idealism and faith of the civil rights movement, Vietnam's heroic and increasingly successful resistance began to give people faith in human beings again. Perhaps man could stand up to the monster after all. Perhaps love and decency and human solidarity were not mere romantic indulgences condemned to exist around the edges of society and doomed to be crushed when they challenged the awesome power and cynical prerogatives of corporate capitalism.

Daniel Cohn-Bendit writes of the influence of Cuba and Vietnam in creating the psychological climate that made possible the May-June 1968 student revolts in France:

> In Vietnam, a small peasant country was withstanding the aggression of the greatest military power on earth. . . . Though there was much to criticize in the National Liberation Front and in the regime of North Vietnam and, for that matter, in Castro's Cuba, the defiant and unshakable resistance of ordinary Vietnamese and Cubans alike had proved that a super-organized and super-armed capitalist society is not invincible. (D. & G. Cohn-Bendit, *op. cit.,* p. 32.)

Susan Sontag writes of the same phenomenon:

> For the anger an American is likely to direct toward the emblems of his country's imperial dominance isn't founded simply upon their inherent repulsiveness, which permits no reaction other than aversion, but rather upon the despairing conviction that American power in its present form and guided by its present purposes is *invincible.* But this may not be, probably isn't, the case. The Vietnamese, for one, don't think so. And their wilder judgments do, by this

time, have a claim to be taken seriously. After all, who—except the Vietnamese themselves—would have predicted on February 7, 1965, that this small, poor nation could hold out against the awesome cruelty and thoroughness of American military force? But they have. (Susan Sontag, *Trip to Hanoi* [The Noonday Press], p. 8.)

For those who still found it difficult to believe that American power would not prove invincible in the end, it was nonetheless hard not to be prodded and inspired by Vietnamese courage and suffering into making at least minimal gestures against the war. If Vietnam's example encouraged the French students to unanticipated levels of commitment and action, its effect had to be at least as great on Americans who felt the direct shame of American responsibility and faced the impact in their own lives of the draft, taxes, casualty lists, etc. From 1965 to early 1968, the contrast between the movement's communal élan and the sterile official response carried people step by step into new kinds of individual and social awareness. (Beginning in 1968, or thereabouts, the movement's rhetoric and analyses became more revolutionary, but growing factionalism and a new harshness of spirit began to undermine the movement's actual revolutionizing effect on its participants.)

The revolutionary implications of Vietnam's example suggests another reason why the United States has felt it necessary to continue the war long after it has been discredited in the eyes of decent people everywhere. More important at this point than establishing its virtue (a difficult task in any event) the United States finds it necessary to establish its power. It must prove its capitalist will. It must convince the underdeveloped peoples of the world that genuine independence will not be tolerated; that any attempts to build a noncapitalist society will either be crushed or, if that proves impossible, subject to such ghastly reprisals that the attempt is not worthwhile; that the United States will indeed persevere in the punishment ("honor its commitments") long after it has lost all immediate hope of crushing the rebels—as in the economic blockade and other harassments of Cuba; as in the devastating bombing and punitive military sweeps in the unconquerable liberated zones of South Vietnam. The United States can afford to write off its economic losses in Cuba and Vietnam, but it cannot tolerate the political losses. It cannot afford to let the idea get around that freedom is possible or that societies that escape its hegemony will be allowed to flourish.

Clearly some of the same considerations apply domestically. The failure to make any but the most paltry gestures to appease public dissatisfaction, the failure to run even a mildly antiwar, but proestablishment, candidate in the 1968 elections, the government sanctioned "police riot" at the convention, and the subsequent indictments of demonstration leaders—none of these may be quite so shortsighted as they appear at first. In the divisions within the establishment between the liberals and the hard-liners, the hard-liners won hands down at both Miami and Chicago—and therefore inevitably in the election. As Carl Oglesby has pointed out, Chicago proved that "liberalism has no power in this country. . . . This country, in the current situation, is absolutely impotent before the threat of what Fulbright has lately called 'elective fascism.' " ("Notes on a Decade Ready for the Dustbin," *Liberation,* August-September 1969.) There is a logic, however gruesome, to the winning position. Not only in the underdeveloped world but in the United States, people must be taught that in the "real" world there are practical limits to both democracy and decency. Rather than encourage Americans to believe that they can indeed rein in their government when its policies offend their humane and humanitarian impulses, they must be brought back to "the despairing conviction that American power in its present form and guided by its present purposes is invincible." (Sontag, *op. cit.*) Given the dangerous psychic changes first generated in the civil rights movement and lately reappearing in the youth culture and the antiwar resistance, the movement must be shown that any hopes it may have about the possibility of a society based on individual dignity and communal solidarity rather than on property, profit, and power are doomed to disappointment.

Lest this interpretation seem too fanciful, let me quote Susan Sontag again. In the following two passages, she discusses the impact on her own psyche of a trip she took to Hanoi in May 1968 and compares it to the feelings engendered in French acquaintances by their experiences in the May-June revolts:

> I came back from Hanoi considerably chastened. Life here looks both uglier and more promising. To describe what is promising, it's perhaps imprudent to invoke the

promiscuous ideal of revolution. Still it would be a mistake to underestimate the amount of diffuse yearning for radical change pulsing through this society. Increasing numbers of people do realize that we must have a more generous, more humane way of dealing with each other; and great, probably convulsive, social changes are needed to create these psychic changes. To prepare intelligently for radical change requires . . . getting more perspective on the human type that gradually became ascendant in the West from the time of the Reformation to the industrial revolution to modern post-industrial society. Almost everyone would agree that this isn't the only way human beings could have evolved, but very few people in Europe and America really *believe* that there is any other way for a person to be or can *imagine* what they might be like. (*Op. cit.,* p. 88; emphasis in original.)

I recognized a limited analogy to my present state in Paris in early July when, talking to acquaintances who had been on the barricades in May, I discovered they don't really accept the failure of their revolution. The reason for their lack of "realism," I think, is that they're still possessed by the new feelings revealed to them during those weeks— those precious weeks in which vast numbers of ordinarily suspicious, cynical urban people, workers and students, behaved with an unprecedented generosity and warmth and spontaneity toward each other. . . . Someone who has enjoyed new feelings of that kind—a reprieve, however brief, from the inhibitions on love and trust this society enforces—is never the same again. In him, the revolution has just started, and it continues. (*Op. cit.,* p. 90.)

Numerous participants in the civil rights movement and in the less cut-and-dried antiwar demonstrations (such as the August 1965 Assembly of Unrepresentative People, the activities of the Resistance, the demonstrations at the Pentagon in the fall of 1967 and at the Chicago convention, the Oakland Stop the Draft Week, and the struggle over the People's Park in Berkeley) have reported experiencing something of the same liberating dynamics. It is sometimes difficult for people who have these experiences to hold onto their conviction that they are the key to the building of a new society, given the pressures from both the right and sections of the left to think that all power grows out of the barrel of a gun. But they are what gives hope and distinction to the movement.

Obviously there is a gap between a movement whose revolutionary character is nourished by experiences and feelings of this type and the old F.B.I., yellow press stereotype of blind partisans on the Soviet side of the cold war. Vietnam's resistance might be as reminiscent of the heroic struggle of the Russian peasants and workers in 1917 as it is of the struggle for independence by the American colonies in 1776. But the realities of Soviet bureaucracy, its Stalinist past and its post-Stalin suppression of our counterparts in Russia and Eastern Europe have been too well documented for too long for the movement to consider it an ally or to be swayed by its brand of "revolutionary realism."*

Rather it is the controlling sectors of the military-industrial complex who bank their hopes for "peace" on the maturity and reasonableness of the Soviet Union, which will permit the super-powers to divide up the raw materials and human resources of the world in gigantic "spheres of influence." Of course there is very little honor among thieves (and not all the thieves in either country are agreed on the desirability of such a division), so tension and conflict persist, particularly in border-line areas and trouble spots like Vietnam and the Middle East, where one or the other of the two countries sees an opportunity to bleed its rival or gain an advantage. But Lyndon Johnson's great hope for getting off the hook in Vietnam was to work out a major settlement with the Russians, whereby in return for American concessions in other areas the Russians would force the Vietnamese to abandon their struggle for self-determination.

This was a difficult initiative to bring off, particularly in view of the Sino-Soviet split, which weakened the Soviet Union's ability to

---

* *There is a section of the movement (Progressive Labor Party) that slavishly follows its own oversimplified version of Maoism. And for most of us what is going on in China is much more exciting and attractive than Russia's revisionist state capitalism and bureaucratic sludge, but information about China is scanty and unreliable, the idolatry of Mao repulsive, the history of the American Communist Party's subservience to the imperatives of Soviet foreign policy too frightening, and our own firsthand experience too real for most of the movement to subordinate its indigenous quality to China worship.*

ride herd on the Vietnamese. The Vietnamese, who had been victimized by similar big-power pressures in 1954 into accepting temporary partition of their country, were anything but tractable. As I discovered when I visited Hanoi in 1966 and 1967 (and as most other Western visitors have reported as well), they are almost as wary of their big-power friends as of their enemies. Pham Van Dong, the Prime Minister, told me that if either the Soviet Union or China stopped supplying them with arms, they would go back to fighting with sticks and snares—and, of course, the considerable quantities of American arms they get through capture and the black market. "But we are extremely grateful to our Soviet and Chinese friends for their considerable assistance," he said with a smile, "and we do not think they will stop helping us."

Despite the difficulties in any U.S. attempt to resolve the Vietnam dilemma through an accommodation with the Russians, the attempt had to be made. Military defeat, loss of political prestige, and domestic disintegration were staring the United States in the face. The secret of the attempted deal was not too well kept and I was made aware of it sometime in July through contacts at the United Nations and elsewhere. But let me quote Theodore White, cautious traditionalist, trusted friend and confidant of presidents and diplomats:

> For weeks before the convention, an unwritten and unpublished script had governed the high diplomacy of America, a script which Lyndon Johnson hoped would end his Presidency with an outburst of doves, a flourish of trumpets, an end to war in Vietnam, and peace on earth. All through July and August, American diplomats had been preparing for a summit conference of their President with Premier Kosygin of Russia. . . . By Tuesday, August 20, Assistant Secretary of State William Bundy had finished drafting a secret diplomatic note to be sent to all America's major allies abroad informing them of the approaching summit and its purpose: George Christian, the President's press secretary, was on stand-by to inform the nation. . . . for Lyndon Johnson it meant the most dramatically conceivable demonstration of his good will and, if lucky, of his world achievement. From a successful summit in Europe, a quick flight would bring him home as a peacemaker to a cheering convention in

Chicago—and then, who could guess what might happen?
(Theodore H. White, *The Making of the President—1968*
[Atheneum], p. 277.)

Unfortunately for President Johnson and Premier Kosygin, a
new mood of disaffection and alienation from the stifling cynicism of
the super-states, together with the creation of a counterculture of subversive warmth and generosity and spontaneity, were proceeding at a
rapid rate not only in France and the United States but in the Soviet
Union and the satellite countries as well. Kosygin had his own "Vietnam" to deal with. On August 22, the armies of the Soviet Union and
five satellite countries invaded Czechoslovakia.

McCarthy, Humphrey, and Johnson were all caught off balance.
McCarthy dismissed the Soviet invasion as a minor episode, hardly
constituting "a major world crisis." "The White House staff . . . were
quoted as saying that Hubert's been destroyed by the Czechoslovakian
thing." (White, *op. cit.,* p. 279.) Johnson was forced to abandon
his trip to Moscow—and the grandiloquent plans that went with it.
A handful of Old Left ideologues, spending most of their time trying to collar delegates, but also looking in on the demonstrators, were
embarrassed and chagrined, tried to defend the invasion. But the Mobilization Committee and most of the demonstrators unhesitatingly
condemned the Soviet aggression, comparing it in principle if not in
intensity with the American aggression against Vietnam. We organized protests at the Polish Travel Agency, the only office in Chicago
that represented one of the invading countries. We called Chicago
the Prague of the American Midwest, comparing the presence of the
6,000 National Guardsmen, the 6,000 American regulars, the 12,000
Chicago police, the tons of Mace, and the other armaments with the
presence of Soviet troops, tanks and guns in Prague.

We had no doubts that the C.I.A. and numerous other U.S. organizations in the service of imperialism had done their best to stir
up trouble in Czechoslovakia, just as Moscow had hailed the American antiwar movement. We realized that the United States would
now try to interpret the growth of an indigenous Czechoslovakian
liberation movement as pro-American and pro-capitalist rather than
pro-life and pro-man. But we knew that Moscow had no influence on
our movement and we doubted how much influence the United States
had in setting the goals or affecting the quality of life experience of

the movement in Czechoslovakia or other Soviet bloc countries. This was not all reasoning by analogy. Movement representatives had exchanged experiences and life-views with students and intellectuals of Czechoslovakia in the wine-cellars of Prague, Brno and Bratislava. (I myself had visited Czechoslovakia in 1964, 1967 and 1968.)

No matter how offended the government pretended to be (and of course many individuals actually were) by the Soviet-led invasion, the "realists" undoubtedly recognized—and approved—the facts as we had presented them in drawing a parallel between Soviet intervention to protect its power interests in Czechoslovakia and American intervention in Vietnam and the Dominican Republic. In any event, they continued their effort to come to terms with the Soviet Union in order to get a settlement in Vietnam favorable to the interests of the American power elite. The fanfare of the public trip had to be abandoned, but behind-the-scenes negotiations continued throughout September and October. Once again it is useful to quote Theodore White. He writes of a secret meeting in New York, on October 7, between a "key Russian diplomat" and "an influential American political figure":

> . . . the Russian made known to the American that Russia had deep problems of its own, both domestically and in foreign affairs with China; despite the rupture of the summer summit by the Czechoslovakian invasion, Russia still sought rapprochement with America. *On the matter of the war in Asia, Russia wanted it to come to an end. Russia, he said, now finally held the upper hand in Hanoi's Communist government over the pro-Chinese Communist elements.* If America stopped the bombing of the North, Russia could guarantee that a positive response from Hanoi would be forthcoming. (White, *op. cit.*, p. 377; emphasis added.)

Despite the persistent speculation of most American politicians and establishment analysts about the struggle in Hanoi between the pro-Russian and pro-Chinese factions, the Vietnamese are, in reality, of course, neither very pro-Russian or pro-Chinese. They welcome aid from all their "socialist brothers," stay magnificently aloof from the Sino-Soviet conflict, and have the closest relationship of all with tiny Cuba, a love affair which does them little material good and can cause them even less harm. Whatever their heritage of factional conflict from the past,* fifteen years of nationalist struggle have made them all supremely pro-Vietnamese. What other sentiments could have enabled them to survive all that time, locked in mortal conflict first with France and then with the United States? In the war against the French, the United States paid eighty percent of the French costs, but during most of the time the Vietnamese received no aid from either the Russians or the Chinese.

Not knowing how to deal with honest men—finding it hard even to believe in their existence—and therefore reduced to dealing with Russia instead of Vietnam, the United States apparently accepted the misguided assurances from their Russian counterparts as the rationale for instituting the badly needed bombing halt in the North, a few days before the election. It just barely failed to turn the tide in favor of the Democrats. Quite properly the Vietnamese continued to insist on complete withdrawal of all American troops and self-determination for Vietnam. Meanwhile, they continued to press their military and political campaign against the occupying American troops and against the "leftover colonial officers" whom the United States was backing in Saigon. The bombing of the North had been militarily unproductive as well as politically unpopular, so although the United States tried to make political capital out of its claim that the Vietnamese had gone back on the agreement (an agreement which apparently had been made with the Russians, not the Vietnamese), they did not resume the bombing.

Undoubtedly Nixon is now continuing the attempt to solve the war in Vietnam not by listening to the Vietnamese, who insist on complete withdrawal, but by talking with the Russians. It is the only hope the United States can see of ending the war (a military and political necessity) without losing "face."

These last paragraphs carry us well beyond the setting at convention time, but they help underline, retrospectively, the seriousness of the bind in which the power elite found itself as the convention approached. They reveal its characteristic determination to handle the problem through the cynical maneuvers of secret diplomacy and big-power politics with the Russians, rather than by paying heed to the

---

* *In 1946 internecine warfare was quite virulent and apparently led to the shameful physical liquidation of the leading Trotskyists, though Ho and the Lao Dong Party attributed it to bandits.*

sentiments and demands of the American people. To carry through with this plan, it desperately needed to have the administration's foreign policy ratified at a rigged convention in a city purged of all public protest.

The Administration had squeaked through at Atlantic City four years earlier, when the explosive issue had been civil rights and the movement was relatively inexperienced. But between Atlantic City and Chicago great changes had taken place. The amount of public disaffection and alienation had grown immeasurably. The organized movement was far stronger and had grown in political and tactical sophistication. This time there was a resolute core of protesters who would not go away. The attempts to deal with them became an international scandal.

IV

Now let us look at five key areas of comparison and contrast between Atlantic City and Chicago.

1) *The differing role and treatment of antiwar demonstrators.*

The crisis at the Atlantic City convention was precipitated by a predominantly black movement, interspersed with whites; the crisis in Chicago by an essentially white movement, interspersed with blacks. The burning issue at Atlantic City was racism, although a separate group of about two hundred antiwar demonstrators, organized by the Committee for Nonviolent Action, was present. Many of the antiwar demonstrators periodically joined the M.F.D.P. vigil, but even after the debacle of the Atlantic City compromise and the abandonment of the civil rights protest, few if any of the civil rights demonstrators joined the antiwar protest. The psychology of the civil rights movement of the time was to avoid endangering public sympathy by criticizing the war. Not until January 6, 1966 did a major civil rights organization (S.N.C.C.) condemn the war.* If today some sections

---

* *Six months earlier and roughly a year after the Atlantic City convention, movement organizers in McComb, Mississippi, circulated a leaflet giving "five reasons why Negroes should not be in any war fighting for America." This was the first civil rights protest against the war. It was stimulated by the death in Vietnam of John D. Shaw, twenty-three, of McComb, who had participated in the McComb civil rights demonstrations in 1961. Three days after the leaflet was printed in the McComb newsletter of the M.F.D.P., Lawrence*

of the antiwar and black liberation movements seem to go out of their way to alienate public sympathy and offend potential supporters by excoriating everyone who disagrees with them even on seemingly minor matters, it is worth remembering the heritage of public relations opportunism they are working off.

The unifying issue at Chicago was opposition to the war, although signs, speeches, and chants continually called for an end to racism. One reason for the greater focus on Vietnam was that for all its generalized opposition to racism, the white movement had been unsettled by the emergence of black power midway between the Atlantic City and Chicago conventions. The proposed solution in Vietnam was simple and unifying—to stop the bombing, withdraw the troops, and permit self-determination for the Vietnamese. The specific programs for ending racism were both more complex and divisive; the black community itself was divided over them. Some of the rhetoric and programs threatened the privileges or challenged the assumptions of many of the antiwar constituents.

In 1964, the tide of public sentiment had not turned yet against the war, so the antiwar demonstrators did not represent a serious threat at the convention. There was no immediate danger of their crystallizing widespread disenchantment with the convention hypocrisies, the candidates, or the program. So although matters were a little touchy, the demonstrators were allowed to stand with their placards and chants *in the very shadow of Convention Hall.* By 1968, the antiwar demonstrators represented millions of people, with a resulting change in the attitude of the authorities that is exactly the reverse of what one would expect in a genuine democracy: the authorities tried to keep the demonstrators out of sight. The attempt could have succeeded only if the protesters had cooperated in their own demise. When they refused, the attempt backfired and multiplied their visibility many times over. Demonstrators were forbidden to come within approximately six miles of the convention amphi-

---

Guyot, Chairman of the M.F.D.P.'s executive committee, issued a statement saying that it did not represent the position of M.F.D.P., but also saying: "It is very easy to understand why Negro citizens of McComb, themselves the victims of bombings, Klan-inspired terrorism and harassment arrests, should resent the death of a citizen of McComb while fighting in Vietnam for 'freedom' not enjoyed by the Negro community of McComb."

theatre, a ban that was enforced in a manner that turned the stomachs of television viewers all over the country.

The contrast between the treatment of antiwar demonstrators at Atlantic City and Chicago is a perfect example of how the United States tolerates dissent (as a sign of the Freedom under which we live) so long as it is ineffectual, but smashes it when it threatens to become popular or powerful.

2) *The attempt to get demonstrators out of the streets, out of genuine resistance activities, and into the McCarthy campaign*—followed at a later date by the last-minute bombing halt and the attempt to pass off Humphrey as the movement's best friend or lesser evil (whichever of the two would lead the movement to stop its protest activities and vote).

The most obvious parallel between the establishment's approach to the civil rights movement in the period leading up to and including the 1964 convention and its approach to the antiwar movement in 1968 is presented by the McCarthy campaign. In the earlier period, as we have already noted, "much of the flurry of activity by the Federal government was aimed, in the words of President Kennedy, at getting the demonstrators out of the streets and into the courts." This was followed by the diversion of movement energies into the voter registration campaign. Senator Eugene McCarthy, with equal candor, announced that the aim of his campaign for the Democratic nomination was to get the antiwar movement out of the streets and into conventional politics. Although some of his supporters hoped to supplement (or even crown) their street or resistance activities by campaigning for McCarthy, McCarthy himself was intent on getting them to give up street demonstrations and resistance altogether. One interesting sidelight, from my own personal experience in the National Mobilization Committee, is how many of his supporters—unable to renounce demonstrations, yet still clinging to the electoral illusion—never quite heard his repeated words along these lines.

In the original announcement of his candidacy, McCarthy said that he wanted "to provide an alternative for those who 'become cynical and make threats of support for third parties or fourth parties or *other irregular political movements.*'" (Quoted from "An Open Letter to McCarthy Supporters," Carl Oglesby in *The Ramparts Wall Poster;* emphasis added.)

In a speech at the University of Denver, McCarthy said:

> For years you had dissented from the war and you ob-
> tained no tangible results. You got results only when you di-
> rected the fire and spirit of your resistance movement into
> the processes of democratic government. (Quoted in the
> *Boston Globe,* April 7, 1968.)

One must make allowances for "campaign oratory" and in-
group morale building, but it is tempting to ask what *tangible results*
they got. Surely nothing more substantial than primary victories that
were soon to be overruled by the party bosses. So undemocratic is the
nominating procedure that even if McCarthy had entered and won
every primary, this would not have gotten him enough delegates to
secure the nomination. According to Arthur Miller, writing in the
New York Times Magazine after the convention, "of 7.5 million
Democrats who voted in the primaries, eighty percent preferred
McCarthy's and/or Robert Kennedy's Vietnam position. The violence
in the hall, let alone on the streets, was the result of this mockery
of a vast majority who had so little representation . . ." To get the
nomination, McCarthy would have had to bind himself over to the
invisible government that has the power to veto any candidate it
cannot control. So even if the "results" had been McCarthy's nomination and election, this still would have left open the question
of what tangible changes in policy would have followed once he
was in the White House.

One clear contrast between 1964 and 1968 was that in 1968 the
attempt to hook and reel in the movement was carried out not by the
incumbent or his heir-apparent but by a relative outsider. The most
obvious reason was that the opposition had grown in sophistication
and militancy and required bait that could be passed off as anti-estab-
lishment. In part this was inevitable because, whereas in 1964 Johnson and Humphrey could disclaim responsibility for "Southern" racism, they could not so easily divest themselves of responsibility for
the continued aggression in Vietnam. But the crux of the matter was
that the section of the movement that was not susceptible to the type
of self-deception involved in the 1964 moratorium and alliance with
the Democrats had grown and matured in the intervening years. It
was strengthened not only by its own bitter experience but by the
widespread youth revolt against the values and institutions of capitalist culture, and by the emergence of the Black Panthers and the gen-

eral radicalization of the black community. Perhaps Bobby Kennedy, no outsider, could have succeeded in the end in seducing large sections of the movement, if he had not been murdered. But even he was finding it difficult, because such a wide gap had opened up between the movement's politics and the most enlightened politics tolerated by the liberal wing of the establishment. The positions taken by both Kennedy and McCarthy in their TV debate shortly before Kennedy's assassination turned off the movement. In addition, Kennedy got a late and unpopular start, due to the fact that his computers, polls, and analysts had underestimated the unprecedented movement of the country leftward.

The heightened crisis and growing public support for the movement had intensified the internal contradictions within the ruling class, widening the rift between those who thought it best to seduce the movement (the McCarthy and Kennedy campaigns, offering concessions in Vietnam) and those who were itching to crush it. From one point of view, the smart thing to do would have been to undercut the opposition by giving the convention nod to McCarthy (once Bobby Kennedy was gone), just as it would have been smart to withdraw from Vietnam before failure to do so had disillusioned or radicalized millions of Americans. But as in the dying days of every empire, the ingrained prejudices of the ruling elite would not permit such a realistic act. The alternative type of "realism" that they adopted was based on other considerations and included the decision to scrap part of the facade of democracy rather than to encourage movement illusions of relevance to the real world.

It was bad enough that Lyndon was fuming in the wings, worried that the effect of angry demonstrators on the delegates and the public would make it difficult—perhaps impossible—for him to come to Chicago and seize the nomination by acclamation. If worse came to worst, it would be better to try to pull it off with Hubert, especially since the Republicans had nominated Nixon, whom nobody could pretend was against the aggression in Vietnam or opposed to current racist institutions and practices. Those sections of the movement that had any sense would have no alternative but to vote for Johnson or Humphrey, whichever it turned out to be, particularly if the government announced a bombing halt before election day. The rest deserved to be crushed anyway, through a strict application of "law and order" in the courts and in the streets.

So a federal grand jury was convened in Chicago before the convention even opened, in order to prepare indictments of any demonstration leaders who insisted on going through with their plans. The Chicago police and the National Guard had been given their battle plans even earlier. Beginning in January, representatives of the Police Department, Secret Service, Military Intelligence and "other governmental agencies . . . met every two weeks through May, and weekly thereafter until mid-August" (The *Walker Report,* p. 95).

Given the alienation and militancy of large sections of the movement and the unwillingness of the power elite to go with McCarthy, the objective that had been foisted on the movement in 1964 through the self-imposed moratorium on demonstrations could best be accomplished in 1968 by serving unmistakable notice that from now on militant demonstrations would not be tolerated. Ideally, if the notice was served drastically enough (through a "police riot"), it would intensify the splits that already existed within the movement, weaken or destroy the antiwar coalition, and drastically reduce the numbers who would respond to future calls for action. At the very least, a sufficiently tough policy in Chicago would turn the clock back to those happier days before the 1967 Pentagon demonstrations when militant demonstrations were small and massive demonstrations docile. If this happened, it might even be possible to tolerate some demonstrations again, as befits a Free Society.

Long before this drastic solution was imposed on the demonstrators, a rather typical symbiotic relationship had been developing between the rival schools of thought within the establishment. They could not come together in their choice of candidates or their programs for Vietnam, but they were agreed that the convention should be freed from the blot of demonstrations. For months Mayor Daley, Sheriff Woods and other members of the "get tough" school issued warnings and threats, while Senator McCarthy made clear his conviction that demonstrations were an intrusion on the democratic process and that he expected his followers to stay away.

After the disturbances in the ghetto that followed the assassination of Martin Luther King on April 4, Daley criticized the Chicago police for not being tough enough, and made his famous order that in future disturbances, the police should "shoot to kill arsonists and shoot to maim looters." Neither arson or looting had ever been contemplated by the demonstrators but the message to expect the worst was unmistakable. Other threats and intimidations followed, including police harassment of known militants, a raid on a Chicago Yippie meeting on April 25 (at which twenty-one were arrested), savage attacks and mass arrests at a peaceful antiwar parade on April 27, and a raid on a Yippie benefit at Chicago's Electric Theatre, at which thirty more were arrested.*

On Friday, August 23, two days before the convention and four days before the intended mass demonstrations outside the Amphitheatre, Brigadier General Richard T. Dunn, commander of the 6,000 Illinois National Guard troops assigned to the convention, translated Daley's earlier statement into a last minute attempt to keep away potential demonstrators and to intimidate those already on hand. He announced that "his men would 'shoot to kill' . . . if there is no other way of preventing the commission of a forcible felony during the convention." He said:

> The troops will be armed and will be carrying ammunition. We use .30-caliber ball ammunition. This kind of ammunition is made to kill. (*Chicago Daily News,* August 25.)

Significantly, the *Walker Report*** fails to quote this statement by General Dunn, although it quotes extensively from the most extreme put-ons by the Yippies, from "unidentified document(s) in police intelligence files," and the wildest imaginings of police informers. After pointing out that such material "could not all be taken seriously," it offers a convenient rationale for the official over-kill (denial of permits, stockpiling of Mace, gas, troops etc.) by saying:

> But since their responsibility takes in the protection of the entire public, they could not take the risk of underestimating any intelligence, however absurd it might seem to a private citizen. (Page 98.)

* See "The Lessons," p. 315-17.
** *The* Walker Report *is a typical liberal document, with its troubled conscience over police "excesses," its obvious attempts to probe honestly what was going on in the minds of the demonstrators, but also with its inability to pin responsibility where it belongs or to understand that when suppression is the order of the day, "excesses" are apt to accompany it. (See Points 3 and 4 below on governmental "impartiality" and on "the erroneous tendency to blame oppressive governmental policy on the mistakes or bad politics of individual villains.")*

These repeated threats and acts of intimidation did, of course, have a chilling effect on potential demonstrators. Thousands who had been planning to come stayed away. I remember a phone conversation with the father of a family of four shortly after the Dunn statement. He explained that although his kids were unhappy with the decision, he and his wife had decided that it would be irresponsible to risk the family's safety by coming.

Throughout all threatening statements and denials of permits, Senator McCarthy had nothing to say about the obvious creation of a police-state atmosphere. But on August 12, he once again urged his followers to stay out of Chicago on convention week, warning against the possibility of "unintended violence." As the Walker Commission delicately puts it, "it was reported that Senator McCarthy had been in contact with Mayor Daley" before issuing the statement. After meeting with Daley,

> he urged (his supporters) to conduct rallies in their own communities rather than to contribute to tensions in Chicago. In addition, telegrams were sent to each of the many campaign headquarters around the country to reinforce the request.
>
> ... The co-chairman of the Pennsylvania Coalition for an Open Convention, for example, announced that his group would comply with Senator McCarthy's request and that they had cancelled plans to take 2,000 persons to Chicago for the mass rally on August 25. (The *Walker Report*, page 54.)

Allard Lowenstein took a similar tack:

> Allard Lowenstein announced a cancellation of the program (for a massive rally in Chicago on Sunday) after Senator McCarthy's public statement urging his followers to avoid Chicago and after an unsuccessful bid to obtain a permit for the use of Soldier Field. (The *Walker Report*, page 53.)

The issue was joined. As at Atlantic City, the liberals had yielded to pressure, had cancelled planned protests, and were using their influence to keep demonstrators away. But the Mobilization and the Yippies refused to withdraw. The Mobilization announced that to yield to such threats was to allow the creation of a police state by default.

The stakes were now higher, the risks greater. The smaller the number of demonstrators, the easier it would be for the forces ostensibly assigned to "protect" the public to crack down on them. Police provocateurs and infiltrators would be more effective in their attempts to provoke violence. It would be easier for Mayor Daley to argue, as he had all along, that we were "nothin' but a small group of troublemakers and terrorists."

But now more than ever it was also important to hold firm. The forces committed to the war in Vietnam and to continued control by the military-industrial complex wanted to pretend that the limits of citizen protest were defined by the electoral process—in which the establishment holds a stacked deck. An absence of protesters during the convention would encourage that illusion. It would also imply that the problems were not so deep-seated and pressing as we knew they were. If in the end we were allowed to protest, we were confident that we would be speaking for and to millions of troubled Americans. If the government persisted in its efforts to stop us, it would have to bring out into the open, on a sensitive occasion, the brute force on which it always relies, in the ghetto, in Vietnam, wherever people are determined to gain control over their own lives and to live in forms of fraternity that are impossible under capitalism.

3) *The attempts of the Federal government to pass itself off as being above partisan conflict and interested only in freedom and justice under an impartially administered system of law and order.*

The myth of the government as impartial referee dies slowly. And the more repressive the society becomes, the more useful the actual decision-makers find it to keep the myth alive. Today it is reflected in virtually all presidential messages and other official utterances.

According to the myth, the norm by which all American administrations are judged is their faithfulness in sitting disinterestedly above the battle, regulating the various conflicts of interest in society without favoritism, with sensitivity to everyone's rights, and in the service of the public. Human nature being what it is, and with the tendency of changes in technology and public taste to open up various "loopholes," things get out of balance occasionally. Sometimes there is even corruption in high places. But under the American system of freedom, there are compensatory pressures from other groups—the free press, the rival party, periodic elections, and the famous checks and balances of the courts, the legislature, and the executive—to keep deviations from getting out of hand. There may be disagreements about policy, but clearly the basic *function* of the government is to balance out all the factors and make any necessary adjustments in behalf of all the people.

Karl Marx knew better. He referred to the government as "the executive committee of the ruling class." If we bear in mind that few executive committees (and no ruling classes) are monolithic, it's an accurate description of how things are in the United States. It's also worth remembering the role of caucuses (formal and informal, visible and invisible) in bringing pressure on executive committees.

We have already noted the failure of American governments, both local and federal, to live up to their claimed function of impartiality in their relations with the civil rights movement. Commenting on the attitude of the French government in the May-June insurgency, the Cohn-Bendits sum up its role in words that apply to all capitalist governments:

> . . . the government was still trying to present itself as the supreme arbiter of all the various interests in society, while trying to keep private property and the means of production in the hands of the bourgeoisie. (*Op. cit.,* p. 24.)

At Chicago the threat to the continuation of private property and the means of production in the hands of the bourgeoisie was perhaps not obvious to the casual observer. (The existence of such a threat seems so *farfetched* in the United States, despite the restiveness of important sections of the population and the increasingly anti-capitalist rhetoric of the movement.) But the government was quite correctly aware that such a threat was implicit in popular attempts to divest the government and the power elite of their power to continue the war in Vietnam and the prevailing racial and economic injustice. Stripped of decision-making power, private ownership does not amount to much—like the supposed ownership of Bell Telephone Company and certain other huge corporations by thousands of small shareholders.

Max Frankel, who, let it be said, was appalled by the crudity of police violence, writes in his introduction to the Bantam edition of the *Walker Report:*

. . . for there in Chicago two fundamental rights in conflict had posed an essential question about our current violence: how can we assure both a people's right to dissent and a community's right to protect its citizens and property.

One does not know whether to congratulate him for being so close to the truth or to chastise him for having, in the end, missed the point altogether. To bring his comment into touch with reality, it is necessary to point out that the *community's* right to protect its citizens and property specifically meant the *government's* right to protect its fictitious citizens, the huge corporations, and their private control of public property, a control which brings with it de facto domination of political conventions and democratic decision-making. Then one can see which of the "rights in conflict" is deserving of support. But I fear that he had something much more prosaic and less real in mind. Something similar to what the authors of the *Walker Report* themselves were thinking of when they wrote euphemistically of the government's responsibility for "the protection of the entire public."

At the hearings of the House Committee on Unamerican Activities on the Chicago disorders, Congressman Albert Watson (South Carolina) sought at one point to reduce the problem to a question of whether it was not true that the marching of antiwar demonstrators "eight abreast down the sidewalk" would interfere with "the right of people to traverse the streets and sidewalks of Chicago in a normal fashion."

> *Mr. Watson.* They can't traverse the streets when you are marching eight abreast. What do they do? Do they lose their rights or do they run over you? (Proceedings, Subcommittee of the Committee on Unamerican Activities, Washington, D.C., December 5, 1968; testimony of David Dellinger; page 945.)

To the best of my knowledge, Chicago has never found it necessary to ban a Chicago Bears football game, or to gas, club and Mace the spectators heading for a World Series baseball game, in order to protect the interests of those who are inevitably victimized by the traffic jams that accompany these events.

But the most ironic example of the government's pretensions of impartiality was its indictment of eight policemen, along with eight demonstrators, under various sections of the civil rights law. By this act it tried, much too mechanistically, to create the appearance of a tie-game, an interim score which it no doubt hoped would give the impression that the government has no vested reason for suppressing the demonstrators' political rights. Who can suspect the umpire when, after a donnybrook breaks out, he throws an equal number of players on both sides out of the game?

By such creaky contrivances do the country's psychological warriors go about their tasks. No wonder American psychological warfare and pacification techniques have been so unsuccessful in Vietnam. Lest this seem an unwarranted extrapolation from the Justice Department's Chicago follies, let me say that when I was in North Vietnam people in some of the villages that I visited told me that sometimes American planes would come with bombs and destruction, and then a few hours later would return, dropping transistor radios and toys for the children, with propaganda leaflets attached telling how much better life was with the Americans. One for death and one for life. One for the generals and one for the humanitarians. What could be fairer than that, in this most evenly balanced of all democratic societies?

Leave aside the American Civil Liberties Union's complaint that the government indicted eight "leaders" on our side and eight rank-and-file policemen on theirs. Or that the penalties are far severer for our charges than theirs—ten years against one. These are peripheral matters. Our role as leaders was minimal. And the movement will not help build an egalitarian future, with grass-roots initiative and responsibility, unless it cherishes these qualities now, by rotating its leaders and not relying unduly on any of them. The demonstrators knew why they came to Chicago, and it wasn't to play "follow the leader." If the government thinks it can cut off a few heads and kill the body, it is in for a shock.

Clearly police brutality was not limited to the eight chosen scapegoats. Hundreds of charging policemen, acting in close formations, succumbed collectively, officers and men alike, to the occupational sickness of their trade. Hundreds of them exceeded the public's approved limits for "game," when the authorities decided to turn the streets of Chicago into a hunting preserve. But there is no way the government, in its pretended impartiality, could even consider indicting them all. For if the government is the executive committee of the ruling class, the police are the government's enforcers. It doesn't pay to bite the hand that protects you. Like J. Edgar Hoover, the police remain in some important respects above the law, even when they offend normal proprieties. So the grand jury (which is invariably dominated by the U.S. Attorney's office) didn't even bother to look at the film clips of what had taken place. (This information was revealed privately by a confidential source high in Chicago's official hierarchy.)

Undoubtedly there would be temporary public advantages in following the A.C.L.U.'s suggestion of indicting the highest Chicago officials, if it could be accomplished politically. But clearly the responsibility for what happened does not stop in Chicago. Nor is the key question whether or not the police could have carried out their assignment with more delicacy and discrimination; for example, clubbing only demonstrators but not newsmen, or only demonstrators and newsmen but not medics and passersby. The excesses which first engage the consciences of the general public (whether in Chicago, in the South during the civil rights demonstrations, or in Vietnam) seem at first glance to be the arbitrary acts of individuals or to result from inadequate training or command. But closer examination usually reveals that they are not quite so arbitrary and flow almost inevitably from the general nature of the struggle that is being waged and the official objectives in that struggle. It is important to combat and expose such "excesses," but it is not realistic to try to clean them up without at the same time exposing the institutional context in which they take place. Otherwise one fights on the level of Ladybird's campaign to beautify America. Not only does he fight in a minor skirmish, he is bound to lose.

There are two key questions that must be answered before one can understand the central issues that led to the "police riot" in Chicago, issues which remain unresolved and have already led to other police riots in other cities.

First, why did the demonstrators have to go to Chicago in the first place? And second, why did top government officials believe that it was necessary to ban demonstrations and to make an example of those who refused to heed the ban?

Most of what I have already written is an attempt to throw light on these two questions. In the present context, it is enough to point out that the demonstrators did not go to Chicago to protest the policies of its police department or the propensities to violence of individual policemen, though naturally they are concerned with both matters all over the country. It was the policies and practices of the Federal government that made it necessary for the demonstrators to go to Chicago. It was the war against Vietnam, the continued racist oppression, the subservience to the military-industrial complex. The Federal government could not be the umpire. It was the enemy.

For its part, the government's major concern was not that the demonstrators might cause inconvenience to pedestrians, shout obscenities, burn trash cans in the street, or even smash a window or two. All these improprieties and worse are regular occurrences at conventions of the American Legion, the Veterans of Foreign Wars and the A.F.L.-C.I.O. Every president goes out of his way to solicit and accept invitations to address such conventions.

If the government has any sense at all (and I must admit that sometimes it is hard to believe that it does), it could not possibly have believed that we would try to invade the convention, though that was the pretext on which the city claimed that we must be kept six miles away. Besides our clear-cut decision against such a tactic and our repeated announcements to that effect, the Federal government's extensive use of bugging, wire-taps and spies must have confirmed that we had no such intentions. They are wasting a lot of the people's money if they did not know. Finally, if there had been any group foolish enough to make the attempt, the government had many times more than enough troops, bayonets, barbed wire, Mace, gas, tanks, helicopters, and guns to frustrate it. Realizing that if it waited for such an attack to take place, it would never happen, the government decided to launch a "search and destroy" mission.

The government was not afraid that we might trample on the rights of others. It was afraid that we might encourage others to assert their rights. It was not our potential misdeeds, real or imagined, that put the city and Federal authorities uptight. It was our politics. It was our views and our attempts to advance them outside the snares of electoral politics. It was the threat of sit-ins and demonstrations at draft boards, induction centers, offices of corporations engaged in war work—at a time when the convention was pretending to provide an adequate opportunity for the redress of grievances. It was the combination of our political demands and our style as a movement. For all these reasons, we were the enemy.

If any additional proof was required to show the government's lack of impartiality, the government itself supplied it when it indicted Bobby Seale, acting national chairman of the Black Panther Party. Everyone on both sides knows that the Panthers were not involved at any stage in the organization or planning of the Chicago protests.

Bobby came to Chicago on the second day of the convention (the fourth day of protests), long after the pattern of police brutality and movement response had been well established. He came at the invitation of the Peace and Freedom Party, as a last-minute replacement for Eldridge Cleaver, Peace and Freedom nominee for president. He spoke at a Peace and Freedom Party rally at Lincoln Park, and again the next morning at a second rally they put on in Grant Park, across from the Conrad Hilton. Then he went home. I did not see him during the few hours he spent in Chicago and did not have the pleasure of meeting him until after we had been indicted as co-conspirators. Six of his "co-conspirators" had never met him before Chicago, the seventh only casually in a crowd.

Where there is a crime, there is generally a motive. It's not hard to discover two possible motives for the government's decision to indict Bobby, one of them clearly established by the pattern of government behavior, the other more speculative. The conjectural one derives from the government's knowledge that the Black Panthers advocate armed self-defense and sometimes speak emotionally on the need for everyone to get a gun.

I do not want to take anything away from the Panther's militancy, which has been tested in the line of fire and is heroic. But some of their speeches, which breathe fire and brimstone, are not a literal guide to their program. This is not an unusual political phenomenon, and is one reason the Bill of Rights and the Supreme Court make a distinction between speech and acts. To use an extreme example from the other side of the spectrum, when President Kennedy spoke in West Berlin in 1963, he sounded as if the United States were about to seize East Germany by force, though his actual policy at the time was to try to cool the Cold War in Europe. When he spoke in Miami, shortly after the Cuban missile crisis, he virtually promised the Cuban counterrevolutionaries that the United States would invade Cuba, although from everything we can determine he had just made a deal with Khrushchev which included a commitment not to do so.

By indicting Bobby Seale, the government has put itself in the position of being able to quote, in court, excerpts from his Chicago speeches in which according to reports he called for people to get guns. If it leaves out his long-run purpose of encouraging the development and training of self-defense forces against unlawful police harassments and arrests (and if the press minimizes or ridicules defense attempts to put the speeches in perspective) it may be able to blur the public's image of unarmed demonstrators being brutally attacked by the police.

The government is anxious to set a psychological climate for the trial, and the battle of public opinion that will surround it, similar to the climate it tried, with some success, to create for the convention hostilities. At that time, it leaked fantastic charges that were never substantiated or borne out by the course of events. One of them was that "an organization was reportedly organized to secure weapons and explosives and to plan a revolution to coincide with the convention." (*Walker Report,* page 97.) Mayor Daley announced that the city had secret information about plots to assassinate leading political figures. This produced the intended result of lurid headlines and public apprehension. To this day he has never produced a shred of evidence, although it would have been to his political advantage to have done so. Even if there had been such a plot it would not have implicated the demonstrators or justified the police violence, but a climate of fear tends to make the public less critical of police brutality—and encourages guilty verdicts.

Not speculative at all is the fact that the convention indictment of Seale coincides with a nation-wide effort of big city police and the Federal government to smash the Black Panther Party. Since the Panthers captured the imagination of large sections of the black community, police have killed or wounded dozens of them in shoot-outs initiated by the police on thinly veiled pretexts or in one-sided attacks. In the attack in which the police wounded Eldridge Cleaver, little Bobby Hutton was shot with his hands in the air. The attack was subsequently used as a pretext to accuse Cleaver of parole violation. In all, over twenty Panthers have been killed in the last three years, most of them by the police. The Panthers claim that all of these were killed by police or police agents, but not surprisingly the circumstances of some of the deaths are not clear to outsiders.

There is no question that the police in a number of cities have shot up Panther headquarters, smashing mimeograph machines, type-writers, and files, and destroying literature and food for their free breakfast program for children. All of these things took place in a raid on the Illinois headquarters in Chicago on the night of July 30, 1969 shortly after I had been there. When I got news of the raid, I returned and saw firsthand the wanton damage. The police claimed that they had attacked because someone had shot at them from a window, but four of us from the New Mobilization Committee, who had been meeting with the Panthers, find this unbelievable. The Panthers were clearly impressed by the fact that the police were in an ugly mood (there had been a raid the previous month, followed by repeated harassments and arrests) and they were determined not to give the police any excuse for further crackdowns. C.B.S. reported it this way: "The police say the Panthers shot first; the Panthers say the police shot first. Civilian witnesses tend to agree with the Panthers." (*Liberation News Service,* Aug. 2, 1969.) Whatever the police may claim about how the shoot-out started, there could be no conceivable excuse for the thoroughness with which they vandalized the headquarters and its contents. After a similar raid on the Panthers' San Francisco headquarters, reporters and public officials were scandalized by the destruction.

The cases are too numerous to itemize, but one woman I know in New York had her door broken down, apartment turned upside down, and her small children terrorized at 3 A.M. In the absence of any incriminating material, she was charged with possession of a dangerous weapon, her bread knife.

One of the government's techniques is to infiltrate black militant groups, and then to arrest a number of persons for allegedly plotting crimes that have been proposed by the infiltrators. The famous "plot" to blow up the Statue of Liberty is an example of the successful use of this technique. (The public didn't seem to care who had planned the event, as long as *someone* had.) I predict that this will be the essence of the government's case against the twenty-one New York Panthers accused of plotting to blow up the Botanical Gardens (someone in the government may have a sense of humor after all), five department stores, railroad yards, etc.

Sabotage is a classical technique all over the world of people who have been struggling for their freedom for a few years—let alone three hundred. In this country we have the hallowed precedent of the

Boston Tea Party, and, as Dr. Spock has pointed out, the injustices imposed on the colonists by the mother country were considerably less than those suffered then and now by black people at the hands of the white society. It would not be surprising if some black liberation forces experimented with some efforts of this general type. If so, the fact that they did should not lead us to side with the police. But the government's charges against the Panthers are so sweeping and heavy-handed as to be ludicrous. I was with Bobby Seale in Oakland when he received a phone call from New York telling the details of the charges. His spontaneous reaction was, "Why, that's stupid! Man, we'd be out of our minds to blow up department stores. That's where the people are and we want to liberate the people."

As nearly as uninformed citizens who are not in on government secrets can ascertain, the purpose of these attacks and wild charges is not simply to destroy the Black Panther Party. From the public statements of top officials, one may deduce that an additional purpose is to manufacture an atmosphere in which a drastic general crackdown would seem justified. By discrediting the Panthers and then establishing their conspiratorial ties with the antiwar movement and the Yippies, the government would be able to move significantly in the direction of political suppression of insurgent groups. Apparently it believes that such a move is necessary in order to continue the present unpopular foreign policy (with or without withdrawal from Vietnam) and to keep blacks, students, and other rebels in line.

On the ideological side, there have been a number of trial balloons sent up by the present administration to test the readiness of the country to accept such a repression. (Or were they simply indiscreet revelations of the way some of its leading officials think?) Let me present some samples from a single department, the Justice Department.

Attorney General John N. Mitchell has proposed controlling "crime" in the District of Columbia by using federal troops and has urged "preventive detention" of suspected criminals who the government thinks might commit crimes if they were free. He has also proposed making "a distinction between 'demonstrators' and 'activists' and spoke of distinguishing between them in order to prevent the latter from being granted permits to protest." (These examples from an article by Elizabeth Drew in *The Atlantic,* May 1969.) "He has significantly loosened the restrictions under which the F.B.I. and other Federal law-enforcement agencies may tap wires. Although he denies being arbitrary . . . he has certainly broken new legal ground by bringing to court the argument that the government can tap the wires of domestic political organizations if it deems their objectives to be subversive." (*New York Times Magazine,* August 10, 1969.) (The argument was made in a pre-trial hearing in connection with the Chicago conspiracy indictments.) Naturally it is the government which decides which organizations are subversive, and the courts whose judges have been appointed by the government which rule on any protests the victims may make.

Mitchell has said that "there's a difference between my philosophy and Ramsey Clark's. I think this is an institution for law enforcement, not social improvement." (*New York Times Magazine.*) Significantly, the *Times* says that "It is John Mitchell's observation that he is the Cabinet member to whom President Nixon pays the most heed—a contention that the men closest to the President rather readily confirm."

Assistant Attorney General Will Wilson has this to offer:

> I don't believe in permissive law enforcement. . . . Clark's trouble was that he was philosophically concerned with the rights of the individual. Our concern is more an orderly society through law enforcement. (*New York Times Magazine.*)

As for student unrest:

> I think if you could get all of them in the penitentiary you'd stop it. The ringleaders I'm talking about. (*The Atlantic.*)

On student unrest, Mitchell has also made his views clear:

> When you get nihilists on campus, the thing to do is to get them into court. (The *New York Times Magazine.*)

Wilson has more to say about free speech and public order:

> In the area of balancing the right of dissent against public order, my heavy leaning would be on the side of public order. On the question of where does free speech move towards public disturbance, my answer would be "pretty soon." . . . I'd call something a riot sooner than

maybe other people might. Don't you think that's the attitude generally of this administration? (*The Atlantic.*)

Deputy Attorney General Richard Kleindienst has called the student dissenter a "modern ideological criminal." In the same statement he affirms that the United States enjoys "the most nearly perfect government which civilization has produced," an observation which must be of great comfort to blacks, G.I.'s dying in Vietnam, and the Vietnamese as I am sure it will be to the people who are rounded up and put in the detention camps he has proposed. "If people demonstrated in a manner that interfered with the rights of others, they should be rounded up and put in a detention camp." (*The Atlantic.*)

It was the considered opinion of both the Democratic administration and the incoming Nixon administration that the 10,000 demonstrators in Chicago tried to demonstrate in a manner that interfered with the rights of others. We have already noted the confusion of the Walker Commission and the *New York Times* expert Max Frankel on this subject. From such clarity on the right and equivocations on the center, concentration camps will be born.

Almost every day brings other revelations of where the government is heading, though it will require time and public complicity to get all the way there. The prosecutions already under way, combined with these little gems of philosophy from the Justice Department, should be enough to remove any lingering doubts we might have. But in fact most of us still find it hard to realize the fate that is being prepared for us. For one thing, in real life such statements are mixed in with reassurances of the government's devotion to democracy and the people's welfare. It is only a handful of terrorists like the Panthers, nihilists like S.D.S., dope addicts like the Yippies, subversives like the Mobe, etc., who have anything to fear. Most Americans are safe—just as most Jews were assured of their safety in Germany in the early years of Hitler as I learned in 1936 when I spent several months there; just as most Czechs are told that they are safe today. But not that safe for that long; and not safe at all without paying a terrible price in subservience and silence, as their former comrades disappear.

I realize that it is offensive to most Americans to make even the slightest comparison between anything that is happening in the

United States and anything that happened at any point in Nazi Germany. But, spurred by Deputy Attorney General Kleindienst's remarks about "ideological criminals" and "detention camps," I have already succumbed to hinting at such a comparison, almost against my will and certainly against my better judgment, so let me point out a strange parallel that is surely a simple matter of historical coincidence, but even so is quite fascinating—dare I say foreboding?

On March 20, 1969 the Federal government indicted eight of us, including Bobby Seale, for conspiracy to organize a riot. There is no real question that in practice either the Federal government sponsored the riot and the Chicago police carried it out (as we tend to believe) or that the Chicago police carried out a riot on their own (as the government's *Walker Report* affirms), and the government is now trying to pin it on us. A few days later, the government accused Bobby Seale's organization of conspiring to terrorize the American people by blowing up various public buildings.

On February 27, 1933 the Hitler government accused four Communists of having set fire to the German Reichstag (parliament). There is no real question that, in practice, either the German government sponsored the act, which was carried out by the Anti-Communist Van Der Lubbe and associates (as most historians believe), or that the fire was set by the anti-Communists Van Der Lubbe and associates on their own and that the German government then tried to pin it on its political opponents, the Communists. On the very next day, the government announced that it had "discovered instructions for the carrying through of a Communist terror. . . . According to these instructions, government buildings, palaces, museums and essential undertakings were to be set on fire." (Bulletin of the German A.P., the German Press Agency, the *Amlitche Preussiche Presse Dienst*, February 28, 1944; quoted in *The Reichstag Fire Trial*, John Lane. The Bodley Head, London: 1934.)

According to the U.S. Attorney's office, "bombs and bomb parts, books and plans on how to make bombs and firearms" were found in the roundup of Panthers. (The *New York Times*, August 27, 1969.) According to an interview with Hitler published in New York on August 6, 1933, "Fuses, cotton-waste soaked in petrol and explosives were found ready." (*The Reichstag Fire Trial*, page 22.)

Although I am serious when I say that the near exactitude between these two double-barrelled attempts to discredit the opposition is coincidental, there are certain general considerations that we ignore at our peril. One is that similar historical conditions produce similar human reactions. The Reichstag Fire Trial and the "discovery" of elaborate plans to set fire to public places took place in the shadowy period of German history when the surrender of Germans to the temptations of fascism had just begun. Hitler and the Nazis, ugly as they were, had not yet consolidated their power and had been constrained by public opinion to launch only a small part of the terror that, during the course of the next few years, was to become their trademark. It was not clear yet whether the right or the center would triumph—or how far the right would go if it did triumph. That was one of the purposes of the trial and the "discovery" of the damning evidence—to inflame public opinion against the left and create an atmosphere in which a general crackdown would be tolerated.

In case anyone doubts this, the trial of the four Communists accused of having set fire to the Reichstag ended in acquittal. The "Not Guilty" verdict came after a trial of four months in Leipzig. I only hope that we shall be as successful in Chicago. Even more I hope that the American people will be more successful in resisting the encroachments of the "orderly society" than the Germans were.

The government's persistence in continuing the war, the terror already visited on the Black Panthers, and the attitudes of the top officials in the government, as revealed in some of their more candid statements, all make it unwise for us to be complacent. The surest way for us to lose the life-or-death struggle now going on is to underestimate *either* the determination of the military-industrial complex to maintain its system of private power, profit, and decision-making, *or* "the amount of diffuse yearning for radical change pulsing through this society (Susan Sontag)," the yearning to "have a more generous, more humane way of dealing with each other."

Statement Before Sentencing
on Anti-Riot Conviction

United States of America vs. David T. Dellinger et al.

1970 THE COURT: All right, Mr. Dellinger; you have the right to speak in your own behalf.

MR. DELLINGER: Well, Judge, before I start, you say that I have the legal right to speak before being sentenced, but last week when I was being sentenced for contempt and attempted to speak, I was not allowed to speak.

THE COURT: Giving you the right to speak means you must be respectful, I said in substance, and I say it again. I don't want you to be anything other than respectful.

MR. DELLINGER: What does that mean? Only say things you agree with, or does it mean I can discuss—

THE COURT: Go ahead. I give you the right to speak, sir, in your own behalf.

MR. DELLINGER: Before I speak I would like to formally object to the fact that my family and friends and fellow members of the movement against war and racism and economic injustice in this country are excluded from the courtroom.

THE COURT: That objection is overruled because of the conduct of certain spectators on previous occasions when there were such disorders that the marshals had difficulty in maintaining order.

MR. DELLINGER: I would like to make four brief points. The first is—

THE COURT: I do not limit you as to time.

MR. DELLINGER: Thank you.

THE COURT: Don't take advantage of that offer.

MR. DELLINGER: It won't be too long.

First, I think that every judge should be required to serve time in prison before sentencing other people there, so that he might become aware of the degrading and anti-human conditions that persist not only in Cook County jail but in the prisons generally of this country.

In a sense, our movement, or the movement in which we play a very small part—much smaller than the government gives us credit for—has helped expose the injustice, the violence, the hypocrisy and illegality of American foreign policy, beginning most notably in 1967. In 1967 the American people as a whole, I think, began to become aware of the futility, the immorality and the illegality of American aggression in Vietnam.

The next year, 1968, at the Democratic Convention, the movement in which we—again—play a small part helped expose to the American people the undemocratic nature of the electoral process in this country. We came to the convention not only objecting to the war and to racism, but believing in democracy and realizing that the present two-party system, the present convention system, the present methods of running the country are not democratic. We came here to ask that the country be returned to the people—the power of decision-making in the country.

The following year, largely 1969 but coming over into 1970, it seems to me that our movement has been subjected to the injustice, the bias, the authoritarian nature of the American judicial system. Let me say that like Mr. Kunstler I feel more compassion for you, sir, than I do hostility. I feel that as a judge you are a man who has had too much power over the lives of too many people for too many years. You have sentenced them to the degrading conditions that I am talking about without being fully aware of what you are doing and undoubtedly feeling correct and righteous, as often happens when people do the most abominable things.

In 1970, I think that perhaps the American people will begin to discover something about the nature of the prison system, the system in which we are now confined and in which thousands of other political prisoners are confined. The Black Panthers have said that all black prisoners are political prisoners, and although it may be hard for people to understand, I think that all people in prison are political prisoners. They are in prison, most of them, because they have violated the property and power concepts of the society. The bank robber I talked to yesterday was only trying to get his in the ways he thought were open to him, just as bankers and businessmen profiteer and try to advance their own economic cause at the expense of their fellows. In a society in which one has to have education, "good family," connections in order to rise to the top economically, it is not surprising if residents of a ghetto and members of the poor white working class and lower middle class often feel that the only way that they can get what everybody else is getting is to get it that way.

I do not think that the property system and the lack of economic egalitarianism in our society are justified in putting a strain on people, holding up the idea of self-advancement and then putting them away under conditions which, when the American people become enlightened, everybody will be ashamed of. I think it is impossible to think of the United States as being a civilized country when it has prisons such as those we are now confined in.

My second point is that whatever happens to us, however unjustified, will be slight compared to what has happened already to the Vietnamese people, to the black people in this country, to the so-called criminals with whom we are now spending our days in Cook County jail.

I have already lived longer than the normal life expectancy of a black person born when I was born—or born now. I have already lived longer—far longer, twenty years longer—than the normal life expectancy in the underdeveloped countries which this country is trying to profiteer from and keep under its domain and control. One of the main reasons for the war against Vietnam is to set an example to the people of the underdeveloped countries that they dare not fight for freedom and self-determination and democracy or else their children will be napalmed, their villages will be bombed and their citizens will be, if not killed, put in concentration camps.

Thirdly, I want to say that sending us to prison, any punishment the government can impose upon us, will not solve the problems that have gotten us into "trouble" with the government and the law in the first place; will not solve the problem of this country's rampant racism; will not solve the problem of its economic injustice; will not solve the problem of its foreign policy and its attacks on the underdeveloped peoples of the world.

The people of this country managed to get rid of President Johnson, but they didn't get rid of the war against Vietnam. They managed to get rid of General Westmoreland, but they didn't get rid of the war. Similarly, the government can put us away, falsely thinking that we are some kind of magical leaders of the antiwar movement and the movement for racial equality in this country, but they will not kill the movement by doing that.

The government has misread the times in which we live. Just as there was a time when it was possible to keep black people in slavery and then it became impossible, so this country is growing out of the time when it is possible to keep young people, black people, Mexican Americans, Puerto Ricans, antiwar people, people who believe in truth and justice and really believe in democracy, when it is going to be possible to keep them quiet or suppress them.

The government misread the Vietnamese people when it thought it could intimidate and terrorize and destroy them, and thus win them over and pacify them. It is similarly misreading the American people today as the war that began as a war against the Vietnamese people has become a war against the American people and against the American ideals of justice and democracy and freedom.

The government is bound to fail in its war against the American people just as it has failed in its war against the Vietnamese people.

Since the time when perhaps ten or fifteen thousand people came to Chicago to oppose having the issue of the war swept under the rug in a rigged convention in a city purged of demonstrations and protest, over ten thousand G.I.'s have been killed because of the government's refusal to listen to what we and others were saying. Perhaps a hundred and fifty thousand Vietnamese people have been wiped out needlessly in that time. For calling attention to that we have been brought up here in the dock and handled in this courtroom by Prosecutors Foran and Schultz in a manner that reminds me of Prosecutor Vyshinsky and the other Russian prosecutors in the time of the political purges in the Soviet Union in the thirties.

Finally, you yourself, for whom I was so happy to read in jail that Bill Kunstler had said he felt more compassion than anger: All the way through this, I have been ambivalent in my attitude toward you, because there is something spunky about you that one has to admire, however misguided and intolerant I believe you are. All the way through the trial, sort of without conscious effort, almost against my own will, I keep comparing you in my mind to George III of England. Perhaps because you are trying to hold back the tide of history, although you will not succeed; perhaps because you are trying to stem and forestall a second American Revolution which is in the cards, which will take place and which neither you nor Foran nor Schultz, nor any of the other people who are doing the dirty work for the Establishment, no matter how convinced they are in many cases of their righteousness in what they are doing—none of them will be able to stop.

Our movement is not very strong today. It is not united; it is not well organized. It is very confused and makes a lot of mistakes. But there is the beginning of an awakening in this country which has been going on for perhaps the last fifteen years, and it is an awakening that will not be denied. Tactics will change, people will err, people will die in the streets and die in prison, but I do not believe that this movement can be denied, because, however falsely applied the American ideal was from the beginning, when it excluded black people and Indians and people without property, nonetheless there was a dream of justice and equality and freedom and brotherhood. I think that that dream is much closer to fulfillment today than it has been at any other time in the history of this country.

I only wish that we were all not just more eloquent—I wish we were smarter, more dedicated, more united. I wish we could work together better. I wish we could reach out even to the Forans and the Schultzes and the Hoffmans, and convince them of the necessity of this revolution.

That is why I said the other day that I don't ever call human beings pigs, and that that was one of the numerous misquotes in my contempt citation. That is why I objected to being accused of having screamed in the courtroom or having been "obscene."

It is an unreal world, typical of the isolation of the court, when the word "bullshit" is considered so obscene that it cannot be spoken among grown people; just as it is an unreality to say to the jury: "Don't read the newspapers; don't listen to the radio; don't look at television; don't discuss the case, even among yourselves." As if somehow that would make them more sanitary and wise and would help resolve the deep problems that underlie the country.

I think that I shall sleep better and happier and with a greater sense of fulfillment in whatever jails I am in for the next however many years, than if I had compromised, if I had pretended that the problems were any less real than they are, or if I had sat here passively in the courtroom while justice was being throttled and the truth was being denied.

I learned that when I spent three years in jail before. When I ended up in the hole and on a hunger strike for sixty-five days, I found out that there are no comforts, no luxuries, no honors, nothing that can compare with having a sense of one's own integrity—not one's infallibility, because I have continued to make mistakes from that day to this, but at least one's knowledge that in his own life, in his own commitment, he is living up to the best that he knows.

I salute my brothers in Vietnam, in the ghetto, in the Women's Liberation movement—all the people all over the world who are struggling to make true and real for all people the ideals on which this country was supposed to have been founded, but never, never has lived up to.